MIMESIS
INTERNATIONAL

ATMOSPHERIC SPACES
n. 17

What is an "Atmosphere"?

According to an aesthetic, phenomenological and ontological view, such a notion can be understood as a sensorial and affective quality widespread in space. It is the particular tone that determines the way one experiences her surroundings.

Air, ambiance, aura, climate, environment, genius loci, milieu, mood, numinous, lived space, Stimmung, but also Umwelt, ki, aida, Zwischen, in-between – all these words are names hiding, in fact, the founding idea of atmospheres: a vague ens or power, without visible and discrete boundaries, which we find around us and, resonating in our lived body, even involves us.

Studying atmospheres means, thus, a parte subjecti, to analyse (above all) the range of unintentional or involuntary experiences and, in particular, those experiences which emotionally "tonalise" our everyday life. A parte objecti, it means however to learn how atmospheres are intentionally (e.g. artistically, politically, socially, etc.) produced and how we can critically evaluate them, thus avoiding being easily manipulated by such feelings.

Atmospheric Spaces is a new book series whose aim is to become a point of reference for a community that works together on this philosophical and transdisciplinary subject and for all those whose research, more broadly, is involved in the so-called "affective turn" of the Social Sciences and Humanities.

WHIMS OF THE WIND

Weightlessness and Thought in Contemporary Literature and Visual Arts

Edited by
Paola Del Zoppo, Rosanna Gangemi and Micaela Latini

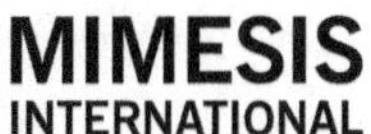

This book was published with the support of the Università degli Studi di Ferrara "Department of Human Studies" (Research Project FAR 2025_ Latini) and the Università degli Studi di Urbino "Carlo Bo".

www.mimesisinternational.com
e-mail: info@mimesisinternational.com

Book series: *Atmospheric Spaces,* n. 17

Series Issn: 3103-4322

Isbn: 9788869774546

P.I. C.F. 0241937030

Cover image:
Victor Hugo (1802-1885), *Arbre couché par le vent*, Maison de Victor Hugo – Hauteville House, Paris
Credits: CC0 Paris Musées / Maisons de Victor Hugo Paris – Guernesey

CONTENTS

III.
PHILOSOPHICAL, AESTHETICAL AND SYMBOLIC STREAMS

Paola Del Zoppo, Rosanna Gangemi, Micaela Latini

Introduction

> To feel the wind is not to make external, tactile contact with our surroundings but to mingle with them. In this mingling, as we live and breathe, the wind, light, and moisture of the sky bind with the substances of the earth in the continual forging of a way through the tangle of life-lines that comprise the land.
>
> Tim Ingold (2007)

In 1919, on the occasion of the marriage of his sister, Marcel Duchamp—well known for pushing the boundaries of artistic experiences as well as the definition of 'art' itself—sent as a gift to the couple in Paris the *Unhappy Readymade* instructions: they had to suspend a geometry book by strings on their balcony, in midair, which was what they did. The wind blew through the volume, chose its own problems, turned and tore out the pages, creating with the rain and the sun unpredictable non-Euclidean shapes, transforming closed knowledge through the "facts of life". This is one of the countless examples of the use of the natural and unpredictable force of the wind as an art instrument inspiring and nourishing the speculative reflection.

The wind, an elusive and invisible element, has always fascinated humans due to its tangible yet intangible presence, capable of affecting bodies, minds, landscapes, architecture, and above all, perceptions and affects. In an era marked by ecological crisis and the urgent need to rethink our way of being in the world, the wind is at once a symbol of instability and openness, of force and lightness, of disappearance and contact.

Within the scope of atmospheric studies, which have developed in recent decades through dialogue with phenomenology, ecology, and aesthetics, the wind has emerged as a paradigmatic figure. As Tonino Griffero notes in *Atmospheres: Aesthetics of Emotional Spaces* (2014), the atmosphere is not merely a background but an affective reality that envelops and influences us pre-reflectively. Atmospheres are not objectively describable entities but emotional backgrounds that shape our relationship with the world. In this sense, the wind is the atmosphere par excellence: the invisible that is felt, the motor of climatic empathy and affective spatiality.

In this theoretical framework, the wind is more than a meteorological event: it is a semiotic and performative force that shapes spatiality and experience—an agent that generates intensity, movement, and interaction. Atmospheric studies emphasize corporeality and spatial sensing: the wind becomes material and a metaphor for this extended corporeality. This "quasi-object", in Latourian terms, is a transpersonal medium that challenges the separations between subject and environment, inside and outside, emotion and perception. Simultaneously, the wind is a privileged figure for thinking about concepts such as transmission, resonance, and diffusion—of ideas, senses, and memories.

This volume arises from the intention to explore such multiplicity, offering a conceptual and sensuous cartography of the wind in its artistic, literary, and speculative articulations to contribute in an original way to atmospheric studies and affective studies by expanding their trajectories into the fields of arts and literature. It gathers, integrates, and extends the papers of the eponymous international Symposium that took place November 24 and 25, 2021, at the University of Tuscia in Viterbo (Italy), and for this the editors are particularly grateful to the scientific committee, notably Jan Baetens, Sara Bédard-Goulet, Isabel Gil, Niccolò Scaffai, Pierre Schoentjes, Maria Stavrinaki.

The wind, here explored not as a monolithic subject but as a rhizomatic and transdisciplinary figure, becomes a heuristic device for interrogating the connections between perception, affect, environment, and creation. The embraced perspective is large, and involves, among others, history of art, ecopoetics, ethnography, mythological studies, and visual studies.

For literary and artistic studies, this publication shows how the wind appears in texts and images not only as a natural element but as a form of thought, a stylistic feature, a generator of narratives and visions. It is a figure of passage, dissolution, healing, and metamorphosis. The air moved by the wind becomes a medium between the sensible and the supersensible, memory and invention. With the point of view of aesthetics and philosophy of art, the wind challenges the concepts of form, substance, and object, suggesting that beauty and meaning can reside in the unstable, the fleeting, the diffuse.

The debate on these pages is enriched by concrete case studies and through aesthetical and philosophical readings that translate abstract concepts into sensorial experiences.

Volume description and sections

This publication unfolds through three thematic sections, each dedicated to distinct aspects of the wind as a natural phenomenon and cultural symbol.

The first section, *Winds of Nature, Science and Design*, explores the relationship between wind and the physical world, both natural and constructed. Monica Fonck and Marcella Pasqualetti open with an in-depth look at the Botanical Garden of Viterbo, where the wind not only influences botanical life but also contributes to the architectural and ecological planning of the space. Tommaso Ariemma follows with a philosophical reflection on how the wind tunnel shaped modern design aesthetics, highlighting the wind's role in forging new paradigms of form and function. Then, Patrizia Mania bridges science and art, reflecting on how the wind can mediate between empirical data and poetic imagination, particularly in the context of eco-art.

In the second section, *Literary Blowings, Artistic and Filmic Atmospheres*, the wind emerges as a powerful literary motif and an affective atmosphere. Niccolò Amelii examines the role of the sirocco in two Italian novels, showing how this hot, oppressive wind embodies existential malaise and symbolic inertia. Daniela Bombara expands on this by analyzing how gusts of wind in Italian fantastic literature introduce madness and mystery, transforming everyday spaces into portals of the uncanny. Simone Pettine offers a delicate reading of Francesco Biamonti's prose, where the breeze becomes an expression of solitude and subtle emotional tension. Stefano Simone brings together the voices of Vian, Montale, and Eliot to reveal how wind can act as a trigger for poetic insight and metaphysical revelation. Peter Schulman investigates the libecciu in Corsican literature and song, exploring its power as a bearer of longing and cultural memory. Focusing on how wind has figured in broader historical and sociopolitical imaginaries, Giuseppe Grilli's essay tracks the symbolism of wind and sails in the aftermath of March Revolutions, suggesting how wind can become a metaphor for transformation, rupture, and the challenges of renewal. Finally, Deianira Amico focusses on the iconographic choice of wind by artists from the 'Corrente' movement, from Birolli to Valenti, and Gioia Sili analyses Joris Ivens' films, where the wind is no longer a background but an expressive agent, both cinematic and lyrical.

The third section, *Philosophical, Aesthetical and Symbolic Streams*, engages with the wind on a conceptual and metaphysical level. Tonino

Griffero's contribution theorizes the wind as an emblem of indeterminacy and ontological openness, in line with his broader work on affective atmospheres. Katia Botta's essay navigates the æsthetic thought of figures like Humboldt and Ritter, showing how the wind structures our visual and imaginative engagement with landscapes. Raffaella Viccei analyses how the wind in Djemila accompanied the short journey of the young Camus, his senses as well as his state of mind. Swaantjie Otto's piece draws on Heidegger to interpret the northeast wind as a poetic opening to memory and thought, revealing the wind's philosophical resonance. Baroque and proto-Baroque forms of the morphological paradigms from Eugenio d'Ors and Hubert Damisch share an intimate, fascinating connection in the essay of Marcello Sessa, arguing how metamorphic mobility theorizations announce modernity.

In conclusion, through its diverse and mutually resonant contributions with a resolutely interdisciplinary perspective, this book does not seek to close but to open: to share with the reader new tools to perceive, think, create, and live in the wind with the wind.

I.
Winds of Nature, Science and Design

Monica Fonck, Marcella Pasqualetti

The Botanical Garden of Viterbo and the Architecture of the Wind

The Hortus botanicus is a semi-natural environment that hosts an extensive range of plants that are collected, cultivated, and conserved according to systematic, geographical, or ecological criteria. Today the Botanical Gardens, particularly the University ones, constitute open-air laboratories functional to scientific research in the various fields of botanical sciences as well as to the dissemination of natural sciences. Plants, both native and exotic, constitute the object of study and primary interest in the Botanical Gardens, and for plants the wind represents a fundamental element.

The wind is functional in many physiological processes. Not only does it favor transpiration, cooling, and gas exchange at the level of the photosynthetic systems, contributing to the fundamental energetic process of the plant, but it is also essential, in many plants, for reproduction, pollination, and seed dispersal.

Anemogamous pollination is the first form of pollen transport that evolved. Still, today, it represents the primary mode of transport of the male gametophyte in many spermatophytes, gymnosperms, and angiosperms, even in those species that present a greater degree of evolution, such as grasses. This mode of transport does not present significant specializations; it is a passive dispersion; the wind cannot guarantee that the pollen arrives on the ovule to be fertilized. Therefore, anemophilous species link their reproductive success to the production of large quantities of pollen. The pollen grains of anemophilous species are light, small (and therefore often allergenic), and sometimes equipped with devices that favor their suspension in the air, for example, air pockets in conifer pollen (Fig. 1). Seed dispersal is also linked to the wind in some species.

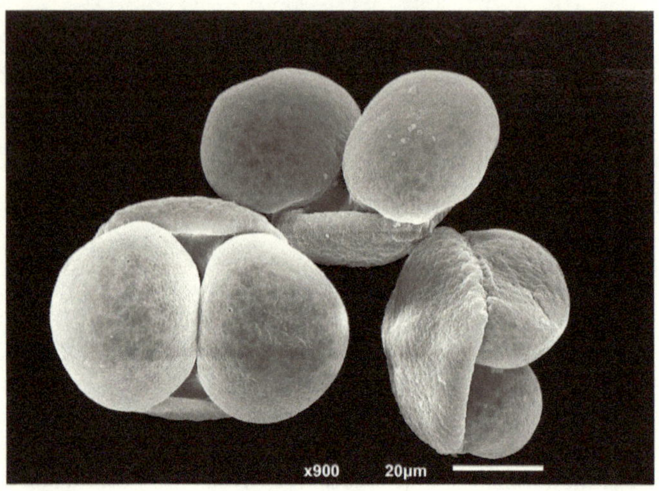

Fig. 1. Ph. by Annarita Taddei

Some fruits are equipped with flight structures (e.g., maples, dandelions, etc.) (Fig. 2), e.g., the fruit of *Alsomitra macrocarpa* (Blume) M. Roem., a cucurbit that grows on the island of Java, reaches heights of over 30 metres and distances of 100 kilometres before descending and germinating. Man has learned from nature, often drawing inspiration, even in the engineering field, from the "flight" structures of plants to exploit the wind to his advantage, draw energy from it, conserve foodstuffs, dissipate pollutants, and much more. For example, Igo Etrich, an Austro-Hungarian aviator and engineer, pioneer of bio-design studies, thoroughly studied the aerodynamic forms in nature to design and build the stable wing (1904) of his hang glider by imitating the structure of the large seed of *A. macrocarpa* (Coineau & Kresling, 1987).

The relationship between wind and plants is limited to the physiological and reproductive aspects outlined above and closely influences many cultivation practices. Every farmer has learned the importance and influence of the wind in tilling the soil, plant treatments, and planting, and has also tried to defend himself from the wind by using, when possible, the same plants to build barriers to calm its effects.

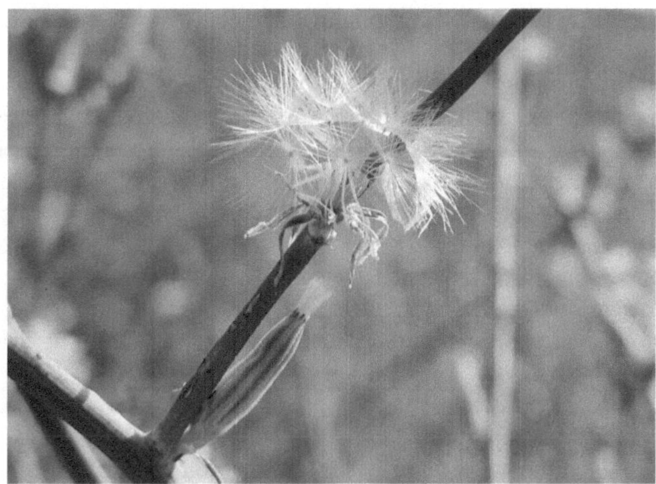

Fig.2.

The very history of the city of Viterbo appears intimately connected to the wind; in fact, in the 13th century, the city was chosen as the papal seat, and it is believed that among the reasons for this choice was the healthiness of the air. Unlike Rome, Viterbo, located on the north-western side of the Cimini mountains, at around 350 m above sea level, enjoys high ventilation which constantly mitigates and cleans the air. Not being excessively far from the sea, about 50 km, the city is affected by the sea breeze and the land breeze in summer. During the day, the warming of the hinterland causes the rise of large air masses, which attract relatively cooler air from the sea, while at night, the opposite phenomenon occurs. In winter, Viterbo is lashed by the north wind, which, finding no barriers in the northern part, cleans the air, making it healthy.

The wind is an element that, as previously observed, characterizes the city of Viterbo, particularly in the winter periods, and was a forcing factor that contributed to outlining the current physiognomy of the "Angelo Rambelli' Botanical Garden. The Botanical Garden stands on the slopes of a hill at the center of which flows the Bulicame thermal spring, whose fame, linked to the thermal waters, dates back to Roman times and, probably, even earlier to the Etruscan era (Fig. 3) area, characterised by strong annual temperature variations (min -10°C, max 40°C), is battered by strong north winds and has a highly calcareous soil. Underground, at depths ranging from 4 to 8 m, numerous aquifers flow with warm waters rich in mineral salts, especially carbonates deposited over millennia forming extensive whitish concretions. This area today represents a true example of "industrial archaeology." Since the early Middle Ages, hemp was processed here using hot water from the thermal spring for the maceration process. The water that flowed from the Bullicame source into unique processing reservoirs through characteristic channels is still visible today. Canalettes and pools are now integrated into the Garden's water system, transformed into lakes and streams that run through the entire structure and host aquatic ecosystems, sometimes enriched by spontaneous herbaceous vegetation. The historical importance of this area is found in the illustrious testimony in the quotes that appear in the *Divine Comedy* in the Canto Inferno, XIV, 79-81, XIV 79-81.

The Botanical Garden covers an area of approximately six hectares. It is in a territory that represented a real challenge and which today, 30 years after its establishment, we can say has been won. It is due to the genius of its founder, Prof. Angelo Rambelli, and his collaborators, that a bare and degraded environment was transformed into a botanical park that today hosts around 20,000 specimens and constitutes a source of naturalistic, landscape, and cultural wealth for the entire scientific community and for the city of Viterbo.

When designing the Botanical Garden, the various limiting factors present in this area, including the wind, were considered. The designers exploited the land's conformation, characterised by a series of steps, to grow plants with different needs, trying to recreate the optimal conditions for the development of the different botanical collections.

The upper part of the Garden is exposed to the north wind, while the lower part is more sheltered. This characteristic was accentuated through the creation of plant barriers placed in succession: the first consisting of a cypress hedge (*Cupressus arizonica Greene*) between the Bulicame Thermal Park and the Botanical Garden; the second a fence covered with climbing plants (*Rosa bracteata* J. C. Wendl); and the third, lower down, a strawberry tree hedge (*Arbutus unedo L.*).

In the northern part of the Garden, close to the *R. bracteata* fence, a Mediterranean scrub reconstruction has been set up; this coenosis constitutes one of the most representative elements of coastal vegetation. It mainly hosts species of evergreen sclerophyll, trees, and shrubs that adapt to summer aridity, such as compact foliage with small, rigid, and leathery leaves. It includes many common species of the Italian coasts, such as *A. unedo* (Corbezzolo or Cerasa marina), *Myrtus communis L.* (Myrtle), *Pistacia lentiscus L.* (Mastic), *Smilax aspera L.* (Stracciabraghe) and *Quercus ilex L.* (Leccio). In the upper part, some *Pinus halepensis Mill* plants have been planted (Aleppo Pine), which have a characteristic shape defined by the strong north winds.

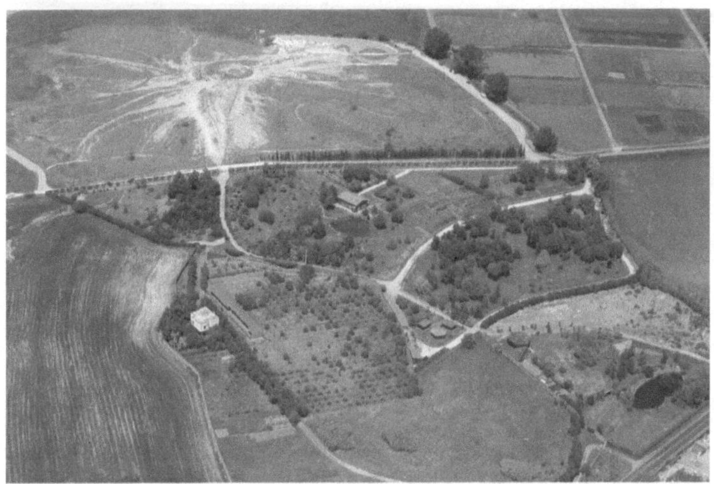

Fig. 3.

In the central part of the Garden, a lush arboretum extends over an area of approximately one hectare, hosting arboreal plants organized based on their geographical origin, partly delimited by the high Corbezzolo hedge. This barrier protects the underlying collections from the wind and allows the creation of a visual screen that hides the reconstruction of the "Desert" from visitors (Fig. 4). This collection, set up with succulent plants from various desert and sub-desert areas around the world (Africa, America, and Europe), can be accessed through narrow passages that separate the lush green of the arboretum from the white rocks and sandy soil that characterize the desert area. A notable difference in temperature can be perceived when going from one room to another. In this area, in the lower part on a prominent rocky ridge, completely sheltered from the winds and exposed to midday, acclimatization tests are underway for some succulent plants, which, thanks to the microenvironment, can grow outside all year round.

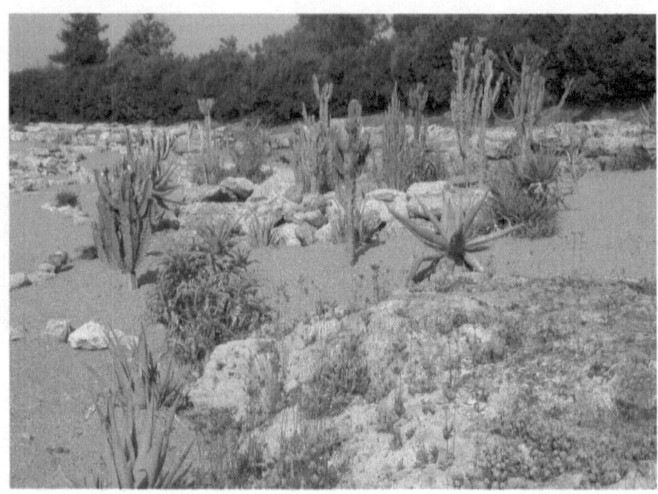

Fig. 4.

Alongside the collections mentioned above, the Garden hosts a significant collection of legumes, a tropical greenhouse, a greenhouse dedicated to the cultivation of pteridophytes, an area dedicated to carnivorous plants, a simple garden, and many other collections aimed at offering visitors a tangible evidence example of plant biodiversity and the many adaptations that plants present.

The "Angelo Rambelli" Botanical Garden presents itself as a training site. It plays a fundamental role in the conservation of biodiversity, research, and environmental education. Numerous thematic courses and events are organized here, which are welcomed every year with enthusiasm and participation.

Translated by Paola Del Zoppo

Tommaso Ariemma

The Birth of Design from the Wind Tunnel

A Thermo-aesthetic Analysis

The domain of air

The 20th century was characterised by the struggle for domination of the air. No longer just land and sea: territories and spaces were traversed by planes, waves, information. Those who ruled the air, ruled the century, as well as our time, because we have not yet abandoned that domination.

In the 1940s, geographers defined their time as the air age. The dominance of the air obliterated geographical and topographical barriers and made the United States a veritable aerocracy.[1]

Power over the air – understood as power not only over war but over transport, logistics and telecommunications – is a global power, immense compared to those of the past. Our atmosphere has become continuously criss-crossed by signals and means of transport, and satellite surveillance has covered every corner of the planet.

Inextricably linked to this political, but above all economic and commercial transformation, industrial design has emerged in the United States courting such power since the 1930s.

The aerodynamic shapes of the objects were enormously successful, as in the case of the famous *Coldspot* refrigerator of 1935, or as in the case of the innovative shape of the *Chrysler Airflow* of 1934, for which the company built a specific "wind tunnel", coordinated by Orville Wright (one of the two inventors of the aircraft), in order to enhance its aerodynamics.[2]

Cars and locomotives could still justify care for aerodynamic forms as a refinement of their function, but what about refrigerators or even telephones? Aerodynamic forms had little to do with function and a lot to do with the ideology of aerial dominance. This is the *streamline style* that gave such fame to designers like Henry Dreyfuss and Raymond Loewy, whose

1 M. Vegetti, *L'invenzione del globo. Spazio, politica, comunicazione nell'epoca dell'aria*, Einaudi, Torino 2017.

2 M. Martinuz, *Design, tecnologia, arte*, LetteraVentidue, Siracusa 2017.

social project was to instil optimism towards technology and celebrate the dynamism of the American way of life by greatly increasing product sales. This is not just any form of design, but the form that has made design a phenomenon of mass culture to such an extent that the term "design" has become synonymous with every creative project.

In 1949, "Time" dedicated its cover to Loewy, emphasising his ability to make the sales curve "aerodynamic".[3] In his autobiography published in 1951, Loewy also declared himself to be a defender of his client's central nervous system and emphasised that the purpose and future of industrial design lay in achieving mental serenity, to which his design contributes, by ensuring that the things surrounding the average American remain in place, discreet and quiet, without sacrificing dynamism[4]. For Loewy, correct design must remove any unpleasant perceptions given by ugly shapes. Particularly interesting is his reading of the shape of the Coca Cola bottle, a shape that the designer considers perfect. However, if in 1915 – thus before the dominance of air – its original designer Alexander Samuelson had thought of it according to the sinuous forms of the actress Mae West,[5] Loewy sees in the double curvature of the bottle a way of favouring the grip and instilling comfort and pleasure.

It could be argued at this point that every future product of industrial design, such as shoes or computers, which has seen in Dreyfuss and Loewy its tutelary deities (or simply in the ideology of the dominion of air its point of reference) was born from the 'wind tunnel', that is, from the search for aerodynamic forms capable of establishing a symbolic link between the ideology of minimum friction, maximum control and the consumer. In this way, a widespread symbolic participation takes place through the forms of the most popular and innovative goods (cars, telephones, shoes, household appliances, computers).

Such an aesthetic offering thus balances, if not normalises, the imbalance produced by the domination of air over a world hitherto founded on the domains of land and sea. The design of aerodynamic forms thus succeeds in the mission that Jacques Rancière identified in design, namely to 'give society its spiritual unity'[6], to define a new structure of common life.

---

3 G. Lipotvesky, J. Serroy, *L'esthétisation du monde : Vivre à l'âge du capitalisme artiste*, Gallimard, Paris 2016, pp. 145-147.

4 R. Loewy, *Never Leave Well Enough Alone* (1951), The Johns Hopkins University Press, Baltimore & London 2002, pp. 418-420.

5 W. Lidwell, G. Manasca, *Deconstructing Product Design*, Rockport Publishers, Massachusetts 2009, pp. 48-49.

6 J. Rancière, *The Future of Images*, Verso, New York 2009.

From domination to ritual

Peter Sloterdijk – defined by Bruno Latour as the *philosopher par excellence* of design[7] for his attention to the form given by human beings to their environments – has given a precise date for the birth of the principle behind industrial design: the use, in 1915, of toxic gases during the First World War. For Sloterdijk, the toxic clouds used during battle are an early form of product "design":

> From its inception, gas warfare combined all three of the 20th century's operative criteria – terrorism, design consciousness, and environmental approach – […] In this movement of explication the principle of design is implicated from the start, since to enable the operational manipulation of gas milieus in open terrain, requires making certain "atmotechnic" innovations. It is these latter that turned the development of chemical war clouds into a product-design-type task.[8]

This is certainly an exaggeration, which nevertheless reaffirms – by attempting to provide a more brutal origin, as original as it is removed, as is customary for many contemporary philosophers – a further element of the connection that industrial design, as it has established itself in the United States, has had with the air.

Sloterdijk is right to identify industrial design as a precise "environmental" creation, not limited to the individual object. Obviously, design contributes to the design of human environments so that people can live and not die, as in the case of gases. But the idea that climate and air quality can somehow be designed has not a little to do with the mission of design, oriented however, and it should be emphasised, to a cooling of a different nature, a symbolic cooling.

If the pages dedicated to toxic gases could refer to a very broad and, in some ways, grotesque concept of design, the reflection that Sloterdijk develops in the pages dedicated to design in his *The Aesthetic Imperative,* on the other hand, comes closer to its symbolic function. Design, according to Sloterdijk, would represent a *simulation of sovereignty,* giving the illusion, especially to the consumer, of power in some way, when one no longer has any power:

---

7 B. Latour, *A Cautious Prometheus? A Few Steps Toward a Philosophy of Design* (with Special Attention to Peter Sloterdijk), "Proceedings of the 2008 Annual International Conference of the Design History Society", pp. 2-10.

8 P. Sloterdijk, *Terror from the Air*, Semiotext(e), Los Angeles 2009, pp. 22-23.

> […] we may define design as simulation of sovereignty: design is when one is capable despite everything. […] Since archaic times, ritual has closed the gap through which impotence, panic and death invade our life. In this sense we can talk of the birth of design out of the spirit of ritual.[9]

A kind of ritual function, then, that cools the spirits, giving an illusion of control. The spirit of the "wind tunnel" has not, therefore, abandoned us: we symbolically participate in the 20th century's dominion over air, a dominion that has set aside all cartographic, purely spatial reason, seeking to limit as much as possible any friction in the flow of life, as with air. The symbolic link with air thus gave an *iconic edge* to products that sought to replicate the enormous success of Loewy's design, as in the case of the design of the 'Air' line that gave so much success to Nike shoes (their air cushioning was above all highly visible, to emphasise the symbolic link beyond the affective function of cushioning shocks) up to the satin-finishing of Apple's iPod and Macbook "Air".

In the case of Nike shoes, the symbolic link with air is made explicit both by the name – a clear reference to the goddess Athena Nike, personification of victory in the guise of a winged woman – and by the logo – the famous *swoosh*, symbolising both a wing and the hissing of air.

The thermo-aesthetic function of design

If we live in a world of design today, if the word design now accompanies any activity, it is because industrial design has embodied, from its origins and in its most widespread manifestations, a kind of low-intensity ritual, of "calming" acceptance of the new domain and illusion of control through the aesthetic coordination of forms. A low-intensity ritual, that is, a low-temperature ritual: design thus belongs to the aesthetic dimension of *coolness*.[10] Design mitigates, reduces friction, "cools down".

The industrial design that imposes itself is a cold design, the coldness of which, however, does not concern industrial production as such, serialised and linked to "inhuman" machines – as indicated by Thomas Maldonado

9 P. Sloterdijk, *The Aesthetic Imperative: Writings on Art*, Polity Press, Cambridge 2017, pp.87-88.

10 D. Pountain, D. Robins, *Cool Rules. Anatomy of an Attitude*, Reaktion Books, London 2000.

in one of his polemical reflections on the contrast between a cold (i.e. industrial) design and a warm (for the few, more artisanal) design.[11]

Industrial design that simulates the domain of air is cool for a specific aesthetic-social function. A *thermo-aesthetic* function. Although our emotions and feelings are culturally associated with warmth and coldness, we still lack an aesthetic understanding of temperature. It is not a matter of emphasising the influence of climate that would distinguish peoples in thinking and creating as Winckelmann indicated in his famous *History of the Art of Antiquity*. A temperature also guides or accompanies images and their production. These are not merely thermal *metaphors,* but *primary metaphors*,[12] a true symbolic temperature. We have no instruments to measure this temperature, but we do have a manifestation of it. Distinct, but obscure. A manifestation, therefore, that is aesthetic, like that of beauty or artistic value, which is not infrequently associated with a certain thrill (without, however, dwelling on the thermal value of this expression) in the user. Although in the philosophical discipline of aesthetics reference to the symbolic temperature is almost completely absent, it is not lacking in other social sciences such as anthropology or mediology.

Famous is, in fact, the theory of the "temperature" of societies according to Lévi-Strauss: according to the anthropologist, there are cold societies and warm societies. Cold, so-called primitive societies, studied by the ethnologist, are societies that produce the least disorder and tend to remain in an initial state, such that they appear without history and progress. Hot societies, on the contrary, so-called civilised, are such because they are governed by imbalances that set conflicts and revolutions in motion.[13]

But the most famous use of thermal categories in the social sciences is the distinction, theorised by McLuhan, between hot and cold media and made explicit in his *Understanding Media* (1964). A distinction, however, that for any reader is far removed from the usual aesthetic perception of temperature. For McLuhan, in fact, a medium is warm if it excludes the active participation of the user (as in the case of the radio); it is cold if it invites the viewer to make an effort or fill in the visual deficiencies of the medium (as in the case of the low definition of the image in early television sets):

11 T. Maldonado, *Il disegno industriale. Un riesame*, Feltrinelli, Milano 1976.

12 G. Lakoff, M. Johnson, *Philosophy in the Flesh. The Embodied Mind and Its Challenge to Western Thought*, Basic Books, New York 1999.

13 G. Charbonnier, *Conversations with Claude Levi-Strauss* (1961), Cape, London 1969.

> There is a basic principle that distinguishes a hot medium like radio from a cool one like the telephone, or a hot medium like the movie from a cool one like TV. A hot medium is one that extends one single sense in "high definition". High definition is the state of being well filled with data. A photograph is, visually, "high definition". A cartoon is "low definition", simply because very little visual information is provided.[14]

It is difficult to understand this "thermal" attribution if we relate it to our aesthetic experience. The reason lies in the fact that McLuhan derives and applies the principle of *cool jazz* to the media in a decidedly singular way[15], thereby creating quite a few misunderstandings, especially from the thermo-aesthetic point of view, i.e. from the point of view of the amount of symbolic, social heat produced within an aesthetic experience.

Cool jazz, like *hot jazz*, did not and does not demand substantially different aesthetic participation from the listener: in any case, one listens to a piece of music. The "cool" element of cool *jazz* was to indicate a "mitigating", "cooling" factor within its composition that incorporated melodic and stylistic elements proper to 'white' culture into a musical genre used, on the other hand, by blacks to express their suffering. McLuhan sees this 'participation' as the reason for 'cool', thus interpreting any medium that requires participation as a "cool" medium. But this makes no sense from a thermo-aesthetic point of view, because this removes the 'mitigating' element at work in the aesthetic dimension of *coolness*. "Cool" is that which is free of friction and conflict, pleasant but not challenging, cute without being excessive. A revolution will never be *cool*. And, curiously enough, this is precisely the epochal change – the cool revolution, one might say – that industrial design has embodied: in having literally replaced the word revolution with the word design[16].

---

14 M. McLuhan, *Understanding media. The extension of man* (1964), The MIT Press, Cambridge 1994, p. 22.

15 J. Rice, *The Rhetoric of Cool. Composition Studies and New Media*, Southern Illinois University Press, Carbondale 2007, pp. 41-42.

16 B. Latour, *op. cit.*

Patrizia Mania

Between Poetry and Science

Ecology of Art and the Wind

The wind – among the most elusive, mobile and impermanent elements – has been an eloquent reminder of the precariousness of our existence over time. From this crucial, but not exclusive starting point, the wind has been articulated in many contemporary works of art and emerges where the active and constitutive components of the work rely on its performing and conforming aspects. Wind machines, air laboratories, poems of life, simple and complex metaphors. The case history of air in art is extremely diversified and, in the light of current emergencies and sensitivities, it would seem to renew a relationship that art has intertwined with this theme a long time ago.

In ancient Greece, the wind was represented by God Aeolus with swollen cheeks, blowing air to release the winds. A particularly happy iconographic invention that alone reveals the importance of this theme and the need to depict it. Over time, thinking about the wind in art has been a challenge and an almost ground-breaking risk that has increasingly united art and science. It would be enough to recall Leonardo, who was persistently committed to study and understand the natural and atmospheric phenomena generated by the movement of air – such as dust, smoke and wind –, and all the questions arising from this. He testified in his writings on air, breath and wind, the importance that he assigned to this in his creative process, which led him to the invention of the aerial perspective, where, starting from a purely physical sphere, he went on to investigate the emotional and sentimental one.

But abandoning distant references and adopting the horizon of here and now, some artistic paths have chosen wind as the driving force of their work, ultimately outlining it as a mnemonic and poetic device for a scientific experiment in an ecological key. This is precisely the trajectory proposed by this intervention, analyzing air as the specific object of reflection of many artists in their poetic and experimental directions. The reason for this is that wind is an element capable of questioning our certainties and bringing to life the palpitating vision of a world, that has always been prone to transform, undergoing variations and oscillations. Whether in allegorical poetic processes, or in functional proposals for rebalancing the ecosystem, the air has been assumed as the vehicle and instrument of aesthetic forms and thoughts, that "vitally" shake contemporary times.[1]

Introducing the subject, it is necessary to recall how it was Marcel Duchamp who pioneeringly turned his gaze to this aspect more than a century ago – confirming once again his fundamental importance – and decided to dedicate one of his first ready-made works to air: *50 cc d'air de Paris*. It was 1919, and the artist, after purchasing an empty glass vial from a Parisian pharmacist, collected some air in it, or rather it would be more appropriate to say, he named the content of it – *50 cc of Paris air* (50 cubic centimetres = 50 millilitres). Once he bought the vial, he left the inscription "serum phisiologique" on it. Intangible – the air was already contained in it – this work is inscribed in the sphere of ready-made, namely those works in which the object is chosen on purely aesthetic basis, extrapolated from its functional context and elected to work of art. The drop-shaped ampoule ending in a glass hook was brought to New York the following year, where Duchamp gifted it to his close friend and patron Walter C. Arensberg. The vial was accidentally broken, and subsequently restored, in 1949. The restored original is now in the Philadelphia Museum of Art. This particular accident made the meaning of the work even more unstable. The breaking, and consequent repair, raised, in fact, a further question, and that is whether the air contained in that ampoule should still be considered the air of Paris. Among other things, there are later and slightly different versions of the work, that testify the constantly cultivated interest by the artist in this field. A vial with nothing in it may be the most insubstantial "work of art" imaginable, but that empty space, displayed and named in an art museum, definitely fits into another category.

Moving forward a few decades, and shifting from the inside to the outside, – from air contained to air containing – Environmental and Land Artists developed the subject in fluid directions, letting the air and the wind make their works susceptible to unpredictable transformations, and turning them somehow into living organisms. As known, for many decades now, art has taken a direction that often disdains the completed form, favoring, on the other hand, its transformation and dissolution and, thus, leaving room for forms, which are rightfully considered "alive" in their constant evolution.

---

1 See N. Bourriaud, *Inclusioni. Estetica del capitolocene*, Postmediabooks, Milano, 2020, pp. 84-90.

Among infinite variations and proposals, one could think, for example, of the empaquetages by Christo and Jeanne Claude and reflect on what they experienced while they were immersed in the air and how they kept changing during their life. Unthinkable, in fact, without the wind and the air to constantly transform them, these works are particularly suitable to a transformation enacted by the atmosphere. Speaking of his latest work, designed together with Jeanne Claude in the early 1960s and realized posthumously and more recently – the wrapping of the Arc de Triomphe in Paris (September 18 – October 3, 2021) – Christo said: "The object will look like it is alive and it will reflect light. The surface of the monument will move and fold and become sensual. People will want to touch the Arc de Triomphe".[2]

But contemporary research has an even more direct approach, contemplating wind as a constituent element of the work.[3] On this occasion, it only seemed fair to propose a few examples that consider wind as a moulding factor from an ecological perspective, which is almost an oxymoron when thinking about its inconsistency.

The threats, in some ways even the debris, brought into play by a distorted relationship with the environment, have been identified by the world of art a long time ago,[4] but the dialogue has become as urgent as ever today.

The examples on which we will briefly dwell certainly do not claim to be exhaustive, compared to the vast field of experiments that have explored this subject, but rather the aim is offering some food for thought, raising some questions on the topic.

Much research has exploited and still uses the energy of the wind to create moving and sound-generating works. Indirectly, air is among the moving elements of some Land Art works. On another level, think of how

2 Christo and Jeanne-Claude's first project, the "empaquetage" of the Arc de Triomphe in Paris dates back to 1961.

3 See also the exhibition *Undercurrents. Experimenta Ecosystems in Recent Art*, Whitney Museum of American Art, New York, May 27 – June 19, 2010.

4 We could certainly say that, as in human history in a more general sense, the issue became irreversible after 8:15 a.m. of August 6, 1945 with the explosion of the atomic bomb in Hiroshima. That something was going wrong and that the relationship with the environment was about to be compromised is a perception that art has been recording since the early years after World War II. Setting aside for a moment the answers that art provided immediately and after a while, and travelling forward in time of a couple of decades, it is only in the 60s and 70s that forms of artistic activism start to tackle the issue of the environment in a systematic way. In fact, many Land Art experiences refer to this idea.

much – especially on an urban scale – the mere act of exhibiting flags and letting them wave has the action of the wind as a necessary condition for it. It is the case, among others, of some installations by Daniel Buren. This uncontrollable action might also have some playful implications, as in the works of Theo Jansen, a Dutch artist who creates sculptures moved by the wind. A kinetic engineer, he has been working on his *Strandbeest*[5] (literally "beach beasts") since 1990. Fast machines, pushed and paced by the wind, made of plastic tubes, pieces of cloth, lightweight plastics and equipped with sensors that can change their course when they get near water. Even for him, this is an attempt to create new forms of life.

In this specific itinerary, the examples can easily show how the terms of the subject have always shifted from poetry to science. The dialogue remains today, in an inevitably changed context and under the threat of an unprecedented climate crisis with harmful consequences. This awareness has prompted us to revisit many of the distorted habits acquired in the exploitation of our planet, to which we had complied, guiltily unaware.

Diving deeper into the dialogue between art and science, it is worth noticing that while, in the past, the place for creating art was the atelier, now an increasing number of artists work in laboratories of various kind – from physical sciences to information technology, biology, climatology, robotics, virtual reality and artificial intelligence. And among those artists engaging with science, an emerging position is undoubtedly occupied by those who deal with the climate in terms of political activism[6].

One of them is David Buckland, film director and producer, responsible for the international project *Cape Farewell 2001*. With *www.capefarewell.com* a community of visionary artists, scientists and educators is trying to build collective international awareness as a cultural response to climate disruption[7].

Shifting the focus on research oriented towards supporting ecological sustainability in a more experimental way, some artists have chosen wind as an engine for natural and social transformation. With *Wind Array Cascade*

5 https://www.strandbeest.com/

6 See: https://www.climateartproject.com/
https://artclimatetransition.eu/about-us/
https://www.climart.info/

7 His work is included in the permanent collections of the National Portrait Gallery in London, the Center Georges Pompidou in Paris, the Michael Wilson Collection in London, the Metropolitan Museum in New York. In 2009, for the Royal Academy he curated *eARTH, Art for a Changing World.* He produced the films *Art from the Arctic*, in 2006 for the BBC and in 2010 *Burning Ice* for Sundance Film Festival.

Machine (2003) Steve Heimbecker translated the data captured from wind detectors into visual sound motifs. The work consists of a 64-channel sensor network, designed to capture in real-time the kinetic wave patterns of the wind on a horizontal surface. It works by analogously reproducing the wind patterns observed blowing across a prairie field of wheat. Translating the action of the wind into sound is a peculiar quality to the research of this artist, who, in 2004, on the occasion of the Les Islomanes symposium held in the Magdalen Islands in Quebec, created the kinetic sound sculpture *Windwaterwall,* swept by the ocean winds. In this case, in the structure of the installation – three windows with hanging shutters – there is a *reference* to the old swings that used to "squeak" in the wind, an autobiographical memory of his childhood, spent in a small prairie village swept by the wind. Beyond the gaze, therefore, the memory.[8]

More recently, the DAMP[9] collective proposed the installation *Anemocorìa* (2021) in the spaces of the Kunsthaus Contemporary Place in Lecce. Honoring the literal meaning of the word – natural dispersion of seeds acted by the wind –, they used an in vitro laboratory to show the close contiguity between decay and transformation resulting from the action of air.

Gaia Bindi writes in *Arte ambiente ecologia* – "When it takes climate from a geographic to a human scale, art succeeds in revealing hidden truths, uncovering dimensions and forms, rhythms and forces, and guarding them for tomorrow. In the presence of the current climate crisis, there is no need to get lost in the romantic idea of the sublime, but rather to prompt culture to resume the dialogue between science and humanity."[10]

On this shared assumption, one can think of Bruna Esposito for specific poetic reference. In many of her research, air is an allegory of lightness and fragility. At first, she used onion skins in the installation *Precipitazioni sparse* (2000-2005), presented in the spaces of the Corderie at Arsenale for the LI Venice Biennale in 2005, and then, more recently, a nostalgic recovery of disused technologies – ceiling fans – where the breath of the wind is evoked to spread and caress (*Altri venti – Ostro*, 2020). Her work *Altri Venti – Ostro* was the first realized for the ongoing series *Altri Venti,* dedicated to the winds of the Mediterranean and offered as a reflection on environmental sustainability, a theme, as mentioned, that the artist has addressed many times in her 40 years of research. In fact, the

---

8 https://www.bucklandart.com/

9 Founded in 2017 by Luisa de Donato, Alessandro Armento, Viviana Marchiò and Adriano Ponte.

10 G. Bindi, *Arte, ambiente, ecologia*, Postmediabooks, Milano, 2019, p. 99.

project *Altri Venti – Ostro* (2020), exhibited in December 2020 at Studio Miscetti in Rome, questioned the overuse of air conditioning systems to reduce the temperature in our rooms. The air conditioner is considered a worldwide commodity, despite its excessive use of electricity and release of pollutants into the environment. According to Bruna Esposito, this prompts the question – what would the world be like, if we abandoned individual comforts from more than just a cultural perspective? Recently, at the Magazzino Italian Art in New York, Domenico Palma presented a video, focusing precisely on the site-specific work that Bruna Esposito had created for the museum, and which was on view until September 11, 2021. This project was realized thanks to the support of the Italian Council fund, a program for the promotion of Italian contemporary art in the world, funded by the Directorate-General for Contemporary Creativity of the MIC[11]. After the New York exhibition, the project stopped in Buenos Aires and in Lisbon to be the quintessential southern wind – the Ostro –; the artist proposes to investigate other winds over time – Scirocco, Libeccio and Grecale. Thus, a work in progress. The artist explained that, in the beginning, the project was born out of her passion for fans – a timeless zero-millimetre breath – the most ancient way of moving air. Against the overwhelming use of air conditioning – one of the most polluting factors for the environment – the artist advocates a future where human beings will prefer fans and ventilators. She had already focused her attention on fans in the past with *Winds of Revolt* or *Revolt of the Winds* (2009), and also on propellers for an exhibition in Murano (2009). In the case of *Ostro,* the double tribute is to a fan activated by photovoltaic energy producing movement and breeze.

Shifting our focus to the atmosphere in general, and to the fog in particular – as a physical composition of droplets suspended in the air – it is worth considering the complex installation proposed by Lara Favaretto at the 58th Venice Biennale – *Thinking Head* (2017 – 2019). With her articulated project, the public at the entrance of the Central Pavilion in the Giardini[12] was suddenly immersed in a thick fog. The steam coming from the roof of the building – through a complex system of water pumps and pipes, smoke pipes and steam nozzles – regularly created a thick fog embracing the public. The idea expanded the sense of bewilderment evoked by the theme of the Biennial curated by Ralph Rugoff – *May You*

11 The Italian Ministry of Culture and Tourism.

12 R. Rugoff, *May You Live in Interesting Times*, 58ª Esposizione Internazionale d'Arte, La Biennale di Venezia, catalogo, 2019, pp. 244, 245.

Live in Interesting Times –, producing an actual state of blurring. As a whole, the work investigated the overall relationship between power and communication through the use of some words considered symbolic of the actual[13] moment. On this subject, the artist organized live streaming discussion groups with artists, intellectuals and scientists, taking place inside a bunker, kept secret to facilitate discussion and not to incur in any form of restriction. The fog embracing the viewers at the entrance – although only a moment in the overall articulation of the project – had somehow the function of dissolving into the vapor that cloaked the façade the sense of rhetorical ambiguity being debated. Ultimately questioning the authority of the Biennale institution, the work invited the viewers – from the very first access to the exhibition spaces – to start a path of exploration on our present and on its (clouded) lack of transparency.

In conclusion, as seen so far, the possible reasons for the use of wind in art are many – from the air contained in objects, to the shaping and sounding effects of its external action, to its induction through devices or its use in vitro laboratory tests, without forgetting ecological poetic digressions and political activism. At least one more level can be added to the suggestions generated by this subject – the air that we inhale and exhale from our body. Piero Manzoni had already made the artist's body the subject of his works with his *Fiato d'artista* (1960). Here, the air that inflated the balloons was produced by his own body, formalized by his life-breath, and then inevitably decaying and dying out over time. To observe the transformation and degradation to mush of his balloons is somehow traumatic.

On this idea, and in new ways aimed at combining artistic research with community participation, Claudia Losi has recently developed some zero-impact environmental experiences.

At the 2021 edition of Biennolo in Milan[14], the artist participated with a work that is part of her installation series entitled *Voce a Vento*. Hand-sewn kites, prayer flags, boat sails, and drying laundry with their light fabrics lift and swell when the wind or the voices of a choir pass them through. This was the case of the performance *Voce a vento (2019),* as described in

13 Consciousness, NDE, Cryo, Solidarity, Amnesia, Phantom, Debit, Flat, Humor, Education, Opacity, Power, Transhuman, Animism, Borders, Self-Doubt, Threshold, Algorithm, Absentee, Evidence, Distraction, Heritage, Insanity, Paradigm, Paradox.

14 BienNolo, the second edition of the contemporary art biennial was held in the Nolo district in Milan from October 1 to 10, 2021 https://www.biennolo.org/

the publication of the same name for the *Passo Chiama Passo*[15] series. To understand *Voce a vento,* we can let ourselves be guided by the words of the artist herself who, in a text co-written with Meike Clarelli, declared: "To inhabit territories is to leave a mark. A few years ago – on an exposed and treeless trail in Mount Bulgheria – we mixed our experiences with the desire to inhabit those territories, in an activity that would create the memory of a temporary and shared action for the people who were present."[16] On that occasion, 30 women, who were part of different choirs, sang their way slowly through a path marked by large wind socks sewn into the shape of an amphora. The performance had precisely the intention of inhabiting the landscape with voices and with their interactions with the wind.

Shared poetic action of a visual and sound nature, the performance was a crossing, a collective ritual, ultimately aimed at rekindling the memory of that place.

In this case, it was the voice, the wind, the community breath that rendered and built the experience and the work. Ultimately almost to cohabit in an ecosystem.

With this last "holistic" suggestion, the power and complexity of the art/air exchange is strengthened even more.

Breezes that caress, that sinuously shape, that mess up with our certainties, that interact to reflect on the preservation of the environment. In this diverse itinerary, they are the constant of an ephemeral and impermanent time that art, with poetry, science and politics, stubbornly and despite everything, is trying to take care of.

Translated by Eugenia Rodella

15 Claudia Losi with Meike Clarelli, *Voices in the Wind*, Step by Step, Milano, Kunstverein Publishing, 2021.

16 *Ibidem.*

II.
Literary Blowings, Artistic and Filmic Atmospheres

Niccolò Amelii

Turbidus Auster

Narrative and Symbolic Declinations of the South-East Wind in *Gli inganni* by Sandro De Feo and in *Scirocco* by Romualdo Romano

Ogni tanto dall'Africa arriva un veloce vento di fuoco, il temuto vento del sud: le piazze si arroventano in tal modo che i bambini scalzi, uscendo di casa al mattino, si bruciano le calcagna e mandano un grido, come se corressero sui mattoni di un forno; poco dopo si avvolgono i piedi con fasci di giornali e camminano lenti e circospetti, seguiti dai più selvaggi cani del quartiere che, in quel giorno, sono diventati buoni, stanchi e bisognosi di un padrone. I cittadini di X cercano ristoro nel mare, dove li reca una fila di tranvai, lenti e sobbalzanti come le ceste che, sopra i carri, portano le galline da un paese all'altro. Per tre giorni dura il vento del sud, poi cade; e giunge lo scirocco. Lo scirocco è meno furente, ma più sottile nel tormentare gli uomini. L'aria si svuota, e i cervelli, secondo la felice espressione di Masolino Ricasoli, giovane umorista della città, noto in quasi tutta l'Italia e residente a Milano, "i cervelli salgono nei crani come l'acqua gassata nel collo della bottiglia dalla quale è saltato il turacciolo". Il mare diventa paludoso e pesante, il cielo si sporca e, a causa dell'umidità, si ha l'impressione di aver messo la mano sul ventre di un pipistrello.[1]

1 "Every so often, from Africa comes a swift wind of fire—the dreaded wind from the south. The squares grow so scorching that the barefoot children, stepping out of their houses in the morning, burn their heels and cry out, as though they were running over the bricks of an oven. Soon after, they wrap their feet in bundles of newspapers and walk slowly and cautiously, followed by the wildest dogs of the neighborhood, who on that day have become gentle, weary, and in need of a master. The citizens of X seek relief in the sea, where a line of trams takes them—slow and jolting, like the baskets that, atop carts, carry hens from one village to another. For three days the south wind lasts, then it falls; and the sirocco arrives. The sirocco is less furious, yet subtler in tormenting men. The air empties, and the brains, according to the apt expression of Masolino Ricasoli, a young humorist of the city, known throughout almost all of Italy and residing in Milan, "the brains rise inside the skulls like sparkling water in the neck of a bottle from which the cork has just popped." The sea turns stagnant and heavy, the sky grows soiled, and because of the humidity one feels as though one had laid a hand upon the belly of a bat." V. Brancati, *Scirocco*, in Id., *Racconti, teatro e scritti giornalistici*, a cura di M. Dondero, Mondadori, Milano, p. 561 (the translations of the excerpts, prepared for reference purposes, were made by Paola Del Zoppo).

With his recognizable, sinuous, and happily evocative prose, Brancati provides in the story mentioned above – entitled *Scirocco* and published the first time in "L'Italiano" in 1936 – one of the most significant literary portraits of the sirocco wind, and, although it seems tautological to have to specify it, portraying a wind is not comparable to portraying a human face or a landscape, it is undoubtedly a more complex narrative operation because there are fewer sensory and perceptual referents to which you can do reliance on descriptive reworking. Representing the wind implies representing more than the wind itself, in its aerial conformation, the humoral and transformative effects it produces on men, animals, environments, and objects at the moment of its passage. In particular, the sirocco is a wind that, being abnormally hot and often humid, has always been associated with atmospheres of torpor and psychophysical malaise, even in its most varied literary representations. It is a south-east wind, initially dry, which reaches the Mediterranean coasts crossing the Sahara. It is loaded with moisture when it flies over the sea and overlooks our coasts, usually blowing no more than three consecutive days.

Because of the intense electricity accumulated in its fogs, the sirocco has been considered since ancient times as an annoying wind, a carrier of disorders both psychic – such as states of apathy, confusion and difficulty concentrating – and physical – such as migraine, hypotension, insomnia. And it is precisely this wind, the same that Orazio in the sixth composition of the second book of *Satire* (entitled *Vita di campagna e vita di città*) has defined as "sultry sirocco", which, in the novels examined – *Gli inganni* (1962) by Sandro De Feo and in *Scirocco* (1950) by Romualdo Romano – ceases to be a mere marginal scenographic element, a trace at most secondary contained in the subtext, to become instead the central vector of the narratives, the founding thematic nucleus around which the development of the works revolves. In the novels mentioned above, the sirocco wind is not limited to framing the fictional events to provide a note of realistic colouring. It also conditions the plot at the bottom by its dense symbolic bearing.

The meteorological and climatic element within the two diegetic constructions is cloaked in a pregnant metaphorical value when it rises to objective correlative not only of the numerous character and psychological nuances of the characters that populate the two novels – indolence, laziness, sadness – but also of the fundamental nature of the environments described, on the one hand, an illanguidized Rome, inebriated and harassed by the most sinister monotony, on the other a turbid Sicily, a remote corner of land inhabited by extreme characters to the point of paroxysm, and in which time seems to have stopped in a cyclical repetition, in the name of an existential tedium that casts a shadow of a grey sloth on everything. In *Scirocco*, winner in 1949 of the first edition of the "Hemingway Prize", the active presence of the homonymous wind is so widespread that the work seems to be written by the "strong wind of the South", as we read on the anonymous presentation of the volume, this sirocco that, investing men and things indifferently, "is born and lives in a logical conclusion like the Truth". Without precise temporal coordinates (we are presumably in the last years of the Second World War), the novel tells, within a chronological period that unfolds for three days, the vicissitudes rushed to a teacher – the protagonist of the story and at the same time the homodiegetic narrator – with timid literary ambitions who has recently moved to the remote village of Castagneto, hidden in the Peloritani mountains (near Messina):

> Da qualche tempo insegnavo a Castagneto, un villaggio sperduto sui monti Peloritani, e l'uggia mia saliva sino ai capelli. Non è facile vivere di noia. Ma lassù, tutti vivevano felicemente di noia![2]

The incipit immediately signals, with a prose that already reveals an evident figurative charge, the emotional and psychological tonality that characterizes the place of the events and, consequently, the everyday life of those who live there and that of the protagonist. The space within which the narrator's novel process develops is a space of existential immobility, in which nothing is destined to happen, characterised by a dull and frustrating monotony that goes well with the descriptions of loneliness, silence, and desolation that follow one another with a specific frequency. The protagonist repeatedly complains of a condition of boredom (similar to that experienced by Domenico Vannantò in Brancati's story entitled *La noia del "937* and set in Caltanissetta), and apparently irrepressible exhaustion, which then reverberates on every sketchy attempt at artistic momentum and sexual enjoyment. Introjected into this aura of overflowing tedium, even the erotic act, which the protagonist lives with impatience and, at times, disgust (to note, again, certain assonance with the frustrated "gallism" of the last Brancati), is destined to become, once extinguished every trace of ancient jouissance, a disturbing element, a mechanical

---

2 "For some time I had been teaching in Castagneto, a remote village in the Peloritani Mountains, and my tedium had risen all the way to my hair. It is not easy to live on boredom. But up there, everyone lived happily on boredom." R. Romano, *Scirocco*, Mondadori, Milano, 1950, p. 11.

repetition of a sequence of gestures carried out for passivity and inertia and not for the genuine desire for love fulfilment.

The sexual excitement that the protagonist feels because of the repeated advances of the daughter of his landlady, who tries in various ways to escape, without ever really opposing it, not only does not result in a satisfactory and serene emotional relationship but instead turns into an insurmountable obstacle for the literary vocation of the same, who feels hunted in the few free moments in which he would like to devote himself to writing. At the same time, however, the hypocrisy and duplicity with which the narrator himself explicitly alludes to the advantages of such intimacy while mocking and blaming the young woman's behaviour are evident. Within a diegetic architecture in which the only perspective of thought deducible from the text is that of the narrator, the effect of ambiguous slippage between the supposed beliefs that emerge from the homodiegetic discourse and the actions affects the degree of trust to be recognized to the narrator who writes "I", who betrays himself in different passages of the story – upsetting the supposed symmetry between will, thought and action – and in betraying himself reveals its actual physiognomy:

> Maledicevo il giorno in cui avevo deciso di scegliere quell'alloggio: ma l'avevo scelto appunto perché avevo intravisto quella figliola che, bisogna riconoscerlo, faceva gola a tutti. Tuttavia non riuscivo a tollerare quello stato continuo di eccitamento che, oltre a innervosirmi, mi toglieva la voglia di rimanermene almeno mezz'ora a tavolino.[3]

The boredom that affects every potential creative stimulus and tarnishes the contours of every possible event "out of the norm" – such as the ambush in which the protagonist himself is invited to participate by the Secretary, intending to flush out an alleged collaborator of the Allies – is exacerbated by the arrival of the sirocco, announced by a "striscia bianca di nuvole"[4], making the narrator, according to an apparently opposite motion, increasingly restless and exasperated by the flat repetitiveness of the hours:

---

3 Ivi, p. 14: "I cursed the day I had decided to choose that lodging; yet I had chosen it precisely because I had caught a glimpse of that girl who, one must admit, was a temptation to everyone. Nevertheless, I could not bear that constant state of excitement which, besides making me nervous, robbed me of the desire to remain at my desk even for half an hour."

4 Ivi, p. 16: "White stripe of clouds".

> Però pensavo sempre che a Castagneto doveva venire il diluvio perché si potesse dire che qualcosa di nuovo era accaduto: e non nascondo che lo desideravo, pur di sentirmi implicato in qualcosa.[5]

If man's life is triggered and then flourishes in conscious actions, in the will to be-in-the-world, the repeated impossibility of acting according to one's passions and fantasies inaugurates a gradual process of alienation, thickened by the existential brutalization that characterizes the surrounding society, now fatally accustomed to its individual and collective degeneration. It follows, as the primary form of adaptation, the development of a cynical and disenchanted attitude that the narrator puts between himself and reality to attenuate and defend himself in the wake of a logic of apathetic contempt and supposed moral and intellectual superiority from the distortions, contradictions, and widespread misery of a backward human microcosm, linked inextricably to ancestral rites and superstitions, harassed by legacies and social injustices endured for quiet living, inexorable resignation, inability to self-awareness of its condition as an acting class in history.

In this scenario of repeated and desolate anonymity, the sirocco makes inroads as an atmospheric agent marked by a high transformative power that incessantly invests men and things, coming to condition at the root not only the moods of the inhabitants and their behaviour but also changing the concrete value of places and objects, clouding their meaning, deforming their physiognomy, to the point of exacerbating their original features and making them threatening and disturbing:

> Nel pomeriggio si mise a soffiare lo scirocco. Il segnale lo diede la bandieruola di ferro sul terrazzo di fronte al mio balcone: cigolava sempre, ma quando soffiava lo scirocco pareva impazzisse addirittura e il suo stridìo esasperante penetrava nelle vene.[6]

The sirocco takes full possession of the narrative scene, soon assuming a metaphorical stature that swells its semantic significance, gravitating around words like "fury" and "threat", which return several times in the

5 Ivi, p. 19. "Yet I kept thinking that in Castagneto the flood would have to come before one could say that something new had happened; and I do not hide that I wished for it, if only to feel myself involved in something."

6 Ivi, p. 23. "In the afternoon the sirocco began to blow. The signal was given by the iron weathercock on the terrace opposite my balcony: it always creaked, but when the sirocco blew it seemed to go mad altogether, and its exasperating screech pierced into one's veins."

text always associated, in fact, with the presence of the wind. The same characters depicted – the curved manager of the tavern, the postal officer "piccolo ma enorme di pancia e di testa", his wife "alta almeno due metri" and "mostruosa in viso"[7] – whose physiognomic characteristics are outlined by excess to configure a human fresco that touches the grotesque and the surreal, seem a "filiazione spontanea dell'inquietante rappresentazione dello scirocco"[8]. The paralyzing wind that whips faces and weakens the already weak energies, the sirocco becomes an objective correlative of that "apatia congenita che, in segreto, si tramutava in fervore incredibile di maldicenza e corruzione, ispirato quasi sempre da sentimenti cattivi e perversi"[9]. Since, albeit inadvertently, the surrounding environment always acts on our personality as a whole, the inhabitants of Castagneto, trapped in an arid and inhospitable geographical space, always equal to itself, which seems unable to change and evolve, live in a perimeter of deep existential emptiness, in a perennial condition of inebriation of the senses and intentions, but without having any consciousness, masking their narrow lives behind fatuous vanities and useless arguments.

And it is precisely in the most significant degree of awareness of the trifles and transience of everything that the fundamental gap between the protagonist and the various characters surrounding him is installed. The protagonist seems to be the only fictional actor capable of identifying, recognizing, and denouncing the sloth and emotional torpor from which he is strenuously clinging. However, this apparently salvific awareness is accompanied, as an inescapable counterpart, by another type of awareness, that of not having any willpower or aspiration that can reverse the channeled fortunes of his unhappy life. The collision of these two awarenesses produces that sense of existential malaise and Sartrian boredom from which the narrator cannot free himself. Unable to emancipate himself from the geographical and anthropological reality that he finds himself experiencing, of escaping from the pockets of stagnation in which he slowly sinks, the protagonist of the novel lives earthly furies and not "astratti furori" – like

7 Ivi, p. 20. "small but enormous in belly and head"; "at least two meters tall"; "monstrous of face".

8 "spontaneous offspring of the unsettling representation of the sirocco", in M. Grasso, *Romualdo Romano, lo scrittore siciliano che vinse il primo premio letterario voluto da Hemingway*, in "Esperonews", https://www.esperonews.it/20200427111861/rubriche/medaglioni/romualdo-romano-lo-scrittore-siciliano-che-vinse-il-primo-premio-letterario-voluto-da-hemingway.html, consultato il 10/11/21.

9 "a congenital apathy which, in secret, turned into an incredible fervor of slander and corruption, almost always inspired by wicked and perverse feelings."

those of Vittorini's protagonist in *Conversazione in Sicilia* – that the sirocco wind – absolute antagonist, entity against which to fight – feeds and swells until it definitively wears out his capacity for endurance and tolerance: "Il fischio del vento m'infastidiva […]. La verità era che non tolleravo più nulla."; "Come odiavo quel vento, di notte!"[10].

The prevailing repetitiveness of the narration is interrupted by a series of events – a hunt, the death of the daughter of the wealthiest man in the country, the burning of a bakery, and the murder of the contractor – around which the novel dissolution then thickens. Yet, even the events that seem destined, at least for a moment, to shake the community from its atavistic drowsiness remain encapsulated in an atmosphere of resigned fatalism, wrapped in the coils of a sirocco that oppresses any potential awakening: "Tranne quel morto (ne muoion tanti!) non vedevo proprio quali cose succedessero. Il vento? ma quello non era un avvenimento: soffiava sempre, lassù."[11]

Just as the literary ambitions of the protagonist remain abstract digressions, unable to materialize, to incarnate in form and words, so the events that affect the flat surface of the life of the country occur without causing any immediate effect, extemporaneous moments of deviation immediately re-incorporated into absolute and general indolence. The existential malaise that snakes like an unshakeable curse through the claustrophobic streets of the country digs into the soul of the protagonist, helped by the incessant sirocco – symbolic vector of languidization and loss of desire – and internally projects the darkest and deepest shadows: "Mi alzai e mi buttai sul letto senza voglia nemmeno di dormire. Di che cosa avevo voglia? È terribile sentirsi vuoti, senza lo spunto indistinto che spinge di dentro e fa espandere nel mondo circostante!"[12]; "Io invece mangiavo, o meglio, non mangiavo più, perché mi sentivo nauseato. Mi sembrava di avere gli occhi piatti e il cervello vuoto. La radio del circolo urlava maledettamente e il vento mi fischiava nelle orecchie"[13].

---

10 R. Romano, *Scirocco*, *op cit.*, p. 39: "The whistling of the wind irritated me […]. The truth was that I could no longer endure anything."; Ivi, p. 45: "How I hated that wind, at night!"

11 Ivi, p. 82. "Except for that dead man (so many die!), I really couldn't see what things were happening. The wind? But that wasn't an event — it blew all the time, up there."

12 Ivi. P. 90. "I got up and threw myself on the bed, without even the wish to sleep. What was it I wanted? It is terrible to feel empty, without that indistinct impulse that stirs within and makes one expand into the surrounding world!"

13 Ivi, p. 92. "As for me, I ate—or rather, I no longer ate, for I felt nauseated. It seemed to me that my eyes were flat and my brain empty. The radio in the club

And further, in a crescendo of self-pity and self-destruction:

> Pensavo dentro di me a cose opache, indistinte, che avevano una testa enorme, una bocca grande e animalesca. [...] Pensavo all'inutilità delle cose che diciamo, quando riusciamo a dirle, alla povertà assoluta della nostra fantasia e al malanno d'esser nati in mezzo ai parassiti in un angolo qualunque della terra.[14]

As well as "Il vento che gradatamente cadeva mi lasciò illanguidire sul letto. [...] Rimasi supino a lungo e dimenticai persino d'esser nato e di pensare"[15].

The sirocco wind seems, once sublimated its atmospheric connotations, to become an all-pervasive and all-encompassing dimension, a substitute agent of a human will be now annihilated by a sense of cyclopean powerlessness:

> Pensavo disperatamente alla vita che lasciavo scorrer come un tappeto, ma non riuscivo a immaginarmene una migliore, altrove. E non mi sentivo capace di risvegliare negli altri, in quelle creature che mi stavan davanti, sentimenti diversi. Chi sa, pensavo, che finalmente non venga il diluvio![16]

However, the flood does not arrive, thoughts do not turn into fact, and things proceed as usual in the infinite wheel of time; the souls of the country, which metaphorically translated rise to represent the entire human condition, brutalized by selfishness, ignorance, indifference and pettiness of all sorts, remain unredeemable. The sirocco ceases to blow after the three canonical days and marks the end of this desperate tragedy of inaction. When reality severs all dialogue and denies itself, made elusive and incommunicable by the blows of the wing of a wind that so resembles

---

was screaming damnably, and the wind was whistling in my ears."

14 Ivi. p. 120: "I was thinking to myself of opaque, indistinct things that had an enormous head, a large, animal-like mouth. [...] I was thinking of the uselessness of the things we say, when we manage to say them, of the absolute poverty of our imagination, and of the misfortune of having been born among parasites in some random corner of the earth."

15 Ibidem: "The wind, gradually dying down, left me languishing on the bed. [...] I remained on my back for a long time and even forgot that I had been born and that I could think."

16 Ivi, p. 116: "I was thinking desperately of the life I was letting slip by like a carpet, yet I could not imagine a better one elsewhere. Nor did I feel able to awaken in others, in those creatures before me, different feelings. Who knows, I thought, whether at last the flood might come!"

the "cocci aguzzi" of Montale's poetry, it can neither be lived nor thought nor written:

> Guardavo trasognato, dimentico d'ogni cosa, come sempre, qui, in questo selvaggiume sperduto, solo come tutte le cose sole. Potevo scrivere qualche pagina chiudendomi con il chiavistello: perché? [...] Il vento era completamente caduto e l'aria era tranquilla. Rientrai e mi misi a tavolino. Guardai a lungo il foglio bianco: perché? Dicevo. E non scrivevo nulla. [...] Io non scrivevo e non pensavo: temevo di premere un solo tasto della macchina, perché mi sembrava di sentir dire "è pronto" e io non ero pronto, non ero mai pronto, non sarei mai stato pronto, perché ero poeta e non facevo poesie, ero giornalista e non scrivevo sui giornali, ero asino e non ragliavo! Allora presi un foglio bianco, lo infilai nella macchina e con mano sicura e tranquilla pressai i tasti e scrissi nel mezzo "FINE".[17]

Even in *Gli Inganni*, Sandro De Feo's first novel, published in 1962, the events that emerge in the arc of the narrative never represent fictional closed units, but serve, on the contrary, as narrative pretexts that the narrator (the protagonist of the work, Antonio) uses to feed his reflections and his incessant mental monologue. Adopting the Aristotelian units of space, time and action, and a narrative structure that unfolds in episodes, De Feo's text can be read as a "romanzo di bilancio, in filigrana autobiografica, della già trascorsa giovinezza"[18], a showdown that Antonio, a middle-aged intellectual who moved from Puglia to Rome to write for the cinema and transparent alter-ego of the author, he carries on with himself, with his lost illusions and above all with the city of Rome, a stage mythologized by his now predominant cinematographic counterpart, which contends with the reality of the places – the cafes of Via Veneto, Piazza del Popolo, Caffè Rosati – the very sense with which to experience them.

17 Ivi, p. 138-139. "I gazed dreamily, forgetful of everything, as always here, in this remote wilderness, alone as all things alone. I could have written a few pages by bolting myself in: but why? [...] The wind had completely fallen and the air was still. I went back inside and sat at my desk. I looked for a long time at the blank sheet: why? I asked myself. And I wrote nothing. [...] I did not write and I did not think: I was afraid to press a single key of the typewriter, because it seemed to me I heard it say "it's ready," and I was not ready, I had never been ready, I would never be ready, because I was a poet and I did not write poems, I was a journalist and I did not write for newspapers, I was a donkey and I did not bray! Then I took a blank sheet, slipped it into the machine, and with a steady and tranquil hand pressed the keys and wrote in the middle 'THE END.'"

18 M. Raffaeli, *Prefazione*, in S. De Feo, *Gli inganni*, Cliquot, Roma, 2020, p. 5: "a novel of reckoning, with an autobiographical watermark, of a youth already past".

The Rome of *La dolce vita* (the film comes out in 1960), therefore, but also the Rome of *La noia* by Moravia (novel published in the same year), invaded by old and new movie stars, producers, screenwriters, directors, aspiring divas, journalists, paparazzi, and impostors more than actual characters (in this regard, Arbasino writes: "Roma, in sostanza, secerne umori, mi pare, più che non esprimere personaggi"[19]). Adapted to the new scenario of a thousand-year-old Rome, always the same, but cloaked in false and mannerist pomp, Antonio "conduce la sua empirica esistenza come uno spettatore nella platea di un cinema o di un teatro"[20], and interprets the ambivalent signs of the city as a man from the South who has not yet wholly managed to free himself from his family legacies, from certain forms of ancestral superstition, and also from a latent nostalgia for youth spent carefree in the provinces, in the countryside and in the farms.

Between Puglia's open and airy spaces and the excessive opulence of a hyper-busy Rome, which always appears disfigured, a step away from crumpling on itself, to change above all is the wind that blows. The sirocco that annoyingly rages on Antonio's Rome, in the little more than twenty-four hours staged in the novel and that accompanies him since the livid awakening, immediately rises to an atmospheric-meteorological agent bearing in itself a veiled physical and at the same time metaphysical tension, which "ipoteca il comportamento di chi vive a Roma, lo intride di una ambigua inerzia, lo spinge alla dilettazione morosa, a un ozio senza dignità e che tale vuole rimanere"[21]. And it is precisely the condition of languid otium that is subtly instilled in the daily succession of facts, mirages and thoughts, to induce in the protagonist a contemplative and introspective attitude, bearer of memories that collaborate to weld the already thick membrane that separates him from a direct, unmediated, non-spurious contact with the surrounding reality. The meteropathic alienation that descends from the very beginning of the novel about Antonio, whose nervous system turns out to be particularly sensitive to the changes of the weather and "in generale al clima orribile di questa città" ("in general to

19 A. Arbasino, *L'ingegnere in blu*, Adelphi, Milano, 2008, p. 184: "Rome, essentially, secretes humors, it seems to me, rather than expressing characters."

20 S. Corriero, *Scetticismo e idealismo negli "Inganni" di Sandro De Feo*, in *Atti del convegno. Il mondo di Sandro De Feo*, a cura di P. Bianchi, C. Novielli, in "Nuovi Orientamenti", gennaio-aprile 1989, p. 13: "he conducts his empirical existence like a spectator in the stalls of a cinema or a theatre."

21 M. Raffaeli, *op. cit.*, p. 7: "it pre-determines the behaviour of those who live in Rome, saturates it with an ambiguous inertia, drives it toward morose delectation, toward an idleness without dignity — and determined to remain so."

the dreadful climate of this city", p. 16), continues like a shadow over the entire arc of the narrative, configuring itself as a separative and liminal condition through which to introject and then rework the impressions and intuitions accumulated during the day.

It is for this reason that Antonio seems to experience the outside world with a certain haughty detachment, more interested in embroidering and connecting in himself the image of that "coffee society" (parody of the original eighteenth-century matrix) that fascinates and rejects him than to live it in first person. As happens to the protagonist of *Scirocco*, Antonio also lives a continuous weakening of the will, so the intentions and promises he makes to himself and others never match, for laziness, indolence and fatalism, with the actions undertaken. The "mollaccia romana" – autochthonous and papal declination of Sartrian "nausea" – incorporates within its magnetic coils every flicker of sincere impulse and free desire, flattening any purpose or desire that goes beyond the voyeuristic dimension of watching live and letting oneself live:

> Che cos'è questo "ribollire"? Altro che ribollire. Con la mollaccia che c'è nell'aria stamattina, il fiato e il sangue mi stanno scendendo nelle scarpe, anzi nelle pantofole, e mi ributterei sul letto non appena messo a piede a terra. Macché ribollire, è stata un po' di stizza ecco tutto, ed è scesa giù anch'essa insieme a tutto il resto, voglia di uscire, voglia di scrivere, voglia di leggere, voglia di voler male o voler bene, tutto sceso giù nelle pantofole che trascino sul parquet mentre mi avvio al bagno.[22]

When the threads that bind the subject to his reality frayed so much that they risk breaking completely, the things that happen outside always appear unimportant, laughable, and dull. That is why Antonio is always listless, contrite and out of focus and has no interest in accompanying Vituccio, the childhood friend who came to visit him to get help in solving minor skirmishes created in his village, by his cousin Alfonso, a Jesuit belonging to a vital congregation. Vituccio represents the eternal face of the province, a native legacy that cannot be severed and that intermittently

---

22 S. De Feo, *Gli inganni*, *op. cit.*, p. 26: "What is this "boiling over"? Boiling over, my foot. With the sticky heaviness in the air this morning, my breath and my blood are sinking into my shoes—no, into my slippers—and I'd throw myself back into bed the moment I set foot on the floor. Boiling over, nonsense; it was only a fit of irritation, that's all, and it too has gone down with everything else—the wish to go out, the wish to write, the wish to read, the wish to hate or to love—all of it sunk down into the slippers I drag across the parquet as I make my way to the bathroom."

reappears, despite attempts to emancipate itself, with its bizarre ways, its linguistic tics, its swampy convictions, its latent vices, and being a privileged spokesman of this microcosm is a character that turns out to be gifted, at least apparently, of robust and well-expressed identity features. However, they are pathetic, ridiculous, and anachronistic.

This, however, cannot be said of Antonio, aware that his existential displacement has caused a traumatic identity disruption, which needs to be systematically propped up through a re-enactment of his past, his roots and a repeated dialogue with the figures – his mother, Raffaele "il familio", now Vituccio – who inhabited that past, filled and project it into a present emptied of meaning and, therefore, deprived of specific taxonomies and paradigms with which to continue to read and interpret one's journey in the world. Moreover, as Norberg-Schulz explains, "l'identità dell'uomo presuppone l'identità del luogo"[23], therefore, when a given place belongs to a man only half, its identity connotations are destined to remain uncertain and indefinable:

> Ma una spiegazione che a qualcuno parrà banale o sentimentale o da reazionario, ma è forse la più vera di tutte, è che io ho paura di sentirmi tagliato fuori, "alienato" si usa dire adesso, dalla mia realtà naturale, déraciné, strappato dalla mie radici. Io non sarei più tranquillo, non sarei più tanto sicuro della mia identità se mi sentissi tagliato fuori completamente dalle mie radici.[24] (p.31)

To survive within a society that changes rapidly and chaotically, in search of new myths and false idols, and that seems totally disinterested in enhancing its true millennial heritage, to act as an intermediary between yesterday and tomorrow, Antonio is aware that it is necessary to have his own personal history to recover. This experience must return to illuminate when it becomes labile and confused. Even in boredom, in exhaustion, in existential tedium exacerbated by the sirocco, it is necessary to leverage what keeps us most firmly on the ground, our roots:

> Così, in una città come Roma io posso trovarmici a mio agio anche quando mi annoia, e spesso mi annoia da morire, anche quando i venti molli mi

23 C. Norberg-Schulz, *Genius Loci. Paesaggi Ambiente Architettura*, Electa, Milano, 1986, p. 22: "the identity of man presupposes the identity of place."

24 S. De Feo, *op. cit.*, p. 31: "But an explanation that to some may seem banal, sentimental, or reactionary — yet perhaps the truest of all — is that I am afraid of feeling cut off, "alienated," as one says now, from my natural reality, *déraciné*, torn from my roots. I would no longer be at peace; I would no longer be sure of my identity if I felt myself completely cut off from my roots."

riducono uno straccio come fanno oggi, solo perché mi ci sono trapiantato tanti anni fa con una o due radici, ripeto non ne occorrono poi tante. Ma strapparle da me vorrebbe dire alienarmi non solo dalla mia natura e da me stesso, ma anche da Roma e da tutto.[25]

However, the memory can become fallacious and deceptive if constantly fed by an imaginative tension that strives to increase some specific traits and to overshadow others, according to trajectories of accommodation capable of architecting reassuring personal myths with greater pleasure and joy. The endemic lethargy and sloth accompanying Antonio's actions and reflections reinforce his tendency to infer his pre-established convictions, and his sample of moral evaluations and social prejudices is preserved and kept available for moments of more significant disorientation. Within the novel there is only one passage in which the cloth of skepticism and indolence that surrounds Antonio and his easy considerations is torn apart, albeit temporarily, reshuffling for a moment the categories with which he is interpreting the people he meets. It is when Antonio and Vituccio himself head to the hospital to try to save a little girl who was involved in a car accident. The mad race against time undertaken by the two disrupts the picture of false knowledge and assumptions in which Antonio has been ensnared for years, and reveals in Vituccio traces of human *pietas* that Antonio would not have imagined even in the slightest:

Mi dà proprio da pensare, non si finisce mai di sbagliare a questo mondo e di apprendere cose nuove. Vituccio fa certe smorfie curiose, inghiotte saliva come uno che vuol mandare giù qualcosa e potrebb'essere il voltastomaco. Ma se fosse pianto? Perché egli si morde il labbro superiore come chi non vuol piangere, lo vedo benissimo nello specchietto retrovisivo, do una occhiata alla strada dinanzi, un'occhiata allo specchietto, vedo benissimo lui e vedo lei che per me è morta, e forse anche per Vituccio, altrimenti perché avrebbe voglia di piangere, un omaccio come lui? E d'altro canto se Vituccio comincia a rendersi conto che la bambina non è più viva, forse perché la sente a mano a mano raffreddarsi, come mai, lui così superstizioso e che ha un po' del sangue di Raffaele nelle vene, come mai invece di scostarsi da lei, le si accosta sempre

25 Ivi, p. 32: "Thus, in a city like Rome I can feel at ease even when it bores me — and often it bores me to death — even when the soft winds reduce me to a rag as they do today, simply because I transplanted myself here many years ago with one or two roots; I repeat, not many are needed. But to tear them from me would mean alienating myself not only from my own nature and from myself, but also from Rome and from everything."

più e la passa due dita sulla fronte che, sono sicuro, si va raffreddando a mano a mano?[26]

The violent encounter with a reality no longer phantasmagorical, but now alive, pulsating, tragic seems to reactivate the sense of time and the mutability of things, thus revitalizing the subtle existential inspiration. The reality of the child to be saved is an immanent, desperate, but also revealing, epiphanic reality, capable of awakening the numb soul and untying it from the forcing and monotony to which it is constantly subjected:

> Questa sì che è realtà, per dio, la realtà sono le cose che mutano e diventano diverse per sé, non le cose che a forza di ripetersi ed essere sempre le stesse non sono più nulla perché nemmeno le vediamo più, reali sono le persone che si sottraggono, sia pure per dieci minuti soltanto, o dieci secondi, alla schiavitù, alla routine della loro natura, libere e per ciò stesso reali. [...] E poiché realtà chiama realtà, quel sorriso ha chiamato l'amore reale, perché libero da convenzioni e pregiudizi di uomini fatti, provati, stanchi, spossati da anni e anni di scirocco romano e di favonio pugliese, e che ora, svegli e tutte le energie tese al massimo, come corridori sulla pista, corrono e suonano il clacson all'impazzata per fendere la folla che tarda a farsi da parte, inebetita com'è dallo scirocco che oggi si può tagliare col coltello.[27]

---

26 Ivi, p. 56. "It really makes me think; one never stops making mistakes in this world, nor learning new things. Vituccio makes strange faces, swallows his saliva like someone trying to force something down, and it might be nausea. But what if it were tears? Because he bites his upper lip like a man who doesn't want to cry — I can see it perfectly in the rear-view mirror. I glance at the road ahead, a glance at the mirror: I see him perfectly, and I see her, who to me is dead — and perhaps to Vituccio as well; otherwise, why should he feel like crying, a big man like him? And yet, if Vituccio is beginning to realize that the little girl is no longer alive, perhaps because he feels her growing colder and colder in his hands, how is it, he being so superstitious and having a bit of Raffaele's blood in his veins, that instead of moving away from her, he draws even closer and runs two fingers over her forehead, which, I am sure, is gradually growing cold?"

27 Ivi, p. 58: "This, by God, is reality — reality is the things that change and become different of themselves, not the things that, by endlessly repeating themselves and being always the same, are nothing any longer, because we no longer even see them. Real are the people who escape, even if only for ten minutes, or ten seconds, from the slavery, from the routine of their own nature — free, and by that very fact, real. [...] And since reality calls to reality, that smile has summoned real love, because it is free from the conventions and prejudices of grown men — tried, weary, exhausted by years and years of Roman sirocco and Apulian favonio — who now, awake and with all their energies stretched to the utmost, like runners on the track, drive and sound their horns madly to cut through the crowd that is

However, the wound in reality that opens a window on the actual, tangible meaning of what is there and spreads outside of its subjective space and its annihilating projections, immediately tends to heal, as well as the promise that Antonio makes to himself to go and visit the child in the hospital the following morning is destined to remain a vague and abstract resolution, unable to be respected because immediately wrapped in that skepticism and powerlessness to think and discover oneself better than what one is.

The reality of that absolute moment, which had a contingent meaning and yet radiated as a potential trigger for a universal awareness of one's relationship with the outside world, thins out and does not settle either in Antonio or in Vituccio, becomes at most "un'immagine da mettere in un racconto", one of the many anecdotes to be added "nei magazzini periferici della memoria", a story "da tenere in serbo e tirare fuori all'occasione"[28]. Nothing more can be learned when the mind and heart are saturated with images and previous thoughts that have occupied all the inner space, and the nerves are agitated by a sirocco that acts as an objective correlative of the inability to see clearly in front of it (as happened in Romano's novel, in which the sirocco burned the eyes of the protagonist several times), everything subtends and transcends: friendship, love, memory, personal ambitions. Even in *Gli Inganni,* the emotional component is reduced to caricature, tired parody, and a game of mirrors in which the fatuous illusions of the characters are reflected. It could not be otherwise in Rome, where appearing is more important than being, a place of ostentatious vice and slammed on the front page, in which every possible sincere affection, as well as every potential pure and disinterested falling in love, is cancelled at the beginning. Here, then, the affection that Antonio seems to feel for the young Silvana smacks of compassion more than love, a feeling born in the wake of the supposed belief that Silvana takes pleasure in making others believe that she is what she is not:

> Povera Silvana, un animale è proprio ciò che essa vorrebbe essere e non è. Almeno quello stupido di impotente non ci rimette gran che, tutto si riduce per lui a un po' di smancerie e a qualche bacio dato contro voglia, mentre la mia povera Silvana a letto con gli uomini ci va davvero perché in fondo è seria e il

---

slow to move aside, dazed as it is by the sirocco that today one could cut with a knife."

28 Ivi, p. 65: "an image to be put into a story"; Ivi, p. 66: "in the outlying warehouses of memory", "to be kept in reserve and brought out when the occasion arises".

> problema per lei è di persuadere sé stessa, prima degli altri, che essa è come un bell'animale, coi sensi, la voglia di un bell'animale.[29]

Yet, as we have already seen, in a city like Rome, where everything is stratified, ambiguous and bears the weight of centuries of history, glories and triumphs, and where the sirocco clouds the sharpness of the senses and makes the boundaries between people and their perceptions uncertain, labile, and confused, one can never be sure that has not overinterpreted, that has not unconsciously mythologized the facts and the emotions. The operation of mythologization is also an operation of typing, a process through which the trait that is most considered to define it is extracted from an event or a person and amplified until it matches the entire perimeter of that given event or that given person, thus managing to insert it subsequently and efficiently in the studied classification with which we try to reduce to the extreme the infinite casuistry of actions, counter-actions, feedbacks, causes, as well as the varied and unknown humanity that surrounds us, with its immense baggage of beliefs, feelings, doubts.

Antonio survives through the continuous processes of typification with which he feeds the meaning of his existence. However, when he begins intending the possible discrepancy between what he believes and the fundamental nature that others possess, and with which they are forced to negotiate daily, he is invaded by a sense of loss and despair. In this topical moment, the sirocco takes on a double thematic function. If on the one hand, it seems, in fact, to rekindle the already pungent desolation of having to constantly be oneself, of not being able to emancipate oneself from the cage that was built with one's own hands, supreme symbol of the physical and psychological "insabbiamento" in which the inhabitants of Rome (Anthony in the first place) have slipped, on the other hand it is charged with a complementary metaphorical value, solver and clarifying, able to uncover the self-produced deceptions from which Antonio lets himself be ensnared for years, too lazy and intimidated to really want to face what they hide and touch the truth (after all, writes Flaiano: "la verità fulmina chi osa

29 Ivi, p. 37: "Poor Silvana — an animal is precisely what she would like to be, and is not. At least that fool of an impotent man doesn't lose much by it; for him it all comes down to a few affectations and a few unwilling kisses, while my poor Silvana really does go to bed with men, because, deep down, she is serious — and for her the problem is to persuade herself, before persuading others, that she is like a fine animal, with the senses and the desire of a fine animal."

guardarla in facia"[30]) nested at the bottom of an individual and collective existence now vacuous, in which everything, even art and culture, is pure exhibition, fulfillment of the self, vanity, immoderate chatter, an instrument of power and sexual blackmail (the same deceptions are inseparably assimilated to what Norberg Schulz calls "il carattere ambientale"[31] of the place, this cyclically decadent Rome, which has kept them in its bosom for centuries, cradles them and nourishes them like children and is then betrayed, suffocated and brutalized).

On the other hand, as Flaiano notes in his review of the work, the novel itself can be read metaphorically as "una folata di vento che trasporta polvere, foglie, cartacce e anche qualche materia imponderabile e preziosa, la nostra stessa vita, le illusioni inutili, una fatica di anni, l'amore per una città che è unica e che si lascia amare e detestare, a seconda degli umori e degli spettacoli che offre"[32]. You cannot escape from yourself just as you cannot escape from Rome once you have let yourself be cloaked in its oppressive splendour, repertoire scenes, and baroque melodramas. In the final dissolution of the novel, at the end of this long day in which nothing seems to have happened and instead everything happened, Antonio understands, after trying to unmask the subodorous liaison between Vituccio and Silvana without succeeding, to have unmasked, instead, himself, his cynical and transfigurative nature that pushes him to project his malaise on others constantly. Antonio has assimilated Vituccio and Silvana into stereotyped models, fueled by literary and cinematographic perspectives, which he has built independently of the phenomenological present of their authentic humanity. At the height of his existential crisis, Antonio realizes that he has falsified reality more than it tends to falsify itself, that he has idealized the love of his cousin Alfonso and the infatuation of Silvana, that he has sublimated the physiognomies of the people around him to make them more suitable puppets for the farce he has set up to protect himself from the real world and from the condemnation to loneliness that it brings with it. This epiphanic enlightenment is accompanied by the dramatic awareness that there is no possibility of knowing reality, of putting chaos

30 E. Flaiano, *Autobiografia del blu di Prussia*, Rizzoli, Milano, 1974, p. 124: "truth strikes down whoever dares to look it in the face."

31 C. Norberg-Schulz, *op. cit*., p. 6.

32 E. Flaiano, *La solitudine del satiro*, Rizzoli, Milano, 1973, p. 35: "a gust of wind carrying dust, leaves, scraps of paper, and also some imponderable and precious substance — our very life, our useless illusions, the toil of years, the love for a city that is unique and that lets itself be loved and detested, according to the moods and the spectacles it offers."

in order, if not filtering and courting it through one's distorted imagination, colonized by media and cinematographic archetypes that mystify its direction:

> E di questo si tratta in fondo. In un mondo così assurdo, estroverso e conviviale all'apparenza, ma nel quale la condizione dell'uomo è ogni giorno di più quella del condannato alla segregazione cellulare, il solo modo, se non di conoscere la realtà, almeno di tirare la sua acqua al nostro mulino, di costringerla a starci vicino, sì da non farci sentire troppo soli, è appunto di mitizzarla e, in certo senso, di idealizzarla. [...] Se ora io sento come un dolore acuto la perdita dei miei due amici, non è perché essi mi hanno fatto dei torti o io ne ho fatti a essi, a questo potrei porre riparo, ma perché, essendosi sottratti all'attività ordinatrice e integratrice dei miti che mi ero fatto di essi, si vanno ora dissolvendo, disintegrando in un'infinità di atti, di gesti, parole, sguardi, sorrisi, smorfie, gemiti, gridi di esultanza o di paura o di brama, di ognuno dei quali io potrei dare infinite spiegazioni tutte più o meno vere e quindi tutte più o meno false. E a questa fuga dall'ordine nel caos nessun riparo è possibile.[33]

Extinguished every horizon of human palingenesis, "la conoscenza della realtà reale non porta ad Antonio alcuna gratificazione e alcun sollievo, ma, anzi, lo conduce all'isolamento"[34]. Tragic is the feeling of vertigo that this discovery causes to think of welcoming it, elaborating on it intimately and making it a starting point to inaugurate a new existential parable. It is easier, more welcoming and safer to fall conscientiously into the ancient parental and affective mythologies, into the tried and tested processes of elaboration of promises and excuses and justifications that alternate in an endless vicious circle, the only survival strategies to be implemented to live from day to day and defend itself from the erosive and exhausting

33 S. De Feo, *op. cit.*, p. 136: "And this, in the end, is what it is all about. In a world so absurd, outward-looking and convivial in appearance, yet in which the condition of man is more and more that of one condemned to solitary confinement, the only way — if not to know reality, at least to draw its water to our own mill, to force it to stay close to us so that we may not feel too alone — is precisely to mythicize it and, in a way, to idealize it. [...] If I now feel, as an acute pain, the loss of my two friends, it is not because they have wronged me or I them — that I might repair — but because, having withdrawn from the ordering and integrating activity of the myths I had made of them, they are now dissolving, disintegrating into an infinity of acts, gestures, words, glances, smiles, grimaces, moans, cries of exultation or of fear or of desire, each of which I could explain in infinitely many ways, all of them more or less true, and therefore all of them more or less false. And against this flight from order into chaos, no remedy is possible."

34 S. Corriero, *op. cit.*, p. 13: "The knowledge of actual reality brings Antonio neither gratification nor relief; on the contrary, it leads him to isolation."

doubts of a multifaceted, mobile and impregnable identity, from the suffering inherent in true and all-encompassing love, from the absurdity and senselessness of existence:

> E, del resto, come si dice? Aiutati che il ciel ti aiuta. E io mi aiuto come posso per non finire schiacciato sotto la cappa di un tempo e di tempi come questi [...] mi aiuto facendomi continuamente promesse di azioni civili che poi non mantengo, facendo andare la macina che macina miti, e siamo (siano? Chiedere all'autore) pure un poco o parecchio compiaciuti e corrivi, ma intanto mi fanno sentire meno solo e più umano. Quando fa questo tempo e in tempi come questi, il segreto, non mi stancherò mai di ripeterlo, è di trovare il modo di non ridursi solo e miserabile come un verme, di darsi fiato, di darmi fiato fino a che un bel mattino, aprendo il balcone e uscendo sulla terrazza del piano attico dove abito, vedrò il cielo pulito e celeste dietro la cupola di San Pietro, allora tutto sarà più facile, voglio dire che sarà più facile resistere a stare al mondo.[35]

35 S. De Feo, *op. cit.*, p. 31: "And, after all, as they say? Help yourself and Heaven will help you. And I help myself as best I can so as not to end up crushed beneath the weight of a time and of times like these [...] I help myself by continually making promises of civic action that I then do not keep, by setting the mill to grind myths; and we are (are we? ask the author) perhaps a little or even very much self-satisfied and compliant, but in the meantime they make me feel less alone and more human. When the weather is like this and in times like these, the secret — I will never tire of repeating it — is to find a way not to be reduced to something alone and miserable like a worm, to give oneself breath, to give myself breath until, one fine morning, opening the balcony and stepping out onto the terrace of the attic where I live, I will see the sky clear and blue behind the dome of Saint Peter's — then everything will be easier, I mean it will be easier to go on resisting, to go on living in the world."

Daniela Bombara[1]

Gusts of Mystery and Madness in Italian Fantastic Narratives

Impetuous winds disrupt, devastate and destroy. Yet, even in their mildest form, they can alter the observer's senses, giving rise to a visual and auditory dynamism that blurs and renders fluid the contours and figures of objects and people, thereby producing an uncertain and approximate perception of reality. Such uncertainty of factual data can also contaminate the gazer and lead to a feeling of identity loss.

Science has already explored the connection between wind and mental health[2], whereas popular tradition, which is sometimes echoed by cinema, insists on highlighting the perturbing trait of a natural force that transcends human limits[3]. In the first seminar of *Also sprach Zarathustra,* Jung

1 Daniela Bombara is currently Research Associate at the University of Witwatersrand, Johannesburg.

2 A. Bulbena et al., *Panic Anxiety, under the weather?*, in "International Journal of Biometeorology", vol. 49, n. 4, 2005, pp. 238-243; J.J.A. Denissen et al., *The effects of weather on daily mood: a multilevel approach, in* "Emotion" 8, n. 5, 2008, pp. 662-667. Unless otherwise specified, all translations from Italian scholars and writers are by the author of this essay.

3 Cf. I. Campagna, *Venti di follia,* [*Winds of Madness*] in "Le Scienze", 30 luglio 2019. On wind-related folklore in Italy and bordering regions, one may cite studies focused on specific geographical areas, which in any case provide useful general indications: D. Mortato, *Folletti, verruche e garofani... Saggio sugli anemonimi in Corsica* [*Sprites, Warts and Carnations... An Essay on Anemonyms in Corsica*], in "Géolinguistique", 23, 2023, https://journals.openedition.org/geolinguistique/13904; N. Prantera, *Anemonimia popolare in area calabrese: spunti per una etnotassonomia dei venti* [*Folk Wind-Naming in Calabria: Notes Toward an Ethnotaxonomy of Winds*], in *ὀνόματα διελεῖν. Studi in onore di John Trumper per il suo 75° genetliaco* [*ὀνόματα διελεῖν. Studies in Honour of John Trumper on the Occasion of His 75th Birthday*], Edizioni AICC Castrovillari, Castrovillari 2020, pp. 85–120; R. Sottile, *I nomi dei venti in Sicilia tra toponomastica, geomorfologia e «mondo magico». Possibili itinerari di ricerca* [*The Names of Winds in Sicily between Toponymy, Geomorphology, and the «Magical World»: Possible Research Pathways*], in *Studi linguistici in onore di Lorenzo Massobrio*, [*Linguistic Studies in Honour of Lorenzo Massobrio*], Istituto dell'Atlante Linguistico Italiano (ALI), Torino 2014, pp. 957–970. Albeit

reported a story (perhaps a dream) by Nietzsche: in a forest he encountered a mysterious man, who struck him with such an acute whistle that it made him faint. Jung commented:

> It is Wotan who gets him, the old wind god breaking forth, the god of inspiration, of madness, intoxication and wildness [...]. It is, of course, the shrieking and whistling of the wind in a storm in a nocturnal wood, the unconscious. It is the unconscious itself that breaks forth. This is very beautifully described here: doors fly open and out bursts that wind, bringing a thousand laughters. It is a horrible foreboding of his insanity [...] that is humanly understandable.[4]

The mysterious man – the unconscious in Jung's interpretation – is the numinous incarnation of the wind; an intruding energy between the observer and the world that triggers an estrangement which forces a rethinking of the usual patterns, dismantling the observer's automatisms[5]. The abandonment of rational thought is, on the one hand, an attempt to overcome the narrow boundaries of logic to welcome the divine; on the other hand, it is an expression of the incoercible power of nature, which towers over human beings and leads them to experience the 'sublime', with a sense of horror and fascination[6].

Whether a gust, a flurry, or a breeze, the meteorological shift of air is ultimately the very image of writing. Such a fluid and 'windy' entity fantastically reworks existence, forcing but also inviting authors and readers to wander, as suggested by Gianni Celati in his *Conversazioni del vento volatore* [*Conversations of the Flying Wind*][7]. Writing becomes wandering,

---

geographically and temporally distant, three examples of wind as a complex cinematic subject can be mentioned. First, in Victor Sjöström's *The Wind* (1928), the violence of the gusts, which render uninhabitable the western American lands, haunts, oppresses, and rapes the protagonists. The wind of La Mancha, that drives people crazy, becomes a character in Pedro Almodóvar's *Volver* (2006). Lastly, the wind embodies a mysterious intent of revenge by the terrestrial flora in M. Night Shyamalan's *The Happening* (2008).

4 C. G. Jung, *Nietzsche's Zarathustra: notes of the seminar given in 1934-1939*, J. L. Jarrett ed., vol. 2, Princeton University Press, Princeton 1988, p. 1227.

5 The reference is to V.B. Šklovskij, *Art as Technique*, in *Russian Formalist Criticism: Four Essays*, translated by L. T. Lemon and M. J. Reis, University of Nebraska Press, Lincoln 1965, pp. 3–24.

6 Cf. E. Burke, *A Philosophical Enquiry into the Origin of Our Ideas of the Sublime and Beautiful*, Dodsley, London 1757.

7 G. Celati, *Conversazioni del vento volatore* [*Conversations of the Flying Wind*], Quodlibet, Macerata 2011. In this regard, see A. Rondini, *Gianni Celati e la teoria*

a highly mobile roaming outside the narrow psychological confines of the ego, eliciting visionary processes to return to an ancient, primordial naturalness of narration. The 'flying wind' crushes and scatters words, creating new connections and recreating the tangible world, in opposition to the flat, mercified, banal literature. By following and indulging the wind-like movement, the writer can initiate the creative process.

Nietzsche's dream goes beyond the real into the fantastic, a field in which it seems almost obvious to observe the irrefutable centrality of the various manifestations and forms of wind: mysterious air changes blow out non-electric light sources in 19th century tales, and storms plunge contemporary environments into darkness. In both cases, the unpredictable movement of the wind functions as a 'threshold passage' to an 'other' dimension[8]. It is a means of accessing the irrational, like unleashing subterranean natural forces or unfolding the motions of the subconscious[9], or else it leads to the epiphany of the supernatural. On the other hand, the confusion and bewilderment – both visual and auditory – caused by the eolian phenomenon predisposes readers to experience the fantastic, which is *hésitation* between real and unreal, following Todorov's theory of

---

letteraria del vento volatore [*Gianni Celati and the Literary Theory of the Flying Wind*], Eum, Macerata 2013.

8 "La soglia fra una dimensione ed un'altra, fra identico ed altro, è anche in fin dei conti la soglia fra ciò che è codificato e ciò che non è (non è ancora o non è più) codificato", "The threshold between one dimension and another, between identical and other, is also after all the threshold between what is codified and what is not (not yet or no longer) codified" (L. Lugnani, *Verità e disordine: il dispositivo dell'oggetto mediatore* [*Truth and Disorder: The Mediating-Object Device*] in R. Ceserani, G. Goggi & L. Lugnani (eds.), *La narrazione fantastica* [*The Fantastic Narrative*], Nistri-Lischi, Pisa 1983, pp. 177-288, here p. 196).

9 In Orson Welles' *Macbeth* (1948), when Lady Macbeth is reading her husband's letter, a gust of wind blows out the candle; the queen angrily tears up the sheet, while the darkness brings out her negative instincts. The wind is a frequent element of cinematic landscape and language. With reference to Fellini's cinema (but his words could have a more general meaning), Fabrizio Borin states: "[il vento è] la Soglia del Fantastico e un effetto speciale invisibile, portatore dell'irrazionale inconoscibile, dell'universo sorprendente, dell'invenzione legata all'inconscio e alla consistenza reale dei sogni", "[the wind is] the Threshold of the Fantastic and an invisible special effect, the bearer of the unknowable irrational, of the surprising universe, of invention linked to the subconscious and the real consistency of dreams" (F. Borin, *Federico Fellini. Viaggio sentimentale nell'illusione e nella realtà di un genio* [*Federico Fellini: A Sentimental Journey into the Illusion and Reality of a Genius*], Gremese, Roma 1999, pp. 26-7).

a gnoseological indeterminacy as a constitutive element of the genre[10], or rather, according to Lugnani, utter inexplicability[11].

Furthermore, it should be considered that the approach to the otherness of the fantastic is frequently embodied in the ghost, a figure that is 'windy' by nature because it is imponderable, visible above all in its effects on the surrounding world, and only perceivable under certain conditions through other senses. Wind and ghosts run together, the former announces the latter and instills its essence in them. They are also linked on a semantic level: the synonym 'spirit' – in Hebrew *ruach,* in Greek πνεῦμα or ἄνεμος (all sharing a common Proto-Indo-European root with the Sanskrit *ātmàn*) – means puff, breath, as well as vital essence and divine creative power, embodied in the biblical *Ruach Elohim*, the primordial breath from which the entire universe was generated[12]. Similarly, in Anglo-Saxon, the term

10 T. Todorov, *Introduction à la littérature fantastique*, Editions du Seuil, Paris 1970, pp. 36-37, 46.

11 "L'impasse fantastica [...] [è] uno stato assoluto di stallo, un insuperabile inceppamento del paradigma; insuperabile proprio perché non si riconoscono se non le leggi della natura. All'origine dell'atto di narrazione fantastica e al fondo dell'atto di lettura fantastico c'è il blocco gnoseologico che deriva da questa *inesplicabilità*", "The fantastic impasse [...] [is] an absolute state of standstill, an insuperable jamming of the paradigm; insuperable precisely because nothing but the laws of nature are recognised. At the origin of the fantastic act of narration and at the bottom of the fantastic act of reading is the gnoseological impasse that derives from this *inexplicability*" (L. Lugnani, *Per una delimitazione del «genere»* [*Defining the Genre's Boundaries*], in R. Ceserani, G. Goggi & L. Lugnani (eds.), *La narrazione fantastica* [*The Fantastic Narrative*], Nistri-Lischi, Pisa 1983, pp. 37-73, here p. 72). More recently, Amigoni links the otherness of the fantastic to the semiotic concept of the encyclopedia, arguing that a defining feature of the fantastic lies in "il rapporto contraddittorio che intercorre tra testo ed enciclopedia. Com'è noto, il racconto fantastico presuppone l'iniziale costruzione di un universo diegetico perfettamente verosimile, in cui accade qualcosa di non compatibile con l'enciclopedia postulata dal testo stesso. Lo scrittore fantastico confeziona in altre parole un testo in cui viene denunciata l'incompletezza, l'inaffidabilità del codice su cui si basano il sapere del lettore e la stessa narrazione", "the contradictory relationship between text and encyclopedia. As is well known, the fantastic tale presupposes the initial construction of a diegetic universe that is perfectly verisimilar, in which something happens that is not compatible with the encyclopedia postulated by the text itself. The fantastic writer, in other words, constructs a text in which the incompleteness, the unreliability of the code on which the reader's knowledge and the narration itself are based is denounced." (F. Amigoni, *Fantasmi nel Novecento* [*Ghosts in the Twentieth Century*], Bollati Boringhieri, Torino 2004, here p. 23).

12 "πνεῦμα significa soffio vitale, anima, spirito divino, spirito (in opposizione al corpo), Spirito santo, angelo", "πνεῦμα means life-breath, soul, divine spirit,

'ghost' derives from the Old English gāst, i.e. breath and soul. If the eolian impetus, therefore, depicts in many religious and mythological contexts spiritual power[13], the study of the fantastic *sub specie venti* highlights the connections between this genre – or literary 'mode'[14] – and an understanding of the sacred that is tensive and conflicting. The sacred becomes a force that surmounts human beings' perception and control, confining them within their limits[15]. Likewise, such analysis could emphasize the connection of the fantastic discourse with a perturbing vision of an animated, personified, and deified nature – the wind moans, threatens, sighs, guides – that equally overpowers mankind, reviving "old discarded beliefs"[16]. The flow of air – creator or destroyer; natural, divine or demonic force – frays and deforms reality, both conveying its alienated representation and revealing its inconsistency and its illusory nature[17].

As can be deduced from these initial hints, the presence of the wind in the fantastic is so frequent and pervasive that it would be fruitless to trace its multiple occurrences in a corpus of texts. Hence, we will limit the

---

spirit (as opposed to body), holy Spirit, angel" (M. L. Crosina, *Il vento, respiro del cielo e della terra* [*Wind: the breath of heaven and earth*], in "Annali di studi religiosi", vol. 5, 2004, pp. 229-239, here p. 229, n. 4).

13 See E. Hsu, C. Low, *Wind, life, health: anthropological and historical perspectives. Preface,* in "Journal of the Royal Anthropological Institute", 2007, pp. 1- 17.

14 R. Ceserani, *Il fantastico* [*The Fantastic*], Il Mulino, Bologna 1996, p. 11.

15 According to Farnetti, the experience of fantastic literature should be understood as rooted in an original religious impulse or intuition of the 'sacred': a troubling sense of oppression before a higher, unknowable power (Cf. M. Farnetti, *Il giuoco del maligno. Il racconto fantastico nella letteratura italiana tra Otto e Novecento,* [*The Devil's Game: The Fantastic Tale in Italian Literature between the Nineteenth and Twentieth Centuries*], Vallecchi, Firenze 1988, p. 7, n. 3). The scholar cites an essay by Otto, (R. Otto, *Das Heilige. Über das Irrationale in der Idee des Göttlichen und sein Verhältnis zum Rationalen*, Gotha 1917), but Leopardi in the *Zibaldone* – 9 October 1823; 31 March 1829 – had already linked the representations of the divine in ancient civilizations to fear and the monstrous (G. Leopardi, *Zibaldone,* R. Damiani (ed.), three vols., Mondadori, Milano 2015, p. 2267, p. 3036).

16 S. Freud, *Das Unheimliche*, in "*Imago*" 5(5-6*)*, 1919; tr. by D. McLintock, *The Uncanny,* Penguin Books, New York 2003, p. 154.

17 Angelo M. Mangini (*Letteratura come anamorfosi. Teoria e prassi del fantastico nell'Italia del primo Novecento* [*Literature as Anamorphosis: Theory and Practice of the Fantastic in Early Twentieth-Century Italy*], Bologna University Press, Bologna 2007) states that anamorphosis is the essence of the fantastic as a literary mode: this pictorial technique of distorting perspective eliminates the distinctions that we usually apply to reality, thus nullifying it. Since the 'windy' representation in fantastic writings serves the same, or a similar, function, the wind can be viewed as an anamorphic device.

present study by outlining its depiction in Italian writings between the 19th and 20th centuries through a few essential thematic nodes: the crossing of thresholds, the wind/ghost identification, the highlighting of instances of the subconscious, and lastly, the description of ancestral powers, of hidden or dormant natural forces, or of disturbing and destructive divine/demonic figures.

Disquieting threshold passages

The wind dissolves faint lights as well as the 'paradigm of reality'[18] by introducing the protagonists to a world where different rules apply. Among the many possible examples, a story by Luisa Saredo (1830-1896), *La locanda dell'Orso* [*The Bear Inn*] (1869), can be considered emblematic[19].

After the conclusion of his medical studies[20], the protagonist takes a trip to the mountains of Savoy, where he is caught in a wind and snow storm which compels him to an inevitable stop-over: "Un turbinìo di vento faceva volteggiare certi fiocchi mostruosi di neve, che accecavano il postiglione ed i cavalli: l'ampio strato del bianco lenzuolo non permetteva più di distinguere il sentiero battuto, i cui margini rasentavano pericolosi precipizii".[21]

---

18 L. Lugnani, *Per una delimitazione del «genere»*, *op. cit.*, p. 55.

19 The story is published for the first time on "Rivista Europea", March 1, 1869, then added by the writer in a collection entitled *Racconti* [*Short Stories*], Firenze, Le Monnier 1878. About Luisa Saredo, born Luigia Emanuel, see C. Boninsegni, *Emanuel, Luisa,* "Dizionario Biografico degli Italiani", vol. 42, 1993, https://www.treccani.it/enciclopedia/luisa-emanuel_%28Dizionario-Biografico%29/, and A. Illiano, *Invito al romanzo d'autrice '800 '900. Da Luisa Saredo a Laudomia Bonanni* [*An Invitation to the Women's Novel (19th–20th Centuries): From Luisa Saredo to Laudomia Bonanni*], Cadmo, Fiesole 2001.

20 The doctor is a key character in the late 19th century fantastic stories, " sia come esponente della razionalità, ossia come polo dialettico rispetto alla dimensione dell'irrazionale e dell'inesplicabile, sia come figura demoniaca" "both as an exponent of rationality, that is, as the dialectical counterpart to the realm of the irrational and the inexplicable, and as a demonic figure" (S. Maxia, *Per introdurre* [*To introduce*], in *«Italia magica». Letteratura fantastica e surreale dell'Ottocento e del Novecento* [*«Magical Italy». Fantastic and Surreal Literature of the Nineteenth and Twentieth Centuries*], G. Caltagirone, S. Maxia (eds.), AM&D edizioni, Cagliari 2008, pp. 15-26, here p. 18).

21 "A whirling gust of wind sent monstrous flakes of snow spinning through the air, blinding the postilion and the horses: the broad expanse of that white shroud no longer allowed them to make out the beaten track, whose edges skirted perilous precipices" (L. Saredo, *La locanda dell'Orso* [*The Bear Inn*], in C. Melani (ed.),

The storm drives the plot forward, as it forces the carriage passengers to spend the night at the Locanda dell'Orso, a place that will prove to be steeped in violent impulses and inhuman ferocity. "Un lumicino tremolava sulla porta mal connessa, e sbatacchiata a tutti i venti si vedeva appesa ad un anello di ferro un'insegna, la quale mi assicurarono dovesse rappresentare un orso".[22] Since there is no room for everyone, the landlady reluctantly allows the protagonist to sleep, with another passenger, in a chalet far from the Inn. "La tranquillità più perfetta regnava intorno; il vento solo mugghiava di fuori e, penetrando dalla finestra mal chiusa, faceva vacillare il lume di una fumosa candela di sego, che avevamo deposta sul tavolino".[23] As the candle goes out, a supernatural scenario of mysterious voices and incomprehensible noises unfolds, to the point that the protagonist's companion runs away.

In solitude, a mysterious apparition unveils:

> Una parte dell'impalcatura di legno erasi sollevata quanto bastava per lasciare passare la testa di un essere strano, mostro o fantasma, il quale mi fissava con occhi tremolanti. Era una testa orribilmente scapigliata, una faccia cadaverica, sparuta, colle gote incavate come quelle di un teschio.[24]

In truth, in the basement of the chalet, the landlady had imprisoned her husband's first children for inheritance reasons. It would therefore be a matter of 'simulation of the fantastic'[25]. There is no Todorovian 'hesitation', nor inexplicability, everything is perfectly clear. The incessant wind, which

---

Fantastico italiano. Racconti fantastici dell'Ottocento e del primo Novecento italiano [*Italian Fantastic Fiction: Fantastic Tales from the Nineteenth Century and Early Twentieth-Century Italy*], Bur, Milano 2009, pp. 257-273, here p. 257).

22 "A tiny lamp flickered above the ill-fitting door, battered by every gust of wind; and, hanging from an iron ring, one could see a signboard which, I was assured, was meant to represent a bear" (Ivi, p. 258).

23 "The most perfect calm reigned all around; only the wind roared outside and, filtering through the ill-closed window, made the light of a smoky tallow candle—set on the little table—flicker" (Ivi, p. 261).

24 "A section of the wooden scaffolding had lifted just enough to let the head of a strange being—monster or phantom—push through, staring at me with flickering eyes. It was a horribly dishevelled head: a cadaverous, gaunt face, its cheeks hollowed like those of a skull" (Ivi, p. 263).

25 See M. Farnetti, *Il giuoco del maligno, op. cit.*, p. 24. In Moreni's opinion, the tale reduces the supernatural to a "divertissement" (C. Moreni, *Il linguaggio del fantastico nella pubblicistica scapigliata milanese,* [*The Language of the Fantastic in Milanese Scapigliatura Periodical Writing*], Dissertation, Providence, Rhode Island May 2008, p. 68). This may be seen as a symptom of the decline of the fantastic included in the magazines of Milan of the seventies.

excises the vivid and rational perception of things by blowing out the candle and mingling with the noises of alleged ghosts, constitutes not only a weather phenomenon but also becomes an emblem of the dark, horrible, and devastating passions of the evil woman, who is so attached to money as to condemn innocent children to a slow and atrocious death. The narration does not comprise supernatural elements, but it offers a monstrous and extreme vision of reality, which is exacerbated by the fearful and hostile wind manifestations[26].

The wind preludes the ghostly apparition according to a more complex dynamic in *Confessione postuma* [*Posthumous Confession*] (1897) by Remigio Zena (1850-1917)[27].

A priest, Pietro, tells his superior about a supernatural fact that has happened to him, to understand whether it is a divine or diabolical manifestation. His brother, Claudio, who is a doctor, had just assisted a young girl who died while in delirium without having been able to confess; the girl was a prostitute. "[Q]uand'ecco spegnersi la lampada all'improvviso, come fulminata da un soffio d'uomo"[28].

In this instance as well, the darkness, which is determined by an anthropomorphized puff of wind, marks the entrance into a supernatural dimension[29]. Having heard the doorbell, Claudio asks the protagonist to open the door but, paradoxically, Pietro feels as though he sees outside the building the shadow of his brother, whom he cannot touch and whose

---

26 See also Hipkins, who emphasizes, however, not the windy setting but the realistic depiction of the alleged ghost: "The ghost which appears there is portrayed with such conviction, that when the events are explained away as a tale of female greed and depravity […] this realistic ending seems improbable. The state of the doubt engendered in the reader is a trace of a latent vocation for the fantastic" (D. E. Hipkins, *Contemporary Italian Women Writers and Traces of the Fantastic: The Creation of Literary Space*, Routledge, London and New York 2007, p. 29).

27 The story first appeared in «Almanacco delle famiglie cristiane per l'anno 1897», anno XII. Ed. Benzinger & Co., Einsiedeln, pp. 37-52.

28 "And then, suddenly, the lamp went out, as if struck dead by a man's breath", (R. Zena, *Confessione postuma* [*Posthumous Confession*], in *La tentazione del fantastico. Racconti italiani da Gualdo a Svevo* [*The Temptation of the Fantastic: Italian Tales from Gualdo to Svevo*], A. D'Elia, A. Guarnieri, M. Lanzillotta, G. Lo Castro (eds.), Pellegrini, Cosenza 2007, pp. 341-350, here p. 343).

29 According to Lanzillotta, the flame of the lamp, first on the verge of going out and rekindled by the protagonist, then definitively blown out by the gust of wind, symbolizes the death/resurrection dynamic that is at the center of the story (M. Lanzillotta, *Una storia dell'altro mondo:* Confessione postuma *di Remigio Zena,* [*A Tale from the Other World:* Confessione postuma *by Remigio Zena*], in *La tentazione del fantastico*, *op. cit.*, pp. 351-378, here p. 343).

words he does not understand, awaiting him. Pietro follows the mysterious figure through a labyrinthine and distorted city, where every building is unrecognizable. The two enter a house without being seen by any of the people inside, as they are clearly acting in a different level of reality: "E dietro a Claudio affrontai il buio che si parava davanti, fitto, impenetrabile; e appena varcata la soglia, un buffo di vento freddo mi schiaffeggiò il volto"[30].

The ascending climax of the eolian manifestation corresponds to a greater penetration of the protagonist into the dense darkness and endless spaces of the underworld, at the end of which the body of the woman who had died in sin can be found; the movement of air therefore takes on a macabre connotation, announcing and symbolizing the mystery of death[31]. The confession of the young woman, who resurrects only for this purpose, is also a 'puff' without words that is endowed with a language pertaining the afterlife, which cannot be understood with the normal tools of logic. It is a soul that exhales: "ma quell'alito aveva suono e forma di sillabe, e in un linguaggio non mai ascoltato e che pure comprendevo quanto il mio, netta, spiccata, intera, raccolsi la confessione d'oltre tomba".[32]

---

30 "And behind Claudio I faced the darkness looming ahead, dense and impenetrable; and the moment I crossed the threshold, a gust of cold wind lashed my face" (R. Zena, *Confessione postuma, op. cit.*, p. 346).

31 Indeed, the episode could be considered, from a different point of view, as having a positive connotation, because the supernatural in this story, which alludes to the miracle of the resurrection, is part of a religious discourse that should reduce the feeling of anguish. However, it ought to be noted that the descriptive methods, including hints at the dimension of the wind, which also recall the ghostly and inconsistent figure of the brother, end up causing "la scoperta di uno stato di turbamento più profondo e sofferente: quell'«aldilà interiore» già novecentesco, che neppure il conforto della risoluzione miracolistica è in grado di quietare" "the discovery of a deeper and tormented state of turmoil: that already Twentieth-century «inner hereafter», which not even the comfort of a miraculous resolution could quiet" (I. Piazza, *Il fantastico come "rivelazione dell'invisibile" in Remigio Zena,* [*The Fantastic as a "Revelation of the Invisible" in Remigio Zena*], in *«Italia magica»,* cit, pp. 81-90, here p. 90. In the quotation, reference is made to N. Bonifazi, *Teoria del fantastico e il racconto fantastico in Italia: Tarchetti, Pirandello, Buzzati* [*Theory of the Fantastic and the Fantastic Short Story in Italy: Tarchetti, Pirandello, Buzzati*], Longo, Ravenna 1982, p. 51).

32 "Yet that breath had the sound and shape of syllables, and in a language I had never heard before—yet understood as fully as my own—I clearly grasped, distinct and whole, the confession from beyond the grave" (R. Zena, *Confessione postuma, op. cit.*, p. 349).

Infernal blizzards and spectral reflections

The connection between the blast of wind and the ghost, or the deceased, may appear to the characters to be a coincidence, however disturbing; these strange occurrences constitute, indeed, one of the key elements of the fantastic, according to Lazzarin[33]. They reveal the otherness of the apparitions, which belong to an underworld situated outside a reality immediately perceivable, and sometimes imbued with dark and negative forces. In the short story *Innocenza* [*Innocence*] (1939) by Elsa Morante, the presence of the wind is a sign of the diversity and potential hostility of the ghost. Little Camillo lives with his very old and deaf grandmother; he opens the door to a languid woman, who "[c]osì spettinata, sembrava un nero temporale"[34]. While the woman is running away, after having stolen his grandmother's soul, the child chases her down the stairs: "Ma quella, coi capelli al vento, sempre ridendo orribilmente se ne andò, e pareva il tuono quando dilegua"[35]. The wind that mysteriously accompanies the woman, who had been welcomed inside thanks to the child's innocence, turns out to be Death, an entity that causes disarray and destruction, like the gusts of wind. The apparition scornfully mocks the finitude of the human being, subjected to the inexorable laws of nature[36].

Granted that Morante's twentieth-century fantastic turns away from the positivist supernatural to probe interiority and "si insinua in zone conosciute e quotidiane"[37], it is worth noting that, in her early production—

33 S. Lazzarin, *Il modo fantastico* [*The Fantastic Mode*], Laterza, Bari 2000, p. 11.

34 "so dishevelled, she looked like a black storm cloud" (E. Morante, *Innocenza* [*Innocence*], in *Racconti dimenticati* [*Forgotten Tales*], I. Babbioni, C. Cecchi (eds.), PBE, Torino 2002, pp. 11- 13, here p. 12. The short story was published for the first time on «Oggi», 25 November 1939.

35 "But she, her hair blown by the wind, still laughing horribly, went away, and her laughter seemed like thunder fading into the distance" (Ivi, p. 13).

36 The connection between the malevolent presence and the atypical wind is also to be found in Buzzati's *Il dolore notturno* [*The Night Pain*] (1942). The arrival of a mysterious man, who embodies suffering, is announced by the movement of the plants in the garden, but the sick boy, who is the protagonist of the story, understands that it is not a normal meteorological phenomenon: "Il vento fa un altro rumore, lo so bene, il vento non fa muovere così le piante...", "The wind makes a different sound, I know it well, the wind doesn't make the plants move like this..." (D. Buzzati, *Il dolore notturno* [*The Night Pain*], in *I sette messaggeri* [*The Seven Messengers*], Mondadori, Milano 2018, pp. 122-132, here pp. 128-129).

37 "penetrating into familiar, everyday zones" (S. Zangrandi, *Trasfigurare il mondo con la fantasia. Tracce fantastiche nella narrativa breve di Elsa Morante e Anna*

to which *Innocenza* belongs—, nineteenth-century narrative strategies are also reactivated, albeit in a dreamlike key[38]. Here, the theme of the wind appears particularly significant; its violence sweeps away the ordinary world to bring out an underground reality of horror and madness, as in the story *Il cocchiere* [*The Coachman*] (1939)[39].

A student gets up in the middle of the night in his hosts' haunted house because an eerie song attracts him; along the way, he is disturbed "dai soffi che al mio passaggio mi ventavano addosso, [...] dai fischi brevissimi che si chiamavano su per le pareti"[40]. The delicate auditory movements of air, akin to the spectral motif, prelude to the oxymoronic character of the ghostly apparition that is both attractive and repelling[41]. The protagonist arrives at the old judge and uncle's room; he claims to be in reality the coachman who had killed the old man to avenge his dismissal.

> Fu qui che coi miei occhi vidi l'alcova invasa da una bufera di vento, e, tutto restando immobile e tranquillo intorno a me nella camera, le ciocche bianche

---

Maria Ortese [*Transfiguring the World Through the Imagination: Fantastic Traces in the Short Fiction of Elsa Morante and Anna Maria Ortese*], in "Cuadernos de Filología italiana", 2014, pp. 215- 232, here p. 217).

38 E. Porciani, *Il sogno nella narrativa giovanile di Elsa Morante* [*Dreams in Elsa Morante's Early Fiction*], in *«Italia magica»*, *op. cit.*, pp. 824- 832.

39 The story was published for the first time on «Oggi», 11 November 1939, and then collected in *Racconti dimenticati*, *op. cit.*, pp. 14-16.

40 "from the gusts that, as I passed, blew against me, [...] from the very brief whistles that called to one another along the walls" (E. Morante, *Il cocchiere* [*The Coachman*], in *Racconti dimenticati, op. cit.*, pp. 14- 16, here p. 14).

41 According to Lazzarin, puffs and whistles, which "sembrano voler trattenere o ammonire il protagonista", "seem to be holding or admonishing the protagonist" (S. Lazzarin, *Il racconto fantastico breve e brevissimo nel Novecento italiano* [*Short and Very Short Fantastic Fiction in Twentieth-Century Italy*], in "Italianistica: Rivista di letteratura italiana", vol. 46, n. 2, *Novelle e racconti: teoria secolare, prassi novecentesca*, May/August 2017, pp. 121-138, here p. 133), are ghostly as well. They are part of a detailed phantasmatic proliferation; central is the uncle/ coachman, devastated by a sea storm that alludes to the "Olandese Volante, spettro innominato del racconto morantiano", "Flying Dutchman, unnamed spectre of Morante" (p. 133). Even in a story by Ortese, which Zangrandi compares to Morante in the aforementioned essay (*Trasfigurare il mondo con la fantasia, op. cit.*), the personified wind seems to lead the protagonist to an encounter with a disquieting dimension. In *La casa del bosco* [*The House in the Woods*] (1987), the female narrator is waiting for a plumber, but time passes in terror, augmented by the wind that blows "un canto inarticolato, selvaggio, ora simile a lamento, ora a minaccia, ora a una lunga storia di vittime", "an inarticulate, savage chant, now like a lament, now like a threat, now like a long tale of victims" (A. M. Ortese, *In sonno e in veglia,* Adelphi, Milano 1987, p. 20).

> del vecchio agitarsi furiose, i suoi denti urtarsi, la sua pelle illividire, e lenzuola e drappeggi sbattere come le vele di un vascello sconvolto.[42]

The infernal storm, clearly inspired by Dante – "siamo dannati tutti e due [...] cocchiere e padrone in eterno corriamo sulla carrozza, per una tempesta nera, e non arriveremo mai"[43] –, punishes a double sin, overturning the biblical symbology of the wind as manifestation of the divine.

The theme of the destructive, but also revealing/assisting wind, which accompanies the protagonists into the realms of the supernatural, had already been touched upon by Federigo Verdinois (1844-1927), in *Ida* (1886)[44]. An emotional storm, which will later become an actual atmospheric phenomenon, disrupts the life of the protagonist, who is faced with the silence of his fiancée Ida. Locked in his room, the young man comes out, rushed by a mysterious wind:

> Mi sentii un'aria fresca alle spalle, anzi mi parve proprio che qualcuno mi soffiasse nel collo. Mi voltai, era la porta rimasta socchiusa. Mi alzai pigramente per andare a chiudere e tornare subito al posto: ma poi, non so come, macchinalmente, mi sentii trascinato ad uscire. Traversai una camera, poi un'altra, poi un'altra ancora, sentii da capo il fresco che questa volta mi soffiava sulla faccia, e mi accorsi con molta sorpresa di essere sceso in giardino.[45]

The cherub of the fountain fantastically assumes Ida's shape; the protagonist kisses her to discover that she has marble lips. During the night, a nocturnal storm knocks down the statue, double of the girl, anticipating, or

---

42 "It was here that I saw with my own eyes the alcove overrun by a raging gale; and though everything around me in the room remained still and quiet, the old man's white locks lashed about furiously, his teeth clattered, his skin turned livid, and the sheets and hangings flapped like the sails of a storm-tossed ship" (E. Morante, *Il cocchiere, op. cit.*, p. 16).

43 "We are damned, both of us [...] coachman and master, for all eternity we race on in the carriage through a black storm, and we shall never arrive" (*Ibidem*).

44 The story was published in "Rivista minima", in January 1880, then in "Il Corriere del Mattino", 8 June 1882, with the title *Tempesta* [*Storm*] and lastly as *Ida* in *Racconti inverosimili di Picche* [*Unlikely Tales by Picche*] (1886).

45 "I felt a cool draught at my back—indeed, it seemed as though someone were breathing on the nape of my neck. I turned around: it was the door, left ajar. Lazily I got up to go and close it and return at once to my seat; but then, I don't know how, almost mechanically, I felt myself drawn outside. I crossed one room, then another, then yet another; I felt the coolness again, this time blowing on my face, and, to my great surprise, I realized I had gone down into the garden" (F. Verdinois, *Ida,* in *La tentazione del fantastico, op. cit.*, pp. 213- 221, here p. 217).

perhaps determining, her macabre fate: Ida is actually dying, and before the end, she will give the protagonist a second chilling kiss, which condemns him to a morbid condition of stasis. The wind has scattered the data of reality, first, by leading the young man to experience the mixture between animate and inanimate[46]; then, as 'storm' – the first title of the story – it reveals the mortuary character of the living, because Ida, as an animated statue, is destroyed, and the real Ida dies[47].

In the *Storie del castello di Trezza* [*The Stories of the Castle of Trezza*] (1875), narration itself takes on an intermittent and 'windy' feature, gradually illuminating the legend of Don Garzia and his two wives, Violante and Isabella[48]. In the first part of the told legend, the wind "urla come uno spirito maligno nella gola del camino, e scuote rabbiosamente le imposte tarlate"[49]. The moans of agony of the page, Violante's lover, mix with this dark entity[50]. In the real world, to which Luciano, the narrator, and Matilde,

---

46 Cf. E. A. Jentsch, *Sulla psicologia dell'Unheimliche* [*Zur Psychologie des Unheimlichen,* 1906], in *La narrazione fantastica, op. cit.*, pp. 399- 410.

47 Nigro identifies in this passage a chiastic structure: "l'oggetto inanimato si trasforma in un corpo animato, ma il contatto con la donna riduce il protagonista in una condizione paralizzante", "the inanimate object is transformed into an animate body, but the contact with the woman drives the protagonist into a paralyzing condition" (A. Nigro, Tempesta *e* Ida: *il fantastico rimeditato di Federigo Verdinois* [Tempest *and* Ida: *Federigo Verdinois's Reappraisal of the Fantastic*], in *La tentazione del fantastico, op. cit.*, pp. 223-234, here p. 231).

48 Published in "Nuova illustrazione universale" in 1875, the short story is then included in *Primavera e altri racconti* [*Spring and Other Tales*] (1876). In an initial line, Luciano exposes, in an impressionistic way, through somehow essential traits, the tragedy of the death of the page, who had voluntarily thrown himself into an abyss so as not to be discovered by the baron. He later recounts the appearance of Violante, an atypical ghost, as she was 'killed' by her husband (perhaps a demon who had taken possession of the woman, or a real being who had wandered around the castle after his lover's death). Finally, he extensively narrates the story of the first wife and her lover. Meanwhile, the story turns out to be increasingly similar to the adulterous relationship of Luciano and Matilde, or perhaps it fosters it. In the conclusion Matilde's husband, suddenly calls her throwing her off balance, and the two lovers fall together into the abyss in front of the castle.

49 G. Verga, *Le storie del castello di Trezza,* in *La tentazione del fantastico, op. cit.*, pp. 125-159, here p. 126; "howling like a malignant spirit down the throat of the chimney, and wrathfully shaking the time-worn shutters" (G. Verga, *The Stories of the Castle of Trezza,* in *The Lock and Key Library,* Vol. 2, *Classic Mediterranean Mystery Stories,* Cosimo, New York 2007, pp. 57- 97, here p. 58).

50 With perfect circularity, in the last part of the story "il vento sembrava assumere voci e gemiti umani, e le onde flagellavano la rocca con un rumore come di tonfo che soffocasse un gemito d'agonia" (G. Verga, *Le storie*, *op. cit.*, p. 157); "the

who listens to him, belong, "il vento cacciava le nuvole rapidamente, e di tanto in tanto faceva stormire gli alberi del giardino […]; il mormorio del mare e quel sussurrio delle foglie, sommesso, ad intervalli, a quell'ora aveano un non so che di misterioso"[51]. The wind is therefore a *trait d'union* between reality and fantasy, assimilating not only external landscapes but also the feelings of the characters: the story of adultery reflects, and helps to fuel, the new passion between Luciano and Matilde. In the second storytelling, Isabella finds out about the existence of the first wife's ghost, which appeared as insubstantial as a breath of wind[52]. This phantom is mysteriously linked to wind: during the sirocco nights the windows must be left open so that the ghost can freely enter the rooms, otherwise it dreadfully moans. In the last section, the wind speaks to the unhappy Violante, perhaps predicting her fate, or sharing her pain: "Il gemito del vento le penetrava sin nelle ossa, con parole arcane ch'ella intendeva, che le dicevano arcane cose, e le facevano dirizzare i capelli sul capo"[53]. The motif of the wind acquires a precise hermeneutical function, as, on the one hand, it highlights the disturbing and authentically fantastic recurrence of the narrative[54], on the other hand, it embodies a *vox naturae* that reveals the

---

wind seemed laden with voices and human moans, and the waves beat upon the rocks with the sound of a heavy fall" (G. Verga, *The Stories, op. cit.*, p. 95). It is the voice of the wind, therefore of the dying (perhaps already a ghost) page, which compels Violante to jump from the castle walls.

51 G. Verga, *Le storie, op. cit.*, p. 128; "the wind was sweeping the clouds rapidly onward, and from time to time rustled through the trees in the garden […]; the murmur of the sea and that occasional hushed whispering of the leaves possessed, at this hour, an indefinable mystery" (G. Verga, *The Stories, op. cit.*, p. 61).

52 Cf. G. Verga, *Le storie, op. cit.*, p. 132. Even when the spirit appears before Garzia, the room's door and window are suddenly flung wide open, as if by a violent blast of wind (Cf. G. Verga, *Le storie, op. cit.*, p. 140). Violante's final apparition takes place in a stormy scenario: a gust puts out the lamp and the violent and brutal baron feels a shiver run through his bones (Cf. G. Verga, *Le storie, op. cit.*, p. 142), succumbed to a surreal atmosphere that makes him accept the supernatural.

53 G. Verga, *Le storie, op. cit.*, p. 158; "The moaning of the wind penetrated to her very bones, whispering mysterious words that she alone could understand, telling her hidden secrets that caused each separate hair to rise upon her head" (G. Verga, *The Stories, op. cit.*, p. 95). According to Castiglia, Verga makes the by now worn Gothic landscape a 'landscape of inwardness' (Cf. I. Castiglia, *"Quella fatale tendenza verso l'ignoto": «Le storie del castello di Trezza» di Giovanni Verga,* in *«Italia magica», op. cit.*, pp. 49- 57, here p. 51).

54 Freud considers uncanny "[t]he constant recurrence of the same thing, the repetition of the same facial features, the same characters, the same destinies, the same misdeeds" (S. Freud, *The Uncanny, op. cit.*, p. 142). The legend and related place constitute a trap that forces the surreal repetition of events, in an infinite

negative aspects of reality – the horror of pain, the injustice of oppression – and that accompanies and supports the oppressed characters.

The relationship between wind and an apparition is even closer in a story by Edoardo Calandra (1852-1911), *Dame Isabeau* (1886), where a gust of air coagulates in the ghost of a young woman. The protagonist Emanuele, immersed in the usual stormy landscape that introduces the surreal dimension, finds the skeleton of a woman and a tombstone with her name. Once home, obsessed with the find and the tombstone, he draws a female face, passionately recreating imaginary events, until a ghost takes shape:

> Lo splendore della fiamma nel camino pareva smorzarsi, come dietro un velo di fumo; m'apparve una specie di nebbia leggiera come quella che si mantiene sull'erbe al nascere del sole; si andò raccogliendo, crebbe rapidamente alta, diritta... e si condensò. [...] Non ebbi che il tempo di gettarmi da parte, ella passò rapida e sentii un'impressione di gelo, una sensazione di soffio, come se un'enorme piuma mi avesse sfiorato volando![55]

The rationalizing explanation does not eliminate, rather it accentuates, the inexplicability of the fantastic: the disturbing lack of the find acts as

---

loop. According to Lo Castro, on the other hand, the last lines – "A Trezza si dice che nelle notti di temporale si odano di nuovo dei gemiti, e si vedano dei fantasmi tra le rovine del castello" (G. Verga, *Le storie, op. cit.*, p. 159); "At Trezza it is said that on all but holy nights groans are once more heard, and phantoms are seen wandering among the ruins of the castle" (G. Verga, *The Stories, op. cit.*, p. 97) – could indicate that also Luciano and Matilde's story is a legend. The tension between reality and fantasy would then cease to exist and the text would be written only to test the charms of popular narrative (Cf. G. Lo Castro, *La fatale attrazione della leggenda nelle* Storie del castello di Trezza [*The Fatal Allure of Legend in* The Stories of the Castle of Trezza], in *La tentazione del fantastico, op. cit.*, pp. 161-170). This interpretation, which takes little account of the numerous hints of 'true fantastic' scattered throughout the narrative, is debatable, since the final sentence could have a very different meaning: reality is engulfed in the supernatural, and the 'true' story of the two lovers becomes legend, even if it was not meant to be so originally.

55 "The glow of the flame in the fireplace seemed to dim, as though behind a veil of smoke; a kind of light mist appeared to me, like the one that lingers over the grass at sunrise. It began to gather, rose swiftly, tall and upright... and grew dense. [...] I had only time to fling myself aside; she swept past, and I felt a chill, a sensation like a breath, as if an enormous feather had brushed me as it flew by" (E. Calandra, *Dame Isabeau*, in *Racconti neri e fantastici dell'Ottocento italiano* [*Dark and Fantastic Tales of Nineteenth-Century Italy*], R. Reim (ed.), Newton Compton, Roma 2002, pp. 376-386, here pp. 385-386).

a 'mediating object'[56], which reveals the reality of the ghostly visit. "Il fumo del tizzo, giocato dal vento tra la finestra e la porta, s'era combinato in quel modo straordinario... Certo, mi aveva fatto quel tiro. Ma il cranio, signore mie, e le ossa, non le ho ritrovate mai più"[57]. Emanuele, who believes himself to be the reincarnation of one of Dame Isabeau's lovers, has materialized the ghost by force of love: "È Eros che costringe Thanatos a restituire le sue prede, che forza le porte dell'Ade"[58]. The passionate energy, emblematically correlated to the image of air, in slight or feverish movement, has therefore reshaped reality, unifying past and present, building fluid and iridescent environments, focusing on one of the constitutive elements of supernatural narratives: "le distorsioni del tempo e dello spazio"[59].

Wind and subconscious between desire, madness, terror

In Pirandello's novella *Un soffio* [*A Breath*] (1931), the protagonist seems almost to turn into deadly air when he discovers that he can eliminate other human beings by making a proverbial saying come true: "Ah la vita cos'è! Basta un soffio a portarsela via –; e congiunsi il pollice e l'indice d'una mano per soffiarci su, come a far volare una piuma che tenessi tra quelle due dita. [...] Ero io, ero io; la morte ero io; la avevo lì, nelle due dita e nel fiato; potevo far morire tutti"[60]. Hence, the 'wind' embodied in a person

56 Cf. L. Lugnani, *Verità e disordine: il dispositivo dell'oggetto mediatore* [*Truth and Disorder: The Mediating Object Device*], in *La narrazione fantastica, op. cit.*, pp. 177- 287.

57 "The smoke from the burning log, tossed by the wind between the window and the door, had come together in that extraordinary way... Clearly, it had played that trick on me. But the skull, ladies, and the bones—I never found them again" (E. Calandra, *Dame Isabeau, op. cit.*, p. 386).

58 " It is Eros who forces Thanatos to restore his prey, who forces the gates of Hades" (M. Lanzillotta, *Un racconto archeologico: «Dame Isabeau» di Edoardo Calandra* [*An Archaeological Tale: "Dame Isabeau" by Edoardo Calandra*], in *«Italia magica», op. cit.*, pp. 91-102, here p. 100).

59 "Time and space distortions" (S. Lazzarin, *Il modo fantastico, op. cit.*, p. 12).

60 L. Pirandello, *Un soffio* in Id., *Tutte le novelle,* vol. VI, 1919- 1936, L. Lugnani (ed.), Rizzoli, Milano 2017, pp. 196- 203, here p. 196, 201; "Ah, how flimsy life is! All it takes is a breath and poof—it's gone!"; With that, I held my thumb and index finger together and blew on them, as if to blow away an imaginary feather [...]. I was it, I was it: I was death. I had it right there, between my two fingers and in my breath. I could make anybody die" (L. Pirandello, *A Breath,* tr. Marella

becomes an agent of the supernatural as the explication of a forbidden desire[61], by employing “le potenzialità fantasmatiche del linguaggio”[62].

In another story by Pirandello, *Vittoria delle formiche* [*Victory of the Ants*] (1936), the wind is a devastating impetuous force that is mysteriously allied with invading ants. The two non-human characters, that lie between animalistic and inorganic, personify the hostile *facies* of Nature, and, at the same time, embody the inner anxieties of the protagonist.

> Una cosa per sé forse ridicola ma, agli effetti, terribile: una casa invasa tutta dalle formiche. E questo pensiero folle: che il vento si fosse alleato con esse. Il vento con le formiche.[63]
>
> La raffica si levò d'improvviso a tradimento [...]; l'incendio d'un tratto divampò crepitando e riempiendo tutto di fumo. Come un pazzo, urlando con le braccia levate, lui si cacciò dentro alla fornace, forse sperando di spegnerla [...] Morì poche ore dopo all'ospedale, dove fu trasportato. Nel delirio, sparlava del vento, del vento e delle formiche. – Alleanza... alleanza...[64]

Feltrin-Morris, in *Stories for a Year*, eds. Lisa Sarti and Michael Subialka, Digital Edition, www.pirandellointranslation.org, 2021).

61 M. Vanon Alliata (*Introduzione* [*Introduction*], in *Desiderio e trasgressione nella letteratura fantastica* [*Desire and Transgression in Fantastic Literature*], M. Vanon Alliata (ed.), Marsilio, Venezia 2002, pp. 7-18) pinpoints in the fantastic a “veicolo per l'esplorazione di una geografia interiore di conflitti, passioni”, “vehicle for the exploration of an inner geography of conflicts, passions” (p. 11) and considers it “il linguaggio per eccellenza del desiderio” “the language par excellence of desire” (p. 12).

62 “the phantasmal potentialities of language” (R. Ceserani, *Il fantastico, op. cit.*, p. 78). Todorov considers interpreting a metaphor literally to be one of the generative elements of the fantastic (T. Todorov, *Introduction à la littérature fantastique*, *op. cit.*, pp. 82-83).

63 L. Pirandello, *Vittoria delle formiche*, in Id., *Tutte le novelle,* vol. VI, 1919- 1936, L. Lugnani (ed.), Rizzoli, Milano 2017, pp. 256- 259, here p. 256. “It was perhaps ridiculous in itself, but in effect a terrible thing: a house completely overrun by ants. And a mad thought: that the wind had conspired with them. The wind with the ants.” (L. Pirandello, *Victory of the Ants*, tr. Julia Nelsen, in *Stories for a Year*, eds. Lisa Sarti and Michael Subialka, Digital Edition, www.pirandellointranslation.org, 2024).

64 L. Pirandello, *Vittoria delle formiche*, *op. cit.*, p. 259. “The gust came all of a sudden, by surprise [...]; the blaze exploded in an instant, crackling and filling the house with smoke. Screaming like a madman, arms flailing, he ran into the fire, perhaps hoping to put it out [...]. He died a few hours later at the hospital where they'd transported him. Delirious, he kept muttering about the wind, the wind and the ants. “An alliance... an alliance...” (L. Pirandello, *Victory of the Ants,* tr. Julia Nelsen, cit.).

In Pirandello's story, the image of the wind as an evil force, which not only escapes the control of the helpless individual but plunges him into madness and destruction, has slight Leopardian resonances, however it can also be linked to negative mythologies about the wind: the *Anemoi,* for instance, whom Aeolus can barely keep in check, embody the winds' destructive power in classical epic.

The wind impetus can also reveal ancestral figures of terrifying and agonizing power. In *L'Incantata* [*The Enchanted*] (1908) by an unknown writer, Giacomo Giacomantonio, screaming gusts impersonate the 'Signori del luogo' [Landlords of the place], anticipating Lovecraft's horror mythology.[65]

A young man named Franco tries to climb a sacred and taboo mountain, the 'Incantata' (the Enchanted), home of very ancient deities. Suddenly he is assaulted by gusts of wind.

> Erano ruggiti, bramiti, barriti dilaceranti, tremendi. [...] Ben presto egli si trovò ravvolto in un'aria puzzolente, assai rarefatta, d'un umidore gelido. [...] I rumori erano divenuti delle risate, delle enormi risate, non possibili ad esseri umani. [...] Che ghigni! Che voluttà ultraumana in quelle sembianze embrionali create da un Dio in delirio![66]

The young man is forced by the Lords to 'see' the forbidden peak but, on descending, he discovers that the punishment for his *hybris* is endured by his companion, whom he finds dead. Beastly, chthonic deities – the animal-like cries, the stench –, the monstrous beings show the protagonist how much his dominion over reality, symbolized by the forbidden climb, is illusory and ridiculous.

65 F. Foni, *Alla fiera dei mostri: racconti pulp, orrori e arcane fantasticherie nelle riviste italiane, 1899-1932* [*At the Monsters' Fair: Pulp Tales, Horrors, and Arcane Fantasies in Italian Magazines, 1899–1932*], Latina, Tunuè 2007, pp. 13-14, 16.

66 "They were rending, dreadful roars, bellows, trumpeting cries. [...] Before long he found himself enveloped in a foul-smelling air, heavily rarefied and steeped in an icy damp. [...] The noises had turned into laughter—huge laughter, impossible for human beings. [...] What grins! What ultrahuman voluptuousness in those embryonic shapes fashioned by a God in delirium!" (G. Giacomantonio, *L'Incantata,* in "La Domenica del Corriere", n. 32, 1908, pp. 14- 15, here p. 15). In fact, the episode seems to anticipate Jung's reading of Nietzsche's story, quoted at the beginning of this essay (C. G. Jung, *Nietzsche's Zarathustra*, *op. cit.*): the wildly laughing wind-deities can be understood as an externalization of the explorer's unconscious, the numinous force that erupts between the observer and the world and suspends rational control.

Final remarks

To conclude, the present analysis of fantastic narratives through the lens of the wind shows the productivity of this theme that is fruitfully employed by several authors to question reality, to show its inconsistencies, its limitations, its negative aspects; as Celati suggests, the wind is a true image of writing, a force that dismantles and reconfigures experience. Lastly, the eolian motif is useful to emphasize the lability of the boundary between reason and madness, a thin ridge that can be moved and altered by the slightest puff of wind. If the supernatural is 'squared literature', as Orlando claims[67] – since it specifically focuses on the dialectic between reason and imagination, staging the 'return of the repressed'–, the fantastic literature of the wind intensifies this tension to the extreme. The wind reworks a reality that grows ever more unstable, as it is undermined by endogenous forces external to the human being, thereby rendering the world we live in increasingly fragile and less and less 'true'.

67 Cf. F. Orlando, *Il soprannaturale letterario* [*The Literary Supernatural*], Torino, Einaudi 2017.

Simone Pettine

"Nelle pause della brezza il silenzio si posava sul silenzio"[1]
Vènt-larg and Solitude: an Analysis of Francesco Biamonti's *Vento largo*

Light, wind, sea. Francesco Biamonti's novels are said to contain some recurring image-words, actual semantic focal points transcending the mere descriptive or denotative element; even the casual reader quickly becomes aware of it[2]. The titles of the four novels published during the author's lifetime, however, are not occasional at all, especially considering Biamonti's *modus operandi*: if a single page could keep him busy for days and days in search of the perfect expressive form, of a precise word, of the clear sentence in its exactness, the attention he had to pay to the choice of those few terms aimed at representing the identity of the books was crucial.

Biamonti's titles almost always make the abstract outweigh the reality: *L'angelo di Avrigue* (1983), *Attesa sul mare* (1994), *Le parole la notte* (1998), and the unfinished *Il silenzio* (published posthumously in 2003). The only exception is a single work, in which the author is not satisfied with a mere common name, but requires that of a particular type of wind: *Vento largo* (1991).

The last above-mentioned novel starts from the natural element. This element distinguishes several landscapes and environments (Liguria and France, the sea, and the mountains) representing a diametrically opposite reality: mainly psychological, sometimes moral, more rarely spiritual, and never in a religious way *sensu stricto*. However, it is an unusual case in Italian literature, in which a novel has the wind as protagonist. Nevertheless, even in works vaguely similar to Biamonti's novels, the boundary line between narrative forms is not so precarious as to make such rigorous and complex classification[3].

---

1 *When the breeze paused, silence folded into silence.* Le traduzioni delle citazioni da Biamonti e dalla letteratura critica in questo testo sono di Paola Del Zoppo.

2 At least one of G. Cavallini's studies is essential: *Su alcune parole-immagine: vento, mare, luce* in *Verga, Tozzi, Biamonti. Tre trittici con una premessa in comune*, Bulzoni Editore, Roma, 1998.

3 *Vento largo* properly it is a novel, but the compositional structure oscillates continuously between prose and poetry. See G. Bogliolo, *Presentazione*, in *Atti della tavola rotonda su* Vento Largo *di Francesco Biamonti*, La biblioteca sul

Vento largo is a novel as pleasant to read as complex to fully understand. It is a book that talks about the wind, in which it is the wind that mainly acts, so much that the writing style itself seems to be transported by it:

> [Il romanzo] non ha né inizio né fine, infatti comincia dalla fine (cioè dalla morte di un passeur), e questo regolare non succedere viene recepito come una cosa del tutto naturale, una continuità dell'orizzonte marino oppure del crinale montano, un'estensione non interrotta nel tempo e nello spazio anche della condizione umana.[4]

Due to its deceptive simplicity, *Vento largo* does not only require careful reading, but if possible several successive encounters between narrator and reader, "perché ad ogni nuova lettura si rivela sempre più perfetto e saldo nella sua apparente, cristallina fragilità" ["because with every new reading it reveals itself as ever more perfect and steady in its apparent, crystalline fragility."][5].

In critical contexts, some diametrically opposed points of view speak about the hermeneutic complexity of *Vento largo*. Even before investigating the deep meanings of the text, some have questioned the very relevance of the air within the work. Among others, Härmä (whose analysis of the book is also very penetrating) on the occasion of a round table dedicated to the novel in question at the city of Peagna (Ceriale) in 2009 wrote: "gli elementi che in questo paesaggio sono chiamati ad avere una parte centrale sono la luce, il mare, le rocce e le nuvole, mentre conta meno il vento evocato nel

---

mare, Alassio, 2009, p. 7: "[il libro] è un oggetto così impalpabile e delicato quale può esserlo un racconto che abbia lo stesso valore e lo stesso incanto di un testo poetico" [[the book] is an object as intangible and delicate as a tale that holds the same value and the same enchantment as a poetic text"]; and E. Suomela-Härmä, *La luce in* Vento largo (same volume), p. 44: "è un'opera difficile da classificare: non è né un romanzo, né una raccolta di novelle; caso mai potrebbe essere definita una serie di istantanee relativa all'esistenza di un gruppo di persone" [it is a work difficult to classify: it is neither a novel nor a collection of short stories; at most it could be defined as a series of snapshots of the existence of a group of people.]

4 "[The novel] has neither beginning nor end; in fact, it begins with the end (that is, with the death of a *passeur*), and this regular not-happening is received as something entirely natural, a continuity of the marine horizon or of the mountain ridge, an uninterrupted extension in time and space of the human condition as well." G. Kiselev, *Una scrittura che cambia luogo e consistenza*, in *Atti della tavola rotonda*, *op. cit.*, p. 31.

5 G. Bogliolo, *op. cit.*, p. 7.

titolo"[6]. Clearly a stumbling block, or a choice due to a particular critical cut; but in the same forum other critics have then rightly called attention to the natural element, both from the thematic point of view ("sin dal titolo, il romanzo […] si mette sotto il segno di un'immagine che suggerisce per eccellenza la leggerezza: il vento"[7]) and from the more properly linguistic one. For Rössner, for example, Biamonti's language would be "una lingua stranamente leggera, simile al vento"[8].

Those who prefer to be impartial, will at least have to come to terms with the words spoken by the author himself. Giorgio Ficara, about twenty years ago, reported a very sibylline consideration by Francesco Biamonti, which seems perfect to narrow the discussion (italicized words, here and elsewhere, are always by the writer): "in effetti io non so e non intendo raccontare altro che natura… o forse è la stessa natura che racconta? Vorrei che le mie pagine sembrassero scritte dal vento".[9] The natural element is pivotal for at least two reasons: it emphasizes what usually escapes sight; and this content to be investigated, if it appears in the environment, transcends it in favour of a psychological dimension, or more appropriately existential.

In this regard, another note by Biamonti proves to be clarifying:

> Ho lavorato sempre cercando di portare alla superficie le cose più profonde dell'animo umano. Portarle sul piano della visibilità, o della musicalità, se la visibilità non è possibile. Tra una scelta psicologica e una scelta visiva io scelgo sempre quella visiva, perché la visibilità è più fertile di senso.[10]

---

6 "The elements that in this landscape are called upon to play a central role are the light, the sea, the rocks, and the clouds, while the wind evoked in the title matters less." E. Suomela-Härmä, *op. cit.*, p. 42.

7 "from its very title, the novel […] places itself under the sign of an image that suggests lightness par excellence: the wind." L. Beiu-Paladi, *La leggerezza del vento nel romanzo di Francesco Biamonti*, Vento largo, in *Atti della tavola rotonda*, *op. cit.*, p. 47.

8 "A strangely light language, similar to the wind." M. Rössner, *Il* passeur *e il traduttore. Riflessioni sul* terzo spazio, *margini e confini*, in *Atti della tavola rotonda*, *op. cit.*, p. 58.

9 "In fact, I do not know and do not intend to recount anything other than nature… or perhaps it is nature itself that speaks? I would like my pages to seem written by the wind." G. Ficara, *Francesco e la via difficile*, in *Francesco Biamonti. Le parole, il silenzio*, Atti del Convegno di Studi *Francesco Biamonti: le parole, il silenzio*, San Biagio della Cima – Bordighera, 16-18 ottobre 2003, il melangolo, Genova, 2005, p. 18.

10 "I have always worked seeking to bring to the surface the deepest aspects of the human soul. To bring them onto the plane of visibility, or of musicality, if visibility is not possible. Between a psychological choice and a visual choice I

This explains why in all of Biamonti's novels, especially in *Vento largo*, observing is more important than speaking, and speaking more than acting. The main characters, actually, do not face endeavouring challenges of any kind: they walk between countries of western Liguria suspended in time, they meet with their peers, now recognizing them, now ignoring their identity; even when they set a precise goal, the action is never decisive.

As a matter of fact, *Vento largo* does not even present a precise plot: Varì, the protagonist, finds himself reluctantly exercising the not very legal profession of *passeur*; Sabèl, loved by the man, but prisoner of his existential discomfort and impatient in the broadest sense, escapes from Aurno and hides in the convent of the island of Saint Honoré. Throughout the novel, Varì wonders about Sabèl's escape, and eventually realizes that he must wait for his spontaneous return, if he ever wants to do it. The novel ends with Varì wanting to stop helping illegal immigrants in the risky passage along the Italian-French border, but then persists, driven by a sort of moral duty, and with Sabèl, still undecided whether to return to Aurno. All the other secondary characters, fleeting shadows, quickly disappear as they appeared.

Nothing seems to have happened, and as a matter of fact it is just like that: the real "action" was actually all internal, it took place in Varì and Sabèl's souls. It is not that the two know much more about themselves and the world they live in than before at the end of *Vento largo*; they clarified some few aspects of their lives; above all, they have started a fundamental investigation for itself. And the wind and other natural elements that are certainly not secondary accompanied their actions and reflections on every occasion. In these cases, of course, "parole come vento, mare, luce cessano di avere valore denotativo, oltrepassano l'idea della cosa significata per assumere valore di immagine"[11].

Giorgio Cavallini insisted on this aspect, paying particular attention to *Vento largo* and writing that "nel secondo libro di Biamonti [...] la parola vento, oltre a figurare nel titolo, ricorre in molte pagine, sia da sola sia in unione oppure in alternanza con le sue altre denominazioni"[12]. As a result,

always choose the visual one, because visibility is more fertile in meaning." C. Cazalé-Bérard, *Pazienza nell'azzurro. Una lettura di* Vento largo, in *Atti della tavola rotonda*, *op. cit.*, p. 21.

11 "words such as wind, sea, light cease to have denotative value; they go beyond the idea of the thing signified in order to take on the value of an image." G. Cavallini, *op. cit.*, p. 144.

12 "in Biamonti's second book [...] the word *wind*, besides appearing in the title, recurs on many pages, both on its own and in combination or alternation with its

the image of the wind allows the word to reach a remarkable expressiveness, achieving that suggestion that was probably always central in Biamonti's mind when approaching his typewriter, in the small studio of San Biagio della Cima.

The image of the wind encompasses a highly symbolic-metaphorical value because it is simultaneously a natural element, a physical place, and a character in the novel. This exceptional status becomes clear little by little, while proceeding in the reading. As for the environment where everything takes place, for example, it has been noted that "è lì, nel mondo sospeso tra la luce e l'aria, che è realmente ambientata l'opera di Biamonti"[13]. Considerations of this type often recur in *Vento largo*, as to emphasize the special status of the village of Varì, which sometimes coincides with a mass of air: "Aùrno era ventoso; ma i venti, che lo flagellavano, passavano sul mare che li mitigava"[14]; "era il regno del vento. Un mistral frantumato al suo finire, scuoteva ancora il paese"[15]; "Aùrno sull'altura sembrava errare su lamine d'aria; tutti i paesi lontani, sui crinali, sembravano edificati nell'azzurro"[16]. Biamonti himself once said that Aùrno was a "paese al vento"[17].

They are all images that simultaneously evoke both the sense of fragility and beauty of the places, traceable characteristics, specularly, in the protagonists. Indeed, Beiu-Paladi has wisely observed how both the names of the places and those of the main characters bear a phonic trace of the windiness:

> Nella loro sostanza sonora quasi tutti i nomi hanno una risonanza musicale, che ricorda la ricchezza di effetti onomatopeici con cui viene descritto il suono del vento [...] Nomi dei personaggi (Varì, diminutivo di Evaristo, Sabèl Viria, Vincenzo, Virgil) [...] Toponimi dalla sonorità ligure-provenzale (Luvaira, Cimòn, Aurive) suggeriscono spesso nella vibrazione del suono V, la voce del vento e imprimono al racconto un'aura di magia che incanta il lettore.[18]

---

other designations." Ivi, p. 146.

13 "it is there, in the world suspended between light and air, that Biamonti's work is truly set." G. Kiselev, *op. cit.*, p. 30.

14 "Aùrno was windy; but the winds that scourged it passed over the sea, which tempered them", F. Biamonti, *Vento largo*, Einaudi, Torino, 1991, p. 11.

15 "it was the realm of the wind. A mistral, shattered at its end, still shook the village", Ivi, p. 54.

16 "Aùrno on the height seemed to wander upon sheets of air; all the distant villages on the ridges seemed built in the blue", Ivi, p. 90.

17 C. Cazalé-Bérard, *op. cit.*, p. 18.

18 "In their very sound substance, almost all the names have a musical resonance, recalling the richness of onomatopoeic effects with which the sound of the wind

After distinguishing between wind as a natural element and its symbolic image, one can attempt to interpret the deep meanings of the text. From the novel's beginning, air is linked to two other concepts: the obsessive idea of death and the inability to communicate, which is typical of humans. The emblematic expression at the beginning is the one that accompanies the few words pronounced at the funeral vigil of the *passeur* Andrea, whose profession Varì will inherit: "nelle pause della brezza il silenzio si posava sul silenzio".[19] The displacement of air, in itself impalpable, allows the emergence of the physicality of silence, which assumes a weight and becomes a monolithic block interposed between those present at the funeral who prefer not to speak.

Biamonti constantly returns to underline the impossibility of meaningful dialogue through the image of the wind. A fundamental passage, in this regard, is that of the fifth chapter, filtered from the perspective of Varì: "parlare, parlava, egli pensò, parlava con Sabèl, ma in modo tale che, se anche fosse stata presente, non lo avrebbe capito [...] – parlare con qualcuno è come parlare al vento, – disse"[20] ("speak, he did speak, he thought, he spoke with Sabèl, but in such a way that, even if she had been present, she would not have understood him [...] — to speak with someone is like speaking to the wind, — he said.") This speaking without mutual understanding conceals a vision of the world that is both painful and complex. If the characters do not speak "non è per sfiducia nella possibilità di comunicare" ("it is not out of distrust in the possibility of communication,"), but for a more serious reason: "per la difficoltà a trovare il fondamento metafisico del dire" ("because of the difficulty in finding the metaphysical foundation of speech.").[21] We can then speak only in an ephemeral way, not of what is really fundamental. This would explain the presence of so many dialogues apparently detached from the particular context in which they take place and the predilection for the thoughts of the protagonists, reported, among other things, in hooked quotation marks, as if it were a real traditional dialogue.

---

is described [...] The names of the characters (Varì, diminutive of Evaristo, Sabèl Viria, Vincenzo, Virgil) [...] Place names with a Ligurian-Provençal sonority (Luvaira, Cimòn, Aurive) often suggest, in the vibration of the sound *V*, the voice of the wind and impart to the narrative an aura of magic that enchants the reader", L. Beiu-Paladi, *op. cit.*, pp. 50-51.

19 F. Biamonti, *op. cit.*, p. 3.

20 Ivi, p. 32.

21 V. Coletti, *Introduzione*, in *Francesco Biamonti. Le parole, il silenzio*, *op. cit.*, p. 14.

The characters, however, *also speak to the wind* in another sense: "sembrano scavalcare la loro dimensione di cronaca [...] aprire un colloquio con le forze della natura"[22] ("they seem to go beyond their dimension of chronicle [...] to open a dialogue with the forces of nature.") In this way, an equal relationship between the wind and Varì/Sabèl is established, and a common identity is recognized: the wind, like men, acts implacably, as if destiny were guiding it. Sometimes, it gives life and guarantees consolation; other times, it brings death. The natural element does not care about those present, just as humans seldom care about the consequences of their actions on others.

As mentioned, the wind is also associated with the idea of death: an exasperated disproportion, considering that, after all, the deaths in the novel are only two, the one already mentioned concerning the *passer* Andrea and another concerning a secondary character, Albert. As for the former, immediately after the funeral we can read that Varì "andava su fasce d'argilla marnosa con ulivi grandi agitati da una brezza ch'era come un vento"[23], where the air *carries* his funereal thoughts. Following Albert's death, instead, it is the natural element that must shape the mood of those present, who are still shocked, and so "la notte era serena" ma "con trasalimenti dell'aria improvvisi"[24].

However, there are several other places in the novel where meditation on death is not bound to particular events, so it can assume a more profound symbolic value, referring to the more general destiny of human beings. As in *Avrigue's Angel*, and then in subsequent works, an obsessive idea of consumption hovers over the natural environment: "le case, disabitate, andavano in rovina"[25]; "se Luvaira era in decadenza, Aùrno era morta [...] Se ne andavano anche i segni cristiani: "madonnette" sbrecciate e ròse, e croci, sui bricchi, inclinate dal vento"[26]. The wind marks the end of civilization, but also the impossibility of transcendence, in a world devoid of the presence of God; "spiravano soffi dalla parte del tramonto"[27]; "si sentiva così stanco di càlcari, di rocce, di gente disperata, di sentieri che finivano nel cielo"[28].

22 F. Croce, *Il romanzo-paesaggio in Francesco Biamonti*, in *Francesco Biamonti. Le parole, il silenzio*, *op. cit.*, p. 27.
23 F. Biamonti, *op. cit.*, p. 4.
24 Ivi, p. 69.
25 Ivi, p. 11.
26 *Ibidem*.
27 Ivi, p. 79.
28 Ivi, p. 87.

Sometimes, as in the concise and poetic third chapter, the wind is not simply the means through which death manifests itself, but the bearer of destruction. It is the wind that allows the frost of the mimosa field of Varì, one of the very few lights in its existence (together with Sabèl, who has already fled to France):

> L'inverno s'avviava nel lungo sereno, ed era un inverno mite; le farfalle e gli altri insetti, aggrappati alla vita, trascorrevano la notte sul lato occidentale dei cespugli, sui rami che avevano raccolto il sole della sera. Le mimose gonfiavano i glomureli, stavano per fiorire.
>
> Ma un giorno, dopo lunghe crepe di splendore, dalle nubi venute dal mare scese la neve e ghiacciò sugli alberi investiti da un vento gelido. Cadevano i fiori e si spaccavano le cortecce. Varì passò a scuotere le mimose per liberarle dal manto nevoso, a rialzare quelle che s'erano abbattute. Ma fu inutile. Ben presto divennero un groviglio di fronde arse.
>
> Non era mai venuto, a memoria d'uomo, un gelo simile.
>
> Gli restò solo la voglia di guardare e piangere: s'insediava nel mimoseto, per le terrazze, un'oscurità minerale, una rigidità ostile. Sembrava fosse passato il fuoco, a carbonizzare.[29]

And it is the wind that also closes the entire sequence: "la luce che il vento muoveva non gli offendeva quasi più gli occhi"[30]. A hope of reconciliation with the world, certainly a mute resignation to the fate that we know we cannot defeat.

Sabèl also encounters several eloquent objects or omens along the way. In Saint Honoré, "fuori del monastero, sul vialetto", next to the chapel of the Penitents, she immediately notices a "teschio posato sulla sabbia dentro un'urna di vetro, col cartiglio in pietra: "come tu sei io ero, come sono tu sarai'"; all obviously mediated by natural elements: "i frangenti, la luce sul teschio solitario, i colpi di mare e di vento sul campo di lavanda; tutto,

29 "Winter was setting out into a long spell of calm, and it was a mild winter; butterflies and other insects, clinging to life, spent the night on the western side of the bushes, on the branches that had gathered the evening sun. The mimosas were swelling their little clusters, they were about to bloom. But one day, after long cracks of brilliance, from the clouds coming from the sea snow descended and froze upon the trees struck by an icy wind. The flowers fell and the bark split. Varì went around shaking the mimosas to free them from the snow mantle, to raise those that had collapsed. But it was useless. Soon they became a tangle of scorched foliage. Never in living memory had such a frost come. All that remained to him was the desire to look and weep: in the mimosa grove, across the terraces, there settled a mineral darkness, a hostile rigidity. It seemed as though fire had passed through, carbonizing." Ivi, p. 19.

30 Ivi, p. 20.

dalla sabbia al cielo, aiutava a cancellare ciò che era stato".[31] The call of the life is inaccessible to her: only her friend Hedwig, a fugitive too, is a "cespuglio scosso dal vento"[32] when she dances.

The condition of Sabèl is very often more worrying than that of Varì. While the man meets and touches death in his search for answers, Sabèl seems to consciously chase it[33]. In her case, death is not simply associated with wind, but with a very specific type, the wide wind of the title: "risentì l'odore di morte che l'aveva cercata presso un lentisco. Veniva da lontano come un vento del largo, il "Vènt-di-damo', delle dame bianche".[34] This constitutes a significant difference, which allows to highlight some divergences in the psyche of the protagonists.

That of Varì and Sabèl is an entirely interior journey, in search of some answers in a painful existential investigation. The world, however, does not grant answers of any kind or solutions to the generalized condition of anxiety: this is how *Vento largo* offers "l'ascesi interiore dei due protagonisti principali" until "una rinuncia che sfocia sull'accettazione di un destino segnato dalla morte".[35] What really counts are the stages and methods that mark this path: Sabèl, offended by life and her past, flees into self-isolation, also represented by the image of the island; Varì, instead, remains immersed in the world in consumption and continues to relate to a large number of other characters.

Varì's attitude is thus manifestly different from Sabèl's constant indecision and her longed-for "living-for-dying". The protagonist faces and tries to reflect upon the condition of the world without being fascinated by it:

> Varì disse che al pericolo si poteva guardare in faccia, ma che c'erano cose che non si potevano controllare: stati d'animo, memorie. L'altro guardava con occhi avidi.
>
> – Si invecchia,– indagò.
>
> – Invecchia anche la terra e il vento,– Varì disse.[36]

---

31 Ivi, p. 73.

32 Ivi, p. 75.

33 Of Sabèl it is said that "sentiva una nostalgia che andava al di là degli uomini" [He felt a kind of nostalgia that reached beyond humans] (ivi, p. 94).

34 Ivi, p. 95.

35 C. Cazalé-Bérard, *op. cit.*, p. 18.

36 "Varì said that danger could be faced head-on, but that there were things that could not be controlled: states of mind, memories. The other looked on with eager eyes. – One grows old, – he probed. – The earth and the wind grow old too, — Varì said." F. Biamonti, *op. cit.*, p. 85.

The complete superimposition of the wind over the characters, whose destiny, marked by consumption, must be necessarily shared, does not only prelude the simple image of death but also other meanings that do not allow changes, but the understanding of the condition of the world. And since in Biamonti's works a clear and deep awareness is never predictable, but requires considerable effort, it only comes in the first manifestation of the vast wind, almost at the end of the book (and before the similar scene between the homonymous wind and Sabèl):

> Non sapeva come spiegarla la sua paura. Le cose, a ripensarle ora, erano da nulla. Tuttavia cercò di raccontare.
>
> Sul pianoro, tra i càlcari, sui flutti pietrificati, erano arrivate le punte del "Vènt-larg", notturno e impetuoso, d'altomare. E gli era parso di sentire sonagli e campanacci dei greggi e delle scorte d'un tempo: redon, clarin, chiodato e martelletto. "Anaren vendren, Anderemu vegneremu" sembravano dire con suono di pietra e di rame.[37]

The images of a humanity in disarray and the need for a shepherd to act as a guide are welded into the perception of time passing by. The vast wind crosses the barrier of contingency and connects different eras, revealing, however, that all epochs are marked by the same uncertainty, by the same existential anguish. Varì is the "shepherd of today", who guides illegal immigrants across the Alps instead of animals; analogy is not a mere supposition, because through the animal metaphor, it recurs several times in *Vento largo*.

The wind, in fact, always seems to emphasize an absence: after all, even death and silence are forms of emptiness. In the seventh chapter, the air connects two apparently separate events, the death of the *passeur* and the escape of Sabèl. Varì realizes that there actually is a correlation between what is happening in his life:

> Ne era convinto anche lui: tutto era cominciato da quella morte. "Che cosa faresti se me ne andassi?" era la domanda che si disinsabbiava dalla memoria,

37 "He did not know how to explain his fear. In hindsight, the things were nothing. Yet he tried to recount them. On the plateau, among the limestones, on the petrified waves, came the gusts of the 'Vènt-larg', nocturnal and impetuous, from the open sea. And it seemed to him he heard the bells and clanging cowbells of the flocks and herds of bygone times: *redon, clarin, chiodato* and *martelletto*. 'Anaren vendren, Anderemu vegneremu' they seemed to say, with a sound of stone and copper." *Ibidem*.

> la domanda che Sabèl gli aveva posto [...] Fuori, il silenzio era riempito dal vento che scendeva dalla montagna: flautato su rocce lontane. Portava, quel vento, foglie secche, che i Luvairischi chiamavano i telegrammi di Pietravecchia. Quando arrivò a Aùrno il vento era cessato e la terra a scale si ergeva nell'antico silenzio.[38]

In the above-mentioned passage we can notice the recurrence of all the semantically relevant terms mentioned so far ("vento", "silenzio", "morte": Wind, silence, death) and the disappearance of the beloved woman. It is evident that nature, in this case the air, has no consolation to offer to the characters, nor does it represent a mere mirror of their psychological condition. In short, in Biamonti, the landscape "non rappresenta una compensazione né una consolazione; in un tempo malato [...] anche il paesaggio, infatti, è irrimediabilmente compromesso e contagiato" ("does not represent a compensation nor a consolation; in a sick time [...] even the landscape, in fact, is irreparably compromised and contaminated"), until it becomes "sintomo della malattia del nostro tempo" "a symptom of the illness of our time" or "metafora della condizione, tragica e lacerata, dell'uomo moderno" ("a metaphor of the tragic and torn condition of modern man.")[39] Only a few musical and melancholic echoes remain, carried by the wind, perhaps prompting a different world, or nostalgia for a time which seems to be more pleasant in the dimension of memory, but in any case, everything turns out to be momentary and inaccessible[40].

The lack indicated by the wind, of course, is always an uncovered existential discomfort, beyond the actual events that concern it. In *Vento largo* the nature "sostituisce le relazioni fra i personaggi" "replaces the relationships between the characters," and since each of them is "immobile, offeso, sognatore, gentile, disperato: a un passo dall'autodistruzione" ("motionless, wounded, dreamer, gentle, desperate: one step away

---

38 "He too was convinced of it: everything had begun with that death. 'What would you do if I were to leave?' was the question that resurfaced from memory, the question Sabèl had asked him [...] Outside, the silence was filled by the wind coming down from the mountain: fluted over distant rocks. That wind carried dry leaves, which the people of Luvaira called the telegrams of Pietravecchia. When it reached Aùrno the wind had ceased, and the terraced land rose in its ancient silence." Ivi, p. 39.

39 F. Improta, *La narrativa di Francesco Biamonti: ipotesi di lettura*, in *Francesco Biamonti tra parole e immagini*, Philobiblon edizioni, Ventimiglia, 2003, p. 17.

40 C. Boccadoro, *Prefazione*, in F. Biamonti, *L'angelo di Avrigue. Vento largo. Attesa sul mare*, Einaudi, Torino, 2020, p. IX.

from self-destruction")[41], the air must represent the condition of these protagonists suspended on the abyss and yet so tenaciously attached to life. Here is one of the best examples among many that are possible:

> L'alba lo colse sulle terrazze d'Aùrno. Si fermò a guardare: il cielo a oriente era di un *verde arioso*, da tempo secco [...] ma subito dopo l'alba un *vento fresco* investì rami malandati [...] *era rimasto proprio solo* a coltivare poche terrazze lì ad Aùrno: gli altri, alzato il viso dalla terra, erano partiti.[42]

It is the *windy* image of a man no longer young, almost the last remaining of his fellows. Even the elderly of Aùrno and Luvaira slowly disappear, while the young people have already left to seek their fortune elsewhere; there is no sign of children, as usual, in Biamonti's novels. Western Liguria thus coincides with a world fatally destined to extinction, harassed by a strange disease.

There remains, perhaps, some chance to be saved. Gioanola interpreted the wind of the novel "come traccia di anima in mezzo alla desolazione e all'abbandono", rightly recalling that the air is precisely this, "anemos, spiritus, ha la natura dell'invisibile".[43] Of course, Albert's subsequent answer to the doubts of Varì, who has recently embarked on the profession of *passeur*, is not casual: "– Lei ha troppi scrupoli, vuol salvare l'anima; noi l'anima la consumiamo nella vita, io e Virgin, la esauriamo di prepotenza".[44] Not only theirs, Biamonti seems to mean. The soul of anyone who flies away enraptured by the wind, remains elusive just like the wind.

41 G. Ficara, *op. cit.*, pp. 18-19.

42 "Dawn found him on the terraces of Aùrno. He stopped to look: the sky in the east was of an airy green, from long dry weather [...] but right after dawn a fresh wind struck the ailing branches [...] he was left quite alone to cultivate a few terraces there in Aùrno: the others, having raised their faces from the soil, had departed." F. Biamonti, *Vento largo*, *op. cit.*, p. 9.

43 E. Gioanola, *Il tempo-spazio di Francesco Biamonti, o l'indiscrezione dell'inesprimibile*, in *Francesco Biamonti. Le parole, il silenzio*, *op. cit.*, p. 82.

44 F. Biamonti, *Vento largo*, *op. cit.*, p. 36.

Stefano Simone

The *Insight* of the Wind

A Symbol of Awareness in Boris Vian, Eugenio Montale and T.S. Eliot

1. *Introduction*

In literature, the blowing of the wind may not be perceived as a symbol, for its superfluous, invisible, quite unintentional nature. However, we can notice that when, in a novel or a poem, the wind blows, characters often become more aware of their (fictional) realities, awakening from a sort of torpor. This inner breath may not be fully understood, as it carries significance difficult to accept or, ultimately, frightening.

2. Insight *and literature*

The term *insight* is quite unusual in literary studies, and yet it could reveal some semantic elements otherwise buried. The APA Dictionary of Psychology explains that the term denotes

> the clear and often sudden discernment of a solution to a problem by means that are not obvious and may never become so, even after one has tried hard to work out how one has arrived at the solution.[1]

It describes a process where the perception of reality is altered and the objectual world is somehow reordered by the mind, through a largely unconscious process.

Carl Rogers, the founder of therapeutic counselling, contributed to the exploration of the meanings of this term. In his view, *insight* is acquired through the self-healing skills possessed by the individual mind, with the aid of the therapist. Rogers writes that

1 G. R. VandenBos (ed.), *APA Dictionary of Psychology*, American Psychological Association, Washington D.C. 2015, p. 544.

> the word "insight" has been used [...] in an almost mystical way. [...] Insight here means the self-perception of new meaning in an individual's own experience such that relationships of cause and effect gain new significance.[2]

These are some of its features:

> It consists in seeing new relationships. It is the integration of accumulated experience. It signifies a reorientation of the self. [...] Insight is essentially a new way of perceiving. [...] It often occurs in the solution of a puzzle. [...] Sometimes this experience is called an "Aha!" experience, because of the sudden flash of understanding which accompanies it. This type of perception is possible in counselling and therapy only when the individual is freed from defensiveness through the process of catharsis.[3]

At the end of the therapy, the patient should be able to interpret his past life in a completely new way: writing about one of his patients, Rogers maintains that she

> now sees familiar facts in a definitely new relationship. She has learned no new facts about the problem. The problem itself is an objective reality that has not been altered. But the problem as she sees it has been decidedly changed.[4]

The person may have some resistances that can hinder this self-comprehension, as it is natural for the patient to deny "certain attitudes which he finds within himself [...] When he can face clearly, and can accept as a part of himself, these less praiseworthy feelings, the need for defensive reactions tends to disappear'[5]. Our tenet is that this encounter with the self may be painful. It is not easy to deal with one's own image, as if disrupted in many different directions, not all equally acceptable.

We should add that, so far, the definition of *insight* appears quite similar to the notion of *epiphany*, as it was developed by modernist writers[6]. Nonetheless, *insight* includes in its meaning also the effect of the term,

---

2 C. Rogers, *Counseling and Psychotherapy: Newer Concepts in Practice*, Houghton Mifflin Company, Boston-New York, 1942, p. vi.

3 Ivi, pp. 206-207.

4 Ivi, p. 176.

5 Ivi, pp. 179-180.

6 In *Stephen Hero* "Joyce defined an epiphany as "a sudden spiritual manifestation" in which the "whatness" of a common object or gesture appears radiant to the observer. Much of Joyce's fiction is built around such special moments of sudden insight". See C. Baldick, *The Concise Oxford Dictionary of Literary Terms*, Oxford University Press, New York 2001, p. 84.

whereas *epiphany* describes just the punctual moment of the ecstatic revelation, without referring to the output of the action. For this reason, the notion of *epiphany* does not seem to refer to any therapeutic effect, unlike *insight*.

So, why analyse this psychological concept in a literary criticism essay? And why apply it to the interpretation of the literary connotations of a natural element, the wind? Taking concepts from other disciplines can support the work of literary criticism and the comprehension of 20th-century literature. Despite its extremely different literary forms, it may be argued that the wind as a symbol bears some similarities in certain authors. It seems to us that, in the minds of novelists and poets, the wind is associated with certain meanings and that the critics should not ignore the contributions of other disciplines – like psychology. We will try to draft an exploration of the possibilities of a (so far) unfathomed union between the wind and the *insight* through a comparative analysis of three writers, Boris Vian, Eugenio Montale, and T.S. Eliot.

3. *Boris Vian and the wind*

We will first analyse *L'Automne à Pékin*. For different and paradoxical reasons, some characters end up in an imaginary desert (the *Exopotamie*) to build a railway (a useless infrastructure, that will collapse at the end of the novel). The many plots of the novel revolve around this narrative core. Among the most important, is the one starring Anne, Rochelle, and Angel, the threesome where Anne and Angel compete for Rochelle's love. Almost all the narrative events take place in the desert, such as Angel murdering Anne, the deaths of almost all other characters and, finally, the destruction of the railway, swallowed by the sands of the desert.

The *désert* differs quite a lot from the real desert, as the wind is absent ("Il n'y a jamais de vent'[7]). The desert is a kind of "sieve' ("*il suffit de tamiser le sable*'[8]), which means that it resembles to a model, levelling out differences to devise an ideal world. In the "Notes manuscrites inédites préparatoires à *L'Automne à Pékin*' we read this: "*Angel expliquera sur cette question de choses à voir. Tant de choses à voir et après, tant de*

7 B. Vian, *Romans, nouvelles, œuvres diverses*, ed. by Gilbert Pestureau, Le livre de poche, Paris 2016, p. 264.

8 Ivi, p. 257.

choses à faire lui répondra qqu. Mais il faut d'abord voir, dit Angel'[9]. In fact, *L'Automne à Pékin* is a meta-pataphysique narrative about the disclosure to the consciousness of a different, more truthful reality. And yet it is also the failure of this perspective: the desire to give order to a chaotic reality is not accomplished[10].

The meaning expressed by the note is related to the domain of the sight. Critics have highlighted that the many descriptions of *loci amœni* in the novel hide the desire the characters feel to dwell in those places as if this would match with the ultimate aim of the novel itself. This analysis does not consider the meaning of "voir': "opening the eyes" also means sacrificing these ephemeral images and the desires they bear. They are ephemeral because their sole function is to conceal a frustrating reality with soothing images, which are not truthful – just a mere diversion. "Voir' means becoming aware of this reality, which may be a painful process.

The desert itself behaves uncannily: all the characters see their consciousness slipping away, as if the sand is slowly eroding it[11]. In this fictional word, the wind comes to their aid: their self-awareness comes back in those insightful moments when the wind blows: "À l'extrémité du couloir, un faible courant d'air agitait une lourde branche d'hépatrol devant la fenêtre. Angel eut de nouveau cette sensation de s'éveiller'[12], and "les herbes vertes et pointues s'agitèrent légèrement au passage du courant d'air. […] "Ils ont construit juste au-dessus d'un trou"'[13]. Anne's *locus amoenus* consists in "*être par terre sur ce sable avec un peu de vent et la tête vide*'[14]: consciousness is consumed by the sand, and thinking is impossible, as "*il n'y a jamais de vent : le sable s'est pétrifié*'[15]. Therefore, the core sense of *L'Automne à Pékin* is the unveiling of a more truthful reality. Images created by men are ephemeral appearances, whose scope is just to avoid the sole truth, the certainty of death. The murmur of the wind is thus a *memento mori*, a negative insight about the precariousness of life.

9 A. Costes, *Boris Vian : Le corps de l'écriture. Une lecture psychanalytique du désir d›écrire vianesque*, Lambert-Lucas, Limoges 2009, p. 234.

10 "*L'Automne à Pekin is simply set in the era of bad light; everything is situated one remove nearer to oblivion*", A. Rolls, *The flight of the angels: Intertextuality in four novels by Boris Vian*, Editions Rodopi B.V, Amsterdam-Atlanta 1999, p. 120.

11 "J'ai le cafard." "Ça va se passer. C'est ce sable"' (Vian, *op. cit.* p. 343) and "Athanagore avait un mal fou à réfléchir, car c'est une habitude qu'on perd très rapidement dans le désert" (Vian, *op. cit.* p. 293).

12 Ivi, p. 319.

13 Ivi, p. 418.

14 Ivi, p. 321.

15 Ivi, p. 331.

In *L'Arrache-cœur* the wind is less prominent, nonetheless it is symbolically similar to the wind of *L'Automne à Pékin*[16]. Here Clémentine develops a neurosis after giving birth to triplets: she will be obsessively taking care of her children[17] and, wanting to protect them from any potential danger outside, she will end up secluding them in cages – that is why they are often compared to birds, flying freely in the air.

At first, wind is mysterious: "La lumière baissait. [...] La bonne alla regarder. Le jour s'envolait derrière la falaise et un vent silencieux venait de se lever. Elle revint, inquiète. "Je ne sais pas ce qui arrive...", murmura-t-elle'[18]. She is going to deliver and the wind bears uncertainty, throwing the characters' lives into disarray. Jacquemort, a psychiatrist who helps Clémentine to deliver, is transformed into a cat, "un chat sans substance'[19]. The wind, blowing from the sea to the cliffs, is held responsible for this transformation, and the "void cat' is carried by it. Soon after, the wind brings hail and Clémentine, hurrying home, terrified, is quite relieved when she finds her children inside, protected. In this moment she conceives her final plan for her sons: "J'ai toujours senti que je trouverais un jour le moyen de les protéger totalement du mal'[20]. Her objective is finally fulfilled at the end of the novel: she has segregated the triplets in cages, with no external contact. After the golden fence of their house on the cliff is closed, in the very last sentence of the novel the wind appears: "la grille, peut-être poussée par un courant d'air, se referma avec un claquement profond. Le vent passait entre les barreaux'[21]. Significantly, the only external object that penetrates this house-nest is the wind, which bears the memories of a once free life, when, in the fictionality of the novel, the triplets were able to twirl

---

16 The first draft of the plot is contemporary to the writing of *L'Automne à Pékin*: "c'est dès janvier 1947, alors que Vian écrit *L'Automne à Pékin* et attend la publication de *L'écume de jours*, qu'il jette sur le papier l'idée générale de ce roman", G. Pestureau, *Introduction*, in B. Vian, *Romans, nouvelles, œuvres diverses*, Le livre de poche, Paris 2016, p. 533.

17 A hypocritical attitude, because in the first part of the novel she is depressed, and she hates them. In psychoanalytical theory, this defence mechanism is called a reaction-formation, "in which unacceptable or threatening unconscious impulses are denied and are replaced in consciousness with their opposite. For example, [...] to deny feelings of rejection, a mother may be overindulgent toward her child", VandenBos, *op. cit.*, p. 883.

18 B. Vian, p. 543.

19 Ivi, p. 597.

20 Ivi, p. 680.

21 Ivi, p. 688.

in the air like birds, their mother unknowing. The murmur of the wind is the echo of a past life, of childhood[22], severed by parental control[23].

This wind brings self-awareness, and it is not always accepted. As we saw, characters (like Clémentine with her children) tend to refuse vitality and the acquisition of *insight*, which brings the possibility of change. Carl Gustav Jung, in his works on archetypes, explained that the wind, as mysterious and unreachable as the unconscious (which speaks through symbols), may be frightening:

> The breath of the spirit rushing over the dark water is uncanny, like everything whose cause we do not know – since it is not ourselves. It hints at an unseen presence, a numen to which neither human expectations nor the machinations of the will have given life.[24]

While interpreting the dream of a young theologian, he recalls that

> in the dream, he knew that in the middle of the woods, there was a lake [...] As he approached the lake, the atmosphere grew uncanny, and suddenly a light gust of wind passed over the surface of the water, which rippled darkly. He awoke with a cry of terror.[25]

Then Jung explains why the element of the wind was paramount:

> as a theologian, the dreamer should have remembered the "pool' whose waters were stirred by a sudden wind, and in which the sick were bathed – the pool of Bethesda. An angel descended and touched the water, which thereby acquired curative powers. The light wind is the pneuma which bloweth where it listeth. And that terrified the dreamer. [...] He wanted nothing of it [...] Wherever there is a reaching down into innermost experience, into the nucleus

22 "Les trumeaux sont certes prisonniers, mais le vent passe à travers les barreaux – alors que la première rédaction se fermait, semble-t-il, sur la porte de l'enfer. Est-ce le privilège de l'imagination, [...] le signe d'une promesse pour l'avenir ?", É. Carassus, *L'Arrache-cœur*, in *Boris Vian : Colloque de Cérisy*, UGE, Paris 1977, pp. 407-424 (pp. 423-424).

23 The entire plot is autobiographical: Vian suffered from cardiopathy since his childhood and his parents tried to protect him by preventing him from joining the activities of his peers. His mother is allegedly described as "inquiète [...] de caractère anxieux et autoritaire", Philippe Boggio, *Boris Vian*, Flammarion, Paris 1993, p. 12.

24 C.G. Jung, *The Archetypes and the Collective Unconscious*, trans. by R. F. C. Hull, Princeton University Press, New York 1980, pp. 407-424 (p. 17).

25 C.G. Jung, *Memories, dreams, reflections*, ed. by Aniela Jaffé, Random House, Toronto 1973), p. 141.

> of personality, most people are overcome by fright, and many run away. Such was the case with this theologian.[26]

It is evident that sometimes the wind blows too mighty to be heard, and that may be frightening for the person experiencing it.

4. Montale's Ossi di seppia *and the wind*

So far, we have examined that the contemporary man has trouble accepting a complete disruption of his life, even a positive one, basking in the torpor of his routine. In *Ossi di seppia*, the first collection of poems by Eugenio Montale, the wind, the protagonist, tries to awaken the ego from an existence of debris.

The wind is not perhaps the most prominent symbol in the collection: references to sea, light, plants, and animals occur the most. Nonetheless, wind is silently present across the whole book. Not casually, the first poem begins with "Godi se il vento ch'entra nel pomario | vi rimena l'ondata della vita':[27] the first name is the wind itself, and these two verses represent the author's agenda: the wind stirs, troubles, brings the "ondata della vita', the insight's teaching. As we saw for Clémentine, the wind brings vitality, but this view can be refused.

Therefore, the ego contradictorily judges this insightful wind. At first, the "miracle", the scope of this *quête*, is represented as a catalysing and disruptive event, in which the "I", tossed, is almost exhausted by this violent passion. Elsewhere the narrator himself will have no qualms in enjoying, illogically, the "disteso mezzogiorno'[28], of the "svanire' ["vanish'], basking in the waiting, often connoted as very bright and sultry landscapes[29].

---

26 *Ibid.*

27 E. Montale, *Tutte le poesie*, ed. by G. Zampa, Mondadori, Milano 2017, p. 7. Engl.: "Rejoice when the breeze that enters the orchard | brings you back the tidal rush of life", E. Montale, *Cuttlefish bones*, trans. by W. Arrowsmith, W. W. Norton & Company, New York 1994, p. 3 – further references to the translations of verses will be in square brackets and will cite only the page number of this edition.

28 Ivi, p. 39 ["noon outspread", p. 61].

29 This last image is the most used by critics to define the "miracle" for Montale: "atmosfere di una luminosità traslucida [...] che inducono a uno stupore inerte e presago. Dell'età dell'oro [...] si può avere un presentimento nella smemoratezza dell'ora meridiana, nella grande pace. È l'istante della sospensione, dell'abbandono" (*Ibid.*, p. xxvi). The wind is taken into account just as an ornament of the life of the ego ("Vengono ricreate situazioni atmosferiche per significare il

Swirling images of incipient storms and broken branches alternate with moments of stasis beneath the radiation of the sun.

In *Corno inglese*[30], perhaps the most romantic lyric, characterised by the roar of the wind, the latter, like a divinity, powerfully dominates the elements of nature, in front of an astonished narrator. Uncannily, the wind bringing the miracle is dryly defined as "il vento che nasce e muore'[31]. The wind fails to "play' the soul of the ego, and in fact, the lyric ends with an almost crying ego amid the turmoil of nature, wishing to merge with the elements: "suonasse te pure stasera | scordato strumento, | cuore"[32]. As it is a youthful, "protomontalian"[33] poem, we can surmise a very first formulation of the wind as a bearer of a miracle, which is followed, in a second phase, by a more complex dynamic in which the miracle coincides with the "stasis". Indeed the wind seems to lose significance; the poems of *Quasi una fantasia* and *Sarcofaghi* present an atmosphere of suspension, in which the air is motionless. Here we have the second phasis of Montale's conception of miracle: waiting for it seems satisfactory enough for the ego, and desire and lack of appetite are mingled: "in questa valle | non è vicenda di buio e di luce"[34]. Here, the necessary condition for the miracle to appear seems to be the absence of wind.

In the *Ossi brevi* section, the wind seems to disappear to the advantage of solar desolation. The wind, the bearer of *insight*, of new more truthful perspectives on the self, cannot flow freely: the heat is the kingdom of men

---

trascorrere del tempo, il senso del transitorio", *ibid.*, p. xxviii). Quite the opposite, the wind in Montale has a symbolic meaning that is yet to be fully interpreted.

30 The poem was published in the magazine "Primo Tempo", as part of a series of seven poems, *Accordi*, preceded by *Riviere* (cf. Montale 2017, pp. 1062 and 1150). This indicates a first "youthful" formulation of the wind as a bearer of miracle, which is followed, in a second phase, by the conception of the miracle as stasis. See also G. Almansi, *Lettura di "Corno inglese" di Montale*, in *Studi Novecenteschi*, Accademia Editoriale, 2: 6, 1973, pp. 401-405, where the critic highlights the quite artificial structure of the poem and questions if the wind really is an objective correlative, because the symbolic associations are numerous and not clearly attributable to a single meaning ("il vento è troppo occupato ad adempiere una molteplicità di incarichi contrastanti per poter mantenere un suo peso di objective-correlative sul lettore", ivi, p. 405).

31 Montale, *op. cit.*, p. 13 ["this wind that lifts and dies", p. 10].

32 Ivi, ["if only it could play on you | this night, O discordant | heart", p. 11].

33 "Un caso a sé è costituito dagli *Accordi*, che nel 1922 l'autore ritiene degni della pubblicazione in 'Primo Tempo'", Gianfranca Lavezzi, "Ossi di seppia", in *Montale*, ed. by N. Scaffai and P. Marini, Carocci, Roma 2019, pp. 24-47 (p. 29).

34 Montale, p. 21 ["this valley knows no alternation of dark and light", p. 27].

who affirm only "ciò che *non* siamo, ciò che *non* vogliamo"[35]. For them, the greatest miracle is not *insight*, but a sickening life where "nel tuo giro inquieto ormai lo stesso | sapore han miele e assenzio",[36] with the regret of not being able to penetrate the primordial substance of being[37]. This representation of the human condition will be explicit in *Mediterraneo*, the fact of being "vasto e diverso | e insieme fisso"[38], an ironically powerful and tragical existence.

Notwithstanding, the wind comes back in *So l'ora in cui la faccia più impassibile*, where the ego experiences the miracle: his words betray "il morso | secreto, il vento che nel cuore soffia";[39] the ideal stasis emerges as a deception, which the ego imposes on himself for fear of the uncertainty. In fact, elsewhere the heat is negatively connoted: if "la farandola dei fanciulli sul greto | era la vita che scoppia dall'arsura"[40], it means that sultriness is not generative, but infertile[41].

In the *Mediterraneo* section, the ego faces a sea-father and its vastness, whereas the narrator is a finite human being. The term "wind' occurs just once[42], and yet here the movement of the air is a formidable presence. All the senses of the ego are stimulated (like in Gabriele D'Annunzio's imagery) by the encounter with the sea, and he perceives its "legge rischiosa"[43], that is "l'essere vasto e diverso | e insieme fisso"[44]. The man is condemned to "infinitarsi"[45], to perceive transcendence, without the possibility of

35 Ivi, p. 30 ["what we are not, what we do not want", p. 41].

36 Ivi, p. 33 ["in your restless running, wormwood | and honey taste the same", p. 49].

37 "Lo schiudersi d'un'ignita | zolla che mai vedrò", ivi. p. 36, ["the disclosure of the kindled clod | I'll never see", p. 55].

38 Ivi, p. 54 ["vast and various, | but unchanging too", p. 89].

39 Ivi, p. 38 ["the hidden | suffering, the wind gusting in the heart", p. 59].

40 Ivi, p. 45 ["the children's farandole along the shore | was life itself, exploding from drought", p. 72].

41 Alberto Casadei states that: "la linea che gli *Ossi* verranno a incarnare, almeno nei risultati che ora appaiono più duraturi, è quella della lettura problematica del reale, necessaria dopo la scoperta, una volta finita l'infanzia, di una non-corrispondenza fra il singolo-adulto e la natura in tutte le sue manifestazioni. È la certezza del 'male di vivere'"", A. Casadei, *Montale*, Il mulino, Bologna 2008, pp. 8-9.

42 "Erratiche forze di venti", Montale, *op. cit.*, p. 57 ["the wind"s capricious gusting", p. 95].

43 Ivi, p. 54 ["your perilous law", p. 93].

44 Ivi, ["to be vast and various, | but unchanging too", p. 89].

45 "Forse solo chi vuole s'infinita", p. 93 ["transcendence may perhaps be theirs who want it", p. 151].

embracing this totality represented by the sea, with which he dialogues as in a prayer addressed to his father, or to God.

In *Fine dell'infanzia*, we see that the calm achieved by the miracle is "finta", a deception: the true reality, unattainable, is transmitted by the wind. Therefore, its breath is a nuisance for the narrator, as it reveals a past life, very far away, when certainty was not at stake, when "il nostro mondo aveva un centro"[46].

L'agave sullo scoglio is a triptych of poems, each introduced by the name of a wind (and each wind has its semantics). The protagonist is an agave (an objective-correlative for the poet), a monocarpic plant, which means that it can wait many years to flower, only once, and then soon after it dies. For the poet, the flowering coincides with the "miracle".

In the first part, *Scirocco* (a hot and dry south-east wind), the agave, speaking in the first person, says:

> ora son io
> l'agave che si abbarbica al crepaccio
> [...]
> e nel fermento d'ogni essenza
> [...]
> sento la mia immobilità come un tormento.[47]

Then the *tramuntane*, the northern wind comes, and the ego, which rejects *insight*, is now abandoned to his pessimism: "ogni forma si squassa nel subbuglio degli elementi [...] tutto schianta l'ora che passa"[48], and reality is no longer comprehensible. The agave, now no longer an "I" but a "you", now contradictorily adores her immobility. The waiting to flower, to bloom, for the miracle to happen is now no more a desire:

> stringi a te i bracci gonfi
> di fiori non ancora nati;
> [...]
> mia vita sottile, e come ami
> oggi le tue radici.[49]

---

46 Ivi, p. 69 ["our world was centered", p. 111].

47 Ivi, p. 71 ["now I am | the agave that hugs the crevice [...] and in that seething | of every essence [...] I feel this rootedness of mine is torture", p. 115].

48 Ivi, p. 72 ["all things are shaken by | the passing hour", p. 117],

49 *Ibid.* ["hug those branches | great with blossoms almost born [...] o my slim-stalked | life [...] how dearly you love these roots of yours | today", p. 117].

With the *mistral* blowing on the sea "s'è rifatta la calma [...] una carezza disfiora | la linea del mare e la scompiglia"[50]. The pattern of the two previous poems resembled to a rapid descent towards the end, whereas now the rhythm of the strophes (five quatrains) and the alternate rhyme also visually echo the "caress' of the sweeter wind". The agave has finally blossomed, and the miracle has happened, yet something is still missing; the life of the agave is a "vita turbata", compared to the vastness of the sea:

o mio tronco che additi,
in questa ebrietudine tarda,
ogni rinato aspetto coi germogli fioriti
sulle tue mani, guarda:
[...]
tutte le immagini portano scritto:
più in là![51]

The miracle is a dying one because it has an ending and is not infinite. The miracle brought by the wind is fleeting and, if elsewhere it was a kind of rebirth, the ego starts to see it as a "prodigio fallito" (failed prodigy)[52]. The longed-for moment now reveals its disillusion: the miracle is ambiguously craved and, when experienced, rejected – "nasce e muore", it is born and dies. The wind still foreshadows this event: for instance, in *Egloga*, "venta e vanisce bruciata | una bracciata di amara tua scorza, istante",[53] in *Clivo* "s'anche il vento tace | senti la lima che sega | assidua la catena che ci lega"[54].

The miracle in itself is more polymorphic: it can be revealed by humans, transfigured into whistling hares,[55] horns,[56] whispering bamboos[57] or life sprouting thanks to the rain, like in *Arsenio*:

se un gesto ti sfiora
[...]

50 *Ibid.*, p. 73 ["the calm returns [...] a caress skims | the line of the sea, briefly | ruffling", p. 119].
51 *Ibid.* ["O my stalk, you | whose arms, all bursting blossoms | now reveal | rebirth in everything, look [...] images below [say]: Farther, farther!", p. 119]
52 *Ibid.*, p. 88 ["a failed miracle", p. 141].
53 *Ibid.*, p. 75 ["o instant, an armful | of your bitter bark, ashes | blow by, vanish", p. 123].
54 *Ibid.*, p. 79 ["when the wind is still, | you hear the assiduous filesawing | at the chain that binds us", p. 131]
55 *Ibid.*, p. 76, [p. 125].
56 *Ibid.*, p. 80, [p. 133].
57 *Ibid.*, p. 98, [p. 161].

quello è forse, Arsenio,
nell'ora che si scioglie, il cenno d'una
vita strozzata per te sorta, e il vento
la porta con la cenere degli astri.[58]

Finally, the wind appears in the last stanza of the final poem, *Riviere*. The ego's cathartic voyage has come to an end, and he is ready to bloom again ("rifiorire'):

sentire
noi pur domani tra i profumi e i venti
un riaffluir di sogni, un urger folle
di voci verso un esito; e nel sole
che v'investe, riviere,
rifiorire![59]

The wind is a bearer of *insight*, moments in which things *bloom again*, from dead vegetation, they metamorphose into the vitality of a new life. Nevertheless, the urge to bloom again is hindered by the knowledge that the miracle will eventually perish.

5. *T. S. Eliot and the wind*

The Wasteland project burgeoned during the years 1920-21. T.S. Eliot is hospitalized in Lausanne and will say that his nervous illness had

---

58 *Ibid.*, p. 84 ["and should one gesture graze you, one word | fall at your side, perhaps, Arsenio, | in the hour dissolving, this is the call | of some strangled life that emerged on your behalf, | and the wind whirls it away with the ashes of the stars", p. 137]. Here the wind goes upwards, and it is positively linked to the sky. However, critics have read this poem in other ways: "the futility of challenging the stormy wind is entrusted to the image of the blindfolded horses that, motionless ("fermi"), smell the ground, instinctively looking for what seems solid and resistant to the rising turbulence. The horses' sense of smell is a gift denied to the protagonist who tries to see through the thick dust blown by the tempest", Andrea Ciccarelli, *Journey as Stasis: A Reading of Montale's Early Poetics*, *MLN*, 124: 1 (2009), 213-235 (p. 224). Nonetheless, it seems to us that the horses are an objective correlative for the "gente [che] non vede nell'affollato corso" (Montale, p. 38), that is people who ignore truth, who do not want to question themselves about life. The ego is isolated from the rest of humans.

59 *Ibid.*, p. 105 ["I could feel – | even I, tomorrow, among fragrances and winds – | fresh-running dreams, a wild rush of voices | surging toward an outlet; and in the sunlight | that swathes you, seacoasts, | flower anew!", p. 169].

represented the core of the poem – we might say the achievement of *insight* is indeed fundamental:

> Various critics have given me the honour to interpret the poem in terms of criticism of the contemporary world [...] To me it was only the relief of a personal and wholly insignificant grouse against life; it is just a piece of rhythmical grumbling.[60]

From the very beginning, memories are depicted as detached from the infertile present of the "wasteland', and the wind transmits positive values, accompanying either the fantasies of the narrator[61] or light-hearted visions of a mythical and intangible world, separated from the current reality of objective degradation[62]. A gust of wind[63] appears in the description of the Lady's boudoir whose baroque imagery will be replaced, in a crescendo of corruption, by the rape of Philomela, by the conversation between husband and wife, obsessively dominated by the latter, and by the discourses of patrons of a pub.

The dysfunctional conversation of the married couple contains the word "wind'. Here the author (as he writes in the notes) is referring to the Jacobean play *The Devil's Law Case*, by John Webster. In the passage, two surgeons ask themselves whether their patient is still alive or not,

---

60 T. S. Eliot, *The Wasteland, A Facsimile and Transcript of the Original Drafts including the Annotations of Ezra Pound*, ed. by Valerie Eliot (Harcourt Brace Jovanovich: New York, 1971), p. 1.

61 It is difficult to perceive an "I" here: "Il personaggio si frantuma, non meno del paesaggio o dell'ambiente in cui è inserito", Alessandro Serpieri, *Introduzione e note*, T.S. Eliot, *La terra desolata*, ed. by Alessandro Serpieri (Milano: BUR Rizzoli, 2017), p. 5.

62 The wind connotes the romantic love of Tristan and Isolde, which is later contrasted with the infertility of the "hyacinth girl". In the third section the "southwest wind" will appear in the cheerful episode of Elizabeth and Leicester, positively connoted amid a scenery of decay. However, Marianne Thormählen points out that "not even these seemingly welcome breezes imply anything like fulfillment or fruition" *("What is the wind doing?" Winds and their functions in Eliot's poetry*, in *T. S. Eliot A Voice Descanting: Centenary Essays*, ed. by Shyamal Bagchee, Macmillan, London 1990, 122-148 (pp. 131-132). Although her reading does not discard also negative values of the wind, here we tend to uniform to the conception of wind as bearer of insight. Humans do not accept the insight carried by the wind, which is somehow a "neutral" judgement in itself.

63 "And drowned the sense in odours; stirred by the air | That freshened from the window", T. S. Eliot, *The Complete Poems and Plays* (London-Boston: Faber and Faber, 1985), p. 64.

with this metaphor: "Is the wind in that door still?',[64] which indicates their amazement at seeing that he still breathes. If then, through the intertext, the wind is associated with aliveness, these verses are easily interpreted:

> The wind under the door.
> "What is that noise now? What is the wind doing?"
> Nothing again nothing.[65]

If the wasteland is the land of already "dead" men, the fact that "the wind under the door' does "nothing' indicates the complete absence of an *élan vital*: the wind of *insight* is sterile.

From now on, the wind will be deprived of any symbolic power, not *per se*, but because of the context of desolation. For instance, in the third section, the modern Thames is bleak:

> The river's tent is broken: the last fingers of a leaf
> Clutch and sink into the wet bank. The wind
> crosses the brown land, unheard. The nymphs are departed.[66]

Nymphs are replaced by prostitutes. Again, another reference to the wind: the ego invokes the gods of the Arcadian Thames, but the adversative introduces a sudden change in the scenery, through a "cold blast": "But at my back in a cold blast I hear | The rattle of the bones, and chuckle spread from ear to ear"[67]. Here the *insight* is negative, it foreshadows death[68] and desolating images that follow, like the rotted Thames, the metonymy of the gasometer which stands for the City, and the episode of Mrs. Porter. In "This music crept by me upon the waters',[69] even if the wind is not addressed explicitly, the verb "to creep", combined with the reference to water, can make the wind resemble a sweet, pleasant music. Nonetheless, the quote from Shakespeare's *The Tempest* implied a magical wind music,

64 Cf. Allyson Booth, *Reading The Waste Land from the Bottom Up*, Palgrave Macmillan, New York 2015, pp. 105-108.
65 T. S Eliot, *The Complete poems*, p. 65.
66 *Ibid.*, p. 67.
67 *Ibid.*
68 As we read in the note, the theme of death is also mentioned by referring to Andrew Marvell, *To His Coy Mistress*: "but at my back I always hear | time's winged chariot hurrying near' (*ibid.*, p. 77).
69 *Ibid.*, p. 69.

whereas here the music is deprived of any passion[70]. The adverb "leeward" reveals that the sails of the barges drifting on the Thames do not welcome the wind's direction ("windward"), but resist it:

> The river sweats
> Oil and tar
> The barges drift
> With the turning tide
> Red sails
> Wide
> To leeward, swing on the heavy spar.[71]

In the fourth section, a current under sea | Picked his bones in whispers"[72]. Notwithstanding that there is no direct reference to the wind, we can surmise a metaphorical, underwater current, which suggests a myth of failed, infertile regeneration[73]. Then, the narrator addresses the reader:

> Gentile or Jew
> O you who turn the wheel and look to windward,
> Consider Phlebas, who was once handsome and tall as you.[74]

"Turning the wheel" means the unfolding of life, of destiny, and the right direction to follow in life (referred to as "windward") to fulfil the inner desire of the self. But going "windward" also means dealing with decay, and death, with the certainty that everything will come to an end (and in fact "Phlebas *was* handsome").

When Perceval arrives at the Graal chapel, he finds it empty because the Holy Grail is absent; only the wind welcomes him: "There is the empty chapel, only the wind's home"[75]. This progressive devaluation of the wind culminates in the "damp gust" promising the regenerating rain, which, however, will not appear in the poem: "In a flash of lightning. Then a damp

70 "Evidente il contrappunto tra la musica messa dalla dattilografa per distrarsi da questo incontro senza passione e la magica musica di Ariel che condurrà Ferdinando all'incontro d'amore con Miranda' (Serpieri, *Introduzione*, p. 113).

71 T. S Eliot, *The Complete poems*, p. 69.

72 *Ibid.*, p. 71.

73 "Whisper' is often negatively connoted – cf. Serpieri, *Introduzione*, p. 120.

74 Eliot, *The Complete poems*, p. 71.

75 *Ibid.*, p. 73. Alessandro Serpieri gives the following explanation: "Il viaggio coincide qui con quello dei cavalieri alla ricerca del Graal. Ma la cappella è vuota, come i pozzi e le cisterne: è casa solo del vento [...] il vento è il vuoto del Verbo' (*Introduzione*, p. 128-129).

gust | bringing rain"[76]. *The Wasteland* ends with the hope of regeneration, (also) brought by the wind, but which eventually fails[77].

When T.S. Eliot wrote *The Hollow Men,* he had not yet reached the certainties of the Christian faith, but no longer was he the man of *The Wasteland.* The author expresses, at the centre of the poem (the ideal centre of his journey) "the moment of turning, the point where descent becomes ascent"[78] – the pivotal moment of *insight.*

> Our dried voices, when
> We whisper together
> Are quiet and meaningless
> As wind in dry grass[79]

The image of the "dry grass" reappears. Since in *The Wasteland* "dry grass [is] singing"[80] thanks to the presence of water (a pool among the rock"[81]), and since in the whole poem humanity is waiting for a life-giving rain, "dry grass' symbolises humankind. So if the wind, as we have so far maintained, brings vitality and *insight*, the simile "quiet and meaningless | As wind in dry grass" means that the murmur of the "hollow men" is insignificant in the sense that human life is deprived of the energy donated by water (it is "dry grass") and, thus, the breath of the wind cannot reverberate in human souls, without the water.

Later, the ego fears the judgment of the souls of heavens, of those who inhabit the "death's other kingdom",[82] the truthful Kingdom, juxtaposed to the "death's dream kingdom",[83] the mundane life, with its uncertainty, like the vagueness of a dream. The voices of the anointed arrive on earth "in the wind's singing | More distant and more solemn | Than a fading star":[84] distant, because in this phase of Eliot's poetry rebirth remains only a faint hope, like the light of a dying star. Soon after, the ego is in disguise, trying

76 T.S Eliot, *The Complete poems*, p. 74.
77 The moral value of the wind can be found in the teaching of the thunder: "La terza indicazione, infine, è "Controlla" (*Damyata*) […] a simboleggiar[la] è una barca a vela munita anche di remi in un mare calmo percorso da una intermittente brezza', Renzo S. Crivelli, *T. S. Eliot* (Roma: Salerno editrice, 2015), pp. 155-156.
78 Helen Gardner, *The Art of T.S. Eliot* (London: The Cresset Press, 1961), p. 105.
79 T. S Eliot, *The Complete poems*, p. 83.
80 *Ibid.*, p. 73.
81 *Ibid.*, p. 72.
82 *Ibid.*, p. 83.
83 *Ibid.*
84 *Ibid.*, p. 84.

to hide his "hollowness", comparing himself to a scarecrow (a "stuffed man"), shaken by the wind: their desire consists in "behaving as the wind behaves"[85].

On *Ash Wednesday*, again, the wind does not have the prominence it has in the *Wasteland*; a possible explanation for this is

> because these wings are no longer wings to fly
> But merely vans to beat the air
> The air which is now thoroughly small and dry
> Smaller and dryer than the will.[86]

The ego knows that he will never come back to his previous conception of life and poetry; now the "wings" of his imagination can no longer fly in an extremely rarefied air, made simple by faith[87]. In this way, Eliot objectifies the truth revealed by religion. Again, this truth is metaphorically echoed (through Ezekiel) in "Prophesy to the wind, to the wind only for only | The wind will listen"[88]. The wind becomes a divine breath speaking to humans and their precarious existence: "Till the wind shake a thousand whispers from the yew",[89] a dying humanity whose objective-correlative is the yew, a typical English cemeterial tree[90].

Compared to his early poems, the irony conveyed by the "voice" of the wind speaking without being heard is missing. Perhaps now that the *insight*

85 *Ibid.* Cf. "[Kurtz] is really "dead," whereas the hollow men are merely not alive, and cannot make the act of surrender involved in actual death. […] The hollow men respond passively to winds, "behaving as the wind behaves," a parody of the Holy Spirit blowing where it pleases', Northrop Frye, *T.S. Eliot* (Edinburgh: Oliver and Boyd, 1963), p. 53.

86 Eliot, *The Complete poems*, p. 90.

87 "Eliot cattura l'immagine estrosa del grande volatile, la cui facoltà di rigenerarsi viene abbinata nella Bibbia alla giovinezza ritrovata […] e che nella simbologia cristiana può annullare la sua vecchiezza spalancando semplicemente le ali nel sole e bagnandosi a una fonte, per farne un'allegoria della vita spirituale e del battesimo', Crivelli, p. 201.

88 T. S. Eliot, *The Complete poems*, p. 91.

89 *Ibid.*, p. 95.

90 Like in Montale, humans are identified with plants: "But when the voices shaken from the yew-tree drift away | Let the other yew be shaken and reply', that must be interpreted opposing the "voices shaken from the yew-tree drift' (voices of the living) and the "other yew' (voices of the dead) (*ibid.*, p. 98). See also Crivelli, *T. S. Eliot*, where the yew-tree is interpreted as the symbol of mortality that gives access to the truthful life ("simbolo della mortalità, per dare accesso alla vera vita', p. 212-213).

has been reached, its call has been finally accepted, and the prayers can soar carried by the wind.

6. *Conclusions*

With the term *insight,* we wanted to propose a new category to analyse literature. The advantage given by interdisciplinarity lies in the use of more specialized terms. We saw that *insight* can variably be a *memento mori*, a call to life, or a symbol of an ascent of the self. It is just one of the indeterminate ways in which humans can get to know themselves. Accepting the *insight* entails a turning point, a new beginning. Contextualised and discussed, it may disappear, like a symptom. This is what happens for example on *Ash Wednesday*, now that *insight* has been reached: the call of the wind is accepted, its breath fades, and the prayers of men merge into it and vanish in the air. What remains of the reading is just a "whisper" of "dry grass".

Deianira Amico

Reading on the Cultural Significance of the Wind's Image in Corrente's Group

A Breeze circulating in Europe during the Interwar period

One of the identifiable features of paintings realised by a prominent artist in Corrente's group is the representation of human figures or objects caught in movement in an atmospheric spatial setting. They are often seen suspended, hanging, or flying mid-air, floating in a disquieting emptiness. Since the wind's motive implies an anti-classical aesthetic, it also has a philosophical and political meaning, for instance, the desire to distance itself from the totalitarian design of the fascist regime. The image of wind frequently appears to express the connection with transalpine European modern culture, poetry, and art in which the Milanese movement is involved.[1]

The teaching of Antonio Banfi constitutes a guideline for the young intellectuals who work in the magazine "Corrente", founded by Ernesto Treccani in Milan in 1938, the same year of Italian racial laws, and closed by Mussolini the date of entry into the war, on May 10th, 1940.[2] Among Banfi's students who graduated in Aesthetics at the Università Statale di Milano, there are Raffaele De Grada, Vittorio Sereni, Enzo Paci, Mario De Micheli and Luciano Anceschi, all involved in the editorial staff of "Corrente". The anti-fascist evolution of the magazine is testified by the changing of the header's title from "Vita giovanile" to "Corrente di vita

---

1 E. Pontiggia, *Una stagione neo-romantica. Pittura e scultura a Milano negli anni Trenta*, in E. Pontiggia, N. Colombo (eds.), *Milano anni Trenta. L'arte e la città*, exhibition catalogue (Milano, Spazio Oberdan, December 2nd – February 27th, 2005), Mazzotta, Milano, 2004, pp. 9-37; N. Colombo, R. Duilio, D. Amico (eds.), *Corrente e l'Europa*, exhibition catalogue (Milano, Fondazione Corrente, November 21st, 2019 – March 19th, 2020), Edizioni Fondazione Corrente, Milano, 2019.

2 R. De Grada, *Il movimento di Corrente*, Edizioni del Milione, Milano 1952; M. De Micheli (Ed.), *Corrente. Il movimento di arte e cultura di opposizione, 1930-1945*, exhibition catalogue (Milano, Palazzo Reale, January 25th – April 28th ap 1985), Vangelista, Milano, 1985; K. Colombo, *Il "foglio in rossetto e bistro. "Corrente" tra fascismo e antifascismo politica letteratura arte*, Mimesis, Milano-Udine 2019.

giovanile" then "Corrente", which means both something flowing but also a political faction. Even the magazine's graphic eliminates the lictor fasces from the first issues by adopting the title on coloured bands (red, yellow, green) or horizontal stripes instead of the verticality of the fascist emblem.

In contrast to the established function of formal balance that characterised Italian painting in the 1920s,[3] Corrente relaunches the wind's image as a privileged instrument of psychological investigation and expressive freedom. These are concepts borrowed above all from symbolist and romantic poetry, the subject of a passionate rediscovery within the Milanese youth *milieu.*

The cultural meaning of the wind's image in the magazine "Corrente", between poetry and philosophy

"Le vent se lève, il faut tenter de vivre"

(Paul Valéry)

Paul Valéry's verses are published as the epigraph of Banfi's article *Motivi e problemi della estetica contemporanea*, a seminal text published in 1938 that proposes a militant reflection on arts, including plastics, theatre, architecture, cinema, and poetry, all interpreted as intimate reflection against the concept of absolute.[4] The Italian culture of the period is largely imbued with idealism as attested by the mottos "L'Arte è il bello" and "la bellezza è un'espressione riuscita".[5] On the contrary, Banfi's aesthetics introduced a dialectic that embraces a reality *in fieri* and is not perfect.[6] This thought is based on listening to the different expressions of art, according to an approach that combines Kantian relativism, Simmel's existentialism,

---

3 M. Cagnetta, *Il mito di Augusto e la "rivoluzione" fascista*, in *Per una discussione sul classicismo nell'età dell'Imperialismo*, in "Quaderni di Storia", n. 3, 1976, pp. 139-181; J. Nelis, *Constructing Fascist Identity: Benito Mussolini and the Myth of Romanità*, in "Classical World", n. 4, 2007, pp. 391-415.

4 Banfi defines art as "intima riflessione" and "tensione contraria a tutto ciò che è assoluto" in A. Banfi, *Motivi e problemi della estetica contemporanea*, "Valori Primordiali", n. 1, February 1st, 1938, pp. 83-98.

5 B. Croce, *Estetica*, Laterza, Bari 1928, p. 88.

6 On the concept of *arte perfecta*, see B. Croce, *op. cit.*, p. 46. Banfi openly criticises this notion: "La morte dell'arte bella è perciò piuttosto la vita dell'arte, in unam ai risolta intima tensione". In A. Banfi, *op. cit.*, p. 84. The debate is analysed in D. Formaggio, *Fenomenologia della tecnica artistica*, Nuvoletti, Milano, 1953, pp. 35-58.

Bergson's vitalism and Marxism, understood as praxis.[7] The philosopher's essay suggests the need for a new vitalism, as he often recurs on the image of art as belonging to the sphere of shifting and ever-changing existence. Hence, Valéry's lines can be interpreted as a call to the new generation of intellectuals who wanted to place art, in Banfi's words, within "la corrente della vita" (the streaming of life).[8]

Conceiving art with freedom is the premise of Banfi's teaching, summed up in the maxim "l'arte vuole vivere e la vita è una cosa sola con la libertà."[9] That means rethinking the values of freedom as a principle of renewal within art with an ethical attitude. Moreover, the "vita dell'arte" loos to the process of nature as an expression of creativity. It also considers technical skills to be a central element of knowledge, without any difference between plastic and decorative arts.[10] On June 15th 1939, the philosopher published the article *Testimonianza alla poesia* in "Corrente di vita giovanile", which addresses poetry as an instrument to establish a new ethical relationship with reality by restoring the correspondence between existential intimacy and objects.[11] The article includes poetry by several representatives of Italian Ermetismo, including Salvatore Quasimodo, Alfonso Gatto, and Mario Luzi, as well as the recovery of 19th-century Romanticism, in particular Giacomo Leopardi.[12] In the works of those authors, the wind constitutes a poetic image of great diffusion and symbolic value. In Leopardi's *Ricordanze*, the wind carries "il suon dell'ora" (the sound of the hour), thus becoming the symbol of the passing of time and what the passing of time entails. The wind also animates Mario Luzi's early poem: "Il pensiero m'insegue in questo borgo/cupo ove corre un vento

---

7 F. Papi, *Banfi, la ragione, il marxismo*, in AaVv, *Antonio Banfi, tre generazioni dopo*, Il Saggiatore, Milano 1980, pp. 3-11.

8 *Ivi*, p. 92.

9 A. Banfi, *Per la vita dell'arte*, in "Corrente", February 28th, 1939, a. II, n. 4.

10 L. Anceschi (ed.), *Antonio Banfi. I problemi di una estetica filosofica*, Parenti Editore, Firenze 1961.

11 "Nella crisi etica del nostro mondo, religione e poesia o arte in genere possono apparire come forme di evasione spirituale quando non si prostituiscano al servizio di un'ideologia... o non si indugiano in un accademismo... ma la loro verità è più profonda... non è fuga interiore ma radicale coscienza, riconoscimento della concreta realtà... la poesia nella sua intimità, nel suo senso delle cose, novità costruttiva delle cose". A. Banfi, *Testimonianza alla poesia*, in "Corrente di vita giovanile", II, n. 11, June 15th,1939.

12 A. Luzi, *Corrente di Vita Giovanile (1938-1940)*, Edizioni dell'Ateneo, Roma, 1975; G. Benvenuti, *L'esperienza di Corrente di Vita Giovanile*, in *Studi di lingua e letteratura lombarda offerti a Maurizio Vitale*, vol. II, Giardini, Pisa 1983.

d'altipiano".[13] The multiplicity of perspectives of this image innervates Italian literature that matured in the terrible years of the world wars: the unexpected is something profoundly disturbing in the precarious condition of the Twentieth-Century man.[14]

Within Corrente, this tradition is joined by the influence of the French symbolist poetry of Baudelaire, Mallarmé, and Valéry, which are examples of a search for an art that is real and concrete because it encapsulates existence.[15] The impact of traditional natural elements such as air on poetry was common among Symbolist poets such as Rimbaud, whose presence is also found in Thomas Eliot's work. In the Milanese magazine, an Italian translation of *the English poet's Rhapsody of a Windy Night* is published, in which the urban context dissolves, floating through the planes of memory.[16] In the image of desolation emerges the painful existential condition of man and the search for a truth that, in the political climate of dictatorship, takes on both political and intimate meanings. Another central reference is Federico García Lorca: air, wind, breeze, and the general transformation of nature into anthropomorphic images. The Spanish poet's animism combines the sensation of ascension (lightness, airiness, upward movement) with the floating images.[17]

Renato Birolli, a significant figure in the Corrente's group for his mature age, is mainly influenced by poetry. He devotes various passages of his diary to the wind as a theme that alludes to the convergence of visual art and poems:

---

13 The verses correspond to the incipit of *Nell'imminenza dei quarant'anni* in M. Luzi, *La barca*, Guanda, Modena 1935.

14 A. Dolfi (ed.), *L'Ermetismo e Firenze. Critici, traduttori, maestri, modelli,* atti del convegno (Università degli Studi di Firenze, 27-31 ottobre 2014), Firenze University Press, Firenze 2016.

15 Corrente's *milieu* is related to symbolism in M. Luzi, *L'idea simbolista*, Garzanti, Milano 1960.

16 T. S Eliot, *Rhapsody of a Windy Night*, 1917, translated by Franco Rege Gianas, in "Vita Giovanile", anno I, n. 4, February 28th, 1938.

17 His verses are published in the anthology dedicated to poetry by Antonio Banfi: "Due voci suonano: l'orologio ed il vento, / mentre fluttua senza te l'alba bianca", *In morte di Josè de Ciria y Escalante,* translated by Luigi Panarese in "Corrente", III, n. 9, May 31st, 1940; "Vesti e spoglia sempre il tuo pennello nell'aria" in *Ode a Salvador Dalì*, traslated by Oreste Macrì, II, n. 11, June 15th, 1939. See also the translation of *Romance Sonambulo*: "Verde che ti voglio verde. /Verde vento. Verdi rami. / [...] Il fico frega il vento/con la squama dei suoi rami" in C. Bo (edited by), *Lirici spagnoli*, Edizioni di Corrente, Milano 1941, p. 283. About the importance of García Lorca for Corrente's group also see E. Treccani, *Arte per amore*, Feltrinelli, Milano 1973, p. 137 [1966 Milano, Giordano Editore].

> Il vento ha liberato le strade dalla nebbia e ora gli asfalti sono lucidi e scivolosi... Nella lucidità del cielo notturno avverto correnti calde, di scirocco invernale, anticipo di primavera... Riconosco il tempo di notte nelle pause del vento. Su su, soffia, perché sono solo. Palagonia, Palagonia: il ritmo è un'invenzione dell'uomo. Un bisogno di canto e di forme e nei moti. Ogni ora serale ha un suo vento [...] Tutto sciolto nel vento, io, che ridere di me.[18]

The wind has a multifaceted characterisation: it is both a metaphor for solitude and a companion ("soffia, perché sono solo"), a trope of freedom ("il vento ha liberato le strade"), as well as a vital impulse since the wind and the ego are whole ("tutto sciolto nel vento, io "). It is also a source of disquiet, a manifestation of a hostile external reality because, in other passages, Birolli writes: "Guarda le gemme [degli alberi fioriti] che oscillano al pericolo del vento."[19]; since this swaying is linked to a condition of restlessness, as the artist further states: "Io temo il mio disordine".[20] The wind returns, condensing these meanings that intensify following his father's death in the early months of 1937, when Birolli spends nights agitated by "terrori notturni," always shaken by gusts.[21] However, the wind is not the only element punctuating Birolli's states of mind. The wind is a timeless image traditionally presented as embodying the rhythms of the natural world, with its tidal motion, storms, and calm passages making it a tempting metaphor for verse and painting itself. In Birolli's oeuvre, the wind becomes formal research of movement: "un bisogno di forme/e nei moti."

The wind as formal research of movement in Renato Birolli's oeuvre

In the first drawing of Birolli's series *Significati ritmici del vento*, realised in 1935, three natural elements are recognisable: an agave, a tree, and the wind. The rhythm of the composition is tripartite: two horizontal lines mark the space of earth and sky, as in children's drawings, creating three strips of composition; three agave leaves in the foreground create a harmonic connection with the tree's branches, and the three lines represent the wind. [FIG. 1] A second drawing introduces two human figures, and, in the artist's handwritten note, the deletion of the word "tempo" with "vento" reveals the meaning of the overall discourse around a poetic image linked

18 Cf. Birolli, *Nono taccuino*, until December 1st, 1936 (1960), pp. 65-66.
19 *Ivi*, p. 103.
20 *Ivi*, p. 114
21 *Ivi*, p. 69.

to the passing of time. [FIG. 2] The presence of the agave evokes Montale's poetry *L'agave sullo scoglio*, where the poetic self identifies with the plant exposed to the changing of different winds, representing different passages, moods, existential perspectives, and melodic allusions.[22]

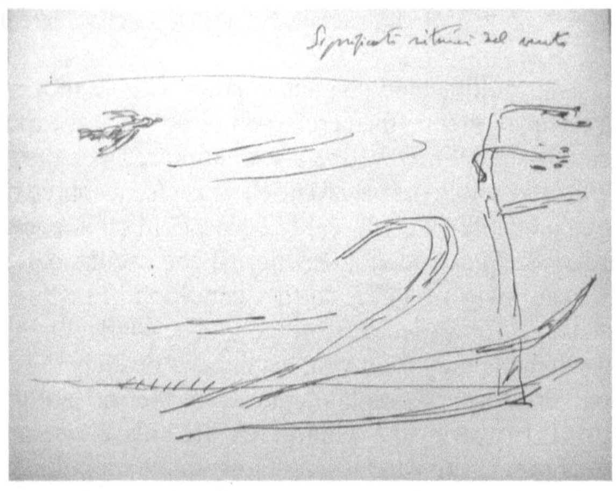

Fig. 1. Renato Birolli, *Significati ritmici del vento*, 1935. In: Renato Birolli, *Metamorfosi*, Edizioni Martano, Torino, 1976, p. 89.

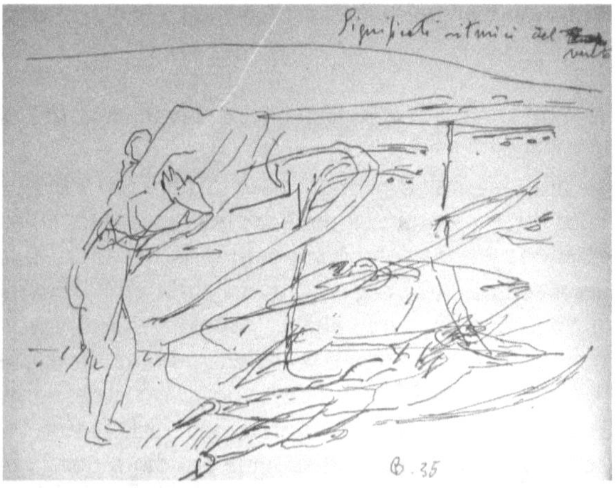

Fig. 2. Renato Birolli, *Significati ritmici del vento*, 1935. In: Renato Birolli, *Metamorfosi*, Edizioni Martano, Torino, 1976, p. 90.

22 G. P. Biasin, *Il vento di Debussy. La poesia di Montale nella cultura del Novecento*, Il Mulino, Bologna 1985.

The association of ideas of wind-rhythm in Birolli's drawings leads back to the musical metaphor, alluding to artistic creation: the wind acts on nature as an element that shapes it, just as the painter's hand engraves on the surface of the drawing. The painter's images are overlaid like a sea of clouds under the pressure of the wind but governed by a compositional principle. For instance, the tree's broken branches transform themselves in the mountain profile, once again preserving the tripartite construction [FIG. 3]. Birolli explores rhythm as a characteristic of memory, motor functions, perception, the natural world, and the art composition. If poetic rhythm shares anything with the painting, it inspires us to search for meaning, tempts us to impose patterns and structures on them, and never confirms whether those patterns have any intrinsic value. As poetic rhythm is not just constructed mechanically, metrically, and predictably but must be complex, shifting, and elusive, the rhythm in painting is not based on geometric rules. Even though Birolli synthesises natural elements as abstract segmented forms on the surface plane [FIG. 4], their movement recalls the laws of nature's internal vitalism without the rigorousness of optical or scientific rules that characterise the period's abstract research.[23] One of his references is Romanticism, as evidenced by the cycle of drawings entitled *Il ritmo in Delacroix* produced during his 1936 trip to Paris. These drawings explore a few paintings by the French master exhibited in the Louvre.[24] The compositions' lines of force are captured through an analysis of the movement, testifying how Birolli found in them the best qualities of Delacroix's Romantic language. As Théophile Gautier already stated, Delacroix's gift was the images flowing in the "tremblement de l'atmosphère."[25]

---

23 About the position of Corrente's group and the critics of geometrical abstract art, see R. De Grada, *Molti astratti e un surrealista al Milione* in "Corrente di vita giovanile", anno I, n. 6, April 15th, 1938.

24 They are published in S. Bini, R. Birolli, F. Bartoli et al. (eds.) *Renato Birolli. Metamorfosi*, Martano, Torino, 1976.

25 T. Gautier, *Les Beaux-Arts en Europe*, Michel Lévy frères, Parigi 1857, p. 172.

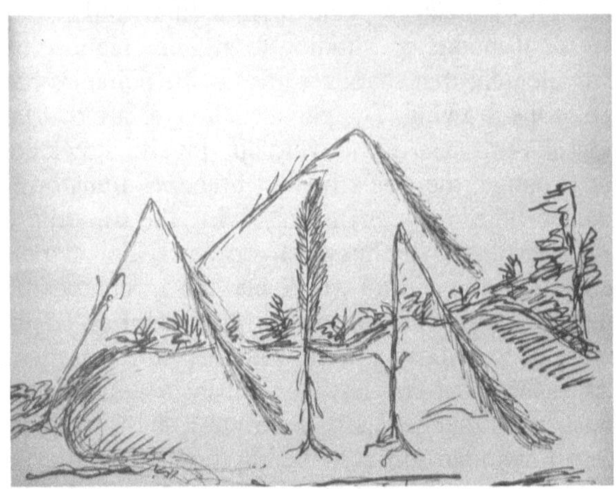

Fig. 3. Renato Birolli, *Significati ritmici del vento*, 1935. In: Renato Birolli, *Metamorfosi*, Edizioni Martano, Torino, 1976, p. 92.

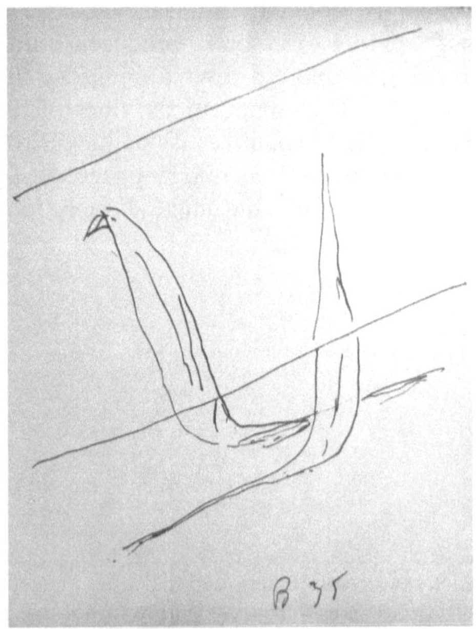

FIg. 4. Renato Birolli, *Significati ritmici del vento*, 1935. In: Renato Birolli, *Metamorfosi*, Edizioni Martano, Torino, 1976, p. 87.

In the same year, Birolli developed an essential nucleus of drawings collected in the volume *Metamorfosi*, curated with his friend, the art critic Sandro Bini, to protest the art system.[26] Indeed, the book was conceived as a stance against the academic *scuola*'s tradition that characterise the culture of the time.[27] Once again, the wind is the protagonist of *Metamorfosi*'s compositions [FIG. 5], and it works as a compositional rhythm governing the human organism and nature as a source of infinite figurative inspiration.[28] Painting, like the wind, is always in process, never fixed; it is always mobile and unstable. It provides no clear answers but rather provokes unanswerable questions, and it is this elusive, challenging, unsettling characteristic that ensures the exploration of what it means to be human and, in the world, teasing us with the promise of answers that it perpetually defers.

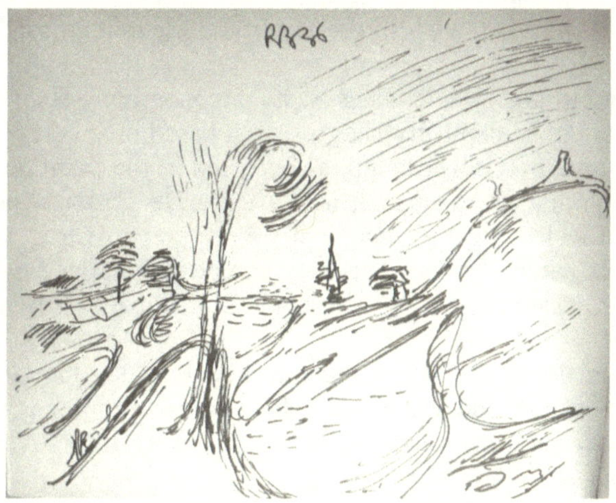

Fig. 5. Renato Birolli, *Metamorfosi V*, 1936. In: Renato Birolli, *Metamorfosi*, Edizioni Martano, Torino, 1976, p. 64.

26 R. Birolli, *Metamorfosi*, Campografico, Milano, 1937. About the volume *Metamorfosi*: P. Rusconi, *Introduzione a Metamorfosi*, in G. Bruno, S. Soldini (eds.), *Renato Birolli. Sentire la natura*, exhibition catalogue (Mendrisio, Museo di Mendrisio, May 1st – July 3rd, 2005), Mendrisio 2005, p. 115 e s.

27 S. Bini, *Nascita delle Metamorfosi* in S. Bini, R. Birolli, F. Bartoli et al, *op. cit*, p. 125.

28 Birolli's images carry with them the imagery of French symbolism: analogies have been found between the artist's inventions and Baudelaire's Charogne. Cf. P. Rusconi, in Gianfranco Bruno e Simone Soldini (ed. by), *Renato Birolli. Sentire la natura*,), testi di G. Bruno, S. Soldini, P. Rusconi, F. Desideri, catalogo della mostra, Museo d'Arte, Mendrisio, 1 maggio-3 luglio 2005, Mendrisio, p. 125

As Valéry states: "Composition is the most human thing about the arts. Nature only offers systems at random; and we have to search for a link which establishes some relation between a whole and its parts. This requires man".[29] Yet the absence of meaning is a terrifying prospect in the great French tradition of Pascal, Baudelaire, and Valéry. It is only human to impose order on the cosmos.[30] Birolli declares the influence of this cultural background, first in the *Self-Portrait* (1934) with Pascal's *Pensées* book open in his hands, then in the recurrence of iconographic themes such as chaos. For instance, in the series of paintings entitled *Caos* (1936-1937),[31] The principles of symmetrical stillness and colouristic sobriety are replaced by movement, ignition, and brushstrokes that create volumes once again moved in a swirling background. Even if the pictorial matter destroys figuration, recognisable elements, such as the shaky sky or pylons dropped as if by a gust of wind, are still present in the Metamorphosis's drawings [FIG. 6].

In addition to poetry references, wind's iconography is an example of a long process of in-depth stylistic research based on a constant dialogue with reality and, precisely, nature, as occurred in the tradition of modern European painting. Furthermore, as Raffaele De Grada wrote in 1938, the model of Delacroix, Cézanne, and Van Gogh consists of the "poetica scoperta della natura."[32] This discovery can be summarized by the master of Aix-en-Provence remark: "Il paesaggio si umanizza, si riflette e pensa in me".[33]

There is an ideal and stylistic connection between the landscapes of Delacroix, Cézanne, and Van Gogh, which Birolli admired at the Louvre. They interpret nature through colour animated by the movement of an inner stream.

---

29 P. Valéry, *Cahiers,* 1931, XIV, P. 808 in J. Robinson-Valéry (eds.), *Paul Valéry. Ego scriptor*, Gallimard, Paris 1992.

30 As Valéry writes in *Ode secrète*: "O quel Taureau, quel Chien, quelle Ourse/ Quels objets de victoire énorme/Quand elle entre aux temps sans ressource/L'âme impose à l'espace informe ! ". Cf. D. Evans, *Paul Valéry and the Search for Poetic Rhythm,* in *Rhythm in Literature after the Crisis in Verse*, "Paragraph", Edinburgh University Press, Vol. 33, No. 2, July 2010, pp. 163-166.

31 About this subject: P. Rusconi, *Renato Birolli. Il Caos,* in *A*. Negri, S. Bignami, P. Rusconi, G. Zanchetti (eds.), *Anni "30. Arti in Italia oltre il fascismo*, Giunti, Firenze 2012, p. 153.

32 R. De Grada, *op. cit.*

33 M. De Micheli, *David, Delacroix, Courbet, Cézanne, Van Gogh, Picasso: le poetiche. Antologia degli scritti*, Feltrinelli, Milano 1978, p. 31.

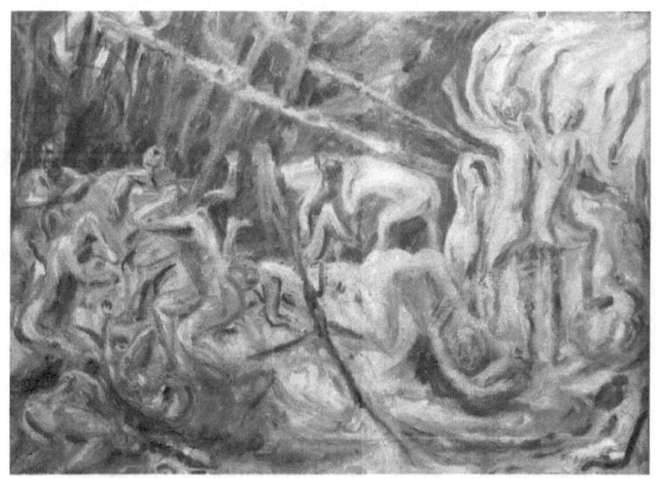

Fig. 6. Renato Birolli, *Il caos (n.2),* 1937, oil on canvas, Milano, Civiche raccolte d'arte, Casa Boschi di Stefano.

Van Gogh's model: the wind as the expression of the relation between subjectivity and reality

> "Ho inteso soltanto ora ciò che voleva Van Gogh
> [...] Sappiamo – io e la foglia – le direzioni fisiche.
> Sappiamo anche d'essere mossi dallo stesso vento".
> (Renato Birolli, *Taccuini*, 1936)

During the 1930s, the solo exhibitions of modern French masters at the Biennale between 1934 and 1938 steered young Italian artists towards colour painting.[34] As Gabriele Mucchi recalls, almost all the group's painters also travel at least once to Paris, the great city of Baudelaire and Delacroix.[35] Thus, another decisive channel for knowledge of contemporary painting is provided by the possibility of leafing through magazines such

34 See the exhibition of Manet, Degas, Renoir, Esposizione internazionale d'arte della città di Venezia, exhibition catalogue n. XIX, 1934, pp. 4, 282-283; n. XX, 1936, pp. 259-260; n. XXI, 1938, pp. 91, 245-246.

35 G. Mucchi, *Le occasioni perdute*, Mazzotta, Milano 2001, p. 105.

as “Cahiers d’art”, “Minotaure”, “Formes”, or “Verve”.[36] Besides these, it must be recalled that Vanni Scheiwiller published the first monographs on the European masters and that postcards and trichomes were widely circulated.[37]

Vincent Van Gogh is the artist to whom Corrente’s group pays close attention, as his name recurs constantly in their writings and correspondence.[38] The volume edited by Lamberto Vitali and published in 1936, which followed a series of initiatives to rediscover the artist’s work in Italy,[39] focusses on an interpretation of the artist as a continuer of the Romantic current[40] understood as an expression of the individual and an ethical dimension.

Van Gogh’s relationship with nature and his work as “colorista arbitrario”, as he calls himself,[41] came, by his own admission, more from Delacroix than from the Impressionists: “Non sarei per nulla stupito se fra poco gli impressionisti trovassero a ridire sul mio modo di dipingere, che è stato fecondato più dalle idee di Delacroix che dalle loro. Perché invece di rendere esattamente ciò che ho davanti agli occhi, mi servo del colore in modo più arbitrario per esprimermi con intensità “.[42] Hence, the atmosphere results from knowledge of reality and emotion, organised by the artist in the image to overcome Impressionist objectivity and Seurat’s lesson. Van Gogh transforms the dots to lengthen; they become lines, then

---

36 R. Guttuso, *Scritti*, ed. by M. Carapezza Guttuso, Bompiani, Milano 2013, p. 659. See also N. Colombo, R. Duilio, D. Amico, *op. cit.*

37 L. Novati (Edited by), *Giovanni e Vanni Scheiwiller editori. Catalogo storico 1925-1999*, Unicopli, Milano 2013.

38 “Leggendo le commissioni di colori di Van Gogh nelle sue lettere al fratello” in R. Guttuso, *Appunti sulla pittura* II, in “Il Selvaggio”, 15 aprile 1940. In a letter sent to the critic in 1938 Birolli jokingly described himself as “il tuo Vincent”. Letter of R. Birolli to S. Bini, 26 novembre 1938, in *Carteggio Bini-Birolli*, edited by G. M. Erbesato, Neri Pozza Editore, Vicenza 1986, p. 32.

39 Among the first review devoted to the Duch artist: L. Vitali, *Epistolario di Van Gogh*, in “L’Ambrosiano”, August 2nd, 1934, October 16th, 1934; L. Vitali, *Precursori: Vincent Van Gogh*, in “Domus”, November 1934, n. 83, pp. 35-38. In 1933, the first monography was published: M. Tinti, *Van Gogh*, Istituto Italiano d’Arti Grafiche, Bergamo 1933 for the first Italian translation of several of Van Gogh’s letters: G. L. Luzzatto, *Vincent Van Gogh*, Guanda Editore, Modena, 1936.

40 “Continuatore della corrente romantica” in L. Vitali, *Vincent Van Gogh*, Hoepli, Milano 1936, p. 15.

41 V. Van Gogh, *Lettere*. This passage is written down by Ernesto Treccani in E. Treccani, *Il sole di Van Gogh*, 1947, in 1.2 Scritti, U. 4, Scritti 1947, n. 4, Archivio della Fondazione Corrente, Milano.

42 V. Van Gogh, *Lettere a Theo*, Guanda Editore, Modena 2021, p. 323.

wavy, circular lines, tangible images of the air and energies that pervade life both in the landscape and the objects. As the Duch painter writes: "L'arte è l'uomo aggiunto alla natura",[43] Art is nature, reality, and truth, but with the meaning that man knows how to draw from it.

Birolli sees Van Gogh's *Epistolary* as fulfilling "un profondo bisogno professionale di chiarezza, né più né meno che un trattato della pittura [...] per un rapporto di colore e linea, un aiuto cioè all'esperienza di dipingere".[44] On several occasions, he annotates in his diary Van Gogh's paintings, dwelling on the presence of the wind as an expression of the feeling of nature and man together: "Quella foglia trema per me", writes Birolli, "Se potesse, quella foglia se ne starebbe ferma; come me, d'altra parte. Sappiamo – io e la foglia – le direzioni fisiche. Sappiamo anche d'essere mossi dallo stesso vento".[45]

Later in his writings, Birolli clearly states that nature represents what brings out the "rapporto di soggettività" for him.[46] In many passages of the diary, the description of the landscape is combined with that of the painting's colours, and the artist identifies himself with both nature and colour, aiming to be a whole thing.[47] Thus, his conscious attention to the element of wind, which returns several times in different compositional keys, brings him humanly and artistically closer to Van Gogh. The Dutch master's paintings that Birolli most loves are those matured in Arles, closely to a warm but hostile nature due to the presence of the mistral.[48] Van Gogh's relationship

---

43 *Ivi*, August 1879, p. 98.

44 R. Birolli, *1960*, Quinto taccuino, August 11th-21st, 1936, p. 37.

45 "Le fronde sono immensi uccelli dal becco voltato in su, corvi. La sua elasticità è armoniosa ed è appena sensibile, caduto il vento, il ricostituirsi dell'usata forma. Elegantissimo tra gli alberi, oppone dignitosa resistenza, cede soltanto con ondulazione sopita. La natura della sua fronda gli impedisce di subire gli eccessi della bufera. Il tempo e lo spazio indietreggiano a primitive posizioni (ho inteso soltanto ora ciò che voleva Van Gogh). [...] quante volte ci siamo detti "quella foglia trema per me". Invece no. La foglia è leggera e c'è un po' di brezza. Questa parrebbe la ragione, si sa che è soltanto questa e tuttavia non basta [...] ogni cosa volge alla propria vita e per la durata propria. Se potesse, quella foglia se ne starebbe ferma; come me, d'altra parte. Sappiamo – io e la foglia – le direzioni fisiche. Sappiamo anche d'essere mossi dallo stesso vento". Cf. anche R. Birolli *1960*, Tredicesimo taccuino, October 1941, p. 89.

46 *Ibidem*.

47 "Tutto è votato a *voler essere quella cosa* [...] Si compie sul monte la metamorfosi della giornata e nell'ora arancione si ferma l'autunno. A striscioni orizzontali è il tramonto. Io sono dentro lo smeraldo". *Ivi*, Settimo taccuino, 1936, p. 54.

48 Birolli most appreciates Van Gogh's last three years of oeuvre. See *Ivi*, Sesto taccuino, September 1936, p. 45.

with nature in the south of France, the sun as a source of life and energy and the disturbance caused by the presence of the mistral is a central issue in his writings: "Ti ho già detto che devo sempre lottare con il *mistral*, che impedisce assolutamente di essere padroni della propria pennellata, da ciò il "selvaggio" degli studi", he writes to his brother Theo.[49] Birolli associates Van Gogh's wind with a form of madness, a psychic malaise.[50] Hence, the persistence of iconographies such as wind, metamorphosis, and chaos are not only influenced by poetry but also respond to a desire to break with the limits imposed by a classicist interpretation towards an expression of art understood as interiority that rises to the consciousness, filtering into it, penetrating its structures, stirring them up, as in the Duch master's paintings. This choice has also a political meaning, as it emerges looking at the painting *Maschere vaganti*, where Birolli describes these masks as carried on by the wind.[51] [FIG. 7] The iconography derived from James Ensor represents the faces of human comedy and hypocritical and grotesque figures and alludes to the falsehood of Italian dictatorship and racial laws.[52] In Birolli's paintings, these masks progressively descend and fall, so even the lie can be unmasked.[53]

The abstracting or personification of wind's natural phenomena, the shrouded sky, the flowering bodies, or objects that appear in Birolli's works is a common motif in Corrente's group. For instance, Giuseppe Migneco's

---

49 "Ti ho già detto che devo sempre lottare con il mistral, che impedisce assolutamente di essere padroni della propria pennellata, da ciò il "selvaggio" degli studi". V. Van Gogh, 2021, p. 320. "È il bel caldo che mi restituisce le forze [...] Purtroppo vicino al sole del buon Dio, c'è, per tre quarti del tempo, un diavolo di mistral". *Ivi*, p. 324. Once again: "Il mistral c'è sempre, ma vi sono degli intervalli di calma, e allora è meraviglioso. Se avessimo meno mistral, questo sarebbe realmente bello e adatto all'arte come in Giappone". *Ivi*, p. 303-304.

50 Vedi gli appunti che ricordano il misconosciuto pittore livornese Mario Puccini, parte del gruppo dei Macchiaioli, ne fanno "il Van Gogh italiano" che "impazzì in un pomeriggio di marzo, per una folata di vento. Chiamiamolo vento". Birolli, *1960*, Ottavo taccuino, 1936, p. 57.

51 "Ora incomincio le maschere vaganti che vorrei passassero portate dal vento sopra le cime di due alberi secchi viola cerulei su un cielo verde di oliva". Letter of Renato Birolli to Giuseppe Marchiori in G. Marchiori et. al. (eds.) *Renato Birolli 1931-1959*, exhibition catalogue (Verona, Palazzo della Gran Guardia, July-August 1963), Edizioni di Comunità, Milano 1963, p 26.

52 Ensor's oeuvre is another artist reference for Corrente's group. His monograph, published in 1929, is preserved in Ernesto Treccani's library. P. Fierens (ed.), *James Ensor*, G. Crès & C, Paris 1929.

53 E. Pontiggia, N. Colombo (ed.), *Milano anni Trenta. L'arte e la città*, exhibition catalogue (Milano, Spazio Oberdan, December 2nd – February 27th, 2005), Mazzotta, Milano 2004, p. 224.

oeuvre is characterised by moving lines that blend human and natural forms. The artist from Messina began painting as a self-taught artist. After 1937, following a police arrest for suspected anti-fascist activity, his painting turned towards the model of Van Gogh as a huge desire for freedom.[54] Migneco embraces the idea of the Sicilian friend Renato Guttuso, who is also interested in Van Gogh's "pennellata organica": an abundant and almost convulsive use of pictorial matter capable of offering a "definizione panica delle cose" and expressing the meaning "dolorosamente terrestre" of his subjects.[55] Migneco expresses the gaze into the abyss of contemporary man, his anguish and loneliness, by breaking the compositions' stillness through serpentines whose dominant colours are yellow and green. The writer Beniamino Joppolo, Migneco's fellow citizen, writes about his painting as a "unico perfetto" with poetry, testifying once again to the research for a relation between literature and visual arts that characterise Corrente's *milieu*.[56] Thus, in *Massaie ubriache* (1938) [FIG. 8] Brushstrokes deform the landscape and bodies in a desperate restlessness as the figures wriggle and sway in the background. At the same time, the subject of drunkenness alludes to mourning, madness, and illness, showing the fragility of life that is invisible to the regime's propaganda narrative.

54 See V. Fagone, *Migneco* in "Galleria", XXII, n.1-2, Ed. Sciascia, Caltanissetta, 1969; V. Fagone, *Migneco* in C. Marsan (ed.), *Migneco*, exhibition catalogue (Firenze, Galleria d'arte Poggiali e Forconi, April 11th – May 9th, 1987), Bonaparte editrice, Milano, 1987, pp. 24-25. It must be remembered that Aligi Sassu and Raffaele De Grada were also arrested in 1937, a year before Renato Birolli. The French press spread the news of this arrest in "L'Intransigeant," "L'Humanité," and other journals. See D. Amico, *Corrente tra Parigi, Roma e Milano* in N. Colombo, R. Duilio, D. Amico, *op. cit.*, 2019, p. 70.

55 R. Guttuso, *Dialogo sulla pittura*, in "Quaderni milanesi", nn. 4-5, Summer – Autumn, 1962.

56 B. Joppolo, *Presentazione* in *Sandro Cherchi Giuseppe Migneco* (Genova, Galleria, March 29th – April 9th, 1940), Genova Galleria Genova, 1940. B. Joppolo, *Giuseppe Migneco*, "Corrente di vita giovanile", II, n. 6, March 31st, 1939; B. Joppolo, *Il pittore Migneco*, III, n. 5, March 15th, 1940.

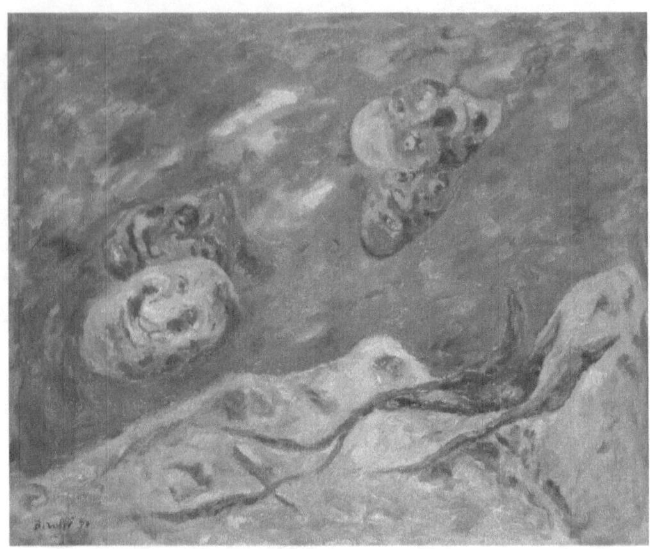

Fig. 7. Renato Birolli, *Maschere*, 1938-1939, oil on canvas, Milano, Collezione Iannaccone.

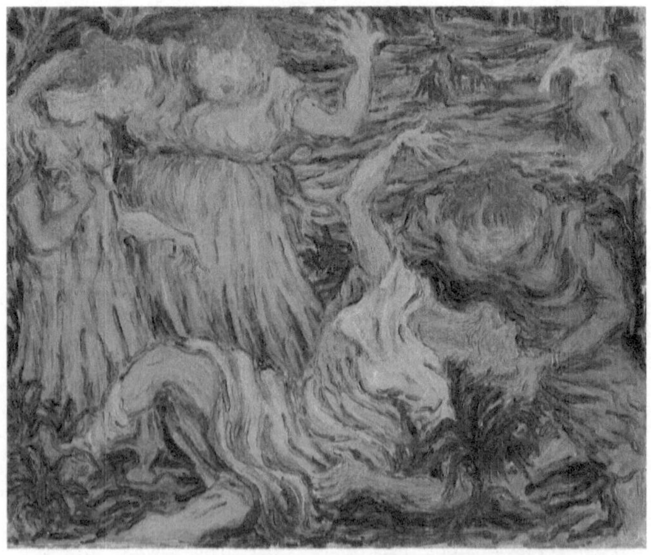

Fig. 8. Giuseppe Migneco, *Massaie ubriache*, 1939, oil on canvas, Milano, Archivio Migneco.

A further feeling emerges in Italo Valenti's oeuvre, fascinated by the "mondo vivo" of French painting.[57] Prerogatives of his poetics of the late 1930s are the suspension of images painted with a deliberately elementary drawing, the not quite-identifiable figures and floating, random quality of the compositions with few and stylised presences. Emblematic is *Gabbiani* (1939),[58] [FIG. 9] where three giant seagulls fly over dry branches of trees unfurled by the wind. The proportions of the birds are oversized, underlying the contrast between their vitality and the barrenness of the landscape. They are reminiscent of Baudelaire's albatross, acting as a metaphor for the artist's existence, who is forced to live in a social environment he does not recognise as his own. Even if Valenti's painting of the period is hardly known, it is innervated by the influence of poetry. For instance, in *Il sogno* (1939), the image of floating card boats exposed to storms suggests restlessness; the boat is also the very instrument of passage, metamorphosis, a symbol frequently used in Ermetismo.[59]

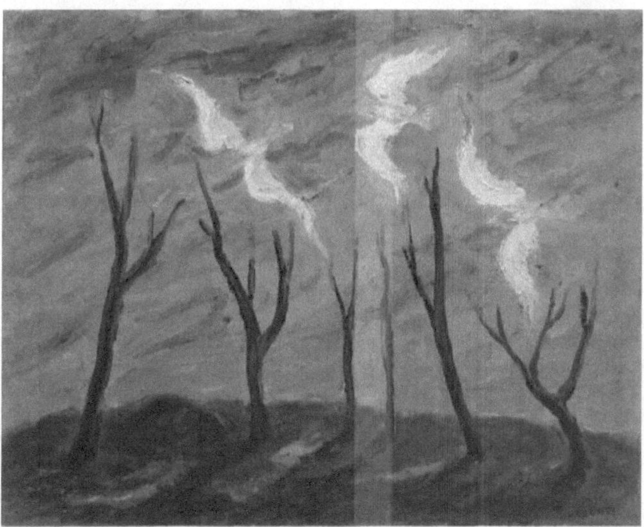

Fig. 9. Italo Valenti, *Gabbiani*, 1939, oil on canvas, Milano, Collezione Iannaccone.

57 "Nel 1935 ebbi il mio primo passaporto per l'estero, e andai per pochi giorni a Parigi e a Bruxelles. La scoperta degli impressionisti, di Cézanne, Van Gogh e Gauguin mi sbalordì; un mondo luminoso e vivo". I. Valenti in *Corrente. Cultura e società 1938-1942*, 1978, p. 29.

58 See A. Salvadori, R. Paterlini (eds.), *Collezione Giuseppe Iannaccone. Italia 1920-1945. Una nuova figurazione e il racconto del sé*, Skira, Milano, 2016, p. 320.

59 See Mario Luzi's poetry *La barca*, infra, footnote 13.

Moreover, the fairy-tale repertoire responds to the search for intimacy as also represented in other paintings such as *I Giovani greci* (1939): the traditional subject of bathers taken from Cézanne is enriched by the image of a flying figure. Suppose the Greek world had been evoked through the myth dear to the *retour à l'ordre*. In that case, Valenti gives it an interpretation that is anything but classical: man and nature are pervaded by the same vitality, and the figures flying in the sky express the state of being free within society from oppressive restrictions. Also, the painting *Gli amanti nel vento* (1939) [FIG. 10], evoking Chagall's model symbolises a utopic expression of a free world.[60] Chagall's breaking of statics and use of vivid colours are accentuated by Valenti, as the red colour blowing follows the movement of the figures. To refer so explicitly to a Jewish painter around those dates is almost like a veritable declaration of independence, at least as much artistic as political.[61]

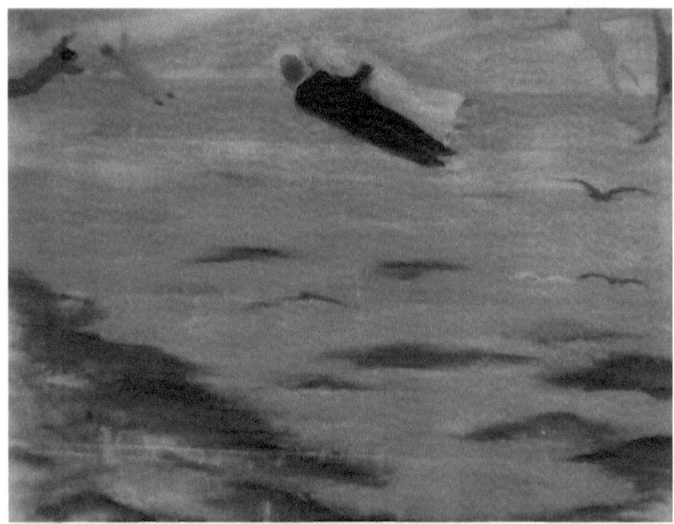

Fig. 10. Italo Valenti, *Gli amanti*, 1939, oil on canvas, Milano, Collezione privata.

60 Chagall is another reference for Valenti since he conjugates imagination and the modern tradition of the most expressive figuration. According to the Italian Jewish-born art critic Guido Ludovico Luzzatto, the Russian painter's movements in the air ("moti per aria") symbolise tension towards "mondo libero." G. L. Luzzatto, *Chagall*, in "La Rassegna Mensile di Israel", June 1930, vol. 5, n. 2, pp. 112-118.

61 An article published on the magazine "Tevere" accuses Italian young artists such as Birolli to represent "un'arte straniera bolscevizzante e giudaica". See T. Interlandi, *Un'autorevole testimonianza a carico dell'arte "moderna". Straniera bolscevizzante e giudaica* in "Tevere", November 24th-25th, 1938.

Birolli, Migneco and Valenti share an attentiveness to the wind's image as an expression of the phenomenological relationship between the cognitive potential of the subject and the inexpressibility of existence's dimension. It concerns Banfi's orientation toward the "libertà estetica" concept, which includes the need for a "primitività vitale", a recovery of the creative tools that allow man not to feel crushed by the anguish of living in a meaningless world.[62] Therefore, the presence of the wind theme in Corrente's group can be read as a precise artistic choice that wants to declare the Milanese group's proximity to an anti-classical aesthetic in the years of Fascist autarchy, a synthesis *in nuce* of what Corrente's "current" is: the blowing of a culture's wind circulating in Europe.

62 A. Banfi, *Motivi e problemi della estetica contemporanea*, *op. cit.*, p. 97. This thinking will be developed by his pupil Remo Cantoni. See C. Gily, *Cosa significa formare. Saggio su Remo Cantoni e il pensare primitivo*, in M. Cappuccio, A. Sardi (eds.), *Remo Cantoni*, Cuem, Milano 2007.

Peter Schulman

Libecciu of Longing

A new Form of "wind energy" in recent Corsican writings and song

Lucretian Wind Energy

The image of the *Libecciu* – the equivalent in Corsica of the more famous *Mistral* in southern France – has long been portrayed in earlier classic novels about Corsica as a symbol of the island's violence. In Prosper Mérimée's famous novel *Colomba*[1], and his brutal short story *Mateo Falcone*[2], for example, the *Libecciu* is seen as a metaphor for pent-up resentment and vengeance leading to *vendettas* and perpetuating conflicts. In the mid-20th century, iconic Corsican writers, such as Marie Susini, would write about the wind in terms of pent-up repression of emotions and the unfulfilled desires of her characters imprisoned by their village lives. Does the wind fulfill a similar function in contemporary Corsican literature as well?

In the works of Cap Corse poet Angèle Paoli, the answer would be "no". In her work, wind and other elements, such as rocks and water, represent chance and the unpredictability of our lives. Although Paoli writes about the beauty and uniqueness of the landscapes she connects with, on an emotional level, the wind she embraces is of a universal nature as well. In her poem "Esprits de la montagne", the wind is seen as a powerful dance, "le vent enfle se boursoufle/se retire s'éloigne flux et reflux de l'air/ puis reprend de plus belle"[3], in a way that suggests danger and death, but leads to a final image of life-affirming sexuality and love: "tu te redresses te retournes/ envers solaire moiteur douce du sexe/ algue serrée sur sa chair/ goût salé d'ivoire lisse/ tu aspires la vie sève."[4] In "La mer comme si de rien n'était," the wind is seen as a continuous source of energy and vitality:

1 P. Mérimée, "Colomba", *Revue des Deux Mondes*, Paris 1840.

2 P. Mérimée, "Mateo Falcone", *Revue de Paris*, 1833.

3 A. Paoli, *Les Feuillets de la Minotaure*, Éditions de Corlevour et Revue Terre des Femmes, Clichy 2015, p. 149.

4 Ivi, p.152.

"l'ensemble pris dans un tourment/ de basses de tambours se chevauchant/ dans le désordre discontinue/ mouvement tournant inépuisable."[5]

Similarly, the fabled music group *I Muvrini*, also uses the wind in their lyrics as symbols of memory and the fight against oblivion. In their famous song, "Ne fermez pas la porte", they urge Corsicans to replace the winds of history that others have written with their own language and voices: "Là-bas où le vent de l'histoire des autres/ A souvent déchiré la paix sur leurs rivages/ Leur laissant au cœur de vieux chagrins/ Ne fermez pas la porte/ Ils viennent d'une mémoire/ Qui n'est pas racontée sur les bancs des écoles."[6] On a wider note, however, in "Dans la main de la terre", they long for a universal wind that will bring all people together in peace: "Le chant d'amour qui fait pleurer/ les yeux d'un peuple/ ne peut à tout jamais laisser/ indifférent/ l'âme du monde."[7] They dream of a wind that will unite all the scattered nations separated by borders and lost memories: "tous ces pays dispersés par le vent/ les chants de blé dans la poche des paysans/ et l'océan qui n'a plus pour frontière/ que la graine emporté par une main d'enfant."[8] Although contemporary Corsican works still associate the wind with unharnessed force, their interpretations lean towards a more inspiring, optimistic vision of a more metaphoric "aeolian energy."

As wind has been a formative element in Ancient Greek and Roman mythology and poetry, one can analyze the emergence of the various facets of the wind in contemporary polyphonic Corsican vocal groups as well as Paoli's poetry, and texts in terms of notions of wind identified by Lucretius in his monumental work *De Rerum Naturae* in which he compartmentalizes the wind into various forms related to humans. As Nathaniel Durant has examined so well in his thesis, "The Importance of the Wind in Book Six of Lucretius' De Rerum Naturae," the soul can be divided into "two distinct but interconnected entities: the mind (animus), which is located in the breast and is the ruling component of the soul, and the spirit (anima) which obeys the mind and is dispersed through the body […]."[9] In Lucretius' breakdown explained by Durant, the soul is divided into four elemental

5 Ivi, p. 111.
6 https://genius.com/I-muvrini-ne-fermez-pas-la-porte-lyrics.
7 https://lyricstranslate.com/i-muvrini-dans-la-main-de-la-terre-lyrics.
8 *Ibid.*
9 N. Durant, *The Importance of the Wind in Book Six of Lucretius'* De Rerum Naturae, 2012, Bachelor of Arts Thesis, Honors College, Wesleyan University, https://digitalcollections.wesleyan.edu/object/ir-1696, p. 6.

constituents: "Wind (*aura*), heat (*vapor*), air (*air*) and a fourth element that is nameless (*east omnino nominis experts*)."[10]

Lucretius also underlines the invisibility of the wind's manifestations – from the inside of human beings and from the outside in sometimes destructive manners. It comprises "unseen bodies of wind, which sweep sea and land, yea, and the clouds of heaven, and tear and harry them with sudden hurricane."[11] Moreover, as Durant adds, Lucretius also uses the word *Ventus* to describe a wind that actively contributes to a natural process and *Aura* as a collective group of winds or breezes."[12] If *Ventus* can generally mean "breeze" for Lucretius, *anima*, Durant explains, "is used by the poet when he wishes to put extra emphasis on the elements' location."[13] As such, if we can use Lucretius's dissection of the wind in terms of spirit, soul, mind, and location, Paoli's poetry, for example, exemplifies all four of Lucretius's definitions as she uses wind alternatively in terms of a healing breeze, a reflection of her soul's love and longing, and of course location: the mountains, cliffs, the *maquis* and shores of Corsica. Similarly, *I Muvrini* and other groups, such as *Voce Ventu*, also use notions of the wind as metaphors for the Corsican spirit, the Corsican land, as well as a type of emotional energy that can sweep into lands as a symbol of freedom.

Wind and Mythology

While freedom can be associated with the wind in Paoli's writing, it is mainly through a process of longing, absence, and desire that the wind is activated within her. Although she does not reference Lucretius directly, her work is immersed in Greek and Roman mythology. In *Les Feuillets du Minotaur*[14], for example, she positions herself as Ariane, the decipherer of the labyrinth, and the Minotaur itself as she seeks a solution to her impossible love for Chloris, who lives across the seas. At times, she uses language to try to capture her love; at other times, she uses metaphors and images to produce a fantastical bubble that can preserve it. It is a "relational labyrinth"[15] she is lost, but her numerous allusions to antiquity help dignify

10 *Ibid.*
11 *Ibid.*
12 Ivi, p. 8.
13 Ivi, p. 11.
14 A. Paoli, *Les Feuillets de la Minoutaure*, *op. cit.*
15 "Que je suis triste, Chloris, de vous voir vous user avec les vôtres dans ces interminables labyrinthes relationnels !", *Les Feuillets de la Minoutaure*, *op. cit.*,

her. She writes of attaining the "burning sources of Phlegéthon."[16] She remarks that since Icarus' fall, La Mugliarese, a rock she frequents, is plagued by the cries of crickets; she admires Zeuxippé's savoir-faire[17]) and looks up to Orion for guidance.[18] At other times, when she is high atop the mountains, the wind gives her a feeling of drunkenness which she compares to Ariane's[19]: "l'ivresses? ivresse des montagnes/ prise dans les cimes du ciel/ ivresse des nuages colporteurs."[20] She compares her emotional liberation to the flight of a kite that spirals towards an Icarian but sweet plunge: "tu te tors autour les demeures anciennes/ te lances dans une inquiétude insolite/ un vol étourdi/ infini transport de ton âme/ un cerf volant effacé/ par une mort douce."[21]

The lightness of the wind is often compared to the earthiness of the *sangliers*, the wild boars that populate the Corsican forests and hills. In her poem, "Orphée," she merges with the ocean breeze to raise herself high among the clouds via ancient Corsican songs: "je me rends aux chants avec des accents solitaires/ fusion avec la force rassurante de la fidèle nature/ seule présence de l'ocean qui monte vers le ciel/ masses de bleue qui se diluent."[22] Sky and sea are inverted as the wild boars bring her back to earth in "Le mugissement des Minotaurs," the book's final poem: "Désire contre désire/ La montagne s'approche de moi, m'offre sa lumière déchirée/ à travers un nuage/ le cri des sangliers dans les feuilles/ [...] les bruits du *maquis* respirent/ font vibrer le silence."[23] The wind acts as a mediation between the sky and the earth, the mountains and the sea in a way that earlier makes the poet cry out in a supra-linguistic extasy: "Yahoouu, Yahouu, Yahouuu et yop, yop, yop/ tu sondes les vibrations de l'air antiques ripailles/ ressens les douces caresses du soleil autour de toi/ au-dessus du ciel/ les oiseaux aussi / nuages/ de vieux arbres dans la brise."[24] *Ventus* and *Aura* combine to elevate the poet spiritually and emotionally.

p. 31.

16 "Il avait atteint les sources brûlantes du Phlégéthon, reconnaissables au lac fétide et huileux aux eaux épaisses qui hantent son marécage", ivi, p. 23.

17 "J'admire le savoir-faire de Zeuxippé, moi qui ne suis pas même capable de coudre une boutonnière !", ivi, p.17.

18 Ivi,p. 77.

19 "Ivresse d'Arianele toit de luzes court/ bel équarrissement de dalles dans les cistes/ équilibre aérien de lignes et de formes", ivi, p. 106.

20 Ivi., p. 107.

21 *Ibid.*

22 Ivi, p. 161.

23 Ivi, p. 166.

24 Ivi, p. 117.

As it elevates, the wind, steeped in antiquity in Paoli's imagination, is also a destructive force that can cathartically cleanse the Corsican landscape and her inner turmoil. In her majestic latest book, *Carnets de marche*, the poet engages in long walks up and down mountains, and from village to village to re-center herself after a devasting loss of love. As she watches the wind agitate the sea with "colères antiques"[25], the tempest excites her as it is the wind that remains the only voice she listens to: "l'au-delà des monts la voix est au vent qui enfle et gonfle secoue et danse et brise tes chimères les feuillages argent."[26] At other moments, the wind shakes her from a somber stupor like a slap across her face as she feels alienated from herself: "Le soleil voile tient la mer à distance. Il semble qu'elle se soit provisoirement absentée,"[27] she writes referring to the anxiety that had kept her up the night before. "Son éloignement m'inquiète. Dans cinquante ans peut-être, l'île ne sera plus que dunes de sable. Ou pire un vaste paysage de détritus encastrés les uns dans les autres. [Mais] le grand vent de dimanche, encore vif sous ma peau, balaie ces images funestes."[28] At other moments, "[le] vent frais ce matin" awakens her as she begins her walk with alacrity:

> De fortes rafales ont balayé la pluie de la nuit. Elle marche vite, s'arrête pour extirper de son sac carnet et crayon. Elle note le vent dans les feuilles. Elle reçoit des gifles d'air par saccades. Elle pense au vent dans les voiles. Ici, plein visage. Le vent enveloppe l'espace. Elle note le mugissement sourd de la mer, celui plus proche du vent dans les feuillages. Moins dense. Des flots d'air froid montent à l'assaut des pentes, puis dévalent en sens inverse, par masses imprévisibles, irrégulières.[29]

At other times, she invokes the figure of Andoar, which in Portuguese means "to walk", as she does throughout the book but also a mythical king of the goats, associated with air in Michel Tournier's take on Robinson Crusoe, *Vendredi ou les limbes du Pacifique*.[30] She dreams of rejoining Andoar one day within her "ma préhistoire inconsciente"[31] to feel the wind through her limbs as she keeps on walking in order to feel like "la bogue verte qui déboule soudain devant moi, me faire caméléon du vent, rejoindre

25 A. Paoli, *Carnets de marche*, Les Éditions du Petit Pois, Béziers 2010, p. 114.
26 Ivi, p. 114.
27 Ivi, p. 54.
28 *Ibid.*
29 Ivi, p. 13.
30 M. Tournier, *Vendredi ou les limbes du Pacifique*, Éditions Gallimard, Paris 1967.
31 A. Paoli, *Carnets de marche*, *op. cit.*, p. 98.

Andoar dans ses cimes, laisser le vide prendre place aux abords du non-désir."[32]

"'Où est son bien ?"[33] she asks. Where can she find her own happiness? In everyday life? But *what* life, she asks? "Sa nature même lui échappe,"[34] she remarks. "Quelle vie ? " she asks again. "La sienne lui manque. Tout est autre. Hanging Rock. Désir intense de grimper là-haut, par-delà des nuages."[35] She seeks to "retrouver l'esprit du vent."[36] She understands that happiness might have taken flight from her, but she might find a sense of restoration by breathing in the air. As she understands it when she watches the plane to Paris from Bastia fly over her every day, she seeks a Zen space where she can be at one with the wind with no prior thoughts or regrets: "Ne plus rien avoir d'autre à faire que d'écouer mugir le vent. Le grand vent d'été tressant novembre. *Raffiche di vento*. [...] Je m'endors bercée par les masses invisibles en bataille au-dessus de moi."[37] Not a panacea for despair but a potential solution to it, the energy of the wind can rattle her from feelings of hopelessness and loneliness: "Balayée par les vents soufflant rafales, *La Mandorle*, lèvres ourlées sur le ciel, est inaccessible. Elle, n'est plus là, mon absente de chaque jour. Le vent ivre secoue les branches. Des griffes enserrent mes cheveux défaits. Je, lutte pour me frayer un passage."[38] Finally, it is in the warm air of the *libecciu* itself that she can create the protective space she needs to come to terms with her solitude, as she describes it: "Le vent souffle par grands rafales. Le maquis ploie sous les à-coups imprévus du *libecciu*. Je ne vais sans doute pas pouvoir marcher très longtemps sur la route. Je n'ai pourtant pas envie de renoncer. Je vais trouver un abri où pelotonner ma solitude."[39]

Songs of Wind, Songs of a People

For the polyphonic group *I Muvrini*, whose name, like Paoli's Andoar, refers to a type of wild sheep which live in the mountains of Corsica, images of the wind are sometimes wistful reminders of what could be or stirring

32 *Ibid.*
33 Ivi, p. 82.
34 Ivi, p. 83.
35 *Ibid.*
36 *Ibid.*
37 Ivi, p. 93.
38 *Ibid.*
39 Ivi, p. 61.

inspirations for a noble future in which humanity is capable of uniting in a beloved brotherhood and sisterhood. As the charitable organization they created, *Umani*, suggests, their prime mission is not to entertain, but to help humanity fight against inhumanity, violence, and intolerance. If Paoli sought inner peace through the wind, *I Muvrini* seek word peace. As the title of their recent songs confirms, *L'Emmigrante*, *Ma sœur musulmane*, and *En 2043*, they are focused on helping people and the planet itself. Born of the Reacquistu Cultural Revival Movement in Corsica in the 1970s, *I Muvrini*, like other groups such as *A Filetta* and *Canta U Populu Corsu*, sing to defend and reappropriate Corsica's cultural heritage through polyphonic song. As Jean-François Bernardini, one of the group's founders advocates in his book *L'Autre enquête Corse*,[40] (The Other Corsican Case), a counter punch to the famous graphic novel and film *L'Enquête Corse*[41], Corsica has suffered a national trauma from centuries of stereotyping from mainland France portraying Corsicans as bandits, terrorists, and violent people. *I Muvrini* seek to unite people by refuting stereotypes rather than propagating them. In their song *A Voce Rivolta* (At the Top of Your Lungs), for example, they sing about the Corsican rivers and winds that lead organically to a sense of freedom: "The river Golu tells/ About hours, drops/ of Eternity/ the libeccio/ caresses the baby hours/ of liberty."[42] The song goes on to lament the rejections the Corsican people have suffered but urges them forward to proclaim their own identity through unified song: "When it's time/ respond you too/ Corsican people/ For the last time/ Tell them that you are/ The loud ones singing."[43]

Similarly, in *Amareni* (Bitterness), they speak of healing the wounds "among all our flowers of love/ and our blossoming auroras/ It was an amazing fragrance/ a gift that came with the day" they begin, but it all leads to "my wounds, my wounds". At the end of the song, fire and wind function as a sad chorus to the island's melancholy: "Wasn't it written somewhere", they ask, "that one day the game would end, the fires would go out leaving a haphazard history behind/ But others after me will say/ that far off suns burn/ the winds cry for fun/ and the poor humans tremble/ poor humans,

---

40 J.-F. Bernardini, *L'Autre enquête corse : le trauma Corsica-France*, Éditions de l'Aube, Collection Mikros, Avignon 2020.

41 R. Pétillon, *Jack Palmer : l'Enquête corse*, Albin Michel, Paris 2003; *L'Enquête corse* (dir. Alain Berberian, 2004), Gaumont.

42 Sung in Corsican: "Golu ci conta/ L'ore candelle/ D'eternità/ Libecciu alliscia/ L'ore zitelle/ Di libertà/ U sole innora/ E cime quassù/ E u mio cantu/ Ti chjama dinù " https://genius.com/I-muvrini-a-voce-rivolta-lyrics.

43 *Ibid.*

poor humans."[44] "The work of the artist", Bernardini explains about one of their albums, *Lucioles* (Fireflies), "is to create light or nothing at all. Were we here just to amuse and entertain, we would be among millions doing that. Today we are called upon to move, enlighten, disturb, and shake up. That is the work of the artist, to perform the world's conscious on stage" (my translation)[45]. For them, the wind, returning to Lucretius, is linked to the gravitas of the soul. It is connected to the human condition.

In their song *The one you think I am*,[46] they focus on being compatible with ones' own sense of identity not what others project upon one: "In the sunlight of a mystery/ I unfurl my sails/ and defy weather and tide/ I am this background/ ruffled by the winds/ I listen to the talks/ and I flash a smile/ Here's to the tune of my language/ and the names of my trees/ and the love of my people."[47] In *Dumanda*, they highlight the bittersweet nature of their songs in which pain and joy converge: "They are like the wind that dances in/ the vastness of an ever happy heart/ they are like a life that opens like that/ onto an infinity that says yes."[48] The song opens cheerily, "They have no chains, they are made of liberty"[49], but then point to a "pain few can imagine."[50] The song concludes with both a tinge of hope and sadness: "My songs are not enough/ tell me if summer will ever return."[51] Finally, in *Vogliu* (I Want), the song begins with the wind carrying off the Corsican people's dreams in a giant gust: "to retrieve/ our dreams when the wind takes them away/ to take our hand/ to open our doors/ to do that trip all over again and answer to our destiny," but ends with a plea to their people to reawaken the songs from within in order to "regain their self-esteem and find joy once more."[52] As the songs in their most recent album, *Portu in*

44 " Ma d'altri cum'è mè ti diceranu/ Quant'ellu scalla u sole luntanu/ Quant'ellu pienghje u ventu veranu/ E face trimulé u core umanu/ U core umanu/ U core umanu… " https://www.muvrini.com.

45 https://www.terracorsa.org/info.

46 "Celle que tu crois".

47 https://lyricstranslate.com/en/celle-que-tu-crois--one-you-think-I-am "Au soleil d'un mystère je déroule mes voiles et je brave les temps/ Et je suis ce décor et je suis ce repère que caressent les vents/ J'écoute les dires et j'adresse un sourire à ces mots que j'entends […]/ Pour le chant de ma langue et le nom de mes arbres et l'amour/ De mes gens."

48 "So cum'è i venti/Chi vanu à ballà/A cori cuntenti/Pè l'immensità" https://www.muvrini.com.

49 "Ùn anu catene sò di libertà," *ibid.*

50 "Ma sò centu pene chì nisunu sà," *ibid.*

51 "Sò e mio cantate chì ùn ponu bastà/ À dimmi l'estate s'ellu venerà," *ibid.*

52 "Pè ritruvà i sogni chì u ventu si porta/ Porghjeci a manu apreci a porta/ Pè rifà u viaghju risponde à la sorte/ Festighjà le dumane e to belle racolte/ Pè cunsulà e

core (What is carried in our hearts) all imply, *Protest Song*, *Missiva*, *Move*, *I Muvrini* is not content to dwell in nostalgia or regret but, like the winds that inspire them, they are eager to move their audiences to perk up and reclaim what they might have lost.

If there are younger heirs to *I Muvrini* who have listened to their call for action, it might be a group with the wind in their very name, *Voce Ventu*. As they have asserted, "Voice/Wind" is the name of their group because wind and voice are intertwined for them into an extraordinary vitality and a unifying message of hope: "We think of the wind as a vehicle for a message of sharing among all people that know no political borders nor cultural limits. *Voce Ventu* – at its origins "the wind voice" and not "the voice of the wind" they explain. "The name comes from the word 'everyone', the group Chjami Aghjalesi that strongly symbolized our humanistic philosophy and our will to weave connections between peoples through messages of peace and sharing."[53] Suppose we began this piece by delving into the inner conflicts in Paoli's works, and the turbulent emotions that the wind helped accentuate and later heal within her. In that case, *I Muvrini*, as well as *Voce Ventu*, give their last word to the wind itself so that it might deliver a new message of human unity and universal connections well beyond the mountains of Corsica and throughout the planet while also preserving and nourishing their own cultural heritage as well.

pene pisà le rivolte/ Tene contu a pace in lu solcu di," *ibid.*

53 Personal email, 11/22/2021.

Giuseppe Grilli

Winds and Sails after March

In the realm of communication, I will proceed axiomatically. However, determining which axiom to start is difficult without a series of reservations and justifications. The first choice would be to opt between the options conceived by Eugenio d'Ors, such as different canonical distinctions, separating category (the movements of the air) from anecdote (the emblematic poetry par excellence of Ausiàs March, *Veles e vents*). The choice is perhaps unavoidable, yet I will not make it, as the category in a volume so programmatically open from the very title, which, in a Mozartian manner, alludes to the idea of caprice (*I capricci dell'aria*), opposes the same concept of a closed or concluded text. I adopt a form of compromise, as Freudian followers of Francesco Orlando's lesson would say, which responds to the only proposal that, at least virtually, I foresee in both fields: inversion. Choosing the anecdote with which March's poem opens, from which I take my starting point, I would be drawn into its evolution into a representation of the so-called macro erotic metaphor that marked the dawn of modern or neoclassical poetry in the geographic and cultural centre of fourteenth-century Tuscany.

I transcribed the text in a note following the edition of RIALC, conceived and directed by Costanzo Di Girolamo in memory of the professor and fellow university student. The numbering of the poem follows the critical edition of Amadeu Pagès, later revised by various twentieth-century authors, XLVI.[1]

1 P. Bohigas (ed. by), *Ausiàs March, Poesies*, rev. Amadeu Soberanas and Noemi Espinàs, Barcelona, Barcino ("ENC"), 2000. Pagès XLVI.

1 Veles e vents han mos desigs complir,
2 ffahent camins duptosos per la mar.
3 Mestre y ponent contra d'ells veig armar;
4 xaloch, levant los deuen subvenir
5 ab lurs amichs lo grech e lo migjorn,
6 ffent humils prechs al vent tremuntanal
7 qu'en son bufar los sia parcial
8 e que tots cinch complesquen mon retorn.
9 Bullira·l mar com la caçola 'n forn,
10 mudant color e l'estat natural,
11 e mostrara voler tota res mal
12 que sobre si atur hun punt al jorn;
13 grans e pochs peixs a recors correran
14 e cerquaran amaguatalls secrets:
15 ffugint al mar, hon son nudrits e fets,
16 per gran remey en terra exiran.
17 Los pelegrins tots ensemps votaran
18 e prometran molts dons de cera fets;
19 la gran paor traura·l lum los secrets
20 que al confes descuberts no seran.
21 En lo perill no·m caureu de l'esment,
22 ans votare hal Deu qui·ns ha ligats,
23 de no minvar mes fermes voluntats
24 e que tots temps me sereu de present.
25 Yo tem la mort per no sser vos absent,
26 per que Amor per mort es anullats;
27 mas yo no creu que mon voler sobrats
28 pusqua esser per tal departiment.
29 Yo so gelos de vostr'escas voler,
30 que, yo morint, no meta mi 'n oblit;
31 sol est penssar me tol del mon delit
32 —car nos vivint, no creu se pusqua fer—:
33 Apres ma mort, d'amar perdau poder,
34 e sia tots en ira convertit,
35 e, yo forçat d'aquest mon ser exit,
36 tot lo meu mal sera vos no veher.
37 O Deu!, per que terme no y a 'n amor,
38 car prop d'aquell yo·m trobara tot sol?
39 Vostre voler sabera quant me vol,
40 tement, fiant de tot l'avenidor.
41 Yo son aquell pus estrem amador,
42 apres d'aquell a qui Deu vida tol:
43 puys yo son viu, mon cor no mostra dol
44 tant com la mort per sa strema dolor.
45 A be o mal d'amor yo so dispost,
46 mas per mon fat Fortuna cas no·m porta;
47 tot esvetlat, ab desbarrada porta,
48 me trobara faent humil respost.

Following my dual reading, both of March and Ors, in their two definitions—the more openly theological one, dear to Petrarch, and Dante's realistic (and materialistic) one—the reasons for both the category and the anecdote can be inscribed.Indeed, we can place *The Caprices of the Air* in that virtual and gentle space that an insightful Shakespearean critic placed after his brilliant essay, as only a stylistic exercise can be. I cite or at least recall Logan Pearsall Smith at the end of his sensible approximation to the writer who, with his genius, literally overturned the fate of literature (*On Reading Shakespeare2*). This is a conclusion particularly relevant to the final phase of his activity as a man when he combines deep thoughts and irony without betraying the serious, melancholic vein of a destiny that is both human and worldly. An exponent or emblem of this phase of the Elizabethan age is probably *The Tempest*. Without intending to be irreverent or excessive, to use a typical Elizabethan lexical term, I recall the latest edition of Ausiàs March's work with a desire for innovation. However, it does not neglect prudence when venturing into turbulent waters. I refer to the edition by Robert Archer in 2017 for the Clásicos Cátedra of Letras Hispánicas. Archer, from whom I omit philological praise, emphasises in the text's presentation the centrality of *Cant* 46 in the canonical order established by the first (and perhaps only[3]) critical edition of March's work by Pagès, justifying its centrality by the historical merit of the musical version elaborated in Valencian phonetics by Raimon, but agreed upon with Martí de Riquer in joint working sessions.

At the same time, the scholar highlights the significance of what I have repeatedly identified in March's work as "windows onto the world," a concept that, in this micro-poem, is entirely dedicated to the apocalyptic imagery of a storm[4]—*corpus* of Ausiàs March between two distinct modes of poetic composition. The first consists of longer poems, the result of the evolution of the *epyllion* in post-medieval and contemporary languages; the second is characterised by brief, compact poems endowed with narrative simultaneity, albeit with certain ambiguities in reference and intertextual allusions. The poem under examination here belongs to the latter category. It follows a *strophic-metric* form that enjoyed significant and enduring success until the twentieth century—apart from exceptional cases such as *I sepolcri*. In these attributions, I draw connections with *The Waste Land*, not only for its role as a literary model in the twentieth century but also concerning *Nabí* in the Catalan tradition or hybrid solutions such as *Poeta en Nueva York*, as well as Pavese's *I mari del Sud*. Although these works belong formally to the *poemetto* tradition, their influence on

---

2 L. P. Smith, *On Reading Shakespeare*, Constable, London 1933; original from the University of Michigan.

3 Archer's edition, like the earlier one by Joan Ferraté, presents some methodological inconsistencies in terms of *collatio* techniques.

4 A myth that remains far from fading—one need only consider the significance of *l'orage* in Camus' *La Peste* (p. 292, 1947 edition). Already Lorca, with *Preciosa y el aire*, had revitalized the epithalamium rhythm in the *Romancero gitano*.

what is conventionally defined as *lyric poetry* has remained profound and pervasive.

To proceed axiomatically, we can identify in Ausiàs March's text, recognised by its first verse functioning as a title, *Veles e vents a mos design complir*, a reference preceding the stormy discussion, commonly accepted as an introduction, but which I propose as an inversion of the psychic content, where air merges with the soul. The poem's second part, in which the poet describes his amorous relationship with the lady in the first person, develops this idea. The lady is not explicitly named but is identified using the old *senhal* stratagem.

Before proceeding further, I would like to recall, in today's general, non-Hispanic, and even non-Romance linguistic environment, that the storm is the theme of the greatest poem of Spain's Golden Age, contained in *Las Soledades* by Luis de Góngora. The first *Soledad* adheres to the canonical *Epillion* style and opens with a tragic shipwreck triggered by a caprice of air and nature, punishing *codicia*, or excessive greed for wealth[5]. Profits are also at stake in March's text, where the poet, a total writer, has been labelled by one of his greatest contemporary exegetes, Costanzo Di Girolamo, as a *forerunner*, indeed as the greatest poet in Europe for an entire century, the fifteenth.

Outside a specific context, it is challenging to understand March's success and corrosive poetry and its decline in favour of a different dynamic in poetic discourse. Between the late fifteenth and early sixteenth centuries, March was perceived as a *Philosopho6*, probably in the wake of the rediscovery of the philosophy of Love with Platonic and inevitably

5 The explicit model is Claudian, as demonstrated by Robert Jammes in his annotated edition of Góngora's masterpiece in *Clásicos Castalia* (Madrid, 1994). Any discussion of the relationship between Golden Age poetry and March would be impossible without first considering M. de Riquer, *Traducciones castellanas de Ausias March en la Edad de Oro,* Instituto Español de Estudios Mediterráneos, Barcelona 1946.

6 I refer to an earlier paper of mine, *Dell'eredità poetica ausiasmarchiana*, in which I reaffirm the validity of the immediate reception of March's poetry in a "traditional" sense, as opposed to later, more normalized readings. A striking example of this is the Spanish translation by the great Montemayor, a spiritualist and mythographer (as seen in his masterpiece *La Diana*, already published under the altered name Jorge de Montemayor): Giuseppe Grilli, *Dell'eredità poetica ausiasmarchiana*, "Aiuon", SR 30 (1988): pp. 249–58. Notably, the omission of *tornadas* in translation was not entirely incidental. In *Cant* 46, March deliberately likens the beloved to a game of dice (*a joc de daus vos acompararé*), a fitting metaphor for the instability of natural order.

Neoplatonic roots[7]. However, this interpretation, which persisted from the earliest reception of his writings, passed through a notable proliferation of manuscript copies and continued in printed editions in Catalan and bilingual Catalan-Spanish versions. This demonstrates a tendency to recognise March not as a troubadour poet but as a thinker.

In recent years, this perspective—though often considered in isolation from its broader implications—has shaped an image of March as a *poet who thinks* or as a figure of *Pensament*. The titles of conferences and scholarly volumes have disseminated and reinforced the idea that this "philosophical" reception of his work has regained relevance. However, it has not been dissociated from the thematic predominance of *erotocentrism* within his textual corpus, as Lola Badia—widely regarded as the leading authority in the field—has affirmed. A series of interconnected consequences emerge from her research and from a determined school of scholars who follow and validate her investigative yet, perhaps, overly *definitive* analyses (though not without internal divergences). Among these, one of particular significance is the idea of thematic *obsessiveness*, which could be summarised in the formula *"fuori dall'eros nulla salus"*—a reading or, at the very least, an interpretation of March that presupposes an exclusive framework, one that cannot extend beyond the so-called *autumn of the Middle Ages* (*Baixa edat mitjana*).

Yet, as already indicated in my introduction, March stands as the poet who categorically rejects not only the validity or persistence of a Middle Ages conceived without temporal or cultural constraints but also—more fundamentally—he is perhaps the first to reflect the conflict of nature within the inner struggle of the human condition. More specifically—and it is necessary to state this explicitly—such a vision is reaffirmed precisely in *Cant* 46, where the poet utters his definitive autobiographical confession: *Jo soc aquell pus extrem amador*. The notion of the *self* as a microcosm—one that is *always*, or nearly always, in tempestuous turmoil—cannot be deemed extraneous to March's thought; instead, its significance becomes all the more evident *ex contrario* when contrasted with its distinct articulation in Lope de Vega, who embraced this idea wholeheartedly, albeit without explicitly claiming it, except in old age (*de senectute*). And yet, it is the

7 The significance of Plotinus' revival within the rediscovery of paganism—as a counterpoint to the dominance of monotheistic traditions, from the decline of classical Islam to the wars of religion fueled by the rise of nation-states—is discussed in *Dialogoi. Rivista di studi comparatistici* 8, Mimesis, Milano.

same *lyric* Lope who, in his youth, was deeply fascinated by the Valencia of his golden exile from Madrid.[8]

Archer rightly argues that the great success of *Cant* 46 is due to its extraordinary and powerful opening, which announces something about to happen. However, he admits that the theme is conventional, insisting on the vicissitudes of unfulfilled love. Here lies the disappointment: from a universal spatiotemporal upheaval, the focus shifts to the personal realisation of being the ultimate lover, the sole survivor among men. Excess transforms into solitude at this point, breaking the possibility of reducing the initial narrative to mere lamentation.

In this dialectic or dispute between the one and the many (including the living and the dead[9]), the living has concentrated on a single subject, highlighting that vitality is an individual rather than a collective or species-wide phenomenon. This reveals a deeper connection to economic and philosophical avarice and a survival mode still alive, though doomed to defeat.

Perhaps not coincidentally, it is precisely in this context that academic criticism of Ausiàs March frequently revisits the theme of the poet's so-called homosexuality.[10] By further intensifying the methodological axiomatism outlined at the outset, the "perverse" impulse toward irregular sexuality is framed as animalistic. Therefore, by that very logic, natural—if not even divine—when interpreted within the framework of emanation, the *Mundo*. This perspective effectively legitimises it on the same level as the diverse temperaments of the winds, which may clash or, conversely, accommodate the varying desires of those who invoke them in a logic reminiscent of mercantile exchange. It is no coincidence, then, that in his nearly "perfect' translation of a revealing selection of *Cants* into Castilian, Pere Gimferrer renders March's *desigs* as *ansias*, employing a Spanish that deliberately echoes the Catalan of the poetic hero of Gandia.

Translated by Paola Del Zoppo

8 I refer to Lope de Vega's reading of Garcilaso, himself a fervent admirer and apologist of March, as attested by a longstanding critical tradition from Lapesa to Gargano. See my auxiliary study, *Intrecci di vite. Intorno a La Dorotea di Lope de Vega*, Il Torcoliere, L'Orientale, Napoli 2008.

9 I explored this topic in G. Grilli, *O vós mesquins…: un poema sobre els temps de l'amor o sobre l'amor d'un temps? [filòlegs i poetes llegeixen Ausiàs March]*, "Cahiers d'Études Hispaniques Médiévales", 14 (2000): 197–221.

10 *Obra poética*, selection and translation by Pere Gimferrer, introduction by Joaquim Molas, Alfaguara, Madrid 1978.

Gioia Sili

Catching the Wind

The Poetic Ambition of Joris Ivens

The essay intends to investigate the role assumed by the wind within the work of Joris Ivens (1898-1989), a Dutch documentary director whose rich production crosses the twentieth-century panorama, with particular reference to two films: *Pour le Mistral* (1965) and *Une histoire de vent* (1988). Far from being defined as a mere atmospheric phenomenon, for the director from Nijmegen, the wind is an element full of meanings that is capable of giving rise to varied interpretative paths. From this perspective, the essay follows the evolution of a complex "visual research."[1] That covers the entire work of the Dutch director like a particular red thread and can reveal the infinite potential of cinema to film the invisible. The itinerary that was chosen to follow is thus divided into three interconnected sections: the first is dedicated to a brief introduction to the cinema of Ivens; the second is focused on specific theoretical and stylistic aspects of *Pour le Mistral*; the third starts from *Une histoire de vent*, the author's poetic testament from which a reflection on the link between the wind and the vital breath is developed, finding, in this sense, suggestive interpretative stimuli in some sequences of the animation film *The Wind Rises* (Miyazaki, 2013).

Ivens' long documentary production is characterised by the desire to film what by definition cannot be represented: the possibility of giving shape to the unrepresentable runs through the entire itinerary of the Dutch filmmaker, furrowed by different themes and questions that wind around the delicate relationship between human being and the environment, also addressed in a utopian key. Expressly, nature for Ivens neither assumes the form of an idyllic dimension, i.e., a pleasant state towards which it is advisable to tend by abandoning the frenetic rhythms of industrial society nor does it assume the characteristics of the opposite condition theorized by the philosopher Thomas Hobbes, in which coexistence among humans is torn apart by a permanent state of war ("Homo homini

1 V. Tosi, *Joris Ivens. Cinema e utopia*, Bulzoni, Roma 1988, p. 209.

lupus"). Conversely, according to Ivens, it develops the expressive form of the documentary since it can "represent reality in its causal and inevitable aspect."[2], between the natural environment and human activity, there is a dynamic, almost dialectical relationship made up of moments of conflict and subsequent calm.

Except for the more experimental works, connected in large part to the director's youthful production, the industriousness, zeal, and diligence of the individual emerge in Ivens' cinema as precious qualities for stemming the indomitable force of nature. In any case, the conflictual element always remains in the background, just as the Dutch origin of the director appears to be implied through the continuous reference to navigation, water, and the construction of bridges and dams. The power of nature is then made visible to the spectator through the action of all its elements: water, earth, and wind, the great protagonist in the master's work. In this perspective, the territory is frequently described and analyzed in the multiple transformations determined by anthropic activity: on the one hand, the role of industry and large oil plants emerges; on the other, the devastation of the landscape caused by wars appears clearly visible (Spain, China, and Vietnam, for example)[3].

In the wake of other well-known directors such as Agnès Varda, Chris Marker – author of the commentary on the film *Le ciel, la terre* (1966) –, Jean-Daniel Pollet, and Andrej Tarkovskij, Ivens also wishes to investigate the complexity of reality, by expanding "the interpretative modes of imagery, within mélange of practices and gendres that are no longer perceived through traditional hierarchies, but are instead reconfirmed into a plurality of discourses and novel aesthetic experiences"[4]. In other words, it is precisely the dialectical relationship between sound and image that constitutes an indispensable access key to the world's enigma, thus favoring a continuous production of meaning and discourse. In fact, through creative editing, the Dutch filmmaker composes a peculiar visual story, escaping the traditional logic of narration based on mimetic-representative criteria.

In the documentary *Pour le Mistral* (1965), Ivens' ambition emerges clearly: to try to photograph the wind, an intangible and evanescent phenomenon par excellence. It is worth remembering that this project is not a starting point but is configured as the terminal moment of a long

2 J. Ivens, *Quelques réflections sur les documentaires d'avant-garde*, in "La revue des vivants", Paris 1931, pp. 518-520.

3 Cf. V. Tosi, *Joris Ivens. Cinema e utopia*, *op. cit.*, pp. 50-51.

4 M. Bertozzi, *Documentario come arte. Riuso, performance, autobiografia nell'esperienza del cinema contemporaneo*, Marsilio, Venezia 2018, p. 28.

path of studies and research carried out with intensity by the director in previous years. In the past, he had the opportunity to deal directly with the works of Dutch painters, masters in depicting the north-west wind, and with the poems of Percy B. Shelley, Federico García Lorca, Saint-John Perse, and Fréderic Mistral. Among the pages of his autobiographical text, written with Robert Destanque and entitled *Joris Ivens*, or *the memory of a gaze* (1988), the filmmaker also recounts having carefully watched the famous film by Victor Sjoström, *The Wind* (1928), and of having collected, over time, numerous stories and legends about the wind which gradually gave rise to the intention of condensing all these elements into a single monumental cinematographic poem.[5].

Recovering some ideas offered by previous works such as *Rain* (1929) and *When the Seine Meets Paris* (1957), in which the relationship between atmospheric phenomena and poetic elements constitutes a common thread, Ivens takes this film one step further, trying to make the Mistral visible. The main protagonist of the documentary is the icy wind coming from the coasts of Provence, capable of overwhelming everything it encounters in its path. In the initial sequences, the viewer watches helplessly the arrival of the storm: under a sky full of clouds, the frightened animals move agitatedly, while the trees sway and the sea suddenly becomes agitated and threatening. The images of Ivens' video camera capture the effects of the Mistral along the deserted beaches with extraordinary effectiveness, simultaneously showing the gloomy desolation in which the surrounding landscape has sunk. In other scenes, the icy north wind directly affects the behavior of the inhabitants of small and large cities in Provence: not only the consequences of its passage are concretely manifested through the movement of clothes and hats, but they are also clearly visible in the faces of the people who stroll down the street, influencing their mood. The documentary thus constitutes a sophisticated and ambitious work, within which the Mistral is not only an atmospheric phenomenon but represents an original key to understanding the lifestyle in the territories of the French region. However, despite the relevance of the objectives, the rich poeticity of the language, the nuances of the lights, and the change of shadows, the monumental project of *Pour le Mistral* appears, according to Ivens himself, incomplete: the peculiar connection that binds cinema to the wind has not yet found its total fulfillment in this film, leaving the door open to new considerations on this elusive atmospheric phenomenon.

---

5 Cf. R. Destanque, J. Ivens, *Joris Ivens o la memoria di uno sguardo*, tr. it., Bulzoni, Roma 1988, pp. 357-358.

In *Une histoire de vent* (distributed in Italy under the title *Io e il vento*), a film presented at the Venice Film Festival in 1988, the journey begun several years earlier by the Dutch filmmaker is completed: he, now in his nineties, travels to the territories remotest in China to capture the invisible image of the wind. It is not the first time that Ivens has traveled to the Far East: from the 1930s onwards, many documentaries with militant characters were shot in China to give voice to the political and social realities of the territory. Among these, it is worth mentioning, by way of example, *Prima della Primavera* (1958), dedicated to the contrasted relationship between humans and nature, *The 400 Million* (1939), focused on the war of liberation of the Chinese people against the invasion of Japan, *Come Yu Kong spostò le montagne* (1976), a collection of twelve films set in various regions of the country during Mao's cultural revolution.

The trait of originality that distinguishes *Une Histoire de vent* compared to the previous works lies, essentially, in its "avant-garde" character.[6]: it is, in fact, a film testament, in which the traditional style of the documentary merges with fantastic appearances, childhood memories and dragon-shaped kites, dream figures, and fragments of ancient Chinese legends[7]. As Benjamin Thomas writes in this regard in the text *L'attrait du vent* (2016), Ivens' film is, first of all, "a reflection on the breath that still animates a director at the end of his life."[8]. This yearning emerges clearly in one of the best-known sequences of the documentary: Ivens, sitting on the crest of a dune in the Chinese desert of Xinjiang, awaits the arrival of the wind, scanning the sky. With the crew's help, the elderly filmmaker builds a majestic scaffolding, almost an authentic open-air theater, which allows the passage of the wind to be recorded. "Yes, but Feng…It is the wind. It is not coming, doctor", the filmmaker says impatiently to the doctor who has come to check on his health conditions, and, in the next moment, the spectator watches the director fall abruptly from the chair on which he is weakly reclining.

6 V. Tosi, *Joris Ivens. Cinema e utopia*, *op. cit.*, p. 207.

7 In the introductory pages of *Che cos'è la filosofia?* (1991), Gilles Deleuze and Felix Guattari identify old age as the phase of life in which it is possible to respond with a certain freedom to concrete questions. In this regard, the two authors mention the name of Ivens, who in *Une histoire de vent* confuses the sound of her laughter with that of a witch in a raging wind. This last element represents the leitmotif of a crazy and ambitious project created by the Dutch filmmaker through his latest film. Cf. G. Deleuze, F. Guattari, *Che cos'è la filosofia?*, Einaudi, Torino 2002.

8 B. Thomas, *L'attrait du vent*, Crisnée, Editions Yellow Now, 2016, p. 22.

The creative montage of the scenes seems to upset the usual linearity of the narration: the image of the director immersed in the dunes is followed by others, which, although apparently without a logical connection, through mutual superimposition, give rise to what could be defined as a visual poem. Thus, for example, in the first image, we see Ivens lying on a hospital bed after suffering a hit on the head. At the same time, the impetuous wind violently slams the window sash, opening it wide and shattering the glass. A few moments later, a masked monkey can be seen raiding the master's room while a typical Chinese dragon-shaped shadow is projected on the wall. Later, we observe the director coming out of the mouth of a gigantic face representing the full moon: the viewer soon discovers that it is a dream, in which the protagonist is Ivens himself, dressed in a large black cloak over an unusual lunar landscape. He observes the Earth from afar, starting a conversation with the wife of Hou Yi, a character belonging to Chinese mythology and known for having saved the planet by destroying nine of the ten suns.[9]. This sequence, therefore, takes the form of a tribute to the silent film *Le voyage dans la Lune* (1902), a masterpiece by Georges Méliès, inspired in turn by the science fiction novels of Jules Verne and H.G. Wells.

Therefore, the oneiric element takes central importance within the film, allowing the Dutch director to dialogue profitably even with the early cinema, intrinsically connected, as is known, to a dreamlike and imaginative dimension, in which the "visionary spectacle" consists in showing more than in telling[10].

Essentially, for the ninety-year-old Ivens, the wind becomes a metaphor for the vital breath, not by chance; in a scene of the film, the master of Tai Chi, skilled in executing slow and regular movements, explains to

---

9 According to the legend of "Hou Yi, the archer," each sun corresponds to a bird. When Hou Yi destroys nine of the ten suns with his bow, leaving only one alive, he saves the earth devastated by catastrophes and destruction. After the battle, as a sign of gratitude, the queen mother of the West gives the young man an elixir of immortality. Hou Yi does not drink the elixir immediately, choosing to stay with his wife, Cheng'e. However, to prevent an apprentice, called Feng Meng, from taking possession of the elixir, Cheng'e decides to drink the potion in turn, thus finding herself forced to live on the moon, in a border area between Earth and the sky.

10 "Questo tipo di spettacolo, che va dal 1895 al 1915 circa, ha come funzione principale quella di mostrare immagini, alla maniera della lanterna magica, o dei Mondi nuovi, ed è stato chiamato opportunamente cinema delle attrazioni". Cf. S. Bernardi, *L'avventura del cinematografo. Storia di un'arte e di un linguaggio*, Marsilio, Venezia 2007, p. 39.

the old filmmaker who has asthma that the innermost secret of breathing is contained entirely in the "rhythm of the autumn wind." It is worth mentioning that the theme of breathing dealt with by Ivens in this film has its roots in the *Tao tê ching* (literally "Doctrine and Practice of the Way"), the cornerstone book of Taoist philosophy, attributable to the legendary Chinese writer Lao-tzu between 6th and 3rd century B.C.[11] In Chinese thought, the Tao represents the way, i.e., the fundamental principle, the dominant idea of everything that exists in the world. According to ancient cosmology, in the beginning, the Tao gave rise to matter, understood as a set of all the entities that populate the planet, and, later, to Energy. The latter coincides with the "Vital breath of the universe" (*Ch'i*), which permeates and animates matter. It is essential to highlight how, in ancient Chinese philosophy, nature itself can be considered in its entirety as a breathing organism, and the human being appears immersed in this energy, which also invades space. The *Ch'i*, the sign of the universe, also circulates in the human body and is strictly attributable to the individual breath, the vital breath that allows us to exist.

Starting from this theoretical setting, in the final sequences of *Une histoire de vent*, the Dutch filmmaker is again observed intent on scrutinizing the sky from the dune's crest. Now the wind gets up, and the effects of its power are finally visible to the viewer: the sand begins to swirl in the air, the tents of the camp where the *troupe* is staying risk being swept away like leaves, and Ivens decides to abandon his chair standing up. The impetuous breath of the air, the vital breath of the universe, envelops the already weakened body of the director, who lets himself go in an intense embrace of the wind, then disappears from the scene and heads alone towards the unknown.

These scenarios acquire greater resonance through the reference to some sequences of the most recent animated film, *The Wind Rises* (風立ちぬ), Miyazaki Hayao's latest masterpiece, presented in competition at the Venice Film Festival in 2013[12]. Even in the work of the Japanese director, the theme of flight, tackled through irrational elements of

11 The reference is to the edition edited by J.J.L. Duyvendal, *Tao tê ching. Il libro della Via e della Virtù*, Adelphi, Milano 1973.

12 In the making of *The Wind Rises*, Miyazaki drew inspiration from two specific sources. The first was the true story of Horikoshi Jirō (1903–1982), an aeronautical engineer known for having built the deadly fighter aircraft. The second source was the novel *The Wind Has Risen* (風立ちぬ) by the Japanese writer Hori Tatsuo (1904–1953), also admired by Kawabata Yasunari. The book follows the story of the woman loved by the author, ill with tuberculosis and forced to live in a sanatorium in Nagano.

nature and fantastic scenarios, amazing flying machines, and impressive warplanes, proves to be decisive. As Maria Teresa Trisciuzzi precisely writes, "Whether they respond to a spectacular or poetic need, the aerial sequences are a fundamental part of the Japanese master's universe: Miyazaki's fantasy finds its ideal location in the clouds, raising its heroes, light as the air and swift as the wind, above an imperfect world."[13]. In this regard, in one of the last scenes of the feature film signed by the master of the Studio Ghibli, the protagonist Horikoshi Jirō is seen receiving the embrace of the wind together with his imaginary mentor, Giovanni Caproni, depicted at his side on the top of a hill. For the Japanese boy, the dream dimension does not represent a simple hiding place or an attempt to escape from the dangers of the world; on the contrary, the possibility of undertaking an authentic training path lies within it. Echoing the words of Marcello Ghilardi, in the figure of Caproni, Jirō then rediscovers "both the essence of the work to which one dedicates oneself, as well as the self-image one tries to shape."[14]. In the evanescent space of the dream, therefore, the young protagonist and the Italian engineer converse with each other, establishing a relationship that is undoubtedly fictitious yet completely intimate and confidential, capable of transcending the logic of time and history.

The conversation between the two characters on the hill is interrupted by the appearance of Nahoko, whose brief existence the Italian engineer compares to the blowing of a "splendid wind." Together with the young girl, who is ill with tuberculosis, Jirō spent some happy moments in the mountains, opening his heart to the wonder and rediscovery of small daily gestures, such as creating ephemeral paper airplanes. The wind that messes up their clothes and hair wrapped up on that occasion the souls of the two boys, immersed in the silent magic of the mountain peaks in summer, inciting them to live. Throughout the film, the air, with its whims and its sudden and naive jokes, fills the days with a poignant beauty, leaving a sweet melancholy in the eyes of the spectator. A sentiment, the latter, which seems to permeate the Japanese engineer's entire existence. As Alberto Brodesco states in this regard, "Horikoshi's dream must wait for a war to

13 M.T. Trisciuzzi, *Hayao Miyazaki. Sguardi oltre la nebbia*, Carocci, Roma 2013, p. 121.

14 M. Ghilardi, *Tempo, tecnica, esistenza nell'ultimo Miyazaki*, in *I mondi di Miyazaki. Percorsi filosofici negli universi dell'artista giapponese*, a cura di M. Boscarol, Mimesis, Milano 2018, p. 44.

meet its possibility of realization. This contrast between a child's dream and the need for history plunges Jirò into a condition of human weakness."[15].

The contradiction inherent in the technique foreshadows the dramatic outcome to which the inventions of Horikoshi, inventor of the deadly fighter plane used during the Second World War, *Mitsubishi Zero Fighter*, will lead, yet, in the ephemeral beauty of an instant, the wind that no one can see invites you to listen to the voice of nature gently. The breath of air, a vital breath of the universe, thus pushes us to welcome the present in harmony with the flow of time and confront the existing without overwhelming ourselves. In this regard, the film closes with the words of Caproni, who exhorts his pupil to ideally follow him to sip a glass of wine with him immediately after having associated the invention of the airplane with an extraordinary and cursed dream at the same time. The dream image then reveals the two orientations that oppose each other with greater intensity throughout Miyazaki's cinema: on the one hand, the admiration for the products of technology, extraordinary flying machines represented in a thousand different forms; on the other the condemnation of the despicable use that humans make of these means. However, it must be specified that for the Japanese director, this ambivalence does not translate into a clear contrast between positive and negative characters: the outlines are much more blurred and intrinsically furrowed by contradiction.

Therefore, if, on the one hand, as taught by the myth of Prometheus told by Plato in the pages of Protagoras, technical expertise appears indispensable for the fate of humanity, on the other hand, it has become a tool in the hands of the powerful to produce weapons and destroy the territory. In this sense, it is possible to glimpse a common thread running through the heterogeneous production of Ivens and Miyazaki, marked by an ambivalent vision of technique, the bearer of many hopes, and, equally, the harbinger of grand illusions. It is precisely in the impossibility of reaching a synthesis between the two positions that the heart of the imagery offered by the two directors is enclosed, as they are skilled in dealing with the theme of flight through different expressive tools (documentary cinema the first, animation the second)[16], recalling several autobiographical episodes in this direction. On the other hand, as seen from the works examined, both authors share an intense relationship with the element of air, which is also investigated in its

15 A. Brodesco, *La melancolia dell'ingegnere*, in *I mondi di Miyazaki. Percorsi filosofici negli universi dell'artista giapponese*, a cura di M. Boscarol, Mimesis, Milao 2018, p. 21.

16 For a deeper dive into Japanese animation, cf. M.R. Novielli, *Animerama. Storia del cinema d'animazione giapponese*, Marsilio, Venezia 2015.

affective dimension. While Miyazaki, the son of an aeronautical engineer, spent his youth and most of his life in Japan, "torn between the muffled echo of war and proximity to a fragile rural peace."[17]Ivens first moved to Berlin to obtain his diploma in photochemistry and then began to travel the world, remaining still anchored to his country of origin to be nicknamed "the Flying Dutchman."

This appellation reveals the most intimate meaning of the bond between the director from Nijmegen and his native country. Despite the physical distance, he has always given voice to nature and its elements, pursuing an enthusiastic passion for documentary. In this sense, unlike the ghost ship, which in the northern European folk tradition is destined to sail the seas without ever reaching a precise destination, the Dutch director has approached his travels with conscience and a critical spirit, distinguishing himself for an intense desire for militancy and testimony. It is no coincidence that, throughout his life, Ivens has often courageously recounted utopian ideals of peace and freedom, independence, and emancipation, thus giving expression to the multiple political, social, and environmental realities of the varied territories that have been the backdrop for his films, often even in dangerous conditions.[18]. Over the years, he has been able to deftly perceive the ineffectiveness of many regimes and grasp the transitory and changing nature of the different political systems. However, faced with such an awareness, he has never stopped believing in ideals and the possibility of their realization, as demonstrated by his latest work, within which the filmmaker's great desire to give shape to the invisible once again emerges.

17 M.T. Trisciuzzi, *Hayao Miyazaki. Sguardi oltre la nebbia*, Carocci, Roma 2013, p. 29.

18 Cf. V. Tosi, *Joris Ivens. Cinema e utopia*, *op. cit.*, p. 216.

III.
Philosophical, Aesthetical and Symbolic Streams

Tonino Griffero

It Blows where It Wishes

The Wind as a Quasi-Thingly Atmosphere[1]

1. *A Phenomenology of the inapparent and the ephemeral?*

Hardly anything can bring attention to the insidiousness of the air more than the current pandemic. In unravelling once again how harmful the phenomenologically latent can be, the latest coronavirus clearly reveals all the limits of a phenomenology traditionally considered to be thought of as a phenomenon that is identified only with what appears. These limits of phenomenology were first felt very lucidly and precociously by Wilhelm Schapp, one of Edmund Husserl's first pupils:

> Phenomena seem to be solid and resistant, but why should solid and resistant mean real? Phenomena do not show any stable delimitation, but why should the real be stably delimited? Phenomena come and go without leaving a trace, but why should the real leave traces? Phenomena cannot be grasped or weighed, but why should the real be able to be grasped and weighed? … I do not find any principle by which things should be the real. I do not find any principle by which daylight and a foot's distance should present us the world as it is. Why shouldn't twilight and a thousand feet's distance present us the world more exactly?[2]

Taking these caveats seriously and refusing to make phenomenology coincide with the visible, with what lies in the light of day or can fully be brought to light, this essay attempts to broaden the meaning of "phenomenon" (meaning what shows itself) to also include the invisible and un-appearing. What is inapparent is affective and a felt-bodily experience: if not all that epistemically exists appears, all that appears indeed exists and must be taken seriously phenomenologically. This way one can and

1 Version with a few (essentially bibliographical) changes of the article with the same title published in "Venti-Journal. Air-Experience-Aesthetics", I (2020), 1, 31-38.

2 W. Shapp, *Beiträge zur Phänomenologie der Wahrnehmung* (2.nd Edition), Klostermann, Frankfurt a. M. 1981, p. 95.

must challenge the traditional ocular-centrism, completely tantalized by boundaries of stable and knowable objects at a distance, and thus rile up traditional ontology.[3] By overcoming the existential narrowness of philosophers who seemingly limit their scope and case studies to books and desks, one should leave the desk (or, if you prefer, the Lucretian topos of "shipwreck with spectator") and give due attention not only to latency but also to subjective facts.

Traditional Western ontology puts substances, things in themselves, before relations, and the dualism subject/object before the in-between preceding them, thus following the classic hierarchical three-branch system of substance-relation-accident.[4] Similarly, it puts being before becoming, solid bodies — cohesive, solid, continuous objects that are mobile only through contact — and the central field of vision before what is vague, ephemeral, and peripheric. It also puts single entities before situations. I would like instead to understand situations, neo-phenomenologically, as gestaltic wholes made up of an internally diffuse-chaotic meaningfulness and a non-numerical manifoldness whose only unquestionable evidence comes from felt-bodily touching. Traditional ontology defines perception as a distancing-constative, as a merely ocular process and not as a deambulatory, peripheric, and synesthetic experience. Unfortunately, these parametres end up exiling everything that is vague, flowing, atmospheric into an alleged inner and private world of the soul. The soul, in turn, is conceived as a solid and stratified body — as a bundle of perceptions or as an ineffable inner theatre.

In an ontology such as this, atmospheres and quasi-things are obviously not welcome. My argument suggests that instead, ontology should recognize that people are not surrounded by meaningless things whose qualities would be nothing but the outcome of projected physical data, but rather by atmospheric feelings and quasi-things that are innately affectively connoted. Embracing new and unthought ontological categories like those of "atmosphere" and "quasi-thing"[5] allows us to leave behind the pragmatic

3 "There has never been a philosophy so far whose conceptualisation was guided by the possibility of being heard, smelled, and tasted" (L. Klages, *Der Geist als Widersacher der Seele*, Barth, Leipzig 1929-32, p. 296).

4 As when an un-splittable circumstance, characterised by an intensive magnitude, is not yet transformed into a reversible relation.

5 These half-entities were something so unthought of that they didn't even have a name before Schmitz raised them to the status of authentic ontological category (*Halbding*) in the last volumes of his *System*. See H. Schmitz, *Die Wahrnehmung. System der Philosophie* III.5, Bouvier, Bonn 1978, pp. 116-139.

purposes and the representational advantages attributed to objectivity and the artificial denial of invisibility. This acceptance of the elusive permits the admittance that, without being a substance or an accident, felt-bodily experience affects us like an extraneous agent; therefore, in turn, it gives full legitimacy to an expanded ontological repertoire.[6]

My atmospherology aims at developing exactly this suggestion. I assume that the variable and the ephemeral, the fluid and the vague, are no less "real" phenomena than the permanent.[7] This implies that one should not neglect the challenging chaotic character of what one might perceive as an epistemic deficit; however, this can only be achieved by freeing oneself from the overestimated gnostic paradigm in favour of a pathic one.[8] Transforming one's lifeworld into the affective brushstrokes of a painting, rather than the accuracy and schematic simplification of a map, allows us to preserve every sensible-qualitative involvement from scientific reductionism.

This path led me, over time, from a neo-phenomenological atmospherology to an ontological theory of quasi-things.[9] Over time and more recently, I have developed a comprehensive theory of "pathic" aesthetics, which focusses on the ability to let oneself go: a skill largely unacknowledged by the rationalistic post-Enlightenment dogma of subjective autonomy and finalistic action. By "pathic," I refer to the perceiver's affective, life-worldly involvement that belongs to the domain of feeling. The pathic therefore disables the perceiver from reacting critically, and leaves one forced to be amongst the intrusion of experience and the elemental. My atmospherological-pathic approach teaches us how to expose oneself to be a means of what happens rather than as a traditional subject who may transform every instance into reflection and every given

---

6 Which reminds me to some extent of the brilliant Sartrean pages of *Being and Nothingness*, which are devoted to pain as a psychic-affective object with its own reality, with intermittent time and life, habits and "melodic" developments. See J-P. Sartre, *Being and Nothingness: A Phenomenological Essay on Ontology*, Pocket Books, New York 1978, pp. 335–337.

7 T. Griffero, *Atmospheres: Aesthetics of Emotional Spaces*, Routledge, London/ New York 2014; Id., *Places, Affordances, Atmospheres: A Pathic Aesthetics*, Routledge, London/New York 2020; Id., *The Atmospheric "We". Moods and Collective Feelings*, Mimesis International, Milan 2021.

8 E. Straus, *The Primary World of Senses: A Vindication of Sensory Experience*, Free Press of Glencoe, New York 1963.

9 T. Griffero, *Quasi-Things: The Paradigm of Atmospheres*, State University of New York, Albany 2017.

into something done. This approach could and should focus attention on the quiet and indiscernible phenomenon of air. Air is not only weightless, invisible, and imperceptible, but also, unlike things in the proper sense, fully coincides with its affective, continuous, and situational appearance without being reducible to mere components of something else.

Whether they be natural phenomena such as twilight, luminosity, darkness, the seasons, the wind, the weather, the hours of the day, the fog; or relatively artificial ones like townscape, music, soundscape, the numinous, dwelling, charisma, the gaze, shame, quasi-things express themselves as atmospheric influences. As affective affordances they are salient and real in the full sense of the word: not despite their being inapparent and ephemeral, but precisely because of it. They trigger an experience that is epistemologically vague but pathically certain, irreducible to causes or origins. The experience of a quasi-thing expresses (and certifies) our embeddedness in a lived space, reminding us of our being-in-the-word, better than other traditionally privileged states, such as the overestimated *cogito.* Restoring pathic experience (or mineness) to a central position, returns worldliness to a state outside the bounds of cognitive dualism and beyond Husserl's phenomenological method of mediating one's surroundings with one's own ego. Thus, one gradually learns to appreciate the importance of entities that are vaguer than the solid, three-dimensional, cohesive, contoured, identified, and persistent things prevailing in traditional ontologies. Holes and shadows, clouds and waves, atmospheres and the wind play a completely new role within a phenomenologically legitimate ontological inventory, based not only on a material stability at the expense of fluidity or single things and their eventual constellations, but rather on influential qualitative nuances and fluxes with their evanescent yet meaningful impressions.

This is not, of course, the place to delve into my atmospherology; however, let me briefly offer that I understand atmosphere as an influential affective presence: as feeling poured out into lived spaces and thereby resonating with, and even into, felt-bodily processes.[10] The affective presence of atmosphere acts through affordances of environmental invitations (precisely through motor suggestions and synesthetic characters) that are not limited to the visual or pragmatic. The non-objectifying externalization of atmospheres allows them to be perceived as a spatial state of the world rather than a very private psychological state; thus, while their intensity also depends on the

10 For an analysis of the main theories of the lived (or felt) body (from Schopenhauer to Schmitz) see now T. Griffero, *Being a Lived Body. From a Neo-Phenomenological Point of View*, Routledge, London/New York, 2024.

subject, their phenomenological apparition is objective — at least when manifested in prototypic form.[11] Due to this objectivity, atmosphere cannot be explained through conventional and associative language; instead, perceiving atmospheres means to communicate with all that is perceived through the felt-body and the affective charge of things, quasi-things, and situations., thus, arriving at an emotional segmentation of the lifewordly reality. Atmospheres are fully consistent with the neo-phenomenological redefinition of philosophy in terms of "thinking in situations" — in terms of a self-reflection of people regarding their "subjective facts"[12] and how they feel in a certain environment.[13]

---

11 It is worth pointing out that I do not fully embrace the neo-phenomenological campaign of desubjectification of all feelings (See H. Schmitz, *Situationen und Atmosphären. Zur Ästhetik und Onthologie bei Gernot Böhme*, in *Naturerkenntnis und Natursein: Für Gernot Böhme*, ed. by M. Hauskeller, C. Rehmann-Sutter, and G. Schiemann. Suhrkamp, Frankfurt am Main 1998, pp. 176-190; and Id., *Atmospheres*, ed. by T. Griffero, Mimesis International, Milan 2023) and prefer to admit that there are three different types of atmospheres. There are prototypic atmospheres (objective, external, and unintentional and sometimes lacking a precise name), derivative ones (objective, external and intentionally produced), and even some that are quite spurious in their relatedness (subjective and projective). This also leads to different types of emotional games. In a nutshell: (a) an atmosphere can overwhelm us (ingressive encounter) and be refractory to a more or less conscious attempt at a projective reinterpretation; (b) it can find us in tune with it (syntonic encounter), to the point that we don't realize we entered it; (c) it can be recognized (be it felt as antagonistic or not) without being really felt in our body; (d) it can elicit a resistance that pushes us to change it; (e) it may not reach the necessary threshold for sensorial-affective observation, thus causing an embarrassing atmospheric and social inadequacy for oneself and for others; (f) it may (for various reasons, also absolutely idiosyncratic) be perceived differently in the course of time; and (g) it may be so dependent on the perceptual (subjective) form that it concretizes itself even in materials that normally express different moods.

12 The distinction between subjective and objective facts is an ontological one (and not just epistemic). The subjective facts are the meanings that one person, that felt-bodily affected, at most can talk about (using their own name), whereas the objective (or neutral) ones are those that everyone can talk about (and merely name), insofar as they know enough and have the language skills. In other words, only subjective facts prove our absolute identity not requiring any reflexive identification: a kind of absolute subjectivity (*tua res agitur*!). In fact, "the subjective does not consist [...] in a position on the terrain of objective facts (relational subjectivity) but in a different kind of factuality: the factuality of subjective facts for someone". In H. Schmitz, *Der Leib, Der Raum Und Die Gefühle*, Sirius, Bielefeld-Locarno 2005, p. 6.

13 For a brief introduction in English see: H. Schmitz, *New Phenomenology: a Brief Introduction*, ed. by T. Griffero, Mimesis international, Milan 2019.

But let us return to the issue of the phenomenology of the inapparent. We can begin, for example, with an umbrella term like "air." When I mention air, I do not mean in Heidegger's ontological sense,[14] nor in the technological sense of making the invisible-ephemeral airy background visible,[15] nor as a synonym for sociological climate,[16] or as a social-cultural fact. Instead, I would like to apply my neo-phenomenology approach of the inapparent to the more "ontically," quasi-thingly phenomenon of air, particularly its windy atmospheres. This method of inquiry implies the "rediscovery of air" carried out by Hermann Schmitz's phenomenological focus on the quasi-thing, as well as Sloterdijk's rendering of atmoterrorism as an epochal event due to the modern tendency to make explicit the implicit and bring the imperceptible to the fore.[17]

This brings the philosophical thematization of speech as epistemically naive and pathically precise to the fore — such as in phrases like "there is something in the air" or "the wind is changing." Speaking metaphorically like this means that one is feeling what is in the air, and, at the same time, that what is in the air is what one feels. These expressive phrases are both irreducible to cognition and to elementary sense-date; thus, the atmosphere described acts as a scaffolding of affective life. The de-psychologization of the emotional sphere is precisely apparent in the way in which the wind modulates our lived space and resonates with our felt-body.

2. *Windy atmospheres*

Of course, there are many ways of treating air as an atmosphere. Smell, not surprisingly, is often considered the atmospheric phenomenon par excellence. Just because smell has neither "sides and therefore presentations

---

14 Phenomenology is a phenomenology of the inapparent, insofar it "is a path that leads away to come before," from the presencing to the unconcealment. See M. Heidegger, *Four Seminars*, Indiana University Press, Bloomington 2003, p. 80.

15 On how to visualize and design a no-thing (not a nothing) like the air, more exactly not so much air as such as its dynamic and transient, aperiodic and turbulent behaviour (its atmospheric forces), see M. Wagenfeld, *The Phenomenology of Visualizing Atmosphere*, in "Evironmental & Architectural Phenomenology", 26, 2 (2015), pp. 9-15.

16 J. De Rivera, *Emotional Climate: Social Structure and Emotional Dynamics*, in "International Review of Studies on Emotion" 2 (1992), pp. 197-218.

17 See P. Sloterdijk, *Foams: Spheres III: Plural spherology*, "Semiotext(e)", Los Angeles, CA 2016.

per profiles (*Abschattungen*),"[18] nor precise and defined edges, angles, faces and colors, it could be argued that smell is the atmosphere itself. Scent is something that, impregnating the lived space, deeply involves us — namely, a pre-dimensional space without surfaces, lines and points. The olfactory is also something we "breathe in," that penetrates "through all the pores of [our] being" and sometimes "can become unbreathable as much on the physical level as on the moral one."[19] By saying that atmosphere is an affective "air," it is also consistent to say that it is a "more": something beyond language that remains unspoken in many sensory experiences, even though it is felt and evokes value-laden impressions.

Nevertheless, the air's elusiveness — together with its effect on human politics, scientific knowledge, and processes of nature — is not what I want to talk about here. I'd rather focus on the atmospheric specificity of the wind, relying on its phenomenological-ontological analysis as a quasi-thing. The wind thus turns out to belong to a "big and colorful family" of physiognomic "characters"[20]: occupying a vast territory between the (so-called) mere *qualia* and things in the proper sense; exerting on the perceiver a more direct and immediate power than full-fledged things.[21] These qualities allow me, on the one hand, to claim the central role played by an "attenuated reality" in making our everyday life richer and more colorful, and, on the other, to highlight wind's atmospheric charge.

The wind is the topic of a highly desirable "aesthetics of air [that] must first render air sensible by being an aesthesis of air."[22] More specifically, it is a very good example of an atmospheric quasi-thing, as religions have always recognized, pointing out that it blows where it wishes: "you hear its sound, but you do not know where it comes from or where it is going. So it is with everyone born of the Spirit."[23] As something apparently inapparent, air actually occurs mainly *ex negativo,* when one misses it. And yet the wind especially affects us on the affective-bodily level in the form of an atmospheric feeling poured out into pre-dimensional space: that is, as a very concrete experience, significantly both climatic and affective, physically and felt-bodily. Provided, of course, that the wind,

18 H. Tellenbach, *Geschmack und Atmosphäre*, O. Müller, Salzburg 1968, p. 28.

19 E. Minkowski, *Vers une cosmologie : fragments philosophiques*, Aubier, Paris 1936, pp. 117-118.

20 H. Schmitz, *Die Wahrnehmung, op. cit.*, p. 134.

21 See T. Griffero, *Who's Afraid of Atmospheres (And of Their Authority)?*, in "Lebenswelt" 4 (2014), 1, p. 193-213.

22 E. Horn, *Air as medium*, in "Grey Room" 73 (2018), pp. 6-25: 22.

23 John 3:8.

exactly like the weather, is duly subtracted to the prognostic obsession of today, inscribed in the flood of "weather forecasts," and synthetically testifies to the quality of our emotional involvement — exactly like the Japanese notions of *ki* or *fūdo*, understood as pre-dualistic coexistence of self and world.[24] It thus provides a first starting point for a long-awaited philosophical climatology (from Montesquieu and Herder on) mainly based on elemental media — something never realized, also for excessive fear of climate determinism.

The relative phenomenological inaccessibility of air certainly ceases to exist rightly when it comes to the wind. Wind has always been the object of the human attempt to catch it and exploit its power. The wind can be directly experienced thanks to a felt-body resonance even in the absence of optical data as it forcefully hits us. It shows itself indeed not only, for example, in an inflated dress or in the bent branches of a tree, in a waving flag or in its effects on the clouds and on water, but also in how it atmospherically and "ecstatically" affects our surroundings. Fully coinciding with its own flow and thus being an event in the proper sense (a "pure act," in a way), it pervades space with its particular voluminousness, tuning it in this or that way (obviously a breeze is affectively different from a hurricane) and arousing specific motor suggestions and synesthetic affordances.

Since wind is always a mediated and thus indirect manifestation, as a gestalting appearing a back-and-forth switch of figure and background, we are required to observe it in a definite context and perspective. This means wind cannot be experienced in a general or in an abstract way: solid or gentle, still or storm-like in different moments or places. Apparently omnipresent, the wind ignores boundaries, and land-borne boundaries in particular. But, above all, wind is irreducible to air moving, as Western ontology instead usually claims, thus thickening it and turning it into a thing to reduce its intrusiveness.[25]

Maybe it is time to detail its quasi-thingly features better:

A. The wind is not edged, discrete, cohesive, or solid and is therefore hardly penetrable like things. Nor does it properly possess the spatial sides in which things necessarily manifest themselves and from whose ortho-aesthetic coexistence one can usually gather their protensional regularities. Thus, we do not perceive in it a side hiding while announcing the others,

24 See T. Watsuji, *A Climate: A Philosophical Study*, Printing Bureau, Japanese Government, Tokyo 1961.

25 The alternative strategy is tracing a quasi-thing back to perceptions so chaotic and de-contoured that they end up being considered as something anomalous, if not pathological.

which means that if a thing can still deceive us by having concealed sides — temporarily or eternally hidden inner strata and only apparent qualities — a quasi-thing like the wind never deceives, because it totally coincides with its phenomenic appearance.

B. Things possess immanent and regular tendencies. An object weighs and tends to fall; the pages of a book turn yellow; if we don't lift something, it stays on the ground. Because of these immanent dispositions, as well as their compatibility or incompatibility with other bodies, things testify to us of their physical-bodily presence. While things have these tendencies even without interaction (the glass remains frangible even if nobody breaks it), which confer to them a future as well as a past revealed by signs, marks, fractures, etc., because of its relative immateriality the wind does not seem to have actual tendencies (nor does it have a history). In their atmospheric and quasi-thingly effect, night, anxiety, and the wind, for example, don't ever get old and don't show any temporal patina. By its absolute "presentness," the wind is not the continuation of something prior, but something always new and so radically *evenementiel* that it does not require a genetic phenomenology and etiologic explanation.

C. While things transcend their momentary character — in the sense that neither are they born nor can they die all of a sudden, but instead bear the signs of their own specific history; and that one can possess them, portion them, save them, or annihilate them — the wind can appear in a partial form, without this necessarily meaning that it does so through fragments and sides. So, if I can point at a single object made of silver to demonstrate what silver is, in the same way, I can refer to this wind, regardless of its specific present variant, to explain what the wind is in general. This is because a single wind is not the portion of a larger wind-thing but fully expresses the "character" of its appearance. In the same way that a different tone does not make the voice of a person (another quasi-thing) a different one (warm, metallic, polished, hoarse), a quasi-thing like the wind has its own distinct identity, which, within certain limits, can be traced back to types, but not to universal-conceptual genera.

D. Above all, the wind is (felt as) more immediate and intrusive than things because it can generate inhibiting and sometimes even unbearable motor suggestions. The felt-bodily communication triggered by it can be summed up as an alternation of encorporation and excorporation that is much more intense than that triggered by things. As a "centre of incorporation"[26] able to occupy some surfaceless and lived spaces, as a

26 H. Schmitz, *Die Wahrnemung,* cit, p. 169.

violent “attractor of our everyday attention”[27], is often more incisive and demanding than things in the strict sense.

E. But perhaps the most philosophically intriguing point is that the wind dies down with the same inexplicable immediacy with which it rises. Even if, as we have seen, it has a “character,” i.e. it is this or that particular wind (as we say of other quasi-things, “Here’s my usual pain in the shoulder,” “Here’s the melancholy of an autumn evening,” etc.), it doesn’t have the same continuity of existence of things, which as a rule cannot disappear from a point in space and reappear in another. For this reason, the embarrassing question asked by the child (“What does the wind do when it isn’t blowing?”), implying in a thingly way a being separate from feeling it[28], turns out to be an excellent — *qua* upsetting and disturbing — philosophical question. The normalising and reifying answer usually given by the adult (“It has died down,” or even “It went to sleep”) disregards its importance.

Though they are things that are not perceived[29], quasi-things like the wind have rather an intermittent life, and it would make no sense to ask where they are when they are not present yet or when they are no longer there. Their intermittence produces a kind of broken biography that cannot be filled in principle (does the wind, or a certain type of wind, have a history?). It is very different from the latency periods typically belonging to things that are temporarily not perceived. To prevent this uncanny experience — to mitigate the anxiety provoked by the incessant change of *qualia* — standard ontology has no other option than to subsume atmospheric perceptions under genera and to give priority to tangible and well-determined entities, which are endowed with regular, homogeneous, cohesive, and three-dimensional shape and can be singled out through genus and species.

F. Lastly, following Hermann Schmitz again, like all other quasi-things, the wind does not have a threefold causality (cause-action-effect) but a twofold one (cause/action-effect). Very briefly, while a book is a book that eventually falls later on the floor and breaks a glass if it hits it, the wind — which in a certain sense “is precisely this blowing and nothing

27 J. Soentgen, *Das Unscheinbare: Phänomenologische Beschreibungen Von Stoffen, Dingen Und Fraktalen Gebilden*. Akademie Verlag, Berlin 1997, p. 13.

28 A question that can be asked of all quasi-things: “What does a voice do when it is not heard?”; “Where is pain when I do not feel it?”; etc.

29 Even when the waves cease to crease it, we still see the water; but when the wind stops, there is no perceptible air left.

else"[30] — does not exist before and beyond its blowing. So to speak, it is an aggression without an aggressor (a cause) that may be separated from it and be prior to it. In other words, the wind is atmospherically an actual fact (a pure phenomenon) and not a factual fact (the wind as a physical-climatic element). When it hinders our way and perhaps makes us fall, it is an action coinciding with its cause.

Traditional Western ontology felt compelled to transform bipolar causality into a tripolar causality because only if the cause can be separated from effect (i.e. a necessary substrate from its more or less accidental manifestation) can science express its prognosis and operate in a preventive way. This indistinction of cause and action confirms *a fortiori* that the somewhat unexpected appearance of a quasi-thingly configuration is necessarily followed by an involuntary experience. This pathic-atmospheric and felt-bodily involvement is at least initially uncontrollable.

The quasi-thingly wind characteristics examined here apply without doubt to every atmospheric experience and not only to elemental atmosphericness. Here, it should open a long speech on general types of resonance triggered by windy atmospheres (narrowness and vastness) and the resulting felt-bodily communication[31]. Just to give a straightforward example of how the discourse should develop: resonance can be a.) discrepant and b.) syntonic. The atmospheric discrepancy (when you are not friends with the wind when the wind kicks up because it is strong, harsh and biting) induces an epicritic contraction by inhibiting fluid bodily behaviour. It gives birth to individual felt-bodily isles of which the subject was previously unaware. However, awareness can sometimes lead to their pathological disorganisation or independence. On the other side, by facilitating bodily behaviour, the atmospheric syntony (when the wind favours us, is a sweet breeze or gently refreshes a muggy environment) provides a protopathic felt-bodily state of well-being, which momentarily prevents some particular isles from emerging and even promotes an uncritical fusion with external reality.

Obviously, the phenomenological cases of our encounter with the air and the wind (what I called "atmospheric games") is necessarily much

30 A. Grote, *Beiträge zur Phänomenologie der Erkenntnis*, Meiner, Hamburg 1972, p. 251.

31 T. Griffero, *Felt-Bodily Communication: A Neo-phenomenological Approach to Embodied Affects,* in "Studi di estetica", XLV, 8, pp. 71-86 (2017) https://doi.org/10.7413/18258646019.

more complicated.[32] Here, I am merely sketching a phenomenological atmospherology of quasi-things that aims at integrating the traditional ontologic "catalogue" starting precisely from the wind. However, it does not amount to corroborating the universal tendency (onto- and phylogenetic) to reification, whose advantages do not compensate for the loss of the semantic-pathic polyvocity of reality. My double-track aim instead consists of taking relations and events as (quasi-)things while taking many things as less thing-like: in fact, many so-called things (a mountain, a road, etc.) are not much more defined than the atmospheric feelings they irradiate — with the significant difference that the atmospheric quasi-thingly repartition depends on a segmentation of what we "encounter" that is not so much artificial (functional) or cognitive-semantic but rather affective and felt-bodily. In short: quasi-things have quality (intensity), extension (non-geometric dimensionality), relation (to other quasi-things and the perceiver's states of mind), place (they are here and not there, even if only in the lived space) and time (they occur right now, etc.). My aesthetic-phenomenological survey of the windy atmosphere should be seen precisely in this light.

32 T. Griffero, *Felt-Bodily Resonances: Towards a Pathic Aesthetics*, in "Yearbook for Eastern and Western Philosophy", 2 (2017), pp. 149-64.

Katia Botta

Wind Souls[1]

The aesthetic focus on wind, understood today mainly as a valuable resource for *green* energy, has its roots in the 19th century, a period in which its dynamism was elevated as a characterizing presence in the landscape. We see this in works that attempt to depict it. Joachim Ritter (1903-1974), in his commentary on the German naturalist and explorer Alexander von Humboldt[2] (1769-1859), author of *Kosmos. Entwurf einer physischen Weltbeschreibung* (1845-1862) – a fundamental model for the development of the aesthetic discipline in the following decades – explains how landscape aesthetics can be interpreted through "Bildkunst" (pictorial art) and "Dichtung" (poetry)[3]:

> In der geschichtlichen Zeit, in welcher die Natur, ihre Kräfte und Stoffe zum "Objekt" der Naturwissenschaften und der auf diese gegründeten technischen Nutzung und Ausbeutung werden, übernehmen es Dichtung und Bildkunst,

1 Funder: Project funded under the National Recovery and Resilience Plan (NRRP), Mission 4 Component 1 Investment 3.4 and 4.1 – Call for tender No. 351 of 09/04/2022 of Italian Ministry of University and Research funded by the European Union – NextGenerationEU.

2 Alexander Von Humboldt developed a concept of nature presented in terms of the relationship between living things and the environment, referring to Schelling's *Naturphilosophie* and Kant's thought. Humboldt was thus a reference not only for scientific studies made at the time by Darwin and Haeckel, but also, and above all, stands as an indispensable example for 19th century aesthetic research, starting with the European ideas of the relationship between man and nature, and going beyond it, attempting to grasp this reality through an immersive method. Cf. N. Scaffai, *Letteratura e ecologia. Forme e temi di una relazione narrativa*, Carocci Editore, Roma 2017, pp. 50-51. On the proposed overcoming by the Humboldtian model, see: H.D. Thoreau, *Walking* (1862), in Id., *Excursions,* Ticknor and Fields, Boston 1863, pp. 161-214, here p. 194; L. Castelletti, *Introduzione*, in J. Muir, *Una tempesta di vento nella foresta*, testo americano a fronte, ed. by L. Castelletti, La Vita Felice, Milano 2019, pp. 5-12, here p. 6-7.

3 J. Ritter, *Landschaft. Zur Funktion des Ästhetischen in der modernen Gesellschaft*, in Id., *Subjektivität. Sechs Aufsätze* (1974), Suhrkamp Verlag, Frankfurt am Main 2021, pp. 141-163, here p. 153.

> die gleiche Natur – nicht weniger universal – in ihrer Beziehung auf den empfindenden Menschen aufzufassen und "ästhetisch" zu vergegenwärtigen.[4]

In this sense, the presence, and the importance of the role played by the wind, an element characterised by informality and elusiveness, is to be found in poetic expressions and artistic works, especially in pictorial representations.

Starting from Humboldtian thought, two poles of aesthetic ideation emerge, in which an important connection to the wind element is felt: first, the field of English Romantic research, in which the personal events of its very young exponents – Percy Bysshe Shelley (1792-1822), John Keats (1795-1821), and Lord George Gordon Byron (1788-1824) – defined by Roberto Mussapi as *I ragazzi che amavano il vento* (*The Boys Who Loved Wind*), were profoundly affected by this natural element. Wind, as an entity, appears in both biographical notes and poetic works through the water-air dichotomy, best defined by the relationship between sea and wind. Shelley, a few months after the death of his friend John Keats, "il poeta dell'immedesimazione"[5], died in Lerici bay during a squall:

> La barca che si farà costruire, a Lerici, sarà battezzata *Ariel*, il demone buono della *Tempesta* di Shakespeare, che sovrintende ai venti e li governa. Forse l'acqua rappresentava, come per Prospero e i personaggi della *Tempesta*, il purgatorio, il gravame del fondale da superare, il luogo di sfida di un'anima che voleva ascendere bruciando aerea e ventosa.[6]

This identification, or rather, correspondence between the "Wild Spirit"[7] of the wind and the poet's desire to elevate his soul is expressed in the renowned *Ode to the West Wind* (1820). The wind plays a central role here, it is the "destroyer" but also the "preserver" (*Wild Spirit, which art moving everywhere*; *Destroyer and preserver; hear, oh hear!*[8]) of Nature (a dual role that will also appear in subsequent works). Its presence is thus

---

4 Ivi, pp. 153-154.

5 R. Mussapi, *I ragazzi che amavano il vento*, in P. Bysshe Shelley, J. Keats, Lord G. Gordon Byron, *I ragazzi che amavano il vento*, testo originale a fronte, ed. by R. Mussapi, Feltrinelli, Milano 2020, pp. 5-36, here p. 36 ("the poet of immedesimation").

6 Ivi, pp. 28-29.

7 P.B. Shelley, *Ode to the West Wind* (1820), in P. B. Shelley, *Poesie*, facing the original, ed. by Giuseppe Conte, Biblioteca Universale Rizzoli, Milano 1998^4(1989), pp. 188-197, here p. 190.

8 *Ibidem.*

essential in defining that natural "atmosphere"[9] into which storms pour or in which its passage is witnessed by other natural elements such as clouds, leaves and waves (a dimension to which Shelley constantly attempts to rise poetically, but without success):

IV. If I were a dead leaf thou mightest bear;
If I were a swift cloud to fly with thee;
A wave to pant beneath thy power [...]
Oh lift me as a wave, a leaf, a cloud!
I fall upon the thorns of life! I bleed![10]

If this spatiality crested by the relationship between air and water is in *Ode to the West Wind* no less interesting is the reference by George Gordon Byron in Stanza 185 of the second canto of Don Juan (1819-1824):

They look'd up to the sky, whose floating glow
Spread like a rosy ocean, vast and bright;
They gazed upon the glittering sea below,
Whence the broad moon rose circling into sight;
They heard the wave's splash, and the wind so low,
And saw each other's dark eyes darting light
Into each other – and, beholding this,
Their lips drew near, and clung into a kiss;[11]

The chiasmus produced here (sky, sea, wave, wind) entails a double evocation of the sea-wind dialogue, albeit not according to an existential declension in this case, but as evidence of the full unfolding of the act of love. It is interesting to point to some correspondence with Shelley's works, in the "thine aëry surge"[12] of the *Ode* and especially in *The Cloud* (dated 1820):

And I laugh to see them whirl and flee,
Like a swarm of golden bees,
When I widen the rent in my wind-built tent,
Till the calm rivers, lakes and seas,
Like strips of the sky fallen through me on high,
Are each paved with the moon and these.[13]

---

9 Ivi, p. 192.

10 Ivi p. 194.

11 G.G. Byron, *Don Juan*, in Id., *The Major Works*, edited by Jerome J. McGann, Oxford University Press, Oxford 2008, pp. 373-879, here p. 479.

12 P.B. Shelley, *Ode to the West Wind*, in Id., *Poesie*, *op. cit.*, p. 190.

13 P.B. Shelley, *The Cloud* (1820), in Id., *Poesie*, *op. cit.*, pp. 208-215, here p. 212.

A presence, that of the wind, from which even Byron was certainly not immune, so much so that he founded with his poet friend, the journal "The Liberal", in which, Mussapi explains:

> Riusciranno a parlare del vento come di una divinità spietata ma infine buona, delle nuvole, della natura divina del cielo, dei fantasmi che prendono forma in una mascherata, del chiaretto che oscilla nei bicchieri, delle donne, danzanti, mascherate o nude, e della musica e del rimpianto per un'armonia perduta che in quei luoghi pareva rivelare una cerniera, una magica promessa di ricongiunzione, qui, nel regno di Colombo e della Lanterna dove erano state scritte anche le favole reali di Marco Polo. Solo due ragazzi potevano tentare una simile impresa, ma ce la fecero, perché uno sapeva vivere e nuotare, l'altro guardare e desiderare.[14]

This description also makes it possible to recognize certain points of tangency with the essence of the Romantic tradition as nurtured by exponents of the so-called *Goethezeit*; first and foremost, the completion of the tour of Italy, the *Grand Tour* of which Goethe himself was a pioneer, a voyage that had devastating consequences on their lives (Keats died very young from previous illnesses, Shelley died shortly afterwards in Lerici bay in the middle of a storm, and Byron near Missolungi in Greece), but which at the same time brought about an extraordinary poetic elevation for all three of these young Englishmen. Goethe's influence is perceptible not only in the choice of scenes[15] in which they are portrayed but also in the treatment of established themes, such as the Venetian carnival (the connection to the German author's *Italienische Reise* is clear here). On the other hand, Venice, in addition to being one of the obligatory destinations on the *Gran Tour* and a vital object of study by the English critic of art John Ruskin[16] (1819-1900) is also, due to the uniqueness of its setting, the destination of the greatest

---

14 R. Mussapi, *op.cit.*, p. 32.

15 It might be interesting to make an iconographic comparison between the portrait of Goethe in the Roman countryside, painted by Tischbein in 1787, and currently preserved at the Städelsches Kunstinstitut in Frankfurt, and the portraits of the young English poets. See for instance the painting by Joseph Severn entitled *Shelley composing "Prometheus Unbound" in the Baths of Caracalla* (1845), now in the Keats-Shelley House in Rome, and Giacomo Trecourt's painting, *Lord Byron sulle sponde del mare ellenico* (1850 ca), oil on canvas now in the Musei Civici in Pavia. Cf. R. Mussapi, *Dove i poeti si sentivano a casa. Il Grand Tour classico di Goethe, quello "eretico" di Dickens. E la Liguria di Byron e Shelley*, in "Luoghi dell'infinito", n. 269, anno XXVI, febbraio 2022, pp. 44-51.

16 Cf. J. Ruskin, *The Stones of Venice* (1851-1853), trad. it. di P. Bà e I. Loffredo, *Le pietre di Venezia*, introduzione di J.D. Rosenberg, Biblioteca Universale Rizzoli, Milano 1987.

artists of the time, including the English painter Joseph Maillord William Turner (1775-1851), inventor of tonal atmospheres.

Henri Focillon (1881-1943), in *Esthétique des visionnaires* (1926), provides a significant commentary on this:

> Il est avant tout homme de plein ciel, et même, à la fin de sa carrière, le cadre léger d'une composition schématique s'évanouit, pour faire place aux fantasmagories de l'air et de l'eau. [...] un visionnaire comme Turner nous absorbe dans un monde instable, où tout est lueur, reflet et fusion. Lui aussi il a et il nous fait subir l'horreur du gouffre, mais ce gouffre est au-dessus de nous, autour de nous, immense, mais non pas vide, rayonnant, mais non pas incolore. [...] A la terrible magie de la fixité s'oppose la magie des fluides, et la couleur, par les passages, par la pénétration de la lumière, par les halos qui la dispersent et qui la dévorent, par sa décomposition même, traduit l'universel mouvement qui fait onduler et chatoyer les phénomènes de la terre, de la mer, du ciel.[17]

Turner's landscape painting, strongly influenced by the aesthetic research of the English writer and politician Edmund Burke[18] (1729-1797), and increasingly aware of the chromatic theories advanced by Goethe[19], presents an extraordinary number of images of the sea-wind dimension, as these two antipodes inescapably characterize the artist's thematic and chromatic choices. This confirms Focillon's claim that we can distinguish

---

17 H. Focillon, *Esthétique des visionnaires* (1926), in Id., *Maîtres de l'estampe. Peintres graveurs*, Librairie Renouard, H. Laurens Éditeur, Paris 1930, pp. 193-212, here pp. 208-209.

18 It is interesting here to refer to the volume *A Philosophical Enquiry into the Origin of Our Ideas of the Sublime and Beautiful*, printed for R. and J. Dodsley, London 1757. Specifically, reference is made to the "How the Sublime is produced" paragraph, p. 126: "Having considered terror as producing an unnatural tension and certain violent emotions of the nerves; it easily follows, from what we have just said, that whatever is fitted to produce such a tension, must be productive of a passion similar to terror, and consequently must be a source of the sublime, though it should have no idea of danger connected with it".

19 Turner, in addition to being influenced by Burke's thought and being celebrated by contemporaries like John Ruskin, also shows a strong connection to the literary and artistic studies of German Romanticism, specifically Goethe's *Theory of Colours* (1810), that came to the artist in 1843 in a translation edited by C. Lock. Cf. M. Bockemühl, *J.M.W. Turner (1775-1851). The World of Light and Colour*, edited by S. Bald, English translation by M. Claridge, Taschen, Köln 2021, pp. 83-85; G. Buzi, *William Turner in Etruria*, Massari Editore, Bolsena 2004, p. 15; on the artist's criticism and painting styles, see J. Ruskin, *Modern Painters* (1843-1860; first complete edition 1873), edited and abridged by D. Barrie, André Deutsch Limited, London 1987; J. Ruskin, *Turner e i preraffaelliti*, materiali a cura di G. Leoni, Abscondita, Milano 2019.

two types of paintings, in which wind – like water – plays a fundamental role in defining the atmosphere referred to. A first group of works, characterised by the depiction of an "unconquered, alien nature"[20], a source of terror and at the same time of tremendous awe, of sublime interpretation (according to Burke), communicates a sense of the great power and destructive force of the wind, here understood as the "herald and bearer of catastrophe": this is the case with *The Fifth Plague of Egypt* (1800), *The Fall of an Avalanche in the Grisons* (1810), or even *Snow Storm* (1812), the storms and shipwrecks so dear to the artist's profoundly romantic interpretation. In contrast, there is also a positive interpretation of the action of the wind, closer to that creative function expressed by Shelley, i.e. a spatiality within which this element, here described according to an aesthetic-generative vision, actively participates in the definition of an atmosphere that could be defined as akin to the "Arcadian" vision, or perhaps better to the contents of the "picturesque" landscape, examples of which can be found in the works of the other famous English landscape painter, John Constable[21] (1776-1837). The wind's motion, which establishes an almost "harmonious" relationship with the other elements that compose the landscape, is presented through certain natural and cultural details: the rippling waves[22], represented in a "particular position"[23], the clouds present even in the mildest atmospheres, which testify, with their dynamism and volubility of form, to the incidence

20 Michael Bockemühl, *J.M.W. Turner (1775-1851). The World of Light and Colour*, *op. cit.*, p. 11.

21 The Romantic panorama of English painting is characterised by the presence of two exponents, Turner and Constable, who use a different method of investigation, the former more closely linked to a catastrophic, abominable, tragic vision of nature, the latter concentrating on a more moderate approach, still imbued with elements of the picturesque, even though it contrasts with earlier representational techniques. Cf. F. Caroli, *Il volto e l'anima della natura*, Oscar Mondadori, Milano 2010, pp. 68-69; G. Gatt, *Constable*, Sadea/Sansoni Editori, Firenze 1968; R. Milani, *L'arte del paesaggio*, Il Mulino, Bologna 2001.

22 Cf. M. Bockemühl, *op. cit.*, p. 22. The reproduction of a moving wave, a "turbolent wave", is very complex because its representation, as it swells or falls, is the result of a temporal fragment that suggests its direction, but which cannot, according to Bockemühl, be considered actual motion. A visual comparison with Turner's work *Waves Breaking against the Wind* (1840), an oil paint on canvas preserved at the Tate Gallery (London), might be useful to better understand this concept. The process of wave formation, a natural result of the rippling of the water's surface caused by the wind, is also a recurring theme in Thoreau's critical reading of his experience near Walden.

23 *Ibidem*. In the Italian translation, the author uses the term "atteggiamento" (attitude) to explain the movement of waves.

– or as Muir would say – the "caresses" of the breeze, or again, the presence of objects and instruments, such as sails hoisted and propelled by the wind, or in the case of terrestrial representations, the depiction of windmills and the curvatures of tree trunks and crowns[24].

If the wind's motion can already be observed in the European sphere, especially in the English cultural reality, as a positive or negative presence of landscape painting and poetic essence, it will only be in the circle of *American Nature Writing* that a further deepening of this aesthetic theme (whose air-water dichotomy is enriched by a third spatiality, the forest) will be felt, specifically in the reflections of Henry David Thoreau (1817-1862) and John Muir (1838-1914). In line with the ideals of his mentor Ralph Waldo Emerson[25] (1803-1882), Thoreau is currently regarded

24 Turner's participation, on a par with English poets, in the cultural and scenic wonders that characterised the stops on the *Grand Tour* is well known. In the long *iter* across the peninsula, there are particularly sought-after destinations (think of Rome, the ancient cities being rediscovered around Vesuvius volcano, the incredible light that envelops Venice), but also lesser-remembered places whose uniqueness greatly influences the aesthetic perception of artists and writers. On the importance of the stay in Etruria, as a recognized stopover frequented by prominent figures of the time such as Turner and the famous Russian writer Nicolaj Vasil'evič Gogol (1809-1852), see: G. Buzi, *William Turner in Etruria, op. cit.*

25 It might be interesting to mention a passage from Emerson included as a note in Franco Meli's contribution dedicated to Thoreau: "It was a pleasure and a privilege to walk with him. He knew the country like a fox or a bird, and passed through it as freely by paths of his own… One must submit abjectly to such a guide, and the reward was great… His power of observation seemed to indicate additional senses. He saw as with microscope, heard as with ear trumpet, and his memory was a photographic register of all he saw and heard". F. Meli, *H.D. Thoreau, ovvero l'escursionismo come modello di vita e genere letterario*, in H.D. Thoreau, *Camminare*, ed. by F. Meli, transl. by M.A. Prina, SE, Milano 1989, pp. 63-80, here p. 65 (Italian translation of *Walking* (1862)). This citation also highlights another perspective within which the vitality of the wind can be seen, namely the interest (already present in English poetics) in animals, especially ornithology. It is then not so coincidental that, in addition to pikes, perches, and other small woodland dwellers, Thoreau focusses in his description of "a very slight and graceful hawk, like a night-hawk, alternately soaring like a ripple and tumbling a rod or two over and over, showing the underside of its wings, which gleamed like a satin ribbon in the sun […]. It was the most ethereal flight I had ever witnessed. It did not simply flutter like a butterfly, nor soar like the larger hawks, but it sported with proud reliance in the fields of air; mounting again and again with its strange chuckle, it repeated its free and beautiful fall, turning over and over like a kite, and then recovering from its lofty tumbling, as if it had never set its foot on *terra firma*. […] The tenant of the air, it seemed related to the earth but by an egg hatched some time in the crevice of a crag; – or was its native nest

as the leading exponent of the American Transcendentalist group[26]. The philosophical and poetic approach he develops can be described as "eco-aesthetic", as it aims to act in defence of Nature, long disfigured by the consequences of modern progress, without, however, neglecting the deep connection between it and the survival of society.

His thought is strongly discernible in a passage from the essay *Walking* (1862):

> My spirits infallibly rise in proportion to the outward dreariness. Give me the ocean, the desert, or the wilderness! […] When I would recreate myself, I seek the darkest wood, the thickest and most interminable and, to the citizen, the most dismal swamp. I enter a swamp as a sacred place – a *sanctum sanctorum*. There is the strength, the marrow of Nature. […] A man's health requires as many acres of meadow to his prospect as his farm does loads of muck. […] A town is saved, not more by the righteous men in it than by the woods and swamps that surround it.[27]

This aim drives him to seek out and want to preserve the *Wilderness* which becomes strongly felt in his experience near Concord at Lake Walden (Massachusetts) between July 1845 and September 1847. The method of investigation theorised by Thoreau stands in continuity with European models – concerning Alexander von Humboldt – but, at the same time, attempts to go beyond them. Again, in *Walking*, he justifies the need for such a decision in an explicit passage: in the authors of the Old World "there is plenty of genial love of Nature, but not so much of Nature herself"[28]. For Thoreau, the function of the poetic word is to capture the "*Expression*"[29],

---

made in the angle of a cloud, woven of the rainbow's trimmings and the sunset sky, and lined with some soft midsummer haze caught up from earth? Its eyry now some cliffy cloud". H.D. Thoreau, *Walden* (1854), edited by S. Fender, Oxford University Press, Oxford 2008 (1° ed. 1997), pp. 281-282.

26 Cf. F. Meli, *H.D. Thoreau, ovvero l'escursionismo come modello di vita e genere letterario*, in H.D. Thoreau, *Camminare*, *op. cit.*, p. 65.

27 H.D. Thoreau, *Walking* (1862), *op. cit.*, pp. 189-90.

28 Ivi, p. 194.

29 *Ibidem*. "Expression" – in Thoreau's language – or perhaps "essence", "atmosphere". It might be important to reflect on what is presented in *Walking*, or on the descriptions given in *Walden* and Muir's work, and the definition suggested by Tonino Griffero: "atmosphere, first of all, is a colloquial term meaning a "something more" one feels "in the air" without being able to precisely express it – let alone rationally explain it. […] [atmosphere is] a feeling or affect that, being not private and internal but objectively and spatially spread out, "tinctures" the situation in which the perceiver happens to be and affectively involves her". Cf. T. Griffero, *Atmosphere*, in *International Lexicon of Aesthetics*, vol.1, Mimesis

and to do this the poet must be able to "impress the winds and streams into his service, to speak for him"[30]. There are two parametres for reading the experience near the "Lake of Light"[31]: "sunlight" and "wind". In doing so, the latter acquires a fundamental role in philosophical thought, placed at the border between culture and nature and aimed at the intellectual growth of the individual who participates in it:

> Living much out of doors, in the sun and wind, will no doubt produce a certain roughness of character – will cause a thicker cuticle to grow over some of the finer qualities of our nature [...]. Perhaps we should be more susceptible to some influences important to our intellectual and moral growth, if the sun had shone and the wind blown on us a little less.[32]

But it also acts as a ubiquitous element and tool for a reading of the natural atmosphere specific to Walden, within which the author consciously immerses himself in solitude, a choice that enables him to approach nature in a way that seems at times to echo Rousseau: "The indescribable innocence and beneficence of Nature – of sun and wind and rain, of summer and winter, – such health, such cheer, they afford forever!"[33]. The intense perception, the intimate dialogue with nature, within which he took refuge, is developed precisely in the increasingly profound and vivid descriptions he gives of the seasons he spent in his small self-built refuge ("It was worth the while to see the sun shine on these things, and hear the free wind blow on them; so much more interesting most familiar objects look out of doors than in the house"[34]), and especially in the transcriptions of the walks during which he actively participated in the seasonal atmospheric changes: "when I had once gone through the wind blew the oak leaves into my tracks, where they lodged, and by absorbing the rays of the sun melted the snow, and so not only made a dry bed for my feet, but in the night their dark line was my guide"[35]. The continuity with the European tradition can be perceived in the resumption of the water-wind dimension, the central motif of the fragments relating to the walks:

Edizioni, Milano-Udine 2022, pp. 77-81, here p. 77; T. Griffero, *Estetica patica. Appunti per un'atmosferologia neofenomenologica,* in "Studi di Estetica", anno XLII, IV serie, 1-2/2014, pp. 161-183, here p. 179.

30 H.D. Thoreau, Walking (1862), *op. cit.*, p. 194.

31 H.D. Thoreau, *Walden, op. cit.*, p. 180.

32 H.D. Thoreau, *Walking* (1862), *op. cit.*, p. 167.

33 H.D. Thoreau, *Walden, op. cit.*, p. 126.

34 Ivi, p. 104.

35 Ivi, p. 229.

> As I walk along the stony shore of the pond in my shirt sleeves, though it is cool as well as cloudy and windy, and I see nothing special to attract me, all the elements are unusually congenial to me. [...] The note of the whippoorwill is borne on the rippling wind from over the water. [...] Though it is now dark, the wind still blows and roars in the wood, the waves still dash, and some creatures lull the rest with their notes.[36]

Particularly when exploring the lake and observing the organisms that inhabit it (he refers here to small perches):

> In such transparent and seemingly bottomless water, reflecting the clouds, I seemed to be floating through the air as in a balloon, and their swimming impressed me as a kind of flight or hovering, as if they were a compact flock of birds passing just beneath my level on the right or left, their fins, like sails, set all around them.[37]

The search for *Wilderness* and the need for total immersion in nature are two factors common to the work of John Muir, author of one of the most famous volumes entirely dedicated to the items that compose and characterize the mountain landscape of the Sierra, namely *The Mountains of California,* published in 1894, followed by *My First Summer in the Sierra* (1911). As with Thoreau's lagoon experience, Muir settles down for two years in a cabin in the Yosemite Valley, where, in addition to various studies, he walks assiduously[38]. For Muir, too, the experience of nature is articulated in a vision:

> Viva e mutevole del paesaggio naturale della Sierra nel tentativo di immortalare sulla pagina scritta quei "*beautiful fragments*" che i suoi sensi, tutti, percepiscono: la prima luce del mattino che incontra le sommità dei monti, un cielo colmo di torreggianti nubi, i gesti e i suoni degli alberi ondeggianti al vento, gli effluvi e gli aromi trasportati dalla brezza.[39]

A reality, as described by Muir, which not only aims to respond to an idealistic defence of nature, but which will lead towards the end of the century to the first active attempt to protect American natural areas[40]. The

36 Ivi, p. 118.
37 Ivi, p. 171.
38 Cf. L. Castelletti, *Introduzione*, in John Muir, *Una tempesta di vento nella foresta*, *op. cit.*, p. 8.
39 Ivi, pp. 11-12.
40 It is important to remember that Muir's work stands not only as a literary and eco-aesthetic model for interpreting the landscape, in this case the *Wilderness*, but

dynamism of the wind, captured in its universality and omnipresence, is expressed at the beginning of the chapter *A Wind-storm in the Forests*, from a perspective that describes its variable aspects concerning the terrestrial, wooded sphere:

> The mountain winds, like the dew and the rain, sunshine and snow, are measured and bestowed with love on the forests to develop their strength and beauty. However restricted the scope of other forest influences, that of the winds is universal. […] But the winds go to every tree, fingering every leaf and branch and furrowed bole; not one is forgotten; the Mountain Pine towering with outstretched arms on the rugged buttresses of the icy peaks […] they [the winds] seek and find them all, caressing them tenderly, bending them in lusty exercise, stimulating their growth, plucking off a leaf or limb as required, or removing an entire tree or grove, now whispering and cooing through the branches like a sleepy child, now roaring like the ocean; the winds blessing the forests, the forests the winds, with ineffable beauty and harmony as the sure result.[41]

The wind's motion acquires, in some cases, a catastrophic, exterminating power, since its "force […] was such that the most steadfast monarch of them all rocked down to its roots"[42], a violence that the author witnesses from his "lofty perch"[43], where he feels "safe, and free to take the wind into [his] pulses and enjoy the excited forest"[44]; but on just as many occasions it appears as a gentle breeze, a breath capable of carrying "music" and "delicious fragrance"[45], aromas and pollen, for, says Muir, "Winds are advertisements of all they touch"[46], perhaps even of the essence of life. The

---

also as the first example of active defence of naturalistic areas (from which the National Monuments project would develop), for the protection and conservation of which he contributed to the foundation of the Sierra Club in 1892 and worked in close collaboration with Theodore Roosevelt (1858-1919), an understanding currently witnessed by a photographic document dating back to the early 1900s. The last decade of Nineteenth century saw the emergence of numerous protected areas, among which the Yosemite National Park is worth mentioning. Cf. Luca Castelletti, *Introduzione*, in John Muir, *Una tempesta di vento nella foresta*, *op. cit.*, pp. 10-11; P. Mazzarelli, *Postfazione*, in John Muir, *La mia prima estate sulla Sierra*, Keller Editore, Rovereto 2021, pp. 249-254.

41 J. Muir, *The Mountains of California* (1894), foreword by G. Ehrlich, Sierra Club Books, San Francisco 1989, p. 185.

42 Ivi, p. 189.

43 Ivi, p. 192.

44 Ivi, p. 191.

45 Ivi, p. 192.

46 Ivi, p. 193.

years spent in the vicinity of the Sierra (between 1868 and 1870) once again reveal an intense connection between the action of the wind and the fluidity of the water, so much so that one seems to flow into the characteristics of the other: "there is always something deeply exciting, not only in the sounds of winds in the woods, which exert more or less influence over every mind but in their varied waterlike flow as manifested by the movements of the trees, especially those of the conifers"[47]. He further adds:

> Most people like to look at mountain rivers, and bear them in mind; but few care to look at the winds, though far more beautiful and sublime, and though they become at times about as visible as flowing water. [...] And when we look around over an agitated forest, we may see something of the wind that stirs it, by its effects upon the trees. Yonder it descends in a rush of water-like ripples, and sweeps over the bending pines from hill to hill.[48]

If, on the one hand, the literary sphere finds in Thoreau and Muir exponents of great stature, on the other hand, an artistic reference is appropriate, here summarized by the work of the group of painters known as the *Hudson River School*[49], and, specifically, the artist who was best able to translate the elements discussed so far by reproducing on canvas those windy, spatial, uncontaminated atmospheres so dear to naturalists. It is therefore with a glance at the work of Albert Bierstadt (1830-1902) that these reflections conclude, a pictorial interpretation whose content recalls and consecrates the research, elements and tones of the windblown atmospheres of the Nineteenth century.

47 Ivi, p. 187.

48 Ivi, pp. 193-194.

49 The Hudson River School, founded by Thomas Cole in the first half of the Nineteenth century, stands as the highest pictorial expression of American landscape research of the period. Among the numerous exponents who collaborated in his stylistic elevation was the artist Albert Bierstadt, who not only shared Muir's Old-World origin (Muir was of Scottish origin, Bierstadt German), but also had a keen interest in the Sierra Nevada, of which he left numerous testimonies in memory of his mid-century voyage here. Cf. B.D. Yaeger, *The Hudson River School. American Landscape Artists*, Smithmark Publishers, New York 1996; K. Manthorne, T. Laughlin Bloom (ed. by), *The Rockies and the Alps: Bierstadt, Calame, and the Romance of the Mountains*, exhibition catalog (Newark Museum, 24th March-19th August 2018), D Giles Ltd, London 2018.

Raffaella Viccei

Le Vent à Djémila

The Ruins of a Roman City in Africa and the Wind by Albert Camus

1. *Djemila in the 1930s and the voyage of Albert Camus*

"Pour un 'Romain' en mission en Algérie, pour un archéologue en séjour à Djemila, comme pour un touriste qui n'y fut que le temps d'une visite, évoquer le souvenir de ce site – un des plus beaux d'Afrique du Nord – c'est aussitôt penser à Yvonne Allais"[1]: the archaeologists Jean Lassus and Marcel Le Glay thus began their remembrance of their recently deceased colleague. Yvonne Allais (1891-1981) came to Algiers in 1925 to teach at *Lycée de jeunes filles d'Alger*. She began working at the archaeological site of Djemila immediately and with such passion that she lived in symbiosis with the ruins, almost identifying herself with the Numidian colony founded by the Romans, called Cuicul in Berber and Djemila in Arabic. This word meaning "la Belle" well expresses "le charme et la séduction"[2] exerted

1 J. Lassus, M. Le Glay, *In memoriam. Yvonne Allais (1891-1981)*, in "Antiquités africaines", n. 18, 1982, p. 7.

2 J. Lassus, M. Le Glay, *op. cit.*, p. 8. The French conquest of Algeria marked the beginning of the discovery of ancient Cuicul: the first plan of the ruins, drawn by the architect and archaeologist Bonaventure-Amable Ravoisié, dates from 1840. Excavations in the 19th and especially in the first decades of the 20th century revealed Cuicul's rich archaeological heritage, reflecting this city's key role in the Mediterranean. Regarding this Roman colony, established for strategic, administrative and commercial reasons, regarding the history of the discovery and excavations, the restoration of monuments: N. Duval, Ğemila, in *Enciclopedia dell'Arte Antica*, Treccani, 1994, III, p. 806, p. 806; N. Duval, *Djémila*, in *Encyclopédie berbère*, n. 16, 1995, pp. 2442-2449; N. Abderrahim Zirout, *Le site antique de Djemila (Algérie). Entre découverte et approche de valorisation*, in "Annales d'Université "Valahia" Târgovişte. Section d'Archéologie et d'Histoire", a. XXII, 2020, pp. 47-67 https://www.persee.fr/doc/valah_1584-1855_2020_num_22_1_1440; *T. Soubira, B. Lhoyer, Histoire de la recherche à Djemila, février 2021,* https://taa.africa/histoire-de-la-recherche-a-djemila.html; *T. Soubira, B. Lhoyer, Cuicul/Djemila, février 2021,* https://taa.africa/djemila.html, also for the bibliography. About Djemila UNESCO site: https://whc.unesco.org/en/list/191/; https://www.unesco.cc/djemila.htm.

by this city of Africa. The fruit of Allais's labour was the monograph *Djemila*[3], published in 1938 by the prestigious publisher *Les Belles Lettres*; the *avant-propos* was written by the *Directeur des Antiquités de l'Algérie*, Eugène Albertini, who in the same year printed, with Louis Leschi[4], the book *Djemila, Cuicul de Numidie. Toute une cité de l'Afrique romaine*[5]. In addition to the archaeological remains, especially those testifying to the apogee of Cuicul at the time of the Severans (193-235 A.D.)[6], Allais, Albertini and Leschi had also paid attention to geography and climate of Djemila, showing how much one and the other had conditioned the Roman colonisers' choice of location, the configuration and development of the site[7].

Reading their pages, like those of journalistic reportage, it is clear that Djemila was also enchanting for the landscape, for the nature that had taken possession of the abandoned architecture, for the Arab *gourbis* settled among the ruins and vegetation, for certain atmospheres that made this place memorable: a polyphonic charm that touched the increasingly

3 Y. Allais, *Djemila*, Les Belles Lettres, Paris 1938.

4 J. Despois, *Louis Leschi 1893-1954*, in "Revue Africaine", 1954, pp. 27-40.

5 L. Leschi, E. Albertini, *Djemila, Cuicul de Numidie. Toute une cité de l'Afrique romaine*, F. Fontana, Alger 1938. Also: E. Albertini, *Le villes mortes. L'Afrique Romaine. Timgad. Djemila*, in "L'Afrique du Nord illustrée", n. s., a. XIX, n. 154, 12 Avril 1924, pp. 1-17: pp. 12-17 (Djemila).

6 Y. Allais, *op. cit.*, p. 24: "Cuicul a atteint son apogèe sous les Sévères [...] Petit ville, mais à l'aspect agréable: étagée sur les pentes de son promontoire, resserrée au Nord, largement étalée vers le Sud, l'agglomération épouse les formes du terrain sans souci de la symétrie. Les rues en pente ouvrent des perspectives variées sur les montagnes environnantes; ces rues sont propres, bien dallées, souvent bordées de colonnades [...]. Les deux vastes places ornées d'un peuple de statues, les portiques élégants, les majestueux édifices publics forment un ensemble empreint de noblesse et d'harmonie. Des fontaines placées aux principaux carrefours ajoutent le charme de leurs eaux jaillissantes à la beauté des masses architecturales. Les maisons particulières, dont les pièces plus ou moins nombreuses entourent une cour centrale, sont parfois aménagées avec une certaine recherche de luxe et de confort".

7 Djemila lies in a mountainous area (h. 850 m), more than 300 km south-east of Algiers, not far from the coast. It is on a narrow triangular plateau, gently sloping down to the confluence of two streams, traces of which remain in the *uidiàn*. Bare rocky mountains and changing colours envelop the city. The landscape "sévère" (Y. Allais, *op. cit.*, p. 8) at various times of the year is clothed in rich vegetation. The sun is blazing and, in winter, the mountains are covered in snow; the air is pure and healthy (Y. Allais, *op. cit.*, pp. 7-10. L. Leschi, *Djemila, antique Cuicul*, Alger 1953[3], pp. 17-18, 34).

numerous tourists[8], and which had also affected Albert Camus[9] from his first excursions in the mid-1930s when, in the company of friends, had spent a few Sundays in and around Djemila.

In the spring of 1937, Camus returned to Djemila: he arrived there not by car, as usual, and faced a particularly tiring journey[10], but aboard a small aeroplane piloted by Marie Viton[11]. With his friend, he spent a special day, which would inspire him to the dazzling pages of *Le Vent à Djémila*[12]. The

8 Since the 1920s, thanks to the official opening of the archaeological site in 1925, thanks to events (H. C., *Les fêtes de Djemila*, in "L'Afrique du Nord illustrée", n. s., a. XX, n. 231, 3 Octobre 1925, pp. 4-5) and publications, the ruins of Djemila were a popular destination for travellers who were even prepared to "subir le supplice de la route Alger-Bouïra pour se rendre à Djemila" (*Le tourisme et nos routes*, in "L'Afrique du Nord illustrée", n. s., a. XIX, n. 180, 11 Octobre 1924, p. 5).

9 Camus bibliography (1913-1960) is endless. For a comprehensive overview, at least: O. Todd, *Albert Camus: A Life*, Chatto & Windus, London 1997 (*Albert Camus: une vie* Gallimard, Paris 1996); E. J. Hughes (ed.), *The Cambridge Companion to Camus*, Cambridge University Press, Cambridge 2007; J. Guérin (éd.), *Dictionnaire Albert Camus*, R. Laffont, Paris 2009; R. Zaretsky, *Albert Camus. Elements of a Life*, Cornell University Press, Ithaca and London; R. Gay-Crosier, A. Spiquel Courdille (éd.), *Albert Camus*, Édition de l'Herne, Paris 2013; J. Herbeck, V. Grégoire, *A Writer's Topography: Space and Place in the Life and Works of Albert Camus*, Brill, Leiden Boston 2015; C. Hermans, *The Algerian*, in C. Hermans, *Interbellum Literature. Writing in a Season of Nihilism*, Brill, Leiden 2017, pp. 9-28; website of *SEC-Société des Études Camusiennes* https://www.etudes-camusiennes.fr/. Essential works: A. Camus, *OEuvres complètes, I: 1931-1944*, Gallimard, Paris 2006; Albert Camus, *OEuvres complètes, II: 1944-1948*, Gallimard, Paris 2006; A. Camus, *OEuvres complètes, III: 1949-1956*, Gallimard, Paris 2008; A. Camus, *OEuvres complètes, IV: 1957-1959*, Gallimard, Paris 2008.

10 Camus mentions to the difficulty of the route in *Le vent à Djèmila*: "Il faut beacoup de temps pour aller à Djémila. […] La ville morte est au terme d'une longue route en lacet qui semble la promettre à chacun de ses tournants et paraît d'autant plus longue" (Albert Camus, *OEuvres complètes, I, op. cit.*, pp. 111-112).

11 Z. Abdelkrim, *Noces. Notice*, in Albert Camus, *OEuvres complètes, I, op. cit.*, pp. 1230, 1236. Regarding Marie Viton, amateur airline pilot and, above all, theatre costume designer and painter: P.-F. Astor, *La créativité et l'effacement dans l'entourage féminin d'Albert Camus*, in L. Bergès (éd.), *La construction du grand auteur*. Actes du 134e Congrès national des sociétés historiques et scientifiques, "Célèbres ou obscurs : hommes et femmes dans leurs territoires et leur histoire", Bordeaux, 2009, Editions du CTHS, Paris 2011, pp. 9-20. https://www.persee.fr/doc/acths_1764-7355_2011_act_134_7_2041.

12 Text of *Le Vent à Djémila*: Albert Camus, *OEuvres complètes, I, op. cit.*, pp. 111-116.

essai[13], which also has some traits from *cahier de voyage*, was published, with *Noces à Tipasa* (first essay)[14], *L'Été à Alger* (third), *Le Désert* (fourth and last), in the collection *Noces*, drafted in 1936, written in 1937-1938, published in a few copies in May 1939 by the Algerian publisher Edmond Charlot[15].

Regarding the Roman city Camus mentions "les restes des maisons, grandes rues dallées sous les colonnes luisantes, forum immense entre l'arc de triomphe et le temple sur une éminence"[16]; because he was impressed, he dwells on the detail of "le visage vivant d'un dieu à cornes au fronton d'un autel"[17]; he mentions the Christian area, quoting the words of a guide through which he shows interest in the Christian remains revealing transformations of the pagan city: "Ici se trouve la ville païenne; ce quartier qui se pousse hors des terres, c'est celui des chrétiens. Plus

13 According to the definition by Camus: A. Camus, *Carnets 1935-1948*, in Albert Camus, *OEuvres complètes, II, op. cit.*, p. 814. Also, Z. Abdelkrim, *op. cit.*, p. 1227.

14 Jacques Heurgon had dedicated research and an essay to Tipasa: *Nouvelles recherches à Tipasa, ville de Maurétanie césarienne*, in "Mélanges de l'École Française de Rome", a. XLVII, 1930, pp. 182-201.

15 Z. Abdelkrim, *op. cit.*, pp. 1228, 1233-1234. The first lines of *Le Vent à Djémila* were anticipated at the beginning of 1939 in the magazine Mithra (no. 2, January-February 1939). Regarding *Le Vent à Djémila*: K. Stephenson, *The Signifying Decor in Camus' "The Wind at Djémila"*, in "The American Journal of Semiotics", 1985, pp. 357-365; J. W. Brown, *'Sensing', 'seeing', 'staying' in Camus' Noces: A Meditative Essay*, Brill, Leiden-Boston 2004, pp. 35-38, 65-78, 82-83; V. Turra, *Albert Camus, figure dell'antico. Il mito di fronte all'assurdo*, Edizioni Fiorini, Verona 2010, pp. 66-69.

16 A. Camus, *OEuvres complètes, I, op. cit.*, p. 111. Comparing textual segments, Camus' very brief description seems to echo Allais' detailed one (*op. cit.*, especially pp. 21-22, 24) regarding the sequence of structures and monuments (from the Severan age) and certain expressions: "les maisons" (p. 21), "[...] de nouvelles entrées monumentales donnèrent aussi accès au forum des Sévères ; la plus majesteueuse était formée par l'arc triomphal [...]. Dressé au sommet d'un perron très élevé, le sanctuaire dominait toute la ville" (p. 22), "ces rues sont propres, bien dallées, souvent bordées de colonnades" (p. 23). Now, "[b]ien que la composition" of *Le Vent à Djémila* "en soit achevée pour la majeure partie en juin 1937 (date figurant sur *dactyl. 3*), les rectificatis ultérieurs révèlent un texte souvent remis sur le métier" (Z. Abdelkrim, *op. cit.*, p. 1236): so Camus' reading of Y. Allais, *op. cit.* and/or of L. Leschi, E. Albertini, *op. cit.*, during the revision process of the essay cannot be ruled out, as well as the editing of *Le Vent*, on the basis of one or both books, relating to the part limited to the ruins. The photos of the city's remains published in the aforementioned 1938 books by Allais, Leschi and Albertini are valuable to get an idea of Djemila as seen by Camus.

17 A. Camus, *OEuvres complètes, I, op. cit.*, p. 116.

tard… "[18]. The 1937 *voyage* to Djemila and Camus' previous visits to other Algerian archaeological sites[19] are part of the interest alive in the 1930s in the fascination-filled rediscovery of ancient Roman cities. However, what prompted the young Albert to see these sites were stimuli and motivations that were in substance different from the more common ones and certainly contrasting with the reading of the archaeological remains of the Roman Empire that was most widespread at the time: a reading aimed at historically and culturally legitimising European imperialist and colonial policies perpetrated in Africa (and beyond) in the opening decades of the 20th century[20].

In Camus, the desire to visit 'dead cities' and the need to write about them date back to crucial years in his intellectual and cultural formation and are linked to fundamental encounters: among these, the encounter with Jacques Heurgon[21] and, above all, the indelible one with Jean Grenier[22]. Two works by Grenier were essential for the Camus of the 1930s and of *Noces*: *Les îles* (1933) and *Santa Cruz et autres paysages africains* (1937). Among Grenier's *paysages africains* appears, along with Tipasa, Djemila[23], and along with Tipasa, Djemila will appear soon afterwards in *Noces*.

---

18 Ivi, p. 115. *On the Christian ruins*, Y. Allais, *op. cit.*, pp. 28-30, 57-62.

19 I think especially of Tipasa. *Infra*, paragraph 2: *Le Vent à Djémila* in *Noces* (1939).

20 With regard to this issue, see for example: M. Munzi, *L'Epica del ritorno: archeologia e politica nella Tripolitania italiana*, L'Erma di Bretschneider, Roma 2001; N. Oulebsir, *Les usages du patrimoine. Monuments, musées et politique coloniale en Algérie (1830-1930)*, Éditions de la Maison des sciences de l'homme, Paris 2004; S. Troilo, *Pietre d'oltremare. Scavare, conservare, immaginare l'impero (1899-1940)*, Laterza, Roma-Bari 2021.

21 Camus was bound to Heurgon not only for university reasons (he was his student at the *Faculté des lettres d'Alger* in 1934), but also by a deep friendship and sharing of ideas, ideals, passions – above all, theatre –. R. Gay-Crosier, A. Spiquel Courdille (éd.), *op. cit.*, pp. 160-170.

22 Camus' philosophy professor at the *Grand Lycée d'Alger*. Camus had a deep, lifelong, and elective bond with Jean Grenier. J. Grenier, *Albert Camus. Souvenirs*, Gallimard, Paris 1968; L. Cammarano, *Jean Grenier y Albert Camus*, in "Diálogos: Artes, Letras, Ciencias humanas", a. XII, n. 5, 1976, pp. 7-11; A. Camus, J. Grenier, *Correspondence (1932-1960)*, Gallimard, Paris 1981; T. Garfitt, *Situating Camus: the formative influences*, in E. J. Hughes (ed.), *The Cambridge Companion to Camus*, Cambridge University Press, Cambridge 2007, pp. 26-38.

23 Regarding the influence of *Les îles* (1933) and *Santa Cruz et autres paysages africains* in *Noces*: Z. Abdelkrim, *op. cit.*, p. 1229; P.-L. Rey, *Noces*, in J. Guérin, *op. cit.*, pp. 616-620; T. Garfitt, *op. cit.*, pp. 30-32.

2. *Le Vent à Djémila in Noces (1939)*

Camus devoted himself to the conception and writing of *Le Vent à Djémila* in 1937, between April, when in the *Carnets* notes "Pour l'essai sur les ruines: Le vent desséchant – le vieil homme aussi dénudé qu'un olivier du Sahel. 1) Essai sur les ruines: le vent dans les ruines ou la mort au soleil […]"[24], and June; he would then review the *essai* before releasing it in 1939[25].

The little more than 20-year-old Albert wrote the essays that make up *Noces* driven by a "force de vie, éclatante"[26] and accompanied, in the *voyages*, by the voices of life (and death) echoing among the ruins of Tipasa (*Noces à Tipasa*) and Djemila (*Le Vent à Djémila*), that re-echoed in Algiers (*L'Été à Alger*) and in Italy – between Fiesole, Florence, Pisa – (*Le Désert*); accompanied by the voice of "ceux qui ont compris", like Jacques Heurgon and especially Jean Grenier, to whom he dedicated respectively *L'Été à Alger* and *Le Désert*. The four essays are linked by a *fil rouge* stated in the title *Noces*: the 'wedding' between man and world, which is sun, sea, sky, wind, olive trees, earth, birds[27]. This connection is crossed and questioned by Camus, who is eager to harmonise with it, especially through the senses and memory. The expression of the emotions and thoughts that arise from such explorations is entrusted by the author of *Noces* to physical and lyrical writing. More precisely: the priority Camus gives to the symbiosis with nature – a symbiosis stretched between happiness and the cognition of being in the world as mortals – requires a writing of *fusion*, on the one hand capable of describing the experience of the I-Camus (in which "l'écrivain et l'être ne se dissocient pas"[28])

24 A. Camus, *Carnets 1935-1948*, *op. cit.*, p. 814.

25 For *Le Vent à Djémila* "[o]n dispose de cinq documents dactylographiés grâce auxquels nous pouvons reconstituer trois versions successives pour cet essai. Seuls nous intéressent les dactylogrammes corrigés à la main par Camus (*dactyl. 1*, *dactyl. 2*, *dactyl. 3*). Il existe aussi un manuscrit de 5 feuillets, très difficilement déchiffrable […]. De tous les essais pour lesquels nous avons pu consulter des dactylogrammes, "Le Vent à Djémila" est celui qui a subi les retouches les plus notables […]", Z. Abdelkrim, *op. cit.*, p. 1236.

26 Z. Abdelkrim, *Noces (1939)* https://www.etudes-camusiennes.fr/noces-1938/.

27 Regarding *Noces*, see especially: M. Monte, *Sobriété et profusion: une rhétorique du paysage dans Noces et L'été* d'Albert Camus, in "*Babel*", n. 7, 2003, pp. 230-254; J. W. Brown, *op. cit.*; P. Dunwoodie, *From Noces to L'Etranger*, in E. J. Hughes (ed.), *The Cambridge Companion to Camus*, Cambridge University Press, Cambridge 2007, in particular, pp. 147-156; A. Quinney, *Albert Camus' Algerian Honeymoon*, in "South Central Review", a. XXXI, n. 3, 2014, pp. 72-81.

28 J. Lévi-Valensi, *Introduction*, in A. Camus, *op. cit.*, p. XII.

that merges and loses itself in the nature, on the other hand, capable of captivating the reader to the point of bringing him into the author's fusion and making him a participant in Nature and the Mediterranean landscapes with Camus himself.

In the 1930s, landscapes flooded by the sun and touched by the sea were at the centre of a cultural and philosophical vision that had its beating heart in the Mediterranean, in an idea of the Mediterranean well summed up by Zedjiga Abdelkrim[29]. Despite the references to this horizon, marked by tangencies and distances, *la pensée de Midi* and Camus' Mediterranean pages, including many from *Noces*, have several unique features[30]: the main one lies in the fact that the Mediterranean of the French-Algerian writer is a place not (only and not so much) literary or a place of the thought but a lived-in place, a place written on the skin; it is above all the place of the Algerian sky and sun that saw Albert come into the world, that saw his illness, his silent mother, the "main affectueuse" outstretched to the "petit enfant pauvre" by the primary school teacher Louis Germain, finally, the "enseignement" and the "exemple" of Germain without which "rien de tout cela ne serait arrivé"[31] – Camus recalls after receiving the Nobel Prize –.

Precisely because Camus experienced the Mediterranean, its nature and its atmosphere, he cannot help but speak of it. "Je ne suis pas un philosophe, en effet, et je ne sais parler que de ce que j'ai vécu"[32].

---

29 Z. Abdelkrim, *op. cit.*, pp. 1228-1230.

30 Among the many studies on Camus and the Mediterraneo, I would like to mention: P. Dunwoodie, *op. cit.*; J.-F. Mattéi (éd.), *Albert Camus et la pensée de Midi*, éd. Ovadia, Nice 2008; A. Baylee Toumi (éd.), *Albert Camus précurseur. Méditerranée d'hier et d'aujourd'hui*, Peter Lang, New York 2009; H. Rufat, *Du mythe à la rêverie méditerranéenne, autour d'Albert Camus*, in "*Caliban*", n. 58, 2017, pp. 269-282; S. Novello, *Albert Camus fenomenologo del Mediterraneo*, in A. Emina (a cura di), *Territori e Scenari. Ripensare il Mediterraneo*, in "Quaderni IRCrES-CNR", a. III, n. 2, 2018, pp. 35-53; Y. Fracassetti, *Camus e il Mediterraneo. Un desiderio di osmosi*, in A. Emina (a cura di), *Narrazioni del Secolo breve. Ripensare il Mediterraneo*, in "Quaderni IRCrES-CNR", a. III, n. 3, 2018, pp. 35-44.

31 Quote from the letter of 19 November 1957 written by Camus to his primary school teacher immediately after the Nobel. Albert Camus, *« Cher Monsieur Germain, ... » Lettres et extraits*, Gallimard, Paris 2022.

32 A. Camus, *Révolte et Romantisme*, in Albert Camus, *OEuvres complètes, III, op. cit.*, p. 411.

In the landscape suspended of the "ville morte"[33] of Djemila, surrounded by precipices[34], the man/ the I-Camus enters in "le cœur battant du monde"[35]: enters with his body – crucial in the pages of *Le Vent à Djémila* – touched, crossed, moulded by the wind[36] and the wind shows itself as a protagonist of felt-bodily resonances[37].

> The quasi-thingly felt-body is the resonance board of atmospheres and other quasi-things. This is achieved through a felt-bodily (*leiblich*) communication with any really salient object or form, starting from what we dwell in [...], up to the weather, atmospheric feelings and, in general, all *qualia* or *affordances* of the outside, whose intermodal analogousness is precisely grounded in existential and felt-bodily resonances. These resonances, highlighting once again the co-belonging of man and the environment (including other people), are an immediate grasping of outside affordances: in short, they are the answer to the valences of atmospheric spaces, and at the same time an estatic extension of the felt-body's own lived directions. Through this (anti-solipsistic by definition) felt-bodily communication, the body embodies not just its tools, but also all the things we experience in the pericorporeal space whose peculiar voluminosity we also sense [...][38].

3. *Camus's feeling for the wind in the ville morte of Djemila*

> Dans cette splendeur aride, nous avions erré toute la journée. Peu à peau, le vent à peine senti au début de l'après-midi, semblait grandir avec les heures et

33 A. Camus, *OEuvres complètes, I, op. cit.*, p. 111.

34 *Ibidem.*

35 Ivi, p. 112: "Djémila figure [...] le symbole de cette leçon d'amour et de patience qui peut seule nous conduire au cœur battant du monde".

36 Regarding themes, methods, issues: VENTI-journal. Air-Experience-Aesthetics https://www.venti-journal.com/all-issues. In particular, see: T. Griffero, *It Blows where it Wishes: The Wind as a Quasi-Thingly Atmosphere*, in "VENTI-journal. Air-Experience-Aesthetics", a. 1, n. 2, 2020, pp. 31-39, especially pp. 33-37. In addition: T. Griffero, *Atmospheres. Aesthetics of Emotional Spaces*, Ashgate, Farnham 2014 (now Routledge, London-New York); T. Griffero, *Quasi-things: The Paradigm of Atmospheres*, Albany NY, State University of New York 2017; T. Griffero, *Atmosferologia. Estetica degli spazi emozionali*, Mimesis, Sesto San Giovanni 2017[2], especially, paragraph 2.1 (Il paradigma climatico) regarding reflections on the wind; T. Griffero, *Being a Lived Body. From a Neo-phenomenological Point of View*, Routledge, London 2023.

37 T. Griffero, *Felt-Bodily Resonances: Towards a Pathic Aesthetics*, in "Yearbook for Eastern and Western Philosophy", n. 2, 2017, pp. 149-164.

38 T. Griffero, *Felt-Bodily Resonances*, *op. cit.*, p. 154.

remplir tout le paysage. Il soufflait depuis une trouée entre les montagnes, loin vers l'est, accourait du fond de l'horizon et venait bondir en cascades parmi les pierres et le soleil. Sans arrêt, il sifflait avec force à travers les ruines, tournait dans un cirque de pierres et de terre, baignait les amas de blocs grêlés, entourait chaque colonne de son souffle et venait se répandre en cris incessants sur le forum qui s'ouvrait dans le ciel. Je me sentais claquer au vent comme une mâture. Creusé par le milieu, les yeux brûlés, les lèvres craquantes, ma peau se desséchait jusqu'à ne plus être mienne. Par elle, auparavant, je déchiffrais l'écriture du monde. Il y traçait les signes de sa tendresse ou de sa colère, la réchauffant de son souffle d'été ou la mordant de ses dents de givre. Mais si longuement frotté du vent, secoué depuis plus d'une heure, étourdi de résistance, je perdais conscience du dessin que traçait mon corps. Comme le galet verni par les marées, j'étais poli par le vent, usé jusq'à l'âme. J'étais un peu de cette force selon laquelle je flottais, puis beaucoup, puis elle enfin, confondant les battements de mon sang et les grands coups sonores de ce cœur partout présent de la nature. Le vent me façonnait à l'image de l'ardente nudité qui m'entourait. Et sa fugitive étreinte me donnait, pierre parmi les pierres, la solitude d'une colonne ou d'un olivier dans le ciel d'été.

Ce bain violent de soleil et de vent épuisait toutes mes forces de vie. À peine en moi ce battement d'ailes qui affleure, cette vie qui se plaint, cette faible révolte de l'esprit. Bientôt, répandu aux quatre coins du monde, oublieux, oublié de moi-même, je suis ce vent et dans le vent, ces colonnes et cet arc, ces dalles qui sentent chaud et ces montagnes pâles autour de la ville déserte. Et jamais je n'ai senti, si avant, à la fois mon détachement de moi-même et ma présence au monde.[39]

The wind creeps unexpectedly into the arid splendour of Djemila. It touches landscape and ruins with a variety of movements and sounds. It interrupts the silence and performs an unwritten score all in crescendo. The play of the wind between nature and the dead city becomes a bittersweet yoke for Camus, for this traveller for a day, which gradually appears as an allegory of life. As sailors well know, the wind conditions the voyage, with its speed, direction and intensity: and not by chance Camus, in stopping the first instant of the hand-to-hand encounter with the wind, resorts to a similitude between himself and the mast of a ship at the mercy of the winds – "Je me sentais claquer au vent comme une mâture"[40]–.

The body is hollowed out by the wind and consumed down to the soul. The wind exerts several functions on the man-traveller: creative function, metamorphic function, it is bearer of a state of mind – "Le vent me façonnait à l'image de l'ardente nudité qui m'entourait. Et sa fugitive étreinte me

39 A. Camus, *OEuvres complètes*, *I*, *op. cit.*, p. 112.
40 A. Camus, *OEuvres complètes*, *I*, *op. cit.*, p. 112.

donnait, pierre parmi les pierres, la solitude d'une colonne ou d'un olivier dans le ciel d'été"[41]. The power of the wind, which is impossible to resist, makes Camus similar to the surrounding bare landscape and places this man-traveller of a day-life in a condition of vertical solitude, projected towards the sky: the solitude of a column or an olive tree.

The wind erases boundaries between man and world and allows it to be realised the "entente amoureuse de la terre et de l'homme délivré de l'humain"[42], as Camus will say in *Le Désert*. It is – writes well Katherine Stephenson – "the element that tips the scales back to a state of equilibrium, as indicated in the paragraph's final sentence where the relation between man, the site as ruins and the site as a natural landscape is clarified"[43].

The wind appears to be a true agent entity: as the main actor, it performs precise actions on the scene of a landscape of ruins. It is a *person*: a companion of a journey, which is also an exploration of the soul, among what remains of a centuries-old city; a companion of the I-Camus who declares, with lyrical lucidity, his own tension to merge with the wind, expresses his own will, which borders on necessity, to be wind, to "do feel at one with the wind"[44]. The union of body-nature/wind ignites and reinforces the conscious and far-sighted capacity for vision that cancels out the illusions of hope and creates, by contrast, "morts conscientes"[45]: to say yes to the acts of the wind, which smoothes and consumes to the soul ("j'étais poli par le vent, usé jusq'à l'âme"[46]), deprives one of body and self-awareness and removes any possible space for hope in the elsewhere.

The wind in Djemila is a powerful, solitary force, but it is also an allied force of the Mediterranean sun: "Lorsque je suis allé à Djémila, il y avait du vent et du soleil [...]"[47], Camus writes in the first lines of the essay, and this

41 A. Camus, *OEuvres complètes, I, op. cit.*, p. 112. In the first sentence there is an allusion to *Genesis* 1, 27 and *Genesis* 2, 7. M. Monte, *op. cit.*

42 A. Camus, *OEuvres complètes, I, op. cit.*, p. 133. M. Monte, *op. cit.*

43 K. Stephenson, *op. cit.*, p. 361, referring to the part from "Ce bain violent" to "présence au monde".

44 T. Griffero, *Felt-Bodily Resonances*, *op. cit.*, p. 155.

45 A. Camus, *OEuvres complètes, I, op. cit.*, p. 114. "Créer des morts conscientes, c'est diminuer la distance qui nous sépare du monde, et entrer sans joie dans l'accomplissement, conscient des images exaltantes d'un monde à jamais perdu. Et le chant triste des collines de Djémila m'enfonce plus avant dans l'âme l'amertume de cet enseignement", Albert Camus, *OEuvres complètes, I, op. cit.*, p. 115.

46 A. Camus, *OEuvres complètes, I, op. cit.*, p. 112.

47 A. Camus, *OEuvres complètes, I, op. cit.*, p. 111.

combination returns in other places[48]. The sun is an indispensable element of nature, and that of the Mediterranean in particular, and has always been present in the life of Camus: "je fus placé à mi-distance de la misère et du soleil. La misère m'empêcha de croire que tout est bien sous le soleil et dans l'histoire ; le soleil m'apprit que l'histoire n'est pas tout"[49].

In Djemila, "the sun and the wind bring to light the true signification of this place as a privileged site generating an experience of the paradox of the human condition – that it is man's very mortality which gives the ultimate meaning and value to life, that confronting death leads to a revitalization of his concrete experience of life"[50].

Sun, ruins, silence, sounds of footsteps and animal sounds, and wind inhabit Djemila. Here, the wind ignites a process of reduction/depletion, reflected in the desolation of the ancient city. It coincides with the moment of greatest fullness of life, of openness or presence to the world expressed by the image of the "splendeur aride"[51]. It is in deserts like Djémila, "lieux où meurt l'esprit pour que naisse une vérité qui est sa négation même"[52], as well as in front of his mother that Camus discovers that extreme deprivation – *dénuement* – uncovers all the richness of the world[53]. Under the actions of the wind, the ruins of the Roman Empire, which went even to Djemila with its "idée basse et ridicule de la grandeur" measured by the "surface qu'il couvrait", appear even more "la négation même" of the "idéal"[54] of eternity pursued by Rome's will to power. The "ville squelette" of Djemila does not trace on the sky – crossed by the plane in which Albert Camus

48 "Ce bain violent de soleil et de vent épusait toutes mes forces de vie" (Albert Camus, *OEuvres complètes, I, op. cit.*, p. 112), for example.

49 So in the *Préface* to *L'Envers et l'Endroit*: Albert Camus, *OEuvres complètes, I, op. cit.*, p. 32.

50 K. Stephenson, *op. cit.*, p. 361.

51 A. Camus, *OEuvres complètes, I, op. cit.*, p. 112. S. Novello, *op. cit.*, p. 43, n. 10.

52 A. Camus, *OEuvres complètes, I, op. cit.*, p. 111. Here, in the *incipit* of the *essai*, and elsewhere, Camus evokes Maurice Barrès and Charles Maurras, ideologues of *Action Française*, an influential extreme right-wing movement, with the aim of declaring his convinced distance from both. In particular, at the beginning of *Le Vent à Djémila*, "Il est des lieux […]", Camus takes up the title of chapter I of *La Colline inspirée* (1913) of Barrès – *Il est des lieux où souffle l'esprit* – but with opposite meaning. Regarding the cultural and ideological significance of the hill in Barrès' novel – that of Sion-Vaudémont in the Lorraine –, regarding the historical significance of Lorraine in the First World War and personal meaning – death of Camus' father in 1914, wounded in the Battle of the Marna –: S. Novello, *op. cit.*, p. 47; O. Todd, *op. cit.*, p. 14.

53 S. Novello 2018, *op. cit.*, p. 41.

54 A. Camus, *OEuvres complètes, I, op. cit.*, p. 115.

and Marie Viton leave the city, seeing it from above for the last time[55] – "les signes de la conquête et de l'ambition. Le monde finit toujours par vaincre l'histoire"[56]. The most iconic ruin from the history of this Empire in Djemila, namely "l'arc de triomphe" of the Severan dynasty, surrounded by "le vols blancs de pigeons"[57], clearly illustrates all of this.

Nature, therefore, remains, and the wind, which is one of the eternal faces of nature, is for Camus the only truth before the absurdity of life. Recognising the eternity, beauty and power of the wind (as of the sun, the sea, the sky), and accepting them, implies man's awareness of finitude. Conscious man says yes to the need for a life free of hope, namely of "résignation"[58], and free from its deception; says no to a world other than the only possible: the world where he lives and breathes, the world inhabited (also) by the wind.

In order to gain this awareness, the body must be reborn, re-mould itself: the wind plays a fundamental role for this regeneration. This vital force moves through the ruins of a city created and lived in by men and, like them, dead; it moves around Camus' body and on Camus' skin. In the wind and forged by it, man immerses himself in a *ville morte*, in a still space and time that are the image of nothingness beyond death. To the consciousness of this nothingness, the man-Camus comes (also) through walking in the wind in the "squelette jaunâtre" of Djémila, similar to a "forêt d'ossements"[59]. This experience of life, marked by the ruins and the wind, is one of those trials that offer man the opportunity to measure himself against death without lowering his gaze and without giving in to mirages that exile from the truth: "[...] les hommes meurent malgré leurs, malgré leur décors"[60]. The *voyage* in the dead city is to enter the breath of the world. In this infinite breath, which takes hold of the traces of man, of "les amas de blocs grêlés"[61] that are a sign and symbol of finite time and the precariousness of human life, Camus goes in search of the meaning of life. "Le vent, une des rares choses propres du monde"[62], is (also) an epiphany

55 "Car cette ville squelette, vue de si haut dans le soir finissant", Albert Camus, *OEuvres complètes*, *I*, *op. cit.*, p. 115.

56 A. Camus, *OEuvres complètes*, *I*, *op. cit.*, p. 115.

57 A. Camus, *OEuvres complètes*, *I*, *op. cit.*, p. 115.

58 So Camus, at the end of *L'Été à Alger*: "Car l'espoir, au contraire de ce qu'on croit, équivaut à la résignation. Et vivre, c'est ne pas se résigner" (Albert Camus, *OEuvres complètes*, *I*, *op. cit.*, p. 126)

59 A. Camus, *OEuvres complètes*, *I*, *op. cit.*, p. 112.

60 A. Camus, *OEuvres complètes*, *I*, *op. cit.*, p. 115.

61 A. Camus, *OEuvres complètes*, *I*, *op. cit.*, p. 112.

62 A. Camus, *Carnets 1935-1948*, *op. cit.*, p. 932.

of that breath and the man, in abandoning himself to the wind and allowing himself to be moulded by it to the point of being wind, comes to feel the "détachement" from himself and his "présence au monde"[63] with a great and unknown intensity.

At the end of *Le Vent à Djémila,* Camus takes up, and varies, some natural elements of the first lines[64]. At the end, the sprawl of the *ville morte*, with its columns, houses, with its forums, arches, temples, is summarised emblematically in the "visage vivant d'un dieu à cornes au fronton d'un autel"[65], namely in the image of a god sculpted by men who are no longer, inhabitants of a *ville* which is no longer. Well before the end of the journey, the wind had run its course in the Djemila of Albert Camus. The absence of the wind in the epilogue of the *essai* says that the wind, which has been inside the *ville morte*, inside its nature and its atmospheres, inside Camus, is also beyond and outside all of this: the wind absent in the epilogue, as opposed to the wind present at the beginning ("Lorsque je suis allè à Djémila, il y avait du vent et du soleil"[66]), is the knowable – so in one part of the *voyage* – that is unknowable – so in the rest – and, as such, the wind is the image of life.

4. *The wind beyond Djemila*

Camus writes the *essai* when the *voyage* is over: the wind of Djemila is therefore also the wind of the memory and is imprinted in the memory of the body that has been in the *ville morte*. Retracing this memory of a single day, Camus re-feels the wind on his skin, re-sees the wind, re-hears the voice of the wind in the ruins and mountains. In the *essai,* there is thus a double time: the time of the experience of the wind and of the concrete osmotic co-presence of man-wind, here and now; the time of remembrance. In this temporal dimension, the wind re-lives through, bodily/sensory and emotional memory, and through writing, which on the one hand is a way to share[67], on the other is the body's need and the body's desire: "Il me faut

63 A. Camus, *OEuvres complètes*, *I*, *op. cit.*, p. 112.

64 The initial "cris d'oiseaux" become "chant d'oiseaux", the "piétinement de chèvres" becomes "brefs ruissellements de chèvres", the "rumeurs venues du ciel" appear, at the end of the journey, "le crépuscule détendu et sonore", Albert Camus, *OEuvres complètes*, *I*, *op. cit.*, pp. 111, 116; Monte, *op. cit.*, p. 40 (online).

65 A. Camus, *OEuvres complètes*, *I*, *op. cit.*, p. 116.

66 Ivi, p. 111.

67 J. Lévi-Valensi, *op. cit.*, p. XV.

écrire comme il me faut nager, parce que mon corps l'exige", Camus writes as he begins thinking about *Noces*[68].

Djemila is not the only *ville morte* crossed by the wind, and it is not only there that Camus is touched by the wind: the same happens in other 'archaeological' sites in Algeria (Tipasa) and especially in Greece (particularly Athens and Mycenae)[69]. One could say that the wind suits the cities that were and are no more and, specifically, the cities that were born and developed under the sign of the two main Mediterranean civilisations, the Greek and Roman civilisations, which symbolise for Camus almost opposite ways of being Mediterranean. Beyond Djemila, Tipasa, Mycenae, and Athens, the wind blows in *Pour Némésis*. This poem, written by Camus in December 1959, a few days before his death, condenses poetically "la manière d'être au monde chez Camus"[70] and almost seems like a return to the youthful wind of Djemila.

> Dans le jour bref qui t'est donné, réchauffe et illumine, sans dévier de ta course.
> Des millions d'autres soleils viendront pour ton repos.
> Sous la dalle de la joie, le premier sommeil.
> Semé par le vent, moissonné par le vent, et cependant créateur, tel est l'homme, à travers les siècles, et fier
> [de vivre un seul instant].[71]

68 A. Camus, *Carnets 1935-1948*, *op. cit.*, p. 811. T. Regarding these concepts, Griffero, *Atmosferologia*, *op. cit.*

69 D. Leclair, *Le voyage en Grèce dans les Carnets d'Albert Camus: l'expression intime de la joie*, in A. Prouteau, A. Spiquel (éd.), *Lire les Carnets d'Albert Camus*, Villeneuve d'Ascq, Presses Universitaires du Septentrion, 2012, pp. 161-176; M.-T. Blondeau, *Jeu de miroirs: les paysages*, in A. Prouteau, A. Spiquel (éd.), *op. cit.*, pp. 133-145.

70 A. Lager, *Les Carnets ou la tentation du poétique*, in A. Prouteau, A. Spiquel (éd.), *Lire les Carnets d'Albert Camus*, *op. cit.*, pp. 83-98, see, in particular, the paragraph *Dompter l'être* (pp. 35-41 online) and p. 37, for the quotation.

71 *Pour Némésis (*à Lourmarin, décembre 59): A. Camus, *OEuvres complètes, IV*, *op. cit.*, p. 1304. R. L. de Araújo, *Albert Camus et la poétique de Némésis*, in "Loxias", LIV, 2016. http://revel.unice.fr/loxias/index.html?id=8451.

Swaantje Otto

The Beginning of *Andenken*

Der Nordost wehet

1.1 *Research Overview*

Among the numerous research papers on *Andenken*, the poem has six extended interpretations.[1] Most of them, with the exception of Reuß's work, do not analyze and interpret the poem's meter.[2] As a result some possible interpretations of individual verses and basic ideas, such as the sympathy (Mitempfinden) of poetic *Andenken* in relation to Susette

1 M. Heidegger, *Gesamtausgabe. II. Abteilung. Vorlesungen 1923-1944. Bd. 52. Hölderlins Hymne Andenken. Freiburger Vorlesung Wintersemester 1941/42*, Klostermann, Frankfurt a.M. 1982⁴. R. Zuberbühler, *Hölderlins Erneuerung der Sprache aus ihren etymologischen Ursprüngen*, Erich Schmidt Verlag, Berlin 1969. J. Schmidt, *Hölderlins letzte Hymnen. Andenken und Mnemosyne*, Niemeyer, Tübingen 1970. D. Henrich, *Der Gang des Andenkens. Beobachtungen und Gedanken zu Hölderlins Gedicht*, Klett-Cotta, Stuttgart 1986. R. Reuß, "… *Die eigene Rede des anderen*". *Hölderlins Andenken und Mnemosyne*, Stroemfeld, Frankfurt a.M. 1990. T. Poiss, *Momente der Einheit: Interpretationen zu Pindars Epinikion und Hölderlins Andenken. Wiener Studien Beihefte* 18, H. Böhlaus, Wien 1993.

2 W. Binder, *Hölderlin. Andenken*, in U. Hölscher (ed. by), *Turm-Vorträge*, Edition Isele, Eggingen 1986, pp. 5-30, p. 7. Binder suggests metrics: "[…] das Versmaß verlangt diese Betonung, und eine Stelle in einem späten Fragment bestätigt sie." He does not specify a verse meter. R. Reuß, "…*Die eigene Rede des anderen*". *Hölderlins Andenken und Mnemosyne*, *op. cit.*, pp. 90-92, 124, 160, *passim*, also sometimes deals with metrical peculiarities. Other contributions dealing with the form of the late poems omit *Andenken*, such as F. Beißner, *Vom Baugesetz der späten Hymnen Hölderlins*, in "HJb", 4, 1950, pp. 28-46. And M. Vöhler, *Das Hervortreten des Dichters. Zur poetischen Struktur in Hölderlins Hymnik*, in "HJb", 32, 2001/02, pp. 50-68. Both W. Binder, *Hölderlins Verskunst*, in "HJb", 23, 1982/83, pp. 10-33, and F. Beißner, *Dichterberuf*, in "HJb", 5, 1951, pp. 1-18, analyse only the ode stanzas. Otherwise, there are sporadic comments on the metrics in the late poems: W. Binder, *Hölderlins Odenstrophe*, in "HJb", 6, 1952, pp. 85-110, pp. 105s. The only comprehensive study of Hölderlin's metrics is B. Previšić, *Hölderlins Rhythmus. Ein Handbuch*, Stroemfeld, Frankfurt a.M. 2008, but it does not deal with *Andenken*.

Gontard's death, one of the main topics examined here, may have been disregarded.

Metrically speaking, *Andenken* does not seem to have a Pindaric form, which can be found in Hölderlin's late poems but is instead a skillful assemblage of Lesbian meters.[3] In addition to the neglect of metrics, there is a second problem with the scholarship on this topic. Interpreters readily adopt Hölderlin's theory of *Wechsel der Töne*[4] as an approach to textual analysis of *Andenken*,[5] and several studies of the poem try to make the text more comprehensible by dividing it into three parts or spheres[6] based on this doctrine. The beginning is generally described as "naiv", the middle as "heroisch" and the conclusion as "idealisch", in Hölderlin's terms. While the present interpretation of *Andenken* will show that the number three plays a decisive role on many levels, the poem cannot be clearly "cut up" in this way.

---

3 M. L. West, *Introduction to Greek Metre*, Clarendon, Oxford 1987, pp. 32s. West gives an overview of these metres. U. v. Wilamowitz-Moellendorff, *Griechische Verskunst*, Weidmannsche Buchhandlung, Berlin 1921, pp. 104s., and B. Snell, *Griechische Metrik*, Vandenhoeck & Ruprecht, Göttingen 1957, pp. 28s., define them with slight variations. For distinct differences to Pindar, see U.v. Wilamowitz-Moellendorff, *Griechische Verskunst*, *op. cit.*, pp. 418-421, 491; B. Snell, *Griechische Metrik*, *op. cit.*, p. 33; M. L. West, *Introduction to Greek Metre*, *op. cit.*, p. 46.

4 F. Hölderlin, *Sämtliche Werke. Vierter Band. Der Tod des Empedokles. Aufsätze. Erste Hälfte. Text und Erläuterungen*, ed. by F. Beißner, Kohlhammer, Stuttgart 1961, pp. 238-240. M. Corssen, *Der Wechsel der Töne in Hölderlins Lyrik*, in "HJb", 5, 1951, pp. 19-49, has contributed one of the first studies of tonal theory. However, it does not deal with the tremendous free-rhythm poems, but only with the earlier poems in ode stanzas.

5 E.g. J. Schmidt, *Hölderlins letzte Hymnen. Andenken und Mnemosyne*, *op. cit.*

6 R. Zuberbühler, *Hölderlins Erneuerung der Sprache aus ihren etymologischen Ursprüngen*, *op. cit.*, p. 91. J. Schmidt, *Hölderlins letzte Hymnen. Andenken und Mnemosyne*, *op. cit.*, pp. 14s.,34. Also: R. B. Harrison, *Hölderlin and Greek Literature*, Clarendon, Oxford 1975, pp. 271; C. Jamme, *Hölderlin und das Problem der Metaphysik. Zur Diskussion um Andenken*, in ZPhF, 42, 1988, pp. 645-665, p. 646. U. Gaier, *Hölderlins vaterländischer Gesang Andenken*, in "HJb", 26, 1988/89, pp. 175-201, pp. 197s. Gaier suggests in the context of his interpretation of Pindar: "Heroisch ist die Richtung, die die Schiffer nehmen in ihrem Auftrag, dem Geist den Weg zu bereiten […]. Idealische Richtung nach Osten in die Kolonie des Andenkens […] wie sie in Griechenland zum erstenmal sich lebendig gestaltet hatte, heroische Richtung zur Tat stehen einander gegenüber […]." "The task of the speaker is die Idealität und Allgemeinheit des Dichtens mit der praktischen Wirksamkeit des Täters zu verbinden. Die Verbindung von Idealität und Täterschaft ist Stiften."

More philosophical interpretations often focus on Hölderlin's reflections on the philosophy of history in *Andenken*, but this issue will not be discussed here.[7] While Heidegger's language-expanding thinking sometimes goes further than any other philological treatment, he often goes far beyond the text itself, which, coupled with his strong tendency towards ideologisation, is a significant point of criticism levelled against him. Both Heidegger and Henrich quickly end up at a high level of abstraction, in Heidegger's case with a desire to establish an identification between himself and Hölderlin as an autobiographical author.[8] Henrich sharply distances himself from Heidegger's ominous exposition by taking *Heidelberg* as an initial point of comparison, mainly in order to clarify his mode of description for *Andenken.*

Reuß interprets the progression of poem thoroughly and meticulously. His argument is linguistically highly nuanced, mostly rejecting real referents of memory, especially biographical ones. In one of the earliest studies, which had some impact on subsequent research, Zuberbühler argued that the vocabulary and thought of Pietism exercised a strong influence on Hölderlin's early and late works and that some Pietist influence was detectable in *Andenken.*[9] More succinct interpretations of *Andenken* can be

7 M. Heidegger, *Gesamtausgabe. II. Abteilung. Vorlesungen 1923-1944. Bd. 52. Hölderlins Hymne Andenken, op. cit.*, should be mentioned here again, as well as T. W. Adorno, *Parataxis*, in R. Tiedemann (ed.), *Gesammelte Schriften. Bd. II. Noten zur Literatur*, Suhrkamp, Frankfurt a.M. 1990³, pp. 447-491; G. Schmidlin, "*Die Psyche unter Freunden*". *Hölderlins Gespräch mit Schelling*, in "HJb", 19/20, 1975/77, pp. 303-327, and more recently R. Homann, *Das Besondere und das Allgemeine in der Dichtung. Anmerkungen zu Dieter Henrichs Buch "Der Gang des Andenkens. Beobachtungen und Gedanken zu Hölderlins Gedicht"*, in: "ZPhF", 42, 1988, pp. 620-644; C. Jamme, *Hölderlin und das Problem der Metaphysik. Zur Diskussion um Andenken, op. cit.*; A. Haverkamp, *Laub voll Trauer. Hölderlins späte Allegorie*, Fink, München 1991; R. André, *Gespräche von Text zu Text. Celan. Heidegger. Hölderlin*, Meiner, Hamburg 2001; and T. Valk, *Das dunkle Licht der Dichtung. Zur Kunst des Erinnerns in Friedrich Hölderlins Hymne "Andenken"*, in: O. Hildebrand (ed.), *Poetologische Lyrik von Klopstock bis Grünbein*, Böhlau, Wien, 2003, pp. 100-113.

8 H.-G. Gadamer, *Anmerkungen zu Hölderlins Andenken*, in U. Beyer (ed.), *Neue Wege zu Hölderlin*, Königshausen & Neumann, Würzburg 1994, pp. 143-152, p. 143. Gadamer describes with precision "Heidegger's innere Gewißheit [...], daß die Grundhaltung des späten Hölderlin mit seinem eigenen Denkschicksal [...] nahe übereinstimmt und eine überwältigende Aktualität aufweist." This claim is not always at the expense of objectivity, as Gadamer also notes.

9 R. Zuberbühler, *Hölderlins Erneuerung der Sprache aus ihren etymologischen Ursprüngen, op. cit.*, pp. 87, 98. More recently, P. A. Hayden-Roy, *Zwischen Himmel und Erde. Der junge Friedrich Hölderlin und der württembergische*

found in certain more general studies on Hölderlin, and shorter essays that contain insights, stimulating proposals, and interpretative suggestions are also included.[10]

Pietismus, in "HJb", 35, 2006/07, pp. 30-66, offers an overview of sources on the pietistic Hölderlin; Zuberbühler (p. 87) assumes at the outset: "Das Titelwort stammt, ebenso wie die verwandten Termini "Gedenken", "Gedächtniß", "Behalten" aus der christlichen Theologie." C. Jamme, *Hölderlin und das Problem der Metaphysik. Zur Diskussion um Andenken, op. cit.*, p. 645, rejects this assumption.

10 R. B. Harrison, *Hölderlin and Greek Literature, op. cit.*; G. Schmidlin, "*Die Psyche unter Freunden*". *Hölderlins Gespräch mit Schelling, op. cit.*; P. Bertaux, *Hölderlin in und nach Bordeaux. Eine biographische Untersuchung*, in "HJb", 19/20, 1975/77, pp. 94-111; D. E. Sattler, *Friedrich Hölderlin. 144 Fliegende Briefe*, Luchterhand, Darmstadt 1981; C. Middleton, *Syntax and Signification in Hölderlin*, in C. Middleton (ed.): *The pursuit of the kingfisher. Essays*, Carcanet Press, Manchester 1983, pp. 98-119; C. Hamlin, *Die Poetik des Gedächtnisses. Aus einem Gespräch über Hölderlins Andenken*, in "HJb", 24, 1984/85, pp. 119-138. E. L. Santner, *Sober Recollections. Hölderlin's De-idealization of Memory in Andenken*, in "*GR*", 60, 1985, pp. 16-22. W. Binder, *Hölderlin. Andenken, op. cit.*; A. Gethmann-Siefert, *Die "Poesie als Lehrerin der Menschheit" und das "neue Epos" der modernen Welt. Kontextanalysen zur poetologischen Konzeption in Hölderlins Andenken. Kontextanalysen zur poetologischen Konzeption in Hölderlins Andenken"*, in H. Bachmaier, T. Rentsch (ed.): *Poetische Autonomie? Zur Wechselwirkung von Dichtung und Philosophie in der Epoche Goethes und Hölderlins*, Klett-Cotta, Stuttgart 1987, pp. 70-100; C. Jamme, *Hölderlin und das Problem der Metaphysik. Zur Diskussion um Andenken, op. cit.*; R. Homann, *Das Besondere und das Allgemeine in der Dichtung. Anmerkungen zu Dieter Henrichs Buch "Der Gang des Andenkens. Beobachtungen und Gedanken zu Hölderlins Gedicht", op. cit.*; J.-P. Lefebvre, *Auch die Stege sind Holzwege*, in "HJb", 26, 1988/89, pp. 202-223; U. Gaier, *Hölderlins vaterländischer Gesang Andenken, op. cit.*; Adorno, T. W., *Parataxis*, in R. Tiedemann (ed.), *Gesammelte Schriften. Bd. II. Noten zur Literatur*, Suhrkamp, Frankfurt a.M. 1990[3], pp. 447-491; Haverkamp, A., *Laub voll Trauer. Hölderlins späte Allegorie, op. cit.*; Jünger, H.-D., *Mnemosyne und die Musen. Vom Sein des Erinnerns bei Hölderlin*, Königshausen & Neumann, Würzburg 1993; H.-G. Gadamer, *Anmerkungen zu Hölderlins Andenken, op. cit.*; M. Franz, *Hölderlins Gedicht Andenken*, in H. L. Arnold (ed.): *Text und Kritik. Sonderband VII*, edition text + kritik, München 1996, pp. 195-212; A. Ross, *Sinnlichkeit und Gefährdung. Andenken als tragischer Prozeß*, in U. Beyer (ed.): *Hölderlin. Lesarten seines Lebens, Dichtens und Denkens*, Königshausen & Neumann, Würzburg 1997, pp. 75-100; R. André, *Gespräche von Text zu Text. Celan. Heidegger. Hölderlin*, Meiner, Hamburg 2001; T. Valk, *Das dunkle Licht der Dichtung. Zur Kunst des Erinnerns in Friedrich Hölderlins Hymne "Andenken", op. cit.*; C. Martel, *Noch denket mir das wohl... Poetik der Erinnerung in Hölderlins Hymnen Andenken und Mnemosyne*, in: "Euphorion", 98, 2004, pp. 385-406; P. Hühn, *Friedrich Hölderlin. Andenken*, in: P. Hühn, J. Schönert, M. Stein (ed.): *Lyrik und Narratologie. Text-Analysen*

1.2 *Tradition and Dating of the Poem*

With 59 verses,[11] *Andenken* is one of Hölderlin's shortest late free-rhythm poems, alongside *Der Ister* and *Mnemosyne*, which count 72 and 51 verses respectively. Of the three, *Andenken* has the most regular structure, with five stanzas of 12 or 11 verses:[12] the arrangement of *Andenken* is quite sure, although we do not possess a final version by the poet, and the poem is probably finished.[13] The printed version of the first publication in the *Musenalmanach* of 1808[14] contains serious errors.[15] Moreover, it cannot be ruled out that further changes were made to the text by the publicist Leo von Seckendorff.[16] Only the poem's last stanza is attested in manuscript

zu deutschsprachigen Gedichten vom 16. bis zum 20. Jahrhundert, De Gruyter, Berlin 2007, pp. 99-11; J. Hirsch, *Ovid in Andenken*, in "HJb", 36, 2008/09, pp. 253-260; G. Vestrheim, *Der Maler-Vergleich in Hölderlins Andenken*, in "HJb", 40, 2016/17, pp. 252-261.

11 T. Valk, *Das dunkle Licht der Dichtung. Zur Kunst des Erinnerns in Friedrich Hölderlins Hymne "Andenken"*, *op. cit.*, p. 101, considers the poem incomplete, since the manuscript gives two verses instead of v. 59 (*Ein Bleibendes aber / stiften die Dichter*), which was erased by the printer. This is true, and indeed, a beautiful final colon is lost. However, since neither Hellingrath nor Beißner (F. Hölderlin, *Sämtliche Werke. Zweiter Band. Gedichte nach 1800. Erste Hälfte. Text*, ed. by F. Beißner, Kohlhammer, Stuttgart 1951, p. 807; F. Hölderlin, *Sämtliche Werke. Hist.-Krit. Ausgabe. Vierter Band*, ed. by N. v. Hellingrath, F. Seebass, L. v. Pigenot, Propyläen-Verlag, Berlin 1923², p. 301) problematize this, it is necessary to come to terms with it, especially since in the manuscript *ein Bleibendes* seems clearly to have been replaced by *was bleibet aber,* [...]. F. Hölderlin, *Lieder und Hymnen*, ed. by D. E. Sattler, Luchterhand, Frankfurt a.M. 1978, p. 453.

12 Although the printed version of *Mnemosyne* produced by Beißner is nicely ordered in three sets of 17 verses (F. Hölderlin, *Sämtliche Werke. Zweiter Band. Gedichte nach 1800. Erste Hälfte. Text*, *op. cit.*, pp. 197s.), this verse and stanza order remain disputed from a text-critical perspective. F. Beißner, *Hölderlins letzte Hymne*, in "HJb", 3, 1948/49, pp. 66-102, pp. 68, 78; R. Reuß, "*...Die eigene Rede des anderen*". *Hölderlins Andenken und Mnemosyne*, *op. cit.*, pp. 351s.

13 F. Hölderlin, *Sämtliche Werke. Zweiter Band. Gedichte nach 1800. Zweite Hälfte. Lesarten und Erläuterungen*, ed. by F. Beißner, Kohlhammer, Stuttgart 1951, p. 802. W. Binder, *Hölderlin. Andenken*, *op. cit.*, p. 6.

14 F. Hölderlin, *Sämtliche Werke. Hist.-Krit. Ausgabe. Vierter Band*, *op. cit.*, p. 300.

15 We find (v. 12) *Eicheln* instead of *Eichen*; (v. 46) *Most* instead of *Mast*; (v. 51) *an der lustigen Spiz'* instead of *an der luftigen Spiz'* (F. Hölderlin, *Sämtliche Werke. Zweiter Band. Gedichte nach 1800. Zweite Hälfte. Lesarten und Erläuterungen*, *op. cit.*, pp. 801s.).

16 Seckendorff himself complained about this, as Beißner reveals based on a letter Seckendorff wrote to Justinus Kerner on 7 February 1807. F. Beißner, *Hölderlins letzte Hymne*, *op. cit.*, p. 66.

form, together with the draft and main manuscript of *Der Ister*. This means that a textual orientation towards "germinal words" (*Keimwörter*) on Hölderlin's part, as in *Mnemosyne*, for example,[17] cannot be established. A small number of alternative expressions in verses 49–59, which were toyed with in the manuscript but rejected in the final version,[18] have been addressed in some studies, but will not be considered here. Since Hölderlin discarded them, they do not represent variants in the tradition that could be debated on an equal footing with the published version.

While the year of publication of *Andenken* is known, its precise moment of composition cannot be determined. As an autobiographical poem – which it is assumed to be here – it contains clues about its possible dating. It can be assumed to have been written after Hölderlin's stay in Bordeaux as a courtier to the Hamburg consul Daniel Christoph Meyer from 28 January to around mid-May 1802[19] – the descriptions of the landscape and culture of southern France and the theme of memory leave little room for doubt about this.[20] In the scholarship, the proposed date range runs from 1802 to 1806.[21] Those interpreters who have written reviews have mostly avoided

17 F. Beißner, *Hölderlins letzte Hymne*, *op. cit.*, p. 79.

18 F. Hölderlin, *Sämtliche Werke. Zweiter Band. Gedichte nach 1800. Zweite Hälfte. Lesarten und Erläuterungen*, *op. cit.*, p. 801; F. Hölderlin, *Lieder und Hymnen*, *op. cit.*, p. 454.

19 A. Beck, P. Raabe, *Hölderlin. Eine Chronik in Text und Bild*, Insel, Frankfurt a.M. 1970, pp. 63s.

20 J. Schmidt, *Hölderlins letzte Hymnen. Andenken und Mnemosyne*, *op. cit.*, p. 12. Schmidt refers to Beck (F. Hölderlin, *Sämtliche Werke. Sechster Band. Briefe. Erste Hälfte. Text*, *op. cit.*, pp. 71s.) with the information that Consul Meyer owned a country house near the Gironde shore, where Hölderlin may have been a guest.

21 F. Hölderlin, *Sämtliche Werke. Hist.-Krit. Ausgabe. Vierter Band*, *op. cit.*, p. 300, dates the poem "dem Stil nach nicht sehr spät, immerhin geraume Zeit nach *Patmos*, (Anfang 1803)."; Beißner (F. Hölderlin, *Sämtliche Werke. Zweiter Band. Gedichte nach 1800. Zweite Hälfte. Lesarten und Erläuterungen*, *op. cit.*, p. 800): spring 1803; J. Schmidt, *Hölderlins letzte Hymnen. Andenken und Mnemosyne*, *op. cit.*, p. 6. F. Hölderlin, *Sämtliche Gedichte*, ed. by J. Schmidt, Deutscher Klassiker Verlag, Frankfurt a.M. 2019□, p. 1013. Schmidt also assumes 1803 as the year of composition. P. Bertaux, *Hölderlin in und nach Bordeaux. Eine biographische Untersuchung*, *op. cit.*, p. 109, partially dates Hölderlin's *sterblichen Gedanken* to spring 1802, when Hölderlin was still in Bordeaux. G. Schmidlin, "*Die Psyche unter Freunden*". *Hölderlins Gespräch mit Schelling*, in "HJb", 19/20, 1975/77, pp. 303-327, p. 327: on historical-philosophical grounds in relation to "das geschichtliche Feld 1803"; F. Hölderlin, *Lieder und Hymnen*, *op. cit.*, p. 610: March 1805 "nach Wochen tiefster Verzweiflung" following the deaths of Susette Gontard and Wilhelm Heinse; C. Middleton, *Syntax and*

taking a position on its chronological position, as have more philosophically oriented observers. With the exception of Reuß – whose caution is, in my opinion, exemplary[22] – most interpreters accept Beissner's proposal of 1803 without further comment.[23] This date is based on the last stanza, which has survived in handwritten form and has been transmitted with the draft manuscript of *Der Ister*, which can be dated to approximately 1803 only by circular reasoning. Arguments for a chronological determination are found in poetological statements linking *Andenken* to the letters to Casimir Ulrich Boehlendorff from January 1801 to autumn 1802.[24] The letter of 1801 reveals something of Hölderlin's mental preparations for the ideas contained in the letter of 1802 and his expectations about his time abroad.[25] The letter written after his stay in France contains concepts that also appear in *Andenken* and autobiographical and poetological reflections that are potentially put into practice in the poem.[26] The present interpretation assumes that the confirmation in the second Boehlendorff letter of the indications given in the first one is sufficient to cautiously date the writing of the text to, at the earliest, a few months after Hölderlin's

---

Signification in Hölderlin, op. cit., p. 98: Winter 1802/03 U. Gaier, *Hölderlins vaterländischer Gesang Andenken, op. cit.*, p. 176: around 1803, quoting from a letter to the publisher Wilmans 08.12.1803, which deals with "einzelne lyrische größere Gedichte"; B. Böschenstein, "*Frucht des Gewitters*". *Hölderlins Dionysos als Gott der Revolution*, Insel-Verlag, Frankfurt a.M. 1989, p. 145, dates it after 1802 in the context of his interpretation of Hölderlin's Dionysus. M. Franz, *Hölderlins Gedicht Andenken, op. cit.*, p. 198: 1805, as he places *Andenken* – in contrast to other interpreters – in the period of the Homburger *Folioheft* and the *Pindarfragmente*, because of the motif of the "Gegenüberstellung von Hellas und Hesperien", which is missing in his opinion.

22 R. Reuß, "*...Die eigene Rede des anderen*". *Hölderlins Andenken und Mnemosyne, op. cit.*, p. 101: "[…] redlicherweise [ist] nur zu sagen, daß Hölderlin das Gedicht nach dem Aufenthalt in Bordeaux […] und vor seiner Einweisung ins Autenriethsche Klinikum ([…]1806) geschrieben haben muß."

23 M. Heidegger, *Gesamtausgabe. II. Abteilung. Vorlesungen 1923-1944. Bd. 52. Hölderlins Hymne Andenken, op. cit.*, p. 19. C. Hamlin, *Die Poetik des Gedächtnisses. Aus einem Gespräch über Hölderlins Andenken, op. cit.*, p. 122; W. Binder, *Hölderlin. Andenken, op. cit.*, p. 7; J.-P. Lefebvre, *Auch die Stege sind Holzwege, op. cit.*, p. 207; T. Valk, *Das dunkle Licht der Dichtung. Zur Kunst des Erinnerns in Friedrich Hölderlins Hymne "Andenken", op. cit.*, p. 101; C. Martel, *Noch denket mir das wohl... Poetik der Erinnerung in Hölderlins Hymnen Andenken und Mnemosyne, op. cit.*, 386.

24 F. Hölderlin, *Sämtliche Werke. Sechster Band. Briefe. Erste Hälfte. Text*, ed. by A. Beck, Kohlhammer, Stuttgart 1954, pp. 425-428 no. 236; pp. 432s. no. 240.

25 Ivi, pp. 425-428 no. 236, lines 26-29, 37-39, 67s., 82-88.

26 Ivi, pp. 432s. no. 240, lines 7-10, 19-21, 34-36, 53-56.

return to Germany.[27] The supposition that *Andenken* is close in meaning to other late poems, above all the unfinished *Mnemosyne* text,[28] has led it to be assigned a similar date. However, *Mnemosyne* cannot yet be reliably dated to the year 1803 either. Moreover, the supposed similarities in content rest on bold interpretative conjectures – as a text, *Mnemosyne* is scarcely comprehensible – and provide no proof of chronological proximity, since many of Hölderlin's late poems, for example, take up ideas from the odes despite their temporal distance.

The structure of the poem, which in contrast to other late poems is not divided into strophic triads[29] and which is distinguished in other respects from the poems in the "neuen Form der hesperischen Hymne",[30] provides a

---

27 Nevertheless, the letter in no way proves that *Andenken* was written around the time it was sent.

28 R. Reuß, "*...Die eigene Rede des anderen*". *Hölderlins Andenken und Mnemosyne*, *op. cit.*, pp. 697-701; otherwise superficial comparisons, e.g., A. Ross, *Sinnlichkeit und Gefährdung. Andenken als tragischer Prozeß*, p. 78.

29 F. Hölderlin, *Sämtliche Werke. Zweiter Band. Gedichte nach 1800. Zweite Hälfte. Lesarten und Erläuterungen*, *op. cit.*, p. 802. On the face of it, this is clear, but there are also disagreements. For example, the idea has been advanced of a triadic division of periods (C. Middleton, *Syntax and Signification in Hölderlin*, *op. cit.*, p. 100), which may well be based on Pindar, from whom Hölderlin took the classification of strophic triads.

30 D. Henrich, *Der Gang des Andenkens. Beobachtungen und Gedanken zu Hölderlins Gedicht*, *op. cit.*, p. 14.
The "hymnic" has been established as a primary criterion, and although *Andenken* has a different form than the other free-rhythm poems (on this, see above all R. Reuß, "*...Die eigene Rede des anderen*". *Hölderlins Andenken und Mnemosyne*, *op. cit.*, pp. 102s.), the designation has been adopted without comment and the poem has thus been more or less casually classified as a hymn. (U.a. F. Hölderlin, *Sämtliche Werke. Zweiter Band. Gedichte nach 1800. Erste Hälfte. Text*, *op. cit.*, p. 802; D. Henrich, *Der Gang des Andenkens. Beobachtungen und Gedanken zu Hölderlins Gedicht*, *op. cit.*, p. 14; M. Vöhler, "*Danken möcht' ich, aber wofür?*". *Zur Tradition und Komposition von Hölderlins Hymnik*, Fink, München 1997, p. 189; R. André, *Gespräche von Text zu Text. Celan. Heidegger. Hölderlin*, *op. cit.*, p. 163; T. Valk, *Das dunkle Licht der Dichtung. Zur Kunst des Erinnerns in Friedrich Hölderlins Hymne "Andenken"*, *op. cit.*, p. 100; C. Martel, *Noch denket mir das wohl... Poetik der Erinnerung in Hölderlins Hymnen Andenken und Mnemosyne*, *op. cit.*, 385. There are hardly any studies that discuss or reject with justification this classification. This is problematic given the problems in the literary-historical discussion of German-language hymn poetry. Hellingrath, F. Hölderlin, *Sämtliche Werke. Hist.-Krit. Ausgabe. Vierter Band*, *op. cit.*, p. 300, distinguishes it from the hymns and classifies it among the "im engern Sinn lyrischen Gedichte"; W. Binder, *Hölderlin. Andenken*, *op. cit.*, p. 6. Binder clarifies that "Hölderlins Gedichte sind keine heiligen Texte, so oft man sie dazu gemacht hat. Wer meint, sie so lesen zu wollen, vergißt den Schlußsatz des *Einzigen*: *Die*

reason for placing it after *Patmos*, the last triadic poem, which can be dated with certainty, thanks to a fair copy from January 1803.[31] However, it is implausible to assume that *Andenken* was necessarily written after *Patmos* solely because of its scope and form. The poems could have been written in parallel, while the unfinished poem *Der Einzige* – begun in 1801 and probably continued in the autumn of 1802 – could also have been completed simultaneously. The fact is that, apart from *Patmos*, none of the late poems after *Der Rhein* (summer 1801) – namely *Germanien*, *Friedensfeier*, *Der Einzige*, *Andenken*, *Der Ister*, *Mnemosyne* – can be dated with certainty. All previous attempts to arrive at more precise delimitations have been grounded in vague or hypothetical interdependencies.

2.1 *Interpretation*

Andenken is both a personal and a public poem. Its public dimension arises not from political or philosophical statements, but from the complex theme of community. That the poet's memory, which incorporates the memory of others, is intimate and social is shown by the beginning and the ending of the poem. The poet – Hölderlin[32] – names the natural motivation

Dichter müssen auch / Die geistigen weltlich seyn." Binder does not fundamentally question the classification of some poems as hymns, but he does not see *Andenken* as one (ivi. p. 13). R. Zuberbühler, *Hölderlins Erneuerung der Sprache aus ihren etymologischen Ursprüngen, op. cit.*; P. Bertaux, *Hölderlin in und nach Bordeaux. Eine biographische Untersuchung, op. cit.*; U. Gaier, *Hölderlins vaterländischer Gesang Andenken, op. cit.*; R. Homann, *Das Besondere und das Allgemeine in der Dichtung. Anmerkungen zu Dieter Henrichs Buch "Der Gang des Andenkens. Beobachtungen und Gedanken zu Hölderlins Gedicht", op. cit.*; C. Jamme, *Hölderlin und das Problem der Metaphysik. Zur Diskussion um Andenken, op. cit.*; and R. Reuß, "*...Die eigene Rede des anderen*". *Hölderlins Andenken und Mnemosyne, op. cit.*, all refer to it as a poem.

31 W. Binder, *Hölderlin. Andenken, op. cit.*, p. 7.

32 According to Beißner (F. Hölderlin, *Sämtliche Werke. Zweiter Band. Gedichte nach 1800. Zweite Hälfte. Lesarten und Erläuterungen, op. cit.*, p. 802): "Die Unterscheidung des Dichters und des Menschen ist überdies bei Hölderlin wohl von vorneherein wie bei keinem andern fehl am Platze." This opinion is defensible in contemporary research and can be justified by Hölderlin's self-image as a poet concerning the ancient literary tradition. In addition, it has been noted, for example, that the spring equinox fell in the middle of Hölderlin's stay in Bordeaux in the spring of 1802 (arrival: 28/01/1802; return: 10/05/1802 postmark in Paris, thus departure from Bordeaux at the end of April, J.-P. Lefebvre, *Auch die Stege sind Holzwege, op. cit.*, p. 215; P. Bertaux, *Hölderlin in und nach Bordeaux. Eine biographische Untersuchung, op. cit.*, p. 100). *Märzenzeit* in

for the beginning of his poetry: the *Nordost*, which leads him to adopt a communal perspective in the solidarising proem. The poem's narrative is composed with light-hearted seriousness and a metrically peculiar harmony. It is interwoven with elements of drama and develops out of the poet's situation in his German homeland, which he reflects on in the third stanza. The situation at home determines how his ideas are linked in the first two stanzas because of the poetology at the end.

In contrast to *Am Quell der Donau*, *Die Wanderung*, *Der Rhein*, *Germanien*, *Friedensfeier*, *Der Einzige*, *Patmos*, *Der Ister*, and *Mnemosyne*, there is no invocation of God, no explicit presence or naming of the divine in *Andenken*.[33] The descriptions of the landscape differ from the deifying invocation and reverential representation in the other poems.[34] The absence of the divine is notable and conspicuous in the late works of Hölderlin, who was intensely concerned, on both a literary and a personal level, with his own and other gods throughout his life.[35] Allusions to Dionysus and Christ in *Andenken* may exist, but they are not presented as reference figures or active forces. *Andenken* tells of the courage to remember, of foreign landscapes and *Heimat*, of the richness of experience, of uprootedness

---

verse 20 can be interpreted as a reference to Hölderlin's birthday on 20 March (U. Gaier, *Hölderlins vaterländischer Gesang Andenken*, *op. cit.*, p. 182; J. Hirsch, *Ovid in Andenken*, p. 255.) and the embedding of this autobiographical mention in the description of historically verifiable celebrations around 21 March can be interpreted as an autobiographical reference to participation, J.-P. Lefebvre, *Auch die Stege sind Holzwege*, *op. cit.*, p. 214. Biographical references are otherwise found in the poems designated as "late hymns" only in *Die Wanderung* with the salutation and hymnic *epideixis* of Swabia and concrete indications of places in the vicinity of the Neckar and Rhine (F. Hölderlin, *Sämtliche Werke. Zweiter Band. Gedichte nach 1800. Erste Hälfte. Text*, *op. cit.*, p. 139, v. 1-24; 92-96).

33 F. Hölderlin, *Sämtliche Werke. Zweiter Band. Gedichte nach 1800. Erste Hälfte. Text*, *op. cit.*: *Am Quell der Donau*: pp. 126-129, v. 40-45, 50s., 89-91, 111s.; *Die Wanderung*: p. 141, v. 108s.; *Der Rhein*: pp. 142s., v. 24-27; *Germanien*: p. 149, v. 1-4; *Der Einzige*: p. 153, v. 9-12; *Patmos*: p. 173, v. 1-4; *Der Ister*: p. 191, v. 57s.; *Mnemosyne*: p. 198, v. 45-48.

34 Deifying invocation or reverential depiction of a country or landscape. Ivi: *Am Quell der Donau*: p. 127, v. 80; *Die Wanderung*: p. 138, v. 1-24; *Der Rhein* throughout; *Germanien* throughout; *Der Einzige*: p. 153, v. 1-4; *Patmos*: p. 174, v. 27-31; *Der Ister*: p. 190, v. 7-9; *Mnemosyne*: p. 197, v. 25-34.

35 W. F. Otto, *Der griechische Göttermythos bei Goethe und Hölderlin*, H. Küpper, Leipzig 1939, p. 10, and K. Kerényi, *Hölderlin und die Religionsgeschichte*, in "HJb", 8, 1954, pp. 11-24, p. 22, name Zeus, Apollo, Dionysus, Helios and Heracles as the Greek gods most revered by Hölderlin. See also M. L. Baeumer, Dionysos und das Dionysische bei Hölderlin, in "HJb", 18, 1973/74, pp. 97-118, p. 98.

and loneliness, of hope for love, of loss of that hope and consolation – as poetry that understands itself as poetry. It is original poetry in Hölderlin's sense,[36] which expresses itself in his own *Stromsemantik*, which structures *Andenken* in the distance. At home, the poet is homeless and reflects various kinds of absence that he himself has experienced in a short time.[37] The awareness of this state, brought about by the loss of the beloved, is the reason for *Andenken*: the blowing *Nordost* is an impulse, signpost, and mediator, while his recent time abroad is the horizon and point of reference. However, there is no sadness or depression, but from the beginning a calm, albeit not carefree, confidence that shelters the poetic *Andenken* in a safe environment – in the poet's own memory of the distant landscape. The poet's reflections in the present seem to interrupt the poem's course, but it is a mistake to assume, as some do, that there is a formal morbidity and "Pindaric" fragility.[38] In reality, the reflections structure the stream of memories at moments of inflection. From the beginning to the end, the poet speaks: the speaker never changes nor does he "leave" the poem.[39] This is shown, among other things, by repeating specific verse measures that connect critical passages meaningfully. The harmony of the composition and the continuity of the line of thought despite apparent jumps is – to make a comparison with ancient texts – similar to Horatian odes, despite the use of so-called free rhythms advocated by Pindar.

36 This observation goes back to the middle verse in *Der Rhein*, the poem that probably contains the most explicit statements about the mysteries of *Stromdichtung*: "*Ein Räthsel ist Rheinentsprungenes. Auch / Der Gesang kaum darf es enthüllen.*" (F. Hölderlin, *Sämtliche Werke. Zweiter Band. Gedichte nach 1800. Erste Hälfte. Text*, *op. cit.*, p. 143, v. 46s.).

37 He has returned from Bordeaux, where he had set out from his *Heimat* (F. Hölderlin, *Sämtliche Werke. Sechster Band. Briefe. Erste Hälfte. Text*, *op. cit.*, p. 424 no. 235, lines 6-8) with the pain of leaving and the beginnings of homesickness (Ivi, p. 428 no. 236, lines 82-88) and from where he returned after a few months' stay (Ivi, p. 430 no. lines 238, 23-27; p. 432 no. 240, lines 1-21) with signs of physical and psychological *Verwahrlosung*. At about the time of writing *Andenken*, Susette Gontard died (A. Beck, P. Raabe, *Hölderlin. Eine Chronik in Text und Bild*, p. 65).

38 e.g. in A. Ross, *Sinnlichkeit und Gefährdung. Andenken als tragischer Prozeß*, *op. cit.*, p. 78, who assumes "syntaktische [...] und bildliche [...] Brüchigkeiten".

39 In contrast, P. Hühn, *Friedrich Hölderlin. Andenken*, *op. cit.*, pp. 101s., identifies two processes of consciousness in two sequences, the first personal, the second impersonal. Likewise T. Valk, *Das dunkle Licht der Dichtung. Zur Kunst des Erinnerns in Friedrich Hölderlins Hymne "Andenken"*, *op. cit.*, p. 100; and C. Jamme, *Hölderlin und das Problem der Metaphysik. Zur Diskussion um Andenken*, *op. cit.*, pp. 646, 652.

2.2 *Andenken – On the Poem's Title*

The title refers to different forms of *Andenken* in the poem. This interpretation aims to show that an intrinsic force, in need of an impulse, determines the poem's structure and triggers a mental *perpetuum mobile*. The title is *Andenken* and not "Angedachtes", hence referring to the process and product in a nominal, verbal, active, and passive sense.[40] In addition to grammar, the temporal aspect must be considered concerning the question of the essence of *Andenken*. In *Andenken*, the past and the future are conceptualized as one, insofar as memory and anticipation go together.[41] By searching for parallel passages in the letters and poems, we can prove that Hölderlin uses "Andenken" synonymously with "Erinnerung" and "Gedächtnis", but this does not exhaustively explain the meaning of the word in the poem.[42] Hölderlin initially thinks of things without reflecting

40 R. Reuß, "*...Die eigene Rede des anderen*". *Hölderlins Andenken und Mnemosyne*, *op. cit.*, 110-126, provides an extensive and factual analysis of the term and its possible meanings in the title. R. Zuberbühler, *Hölderlins Erneuerung der Sprache aus ihren etymologischen Ursprüngen*, *op. cit.*, pp. 88-90. Zuberbühler strives to interpret *Andenken* in Hölderlin within the framework of Christian theology. He classes the term under "verwandte Termini", such as "Gedenken", "Gedächtnis", "Behalten", which have their origin in the establishment of the Lord's Supper by Jesus Christ. He also cites "Gedanke" as an old secondary meaning of the word "Dank" from contemporary linguistics. Likewise A. Ross, *Sinnlichkeit und Gefährdung. Andenken als tragischer Prozeß*, *op. cit.*, p. 79. H. Hühn, *Mnemosyne. Zeit und Erinnerung in Hölderlins Denken*, J. B. Metzler, Stuttgart 1997, p. 14, in reaction to Henrich's (D. Henrich, *Der Gang des Andenkens. Beobachtungen und Gedanken zu Hölderlins Gedicht*, *op. cit.*, pp. 131-139) remarks, calls for a conceptual differentiation of "Angedenken", "Erinnerung" and "Gedächtnis" in Hölderlin's work.

41 M. Heidegger, *Gesamtausgabe. II. Abteilung. Vorlesungen 1923-1944. Bd. 52. Hölderlins Hymne Andenken*, *op. cit.* Heidegger believes that this is not a matter of thinking back to the past, in the sense of what is irrevocable, but instead of an *Andenken* of what is to come, which can only be "Denken an das Gewesene", which, in contrast to what has passed, is the "fernher noch Wesende" (p. 84). The distinction between two forms of the past, which basically amounts to the difference between the perfect and the imperfect, captures an aspect of remembrance that is moved and determined by the past (*Noch denket das mir wohl* [...]).

42 The possibility of filling out the meaning of the term through textual comparison is limited, because "Andenken" occurs only once in the lyrical corpus (H.-M. Dannhauer, H. O. Horch, K. Schuffels, *Wörterbuch zu Friedrich Hölderlin. I. Teil. Die Gedichte. Auf der Textgrundlage der Großen Stuttgarter Ausgabe*, Niemeyer, Tübingen 1983, p. 22). The related term "*Angedenken*" occurs four times. (Ivi, p. 25) In addition to considerations bearing on differences in meaning, it should also

on them – the latter happens for the first time in the middle stanza. The poem shows that reflection's mental movement differs from "Andenken." The complex *Andenken* found in the poem cannot be equated with reflection, even though it has sometimes been used synonymously with "Erinnerung" (recollection) – a productive memory that comes close to *Andenken* – to designate the poet's activity. In *Andenken*, he joins up with others, whose *Andenken* he shares in and partially identifies with his own. The word is simultaneously to be understood as an infinite verb. At first, it is the *Andenken* of the poet who speaks the titular word, as can be assumed from the first verses, and becomes apparent with the *schöne Garonne* in verse 6.[43] Here, the parallel passage comes into play, whose significance for the poem can be seen in yet other intertextual references. In *Hyperion*, the hero, an image of the poet, upon receiving a letter with news of the passing of Diotima, the idealized literary image of Gontard, utters parting words shortly before his journey to the Germans that exhibit numerous parallels with *Andenken* and contain the core concept of "*Angedenken*".[44] Thus, the title gives a first, essential indication that the "Andenken" of the poem is essentially concerned with the loss of the beloved.[45] However, this

---

be noted that, in sound, sense and as a dactyl, *Andenken* forms a different title than would the term "*Angedenken*" with two prefixes in two trochaea.

43 See note 44.

44 p. 191 "*Und nun lebt wohl, ihr Alle! all ihr Teuern, die ihr mir am Herzen gelegen, Freunde meiner Jugend und ihr Eltern und ihr lieben Griechen all, ihr Leidenden! Ihr Lüfte, die ihr mich genährt, in zarter Kindheit, und ihr dunkeln Lorbeerwälder und ihr Uferfelsen und ihr majestätischen Gewässer, die ihr Großes ahnen meinen Geist gelehrt – und ach! ihr Trauerbilder, ihr, wo meine Schwermut anhub, heilige Mauern, womit die Heldenstädte sich umgürtet und ihr alten Tore, die manch schöner Wanderer durchzog, ihr Tempelsäulen und du Schutt der Götter! und du, o Diotima! und ihr Täler meiner Liebe, und ihr Bäche, die ihr sonst die selige Gestalt gesehn, ihr Bäume, wo sie sich erheitert, ihr Frühlinge, wo sie gelebt, die Holde mit den Blumen, scheidet, scheidet nicht aus mir! doch, soll es sein, ihr süßen Angedenken! so erlöscht auch ihr und laßt mich, denn es kann der Mensch nichts ändern und das Licht des Lebens kommt und scheidet, wie es will.*" It is a farewell to the *Heimat*, containing childhood friends, parents and comrades, the skies, forests and waters, and the walls of heroic cities. The direction of movement of remembrance in *Andenken* is from the poet's homeland towards foreign lands he visited in the south, while in *Hyperion* it is from the *Heimat* towards the foreign north.

45 (Due to this article's focus on the wind, the arguments are presented briefly here and will be published in a second article.) The first thing that reaches the level of consciousness – stretching into the distance with the wind – is the river, the *schöne Garonne,* the third adoneus in *Andenken* and the first freestanding one. Suppose one is prepared to concede a minimum of legitimacy to interpreting letters. In

parallel to *Hyperion* is by no means proof that the poem should be located

that case, one striking feature of this group of words cannot be denied: the river, which – like the wind – moves, accompanies, and structures the poem at every level, has, as the *schöne Garonne*, the same initials as Susette Gontard, that is, the woman whom Hölderlin recognized and loved as a kindred spirit and who died on 22 June 1802. The initials appear first in verse 6 and then again in verse 22. The only interpreters who have discussed a connection between the death of Susette Gontard and *Andenken* are: (i) P. Bertaux, *Hölderlin in und nach Bordeaux. Eine biographische Untersuchung, op. cit.,* who does not mention the *schöne Garonne* as a reference, but only refers to *sterbliche Gedanken* as the poet's thoughts of the beloved, giving no interpretation of the initials; (ii) J.-P. Lefebvre, *Auch die Stege sind Holzwege, op. cit.*, p. 204, contradicts Bertaux, referring to the initials; (iii) D. Henrich, *Der Gang des Andenkens. Beobachtungen und Gedanken zu Hölderlins Gedicht, op. cit.*, pp. 225, fn. 108] Henrich rejects the argument "die Bauform eines Gedichtes verständlich zu machen."; (iv) Reuß calls the whole thing "ein Aperçu, das dem Gehalt der Stelle jedoch äußerlich bleibt" (R. Reuß, "*...Die eigene Rede des anderen*". *Hölderlins Andenken und Mnemosyne, op. cit.*, p. 244, fn. 438); (v) M. Franz, *Hölderlins Gedicht Andenken, op. cit.*, p. 209, has also interpreted the letter sequences in verse 31s. He succinctly argues that the poem is a farewell to the beloved (p. 211).

There are also references to Susette Gontard and Diotima, her ideal equivalent in *Hyperion*. The middle stanza provides the most vital testimony to this, and in the fourth stanza the poet, seeking consolation, asks after the friends in the epistolary novel. In the verses of the opening stanza, the letter G also appears in noticeably central positions: *Geh aber nun und grüße* / [...] / *Und die* G*ärten von Bourdeaux* [...]. In addition to the prominence of the letters, the motif of the garden is also conspicuous here, which, in addition to its connotations of homeliness and cultivated nature in *Hyperion* (F. Hölderlin, *Sämtliche Werke. Dritter Band. Hyperion, op. cit.*, pp. 67, 87, 89) and the poems, is inextricably linked with Diotima and the feminine par excellence in Hölderlin. *Die Eichbäume* (F. Hölderlin, *Sämtliche Werke. Erster Band. Gedichte bis 1800. Erste Hälfte. Text*, ed. by F. Beißner, Cotta, Stuttgart 1943, p. 201, v. 1s.): "*Aus den Gärten komm' ich zu euch, ihr Söhne des Berges! / Aus den Gärten, da lebt die Natur geduldig und häuslich* [...]"; *Der Prinzessin Auguste von Homburg* v. 1-4 "*Noch freundlichzögernd scheidet vom Auge dir / Das Jahr, und in hesperischer Milde glänzt / Der Winterhimmel* über deinen / *Gärten, den dichtrischen, immergrünen*"; *Der Wanderer* (F. Hölderlin, *Sämtliche Werke. Zweiter Band. Gedichte nach 1800. Erste Hälfte. Text, op. cit.*, p. 82, v. 76-78): "*Und der pflükenden Hand reichen die Zweige sich selbst. / Auch zum Walde zieht mich, wie sonst, in die freiere Laube / Aus dem Garten der Pfad oder hinab an den Bach.*" *An Diotima* (F. Hölderlin, *Sämtliche Werke. Erster Band. Gedichte bis 1800. Erste Hälfte. Text, op. cit.*, p. 210, v. 24-27: "*Und das dampfende Tal mit seinen Saaten und Blumen, / Und der Garten vor uns / Nah und fernes entweicht, verliert sich in froher Verwirrung / Und die Sonne verlischt.*"] The adoneus, in which the *schöne Garonne* also appears, is finally a metre that also circumscribes Diotima in the words of farewell in *Hyperion*: "[...] *heilige Flamme,* [...] *du bewahrst im Stillen das Schöne.*" F. Hölderlin, *Sämtliche Werke. Dritter Band. Hyperion*, ed. by

in Greece, nor is it a "*griechische Gedankenwelt*" in which the poet's ego moves in *Andenken.*[46] Instead, the poem looks to the south-west, to the south of France and Swabia, and in the distance the New World.

The title also evokes feeling, which goes hand in hand with *Andenken* but is not expressed in the word itself, thus conferring on it a certain distance, even though it captures the intimate core of the poem.[47] It is a question of the processing and shaping of life experience through *Andenken*, including as a "Medium [...], in welchem das Subjekt die sedimentierte Erfahrung

---

F. Beißner, Kohlhammer, Stuttgart 1957, p. 126. Identifying the Garonne as a woman was popular then, which Hölderlin might have learned of in France (J.-P. Lefebvre, *Auch die Stege sind Holzwege*, *op. cit.*, p. 203) and now takes on a personal meaning. The wind is indeed presented as masculine, driving men, while the river is presented as feminine and is sought out by women. In the poem, the *braunen Frauen* are shown on the dance floors on the banks of the Garonne. The pair of trees in verse 12 are *edel* and *schauet hin* over things from a lofty height. *Dort*, in the foreign land, the trees are side by side. It is also possible to spot an analogy between the relationship between Hyperion and Diotima and the earlier relationship between Hölderlin and Gontard. Even the apparent allusions to love in the poetic landscape can hardly be understood in general terms.
The fact that "Alles in innigem Liebesbezug [steht]" does not explain the verses (R. Zuberbühler, *Hölderlins Erneuerung der Sprache aus ihren etymologischen Ursprüngen*, *op. cit.*, p. 93). By no means is "das Bild einfach mit den Augen [aufzunehmen]", as Binder (W. Binder, *Hölderlin. Andenken*, *op. cit.*, p. 12) assumes, although he rightly rejects mythological interpretation at this point. The poet seeks his beloved in the memory of the distant landscape, remembering her in certain places. The *schöne Garonne* will continue to flow for a long time and the pair of trees there will grow slowly and steadily. If we ask why the poet should remember his beloved in a foreign land, one possible answer could be that when he himself was there, he knew she was alive, and thus the last hope of a worldly reunion existed in the south of France. Thus, the poet consoles himself by fixing the memory of the beloved in experiences of a past shared neither with her nor with living friends from the same environment. It is also preserved by not explicitly discussing it. In the context of the poetry in memory of Gontard, it is consistent that a figure from the circle of characters in the *Hyperion* novel appears. *Mit dem Gefährten* is once again an adoneus: the significant metre of *Andenken* captures the poet's reflection here, as the *schöne Garonne* previously did, as Gontard's *Andenkenort*. The *Reichtum* of the remembered experience and remembered hope for a reunion with Gontard stretches out before the poet. Just as the mariners can lose their lives at sea, he can become *seellos* in *Andenken*. The *schönel Garonne* is the first adoneus of the poetic memory of the landscape of southern France, while the *prächt'ge Garonne is* the last.

46 Heidegger in particular is certain of Greece's status as a place of *Andenken*. M. Heidegger, *Gesamtausgabe. II. Abteilung. Vorlesungen 1923-1944. Bd. 52. Hölderlins Hymne Andenken*, *op. cit.*, pp. 128s.

47 See note 43.

erhält", as Reuß puts it – in which, however, this medium does appear to be actively used, but remains purely passive.

2.3 *Proemium: The Promise of the Nordost*

Der Nordost wehet,
Der liebste unter den Winden
Mir, weil er feurigen Geist
Und gute Fahrt verheißet den Schiffern.

Der Nordost wehet: *Andenken* begins by telling us the direction of the wind. In this way, the reader's imagination is steered in the first verse towards an external natural phenomenon perceptible to the senses.[48] The poem first turns to an external condition in a present lacking temporal and geographical determination. The clarity of this beginning lies in the indication of the direction. The last word of the fourth verse, as a clause following the finite verb, hints at an Interessengemeinschaft in the wind. Here it becomes apparent that the direction of the wind, favourable for sailors, is connected with an auspicious beginning to the *Andenken*.[49] The poem is oriented towards the south-west, towards the Occident.

---

48 Not so Heidegger, for whom a "feststellende Aussage über die Witterung" at the beginning of a poem would be too "prosaisch". M. Heidegger, *Erläuterungen zu Hölderlins Dichtung*, Klostermann, Frankfurt a.M. 1971□, p. 85. "Der Nordost wehet. Das ist weder Feststellung der Windverhältnisse, noch Beschreibung eines zufälligen Witterungszustandes, noch eine "poetische Umrahmung" [...]." M. Heidegger, *Gesamtausgabe. II. Abteilung. Vorlesungen 1923-1944. Bd. 52. Hölderlins Hymne Andenken, op. cit.*, p. 32. Heidegger may not be wrong in this interpretation, but the wind must also be interpreted as a force of nature, because navigational meaning presented in the poem, which cannot be interpreted in purely metaphysical terms. R. Reuß, "*...Die eigene Rede des anderen*". *Hölderlins Andenken und Mnemosyne*, *op. cit.*, p. 129, interprets the beginning in the opposite way: "Im Anfangssatz von Andenken stellt sich das Tun eines Subjektes dar, das sich in die Nichtigkeit eines dürftigen Beobachtungssatzes flüchtet und das Andenken, das ihm zugedacht ist, *in den Wind zu schlagen sucht*." Beginning the poem with the direction of the wind would establish be a certain dependence on natural force (Ivi, p. 131).

49 Whatever else these verses may convey, the concrete factual reference of the words cannot be denied. See also D. Henrich, *Der Gang des Andenkens. Beobachtungen und Gedanken zu Hölderlins Gedicht*, *op. cit.*, p. 82; J.-P. Lefebvre, *Auch die Stege sind Holzwege*, *op. cit.*, p. 204; in contrast M. Heidegger, *Gesamtausgabe. II. Abteilung. Vorlesungen 1923-1944. Bd. 52. Hölderlins Hymne Andenken*, *op. cit.* p. 37; R. Homann, *Das Besondere und das Allgemeine in der Dichtung.*

The wind is only mentioned at the beginning, and only in the third verse of the last stanza – which states the place where the *Männer* depart from the *luftige*[n] *Spiz* – does the *Nordost* presumably blow again in the context of an action that refers back to the initial situation.[50] Although only made explicit with the address in verse 5, the syntactic composition of the poem's beginning already establishes the power of the wind as an impulse for *Andenken*, since within the unit formed by the first four verses, the first verse is an independent main clause. Grammatically and logically, the blowing wind outside is presupposed by the inner *Andenken* of what follows, a dynamic repeated at the end in another, expansive image. The distinctive power of the beginning is also shown by the metre: *Der Nordost wehet*: x ¯ ¯ ˘. The first verse carries weight while speaking of a powerful, weightless movement of the air, which is imperceptible without resistance. It contains a molossus, which occurs three times in *Andenken*.[51] The dactyl of the title is thus followed by a measure otherwise rare in Hölderlin's late poems. In the parallelism between quantifying and accentuating measurement and German prosody (aáàáa[52]), this movement creates a rhythm with a dynamic similar to gusts of wind blowing on three /t/ sounds. The second verse is an apposition of the first: *der Nordost* [ist] *der liebste unter den Winden*. *Unter den Winden* is the first adoneus[53] in the poem, a

---

Anmerkungen zu Dieter Henrichs Buch "Der Gang des Andenkens. Beobachtungen und Gedanken zu Hölderlins Gedicht", *op. cit.*, p. 629.

50 This is also supported by the metrical analysis of verses 3 and 51, which represent the only catalectic dactylic trimetres, 3da^. B. Previšić, *Hölderlins Rhythmus. Ein Handbuch*, *op. cit.*, p. 251, ref. *Friedensfeier*, leaves it at this when designating the measure, which like the first part of epic hexameter is also called hemiepes in Penthemimeres, and, in lyric poetry, Archilochius minor (B. Snell, *Griechische Metrik*, *op. cit.*, p. 26), since it forms a complete verse.

51 The other passages are v. 28: "*Damit ich ruhen möge; denn süß*": ˘ ¯ ˘ | ˘ ¯.
v. 58: "*Und die Lieb' auch heftet dilig die Augen*": x ˘ ¯ ˘ | ¯ ˘ ˘ ¯ ˘.

52 To clarify accents, simple schemes are used in a supplemental way in this study: e.g. aáàáa, according to Heusler's scheme (Heusler, A., *Deutsche Versgeschichte. Mit Einschluss des altenglischen und altnordischen Stabreimverses*, De Gruyter, Berlin 1956, p. 283), which is also occasionally used by R. Reuß, "*...Die eigene Rede des anderen*". *Hölderlins Andenken und Mnemosyne*, *op. cit.*, p. 130. This complementary usage of two sign systems attempts to do justice to a historical-critical claim and, at the same time, to observe the rhythm concerning the metre, as demanded by B. Previšić, *Hölderlins Rhythmus. Ein Handbuch*, *op. cit.* p. 19).

53 M. L. West, *Introduction to Greek Metre*, *op. cit.*, p. 33. West lists the colon, notwithstanding other designations in modern classical philology, among the basic kola of Lesbian poetry from the Aeolic tradition as adonean; it is also called adoneus in this work because this designation seems the least controversial and is still widely used. The term is derived from Sappho's lamentation of Adonis: Sappho

colon found in essential statements and nominal groups in *Andenken.* In his metrically oriented interpretation of *Hälfte des Leben*, Menninghaus has explained the "bewusst forcierte kollaterale Aussagekraft" of metrical features in Hölderlin.[54] The first and last adoneus in *Andenken* stand in a striking relationship to each other: *unter den Winden*, as a definitional postscript, names the group of natural forces, the winds, one of which, the *Nordost,* brings about the first movement in the poem. In a metrically identical way, [...] *stiften die Dichter* at the end evokes the group and the forces that put poetry to work: the poets and *Stiften*, as the "gründende Schenkung des Anfänglichen."[55] The first adoneus realizes a dynamic semantically and rhythmically, while the final one renews this realisation and, using the same rhythm, attributes lasting and sustainable productivity to the poets.

In certain other verses of the late poems, the blowing is not to be interpreted in purely meteorological terms. There, the metonymic reference to wind is the movement of blowing in the sense of an adequate power.[56]

Frg. 168 (E.-M. Voigt (ed.), *Sappho et Alcaeus. Fragmenta*, Polak & van Gennep, Amsterdam 1971); Plotius Sacerdos (*art. gram.* III, 3, v. 57-63: *De adonio dimetro sapphico dactylico.* (*Gramm. Lat. VI, Scriptores artis metricae.* H. Keil (ed. by), *Grammatici Latini VI. Scriptores artis metricae. Fragmenta et Excerpta metrica*, Teubner, Leipzig 1874, pp. 516, 25), who was the first to call the measure *adonius,* maintains that it is a catalectic dactylic dimeter invented by Sappho. The further terminology of the adoneus is, as mentioned, problematic: E.-M. Voigt (ed. by), *Sappho et Alcaeus. Fragmenta, op. cit.*, p. 15, equates an acephalous pherecratic with the reizianum, she thus more often assumes "da+sp" instead of "da+tr" (in contrast U. v. Wilamowitz-Moellendorff, *Griechische Verskunst, op. cit.*, p. 399): "alte Klausel, kein daktylisches Metron"); W. Menninghaus, *Hälfte des Lebens. Versuch über Hölderlins Poetik*, Suhrkamp, Frankfurt a.M. 2005, pp. 21s., thinks Voigt arbitrarily called the adoneus like this and questions it; although he quotes B. Snell, *Griechische Metrik, op. cit.*, p. 29, beforehand, who allows just that (the adoneus is furthermore called akephal Pherekrateus = Reizianum beforehand by F. Crusius, *Römische Metrik. Eine Einführung*, Georg Olms Verlag, München 1955², pp. 130, 116. U. v. Wilamowitz-Moellendorff, *Griechische Verskunst, op. cit.*, pp. 399-404. Wilamowitz' Reizianum passage is scarcely comprehensible.

54 W. Menninghaus, *Hälfte des Lebens. Versuch über Hölderlins Poetik, op. cit.*, p. 31.

55 Heidegger gives this description of the nature of *Stiften.* M. Heidegger, *Gesamtausgabe. II. Abteilung. Vorlesungen 1923-1944. Bd. 52. Hölderlins Hymne Andenken, op. cit.*, p. 193.

56 *Burg Tübingen*, F. Hölderlin, *Sämtliche Werke. Erster Band. Gedichte bis 1800. Erste Hälfte. Text, op. cit.*, p. 102, v. 61s.: "[...] *den Spöttern und Tyrannen / Weht Entsezen ihr Verdammerspruch* [...]"; *Der Frieden*, (F. Hölderlin, *Sämtliche Werke. Zweiter Band. Gedichte nach 1800. Erste Hälfte. Text, op. cit.*, p. 7, v. 45-47): "*Und unstät wehn und irren, dem Chaos gleich, / Dem gährenden*

What is special about the blowing in *Andenken* is that the context gives the blowing of the wind the meaning of a force of nature, but by emphasising the rhythmic force, it stimulates the poet's poetological reflection and personal memory, and is thus more than a mere allegorical wind in a lyrical poem about nature.[57] The wind does not simply blow continuously from here to there throughout the poem, but rather it carries us from the present of the *here* at the beginning of the poem to a distant place. In the body of the poem, its presence is hinted at as a force in the background, which then carries us, at the end of the poem, from the present of the *there* out over the inconceivable vastness of the sea.[58] Natural power initiates and guides the beginning of a process of consciousness with performative poetic power.

The beginning also reveals another crucial difference with respect to Hölderlin's other poetry, for it does not concern the origin of the wind, but rather the places it will go.[59] Only the beginning of the third verse

Geschlechte die Wünsche noch / Umher [...]"; *Der Archipelagus* (F. Hölderlin, *Sämtliche Werke. Zweiter Band. Gedichte nach 1800. Erste Hälfte. Text, op. cit.*, p. 110, v. 249-252): "*Wieder, wie vormals oft, bei Hellas blühenden Kindern, / Wehet in neuer Zeit und über freierer Stirne / Uns der Geist der Natur, der fernherwandelnde, wieder / Stilleweilend der Gott in goldnen Wolken erscheint*"; *Wie wenn am Feiertage*, (F. Hölderlin, *Sämtliche Werke. Zweiter Band. Gedichte nach 1800. Erste Hälfte. Text, op. cit.*, p. 119, v. 35-38): "[...] *Götter. / Erfrägst du sie? im Liede wehet ihr Geist / Wenn es der Sonne des Tags und warmer Erd / Entwächst* [...]"; *Wie Vögel langsam ziehn...* F. Hölderlin, *Sämtliche Werke. Zweiter Band. Gedichte nach 1800. Erste Hälfte. Text, op. cit.*, p. 204, v. 2-5: "*Es bliket voraus / Der Fürst und kühl wehn / An die Brust ihm die Begegnisse wenn / Es um ihn schweiget* [...]".

57 The only comparably complex passage is in the related poem *Mnemosyne*, here with reference to gods or Gods. F. Hölderlin, *Sämtliche Werke. Zweiter Band. Gedichte nach 1800. Erste Hälfte. Text, op. cit.*, p. 195 (2nd ed.), v. 8-13: "*Zweifellos / Ist aber Einer. Der / Kann täglich es ändern. Kaum bedarf er / Gesez. Und es tönet das Blatt und die Eichbäume wehn dann neben / Den Firnen. Denn nicht vermögen / Die Himmlischen alles.*"

58 Possibly the *Ulmwald* inclines *die Gipfel* (v. 14s.) in the wind, another force then moves the cradling air currents. It then returns in verse 51. *Gesamtausgabe. II. Abteilung. Vorlesungen 1923-1944. Bd. 52. Hölderlins Hymne Andenken, op. cit.*, p. 32. Heidegger thinks that the first verse "klingt in jedem folgenden mit" and that one must "im Übergang von jeder Strophe zur nächsten hören". In my opinion, this idea is not comprehensible when applied to the poem as the whole, but it is the *Strom* that is greeted and touched by the wind that runs through the poem.

59 A reference to the gods is suggested at this point. However, it is difficult to contextualize in an interpretation: The *Nordost* blows from the legendary land of Hyperborea, where Apollo winters and celebrates sacrificial festivals with the Hyperboreans, while Dionysus stays in Delphi during this time. Both gods are of

reveals that the wind is the poet's favourite (*der liebste*). Here it can be seen that *Andenken* begins, unlike any other poem from the same period, with a declaration of love by the poet from his own present – which is, incidentally, surprising as a personal assessment of the *Nordost*, for it is an autumn and winter wind, and has been portrayed since ancient times as bringing rain clouds and storms, as the middle wind between the harsh north and the wild east. The north wind or north storm is hostile and tends to be portrayed as destructive in other late poems and in *Hyperion*,[60] while

significance throughout Hölderlin's lyrical work and in *Hyperion*. Hyperborea is not even mentioned in the poems or in *Hyperion* (H.-M. Dannhauer, H. O. Horch, K. Schuffels, *Wörterbuch zu Friedrich Hölderlin. I. Teil. Die Gedichte. Auf der Textgrundlage der Großen Stuttgarter Ausgabe*, *op. cit.*, p. 348; H. O. Horch, K. Schuffels, M. Kammer, *Wörterbuch zu Friedrich Hölderlin. II. Teil. Hyperion. Auf der Textgrundlage der Großen Stuttgarter Ausgabe*, Niemeyer, Tübingen 1992, p. 253), but Delphi and its function, as well as Apollo and Dionysus (mainly in the form of Bacchus or other cults and epithets), are mentioned several times by name and appear in numerous references. Apollo: *Die beschreibende Poesie*, F. Hölderlin, *Sämtliche Werke. Erster Band. Gedichte bis 1800. Erste Hälfte. Text*, *op. cit.*, p. 229, v. 1; *Götter wandelten einst*, Ivi, p. 274, v. 2; *Menons Klagen um Diotima*, F. Hölderlin, *Sämtliche Werke. Zweiter Band. Gedichte nach 1800. Erste Hälfte. Text*, *op. cit.*, p. 78, v. 114; *Der Einzige*, Ivi, p. 153, v. 7; Hymnische Entwürfe: *Der Vatikan*, Ivi, p. 253, v. 41; *Hyperion*, F. Hölderlin, *Sämtliche Werke. Dritter Band. Hyperion*, *op. cit.*, pp. 88, 107, 274; Bacchus, god of joy, Evier, god of wine, the Delphic god, thunderer (not Zeus here): *An unsre großen Dichter*, F. Hölderlin, *Sämtliche Werke. Zweiter Band. Gedichte nach 1800. Erste Hälfte. Text*, *op. cit.*, p. 261, v. 1, 3, 8; *Der Einzige*, Ivi, p. 154, v. 55; *Brod und Wein*, Ivi, pp. 94s., v. 123, 141, 155; *Der Rhein*, Ivi, p. 147, v. 145; *Der Archipelagus*, Ivi, p. 110, v. 228; Hymnische Entwürfe: *Wie Meeresküsten*, Ivi, 1, p. 205, v. 7; Delphi: *Brod und Wein*, Ivi, p. 91, v. 50, 62; Hymnische Entwürfe *Die Titanen*, Ivi, p. 217, v. 5; *Hyperion*, F. Hölderlin, *Sämtliche Werke. Dritter Band. Hyperion*, *op. cit.*, p. 144).

60 *Der Main*, F. Hölderlin, *Sämtliche Werke. Erster Band. Gedichte bis 1800. Erste Hälfte. Text*, *op. cit.*, p. 303, v. 11 (here the *Nordsturm* is as the destroyer of a memorial and thus has the effect to the *Nordost*, which speaks against a text-internal kinship or even identification of *Nord* and *Nordost*): "*Ach! einmal dort an Suniums Küste möcht' / Ich landen, deine Säulen Olympion! Erfragen, dort, noch eh der Nordsturm / Hin in den Schutt der Athenertempel / Und ihrer Götterbilder auch dich begräbt* [...]"; *Der Mutter Erde*, F. Hölderlin, *Sämtliche Werke. Zweiter Band. Gedichte nach 1800. Erste Hälfte. Text*, *op. cit.*, p. 124s., v. 51-54: "*Die Tempelsäulen stehn / Verlassen in Tagen der Noth, / Wohl tönet des Nordsturms Echo / tief in den Hallen* [...]"; [Hymnische Entwürfe] *An die Madonna*, Ivi, p. 213, v. 71-78: "*Darum beschüze / Du Himmlische sie / Die jungen Pflanzen und wenn / Der Nord kömmt oder giftiger Thau weht* [...] *gib erneuertes Wachstum*." *Hyperion*, F. Hölderlin, *Sämtliche Werke. Dritter Band. Hyperion*, *op. cit.*, p. 15: "*Wie ein heulender Nordwind fährt die Gegenwart über die Blüthen*

the *Nordost* in *Andenken* is a welcome trailblazer and companion. This difference is remarkable in view of many other passages of Hölderlin's œuvre where the wind direction is mentioned. Hölderlin otherwise likes to cite topical characteristics of the winds. In this case, the west wind and the north wind (or north-east wind), which also occur under their Greek names Zephyros and Boreas, correspond to the ancient characters of the winds frequently mentioned in Greek and Latin literature.[61] All the north-east wind variants[62] were depicted in ancient times as unpleasant, like

---

unseres Geistes und versengt sie im Entstehen." Hölderlin even sets the North in opposition to love: *Elegie*, F. Hölderlin, *Sämtliche Werke. Zweiter Band. Gedichte nach 1800. Erste Hälfte. Text, op. cit.*, p. 72, v. 45-47: "*Und drohte der Nord auch, er, der Liebenden Feind, sorgenbereitend, und fiel von den Ästen das Laub* [...]". The context is a peaceful love that defied adversity but has now been lost. No spirit of change or courage is stirred up by the wind and set against the sorrow.

61 H.-M. Dannhauer, H. O. Horch, K. Schuffels, *Wörterbuch zu Friedrich Hölderlin. I. Teil. Die Gedichte, op. cit.*, pp. 797, 765, 78: Zephyrus occurs twice in a Latinized form and four times in derived words, while the west wind occurs twice: in the passages in question, the west wind corresponds to its ancient role as a gentle and warm spring wind. Boreas occurs twice, corresponding to its classical role as a troublemaker, Euros – the east wind and south wind – do not occur; (the only passage that mentions south is a reference to the cardinal direction or metonymic region; *Der Wanderer*, F. Hölderlin, *Sämtliche Werke. Zweiter Band. Gedichte nach 1800. Erste Hälfte. Text, op. cit.*, p. 81, v. 44). In a letter to Christian Landauer (February 1801; F. Hölderlin, *Sämtliche Werke. Sechster Band. Briefe. Erste Hälfte. Text, op. cit.*, pp. 415-417, n. 229, lines 56-59), in which he articulates his dissatisfaction with political conditions, Boreas serves as a metaphor in the decisive sense: "Es ist überall ein notwendig Übel, Zwangsgeseze und Executoren derselben haben zu müssen. Ich denke, mit Krieg und Revolution hört auch jener moralische Boreas, der Geist des Neides auf, und eine schönere Geselligkeit, als nur die ehernbürgerliche mag reifen!"

62 Thanks to his extensive reading, Hölderlin was undoubtedly familiar with the variety of winds and wind names in ancient mythology. It is unclear, however, to what extent he was troubled by the factual/terminological problem in his poetry, since there is insufficient textual evidence. If it is an allusion or equation, it is difficult to say which could be the *Nordost* in *Andenken*. In Greek literature, Boreas is still clearly the north wind and the antagonist of Notos (south wind) (H. G. Liddell, R. Scott, H. S. Jones, R. McKenzie, (ed. by), *A Greek-English Lexicon. 9. Auflage,* Clarendon, Oxford 1940[9], p. 322). The Latin authors introduced Boreas as a foreign Greek word, usually denoting the north wind, "eig. Nordost-Drittel-Ostwind (Plin. 2, 119)" (K.-E. Georges, *Ausführliches lateinisch-deutsches Handwörterbuch. Aus den Quellen zusammengetragen und mit besonderer Bezugnahme auf Synonymik und Antiquitäten unter Berücksichtigung der besten Hilfsmittel. 2 Bde*, Hahnsche Buchhandlung, Leipzig 1913[8] 風, vol. 1, sp. 854; at the end it says "Boreas=Aquilo als mythologische Person"), for which they have further designations that are astronomically justified: aquilo "genauer genommen

their leading representative Boreas. By contrast, the opening verses of *Andenken* do not point to a hostile, destructive *Nordost*, nor are there any other allusions to ancient topoi.

While the poet personifies the wind, when he venerates and greets it in a friendly way as something most dear, promising and familiar, this does not amount to deification, in either traditional or modern terms. Here, a first-person relationship is established with the wind as mentor, based solely on the poet's personal experience, which is specific and tied to the present moment. In this individual personification of natural forces, which is specific to the work, the physical-poetical effect is assessed concerning the concrete case in question. It is then emphasized metrically and in the verse construction. While Hölderlin adopts the personification of the north wind according to Greek tradition and identifies it in places with Boreas, and while, in general, wind god topoi do not occur infrequently and the *Nord* and *Nordost* are traditionally closely related or equated, we cannot assume without further evidence in *Andenken* either a mythical

---

Nord-Drittel-Ostwind" (K.-E. Georges, *Ausführliches lateinisch-deutsches Handwörterbuch*, *op. cit.*, vol. 1, sp. 528; here the equation "aquilo=boreas" of the natural scientific designations is written at the beginning), *septentrio* or *septemtrio* (K.-E. Georges, *Ausführliches lateinisch-deutsches Handwörterbuch*, *op. cit.*, vol. 2, sp. 2611s.; here, however, another Greek counterpart is mentioned]. The identification of wind directions in ancient literature, which differ from each other according to the classification of ancient natural science, has thus been handed down. Zedler's contemporary classification (J. H. Zedler, *Großes vollständiges Universal-Lexikon. Bd. 24*, Zedler, Leipzig 1740 (repr. Graz 1995), sp. 609s., under "Wind": sp. 596-649) adheres to the most exact ancient representation in Pliny the Elder's *Naturalis historia* (2, 119-120), which Georges also cite. Here the north is called "Septentrio, Apertias, Apactias", the north-north-east "Aquilo, Boreas", north-east is "Barrhapelliotes, Supernas". In the New Pauly (H. Cancik, H. Schneider, *Der neue Pauly. Enzyklopädie der Antike. Bd. 6*, J. B. Metzler, Stuttgart 1999, sp. 136), for the *Nordost* only "Kaikias" is given as one of the *anemoi katholikoi*, which in Zedler denotes the east-north-east. As a reader, one cannot be sure of the wind direction when reading wind names in Latin or Greek texts. In German translations of Latin poetry, aquilo and boreas or aquilo and boreas are translated as "Nordwind", but with the secondary wind directions it becomes difficult, if the sources contradict each other. The factual-terminological problems further complicate the search for a mythical counterpart to Hölderlin's *Nordost.* All mythical wind characters that could be recognized in Hölderlin's *Nordost* are already rare in the surviving Greek literature and correspondingly have been infrequently taken up in more recent German literature, which bodes ill for the search for a literary model. No source that ascribes to ancient winds the ability to promise *Schiffern feurigen Geist / Und gute Fahrt* or anything comparable could be found.

assimilation of *Nordost* and Boreas in line with ancient literary convention or some other topical reference, or a proximity to the north winds as characterised elsewhere in Hölderlin. The one other passage in which the *Nordost* is mentioned is the only place where a clear indication is given as to its nature. The passage as a whole shows close connections to *Andenken*, which is why it is quoted here in its entirety:

> Drum wie die Staaren / Mit Freudengeschrei, wenn auf Gasgogne, Orten, wo viel Gärten sind,
> / Wenn im Olivenland, und / In liebenswürdiger Fremde [...] / Und das Herz der Erde thuet / Sich auf, wo um / Den Hügel von Eichen / Aus brennendem Lande / Die Ströme und wo / Des Sonntags unter Tänzen / Gastfreundlich die Schwellen sind, / An blüthenbekränzthen Straßen, stillegehend. / Sie spüren nemlich die Heimath, / Wenn grad ... aus falbem Stein / Die Wasser silbern rieseln / Und heilig Grün sich zeigt / Auf feuchter Wiese der Charente, / [Lücke *über* zwei v.] Die klugen Sinne pflegend. ... wenn aber / Die Luft sich bahnt, / Und ihnen machet waker / Scharfwehend die Augen der Nordost, fliegen sie auf, [...].[63]

This part of *Das nächste Beste* is the only other place in Hölderlin's œuvre where the *Nordost* occurs. These verses tell us something about the wind, which the subsequent interpretation of the *feurigen Geist* and the *gute Fahrt* supports. Here, the *Nordost* strengthens the sensory perception of living beings. It thus brings or awakens an ability that has a positive effect on the ability of these living beings to act, as the proleptic attribution *die Augen wacker machen* shows.[64] The term *scharfwehend* emphasizes the immediate effect of the wind on the senses, since the component *scharf-* can be assigned to the semantic fields of seeing and blowing; the word is constructed in a metonymic chiasmus here. It is starlings that experience the effect of the *Nordost* during winter in Gascony (in southern France),

63 Hymnischer Entwurf: *Das nächste Beste*, F. Hölderlin, *Sämtliche Werke. Zweiter Band. Gedichte nach 1800. Erste Hälfte. Text*, *op. cit.*, p. 237, 3. ed, v. 9-12, 16-31s. W. Binder, *Hölderlin. Andenken*, *op. cit.*, p. 13. Binder and Heidegger also cite this passage to give the *Nordost* in *Andenken* the same freshness und sharpness as in the fragment, which is potentially impermissible. M. Heidegger, *Gesamtausgabe. II. Abteilung. Vorlesungen 1923-1944. Bd. 52. Hölderlins Hymne Andenken*, *op. cit.*, p. 31.

64 U. Gaier, *Hölderlins vaterländischer Gesang Andenken*, *op. cit.*, p. 179, has found the expression *wackere Augen* in 1 Sam. 14:27. Here it is Jonathan's eyes that become valiant in the battle of the Israelites against the Philistines, "feurig und mutig" on Gaier's understanding. The existence of a relationship between the passages and above all a reference to *Andenken* is obvious.

while they are *en route* to Africa. Here, the idea of connecting the German *Heimat*, where the starlings breed, with the south of France, where they rest, appears for a second time. Since the context of the verses is fragmentary and obscure anyway, it is safest to stick with this quite general interpretation of the passage.[65]

The *Nordost* is the poet's trailblazer and guide.[66] This is not, however, the explicit justification given for the poet's preference is rather that the *Nordost* ist *der liebste unter den Winden* / [...] *weil er feurigen Geist* / *Und gute Fahrt verheißet den Schiffern*. This reasoning raises questions that the poem only gradually answers but also provides initial clues to the poet's location and undertaking. In navigation, the course determines whether a particular wind direction is favourable or unfavourable. Therefore, it can be assumed at this point that neither the point of departure nor the destination lie in the Mediterranean region of Greece or Italy, where the *Nordost* would not be welcome, since in Greek and Latin narratives north and east winds, whether in the form of mythical persons or pure forces of nature, cause ships to go off course in the Aegean and the Mediterranean. Nevertheless, in poems about lands and shores where Mediterranean winds do not blow, preformed narratives, characters and ancient names are found as topoi. In the case of *Andenken*, this can be definitively ruled out with the fourth verse, since the favourable character of the *Nordost* applies to sea voyages

65 M. Heidegger, *Gesamtausgabe. II. Abteilung. Vorlesungen 1923-1944. Bd. 52. Hölderlins Hymne Andenken, op. cit.*, pp. 31s. Heidegger interprets the passage "vielleicht [...] in Beziehung [...] zu Andenken" in support of his interpretation of the opening verses of *Andenken*: [Zitat v. 1-4 *Andenken*] "[...] jener Wind ist genannt, der in den Breiten der schwäbischen Heimat mit seiner scharfen Kühle den Himmel rein fegt und dem Feuer des Himmels, *der Sonne*, den Raum schafft, in dem ihr Leuchten und Glühen sich entfaltet. Dieser Wind macht die Luft klar. Das Kalte, Kühle, Unbestechliche öffnet sich mit ihr." Hence, while Heidegger interprets the two passages together in a somewhat imprecise way, and departs from both in a few words somewhere between the texts, he captures the significance of the *Nordost* for the beginning of the poem.

66 The other interpretations go in more or less different directions: D. Henrich, *Der Gang des Andenkens. Beobachtungen und Gedanken zu Hölderlins Gedicht, op. cit.*, pp. 66, 91. Henrich calls the *Nordost* motivation, "klare, kühle Luft", which creates "a mood of change". J. Schmidt, *Hölderlins letzte Hymnen. Andenken und Mnemosyne, op. cit.*, p. 24. Schmidt interprets it metaphysically as the pneuma of memory: "Nordost inspiriert und ist Bote und überwindet die Trennung, wie in *Patmos* die *Fittige* und in *Der Ister* die *Schwingen*". R. Reuß, "*...Die eigene Rede des anderen*". *Hölderlins Andenken und Mnemosyne*, *op. cit.*, p. 127, refers to the wind as a "Naturphänomen": "Das Reden im ersten Vers ist profan. Kein Wort lässt vermuten, der Redende werde enthusiasmiert, vom Anhauch eines Geistigen berührt."

to areas that had been opened up by Hölderlin's time. In the sixth and seventh verses, it can be assumed that the *Nordost* promises the *Schiffer* a good voyage through the northern hemisphere, an assumption which is finally confirmed in the last stanza. But the fourth verse already announces that it is heading *ins Offene* (into the open), i.e. into the western ocean. The justification given for the poet's predilect supports this hypothesis, and says something about the connection between poet and *Schiffer*. It is worth looking at the syntax and verse structure first. The *feurigen Geist* is associated with the *gute Fahrt*, and it makes sense to understand this association as a cause-effect sequence. As explained below, the verse structure of the justification suggests a close relationship between the author and the *Schiffer*.[67] With the personal pronoun in the dative case at

67 Several passages in Hölderlin's poem also point to this: *Der Archipelagus*, F. Hölderlin, *Sämtliche Werke. Zweiter Band. Gedichte nach 1800. Erste Hälfte. Text*, *op. cit.*, p. 105, v. 72-75. "*Siehe! da löste sein Schiff der fernhinsinnende Kaufmann, / Froh, denn es wehet' auch ihm die beflügelnde Luft und die Götter / Liebten so, wie den Dichter, auch ihn, dieweil er die guten / Gaaben der Erd' ausglich und Fernes Nahem vereinte*." G. Vestrheim, *Der Maler-Vergleich in Hölderlins Andenken*, *op. cit.*, pp. 258-61, who refers to Heidegger's brief reference to v. 81 of *Archipelagus* (M. Heidegger, *Gesamtausgabe. II. Abteilung. Vorlesungen 1923-1944. Bd. 52. Hölderlins Hymne Andenken, op. cit.*, p. 178), focusses on the motivic linkage of trade and seafaring with art and poetry in *Archipelagus* and *Andenken*. What both poems have in common, he says, is that "sowohl Dichter als auch Schiffer sich an der "beflügelnden Luft" erfreuen können". He equates the sails of ships with the wings of song, claiming that "Auch Liebe der Götter umfasst *Dichter* und *Schiffer* gleichermaßen" is said in both poems. A similarity between *Dichter* and *Schiffer*, which is only implied in *Andenken*, is made explicit in *Archipelagus*. "[…] hier [*Andenken*] sind die Schiffer Metapher für die Dichter […], während der Kaufmann mit ihnen verglichen wird." However, it can be seen from both texts that *Schiffer* and *Dichter* are rather consubstantial for Hölderlin, because of the courage they have to muster. This is supported by two further passages: *Der Wanderer*, F. Hölderlin, *Sämtliche Werke. Zweiter Band. Gedichte nach 1800. Erste Hälfte. Text*, *op. cit.*, p. 82, v. 77-81, v. 103-106: "*Auch zum Walde zieht mich, wie sonst, in die freiere Laube / Aus dem Garten der Pfad oder hinab an den Bach, / Wo ich lag und den Muth erfreut' am Ruhme der Männer / Ahnender Schiffer; und das konnten die Sagen von euch, / Daß in die Meer' ich fort, in die Wüsten ich mußt', ihr Gewalt'gen!*" and Ivi, p. 83, v. 103-106: "*Darum reiche mir nun, bis oben an von des Rheines / Warmen Bergen mit Wein reiche den Becher gefüllt! / Daß ich den Göttern zuerst und das Angedenken der Helden / Trinke, der Schiffer* […]". J. Schmidt, *Hölderlins letzte Hymnen. Andenken und Mnemosyne*, *op. cit.*, p. 15. Schmidt, too, discovered the parallel to *Der Wanderer*, but does not discuss it further, instead taking it as proof for his interpretation: "Hölderlin lebt im Entweder-Oder der Spannung Dichter-Held". However, it may not be a question of an either-or, which Schmidt presumably sees as a result of

the beginning of the third verse, the speaker reveals his preference for the wind as his own in the last possible syntactic position, and then goes on to justify this presence: *der Nordost* is *der liebste*, [...] *weil er feurigen Geist / Und gute Fahrt verheißet den Schiffern*. The justification takes the form of a chiastic structure through the position of the verse-initial and metrically stressed personal pronoun *mir.* In light of the word order and the division of verse, it could be understood that the *Nordost* promises the speaker a *feurigen Geist* and *den Schiffern gute Fahrt*, while syntactically both are promised to the *Schiffern*. The fact that the speaker, as the text clearly states here, has chosen the *Nordost* – even though the syntax indicates that the *Nordost* undoubtedly promises things to the *Schiffer* (despite the hint at a "co-promising" of the *feurige' Geist*) – shows a connection between the speaker and the *Schiffer*. The *mir* in the latest position as enjambment of the second verse in diametrical position of the chiasmus to the *Schiffer* provides formal support for this assumption. In some sense, the speaker identifies with the *Schiffer*, i.e. they are characterised by a common identifying feature or even form a homogeneous group. Another clue is given by the formulation *unter den Winden*, in which *unter* may be understood in two

his strict separation of spheres, but rather, as *Andenken* possibly says in v. 38-41: Hölderlin does not have the choice of becoming a *Schiffer* and thus a hero, but rather his being a poet is based, among other things, on his perception of what is similar between him and the *Schiffer* (courage, an orientation towards what is far away, etc.), but also of what leads them down opposing paths, since the *Schiffer* do not have this perception, since they reverentially bear *Scheue*. Another relevant passage is F. Hölderlin, *Sämtliche Werke. Erster Band. Gedichte bis 1800. Erste Hälfte. Text*, *op. cit.*, p. 226, v. 33-40: p. fn. 109 on *Der Archipelagus*. The most striking comparison between poetry and navigation is in *Der Jüngling an die klugen Rathgeber*, a poetological response by Hölderlin to his critics (Ivi, p. 226, v. 33-40): "*Und könnt ihr ja das Schöne nicht ertragen, / So führt den Krieg mit offner Kraft und That! / Sonst ward der Schwärmer doch ans Kreuz geschlagen, / Jetzt mordet ihn der sanfte kluge Rat; / Wie manchen habt ihr herrlich zubereitet / Fürs Reich die Noth! wie oft auf euern Sand / Den hoffnungsfrohen Steuermann verleitet / Auf kühner Fahrt in's warme Morgenland!*"
In *An die Unerkannte*, the poetic quest, in comparison with the *Schiffer*, is still explicitly situated in the context of Hölderlin's early idealism (Ivi, pp. 197s., v. 1, 7-12, 22-24, 37-42): "*Kennst du sie [...]? / Die uns trifft mit ihren Mittagsstralen / Uns entflammt mit ihren Idealen, / Wie vom Himmel, uns Gebote schickt / Die die Weisen nach dem Wege fragen, / Stumm und ernst, wie von dem Sturm verschlagen / Nach dem Orient der Schiffer blikt?* [...] *Die den Dulder, den der Sturm zertrümmert, / Den sein fernes Ithaka bekümmert, / In Alcinous Gefilde bringt?* [...] */ Die das Eine, das im Raum der Sterne, / Das du suchst in aller Zeiten Ferne / Unter Stürmen, auf verwegner Fahrt, / Das kein sterblicher Verstand ersonnen* [...]."

senses: as a modal preposition indicating a subset, but also as a fixed phrase in seafaring language, according to which one sails "under" a wind.

What connects the speaker and the *Schiffer* is an appreciation of the *Nordost*, which promises *Gutes*. The meaning of this *Gutes* says a good deal upfront about the poem and, as we see at the end, frames it in conjunction with the conclusion. The *feuriger Geist* can be interpreted in the context of the verses, considering its cause-effect relationship to the *gute Fahrt* and within the semantic network of other poems. It has been seen as a reference by Hölderlin to his poetics, which has given rise to interpretations that are far removed from the text. It is the first-named of the promised things, closes the verse that begins with the personal pronoun in the dative, and is more heavily emphasized than the beginning by the catalexes of the third dactyl, thus dominating the third verse. In addition, it carries rhetorical emphasis, as the third noun at the end of the poem's third verse: *Nordost*, *Winde*, *feuriger Geist*. The *feuriger Geist* is not simply passionate drive,[68] kindled by the promising wind, but the bravery of heart and mind in the face of an existential danger to the poet created by the loss of the beloved, and therefore necessitating the comparison with *Schiffer*. The poem will show that seafarers leave their homeland seeking wealth and, in this way, put themselves in mortal danger. The speaker thinks of the mariners when the wind blows, which is favourable to them, and so the *Andenken* begins not in the fifth verse, but with the blowing of the *Nordost* in the first. The poet is familiar with the importance of the wind and empathizes with the *Schiffer*, and this wind thus becomes his favourite. However, not only does he share a sympathetic enthusiasm for

68 Schmidt restricts himself to this interpretation and sees the connection with the justification of the poet's preference in the fact that "[er] damit die mächtige Anziehungskraft hervorhebt, die das heroische Dasein für ihn hat." J. Schmidt, *Hölderlins letzte Hymnen. Andenken und Mnemosyne, op. cit.*, p. 15. This provides the basis for his division of the poem into the three spheres. W., Binder, *Hölderlin. Andenken, op. cit.*, p. 9. Binder, too, first understands "joy of discover" and love of adventure", which are peculiar to the *Schiffer* as *Männern* in the fourth stanza, and, discussing directions of travel (Ivi, pp. 8, 11), he refers to the Greek Hesperian thesis derived from the Böhlendorff letter (No. 236). In connection with verses 39 and 40, he interprets the *feurigen Geist* as "den Willen, der draußen, im Andern und Fremden das Instrument seiner Selbstfindung sucht" (Ivi, p. 10). For Binder, the "Andere, Fremde" "is the infinit", which Hölderlin also refers to as *Reichtum,* although the latter term does have other meanings in the poems. With his interpretation of the *feurigen Geist* as the only one, Binder attempts to strike a compromise between the points of the compass that have been assumed as the orientation of the *Schiffer*: West to contemporary West India, East to the origin of culture, i.e. Mesopotamia and/or India.

their undertaking, but the wind is also favourable for his undertaking, for which he himself needs a *feurigen Geist*.

References to fire and *Geist* obviously occur in essential passages in Hölderlin's poetics, but they are difficult to interpret in detail and differ significantly from each other. The context in *Andenken* is also very specific, but there is a parallel passage to which it potentially has an intellectual connection. In *Wie wenn am Feiertage...* it is also about the project of high poetry (F. Hölderlin, *Sämtliche Werke. Zweiter Band. Gedichte nach 1800. Erste Hälfte. Text*, *op. cit.*, p. 119, v. 28-31): "*Und wie im Aug' ein Feuer dem Manne glänzt, / Wenn hohes er entwarf; so ist / Von neuem an den Zeichen, den Thaten der Welt jetzt / Ein Feuer angezündet in Seelen der Dichter*."[69] The context is that of the power of the celestials in the world and over the poet since he owes them his creative power. But "*ein Feuer* is *angezündet / an den Zeichen, den Thaten der Welt.*" It is the *Thaten* of reality that kindle a poetic fire; in the world there is a close relationship between energy and poetic power, both of which are of divine origin. This is recounted in the hymn, the reference to the later poem lies in that kindling of the fire in the spirit through the memory of the *Schiffer* and their deeds. *Andenken*, however, does not tell of divine activity is a secular poem about what *bleibet* (remains) in the world. It almost seems that *Andenken* has taken up the idea of the hymn, detached it from the divine reference and personified it. The poem's development shows navigation not to be a purely metaphorical frame of reference, but also a practical one, since the poet requires similar mental abilities for his undertaking. He, too, is required to run the greatest risks and make the greatest sacrifices when he leaves his homeland in *Andenken*. Moreover, in the visualisation of cultural experiences in a foreign land that triggers homesickness, as well as fascination, he dispenses with his own culture, his loved ones and the environments in which his memory has grown has been wholly linked – and all this occurs in the awareness that he remembers an irretrievable state in which he could hope to see his beloved again. The poet, like the sailor on the open sea who, surrounded by an alien element without physical or psychological points of connection, has neither his arrival nor his return in view and recognizes in its vastness his condition of being lost in the world, is threatened by a temporary loss of identity. The danger of this loss alone is a reminder of the fate of human beings, namely to end up

69 The fourth stanza ends: "... *Und was zuvor geschah, doch kaum gefühlt, / Ist offenbar erst jezt, / Und die uns lächelnd den Aker gebauet, / In Knechtsgestalt, sie sind erkannt, / Die Alllebendigen, die Kräfte der Götter.*" [v. 32-36].

as non-being despite all hopes for another existence. Unlike the *Schiffer*, the poet has this experience alone, a thought that pervades and structures *Andenken*. It becomes apparent that the first four verses can be regarded as the poem's proem – yet they cannot be understood in isolation because they anticipate what is essential. This is made clear by the chiastic verse structure described above: the speaker may receive *feurigen Geist* from the blowing wind, while the positive result and the verb of promising are in the second verse, with the *Schiffer*. The *gute Fahrt* is in the measure of the fourth verse[117] and receives less emphasis as the second term. What is good is a voyage free from adversity, in which the voyagers reach their destination safely and soundly. The poet says: for the many, this success is promised with the wind, while the individual may hope for *feurigen Geist*. His *Fahrt* is the poet's path and process that requires the favour of the moment, just like a sea voyage. The poem thus unfolds and conveys the meaning of the promise, which is determined by the confidence that what is promised will be received, although it remains unclear when.

Conclusion

The poem's development involves an alternation between active and passive *Andenken*, in which the poet evinces a thorough surrender to fate, simultaneously coupled with initiative, freedom of choice and audacity. At the same time, he can associate and partially identify his personal *Andenken* with those of other existences, both male and female – and this empathy and solidarity, in conjunction with his other qualities, ultimately places him among the ranks of the great poets. Therein lies part of the poetics of *Andenken*. Hölderlin thinks of beauty, holidays, and people in a foreign land, their fate, and *and* his loss of hope for romantic fulfilment, and in doing so he speaks personally. *Andenken* is, therefore, a unique way of thinking because it is purposeful and committed while being filled with humility in the face of nature as a fateful power and of a foreign culture, to which the poet *an-heim-fällt*, by consciously distancing himself from his hometown in the memory of his beloved, and by locating her memory there. The particularities of *Andenken*, evident already in the introduction, become more transparent through interpreting every single verse and the stanzaic contexts. The absence of divine, mythological figures, places of worship or persons from antiquity and Christianity, which strikes the first-time reader, and which clearly distinguishes the poem from other late poems, is explained by the fact that *Andenken* is to be understood as a detached snapshot of the poet's own recent personal experiences and his solidarization and identification that transcends vast spaces and cultures, referring to the New World and contemporary philosophy. The ancient world is subtly conceived but not a place of reference for the poet's experience and free choice to become a poet while remaining bound by fate. The context, which evinces familiarity with antiquity and remoteness from it, tells other things. The wind blows from the northeast, blows toward more recent experiences, stirring up more recent memories. Alongside wind, air and earthly things – like gardens, trees and vineyards – springs, streams and the sea as estuaries provide meaning and structure. However, *Andenken* is seldom counted among Hölderlin's Stromgedichte[70] *Der Nordost wehet* and *feuriger Geist* is promised: movement begins and concludes the *Andenken*, a conclusion that is neither coming to a standstill or turning back in astonishment, but rather a continuation of literature through the *Andenken* of history, both general and personal. Hölderlin does not point out that he has erected a *monumentum aere perennius*. Instead, as one of the poets, he hopes to win a share in the eternal continuum of what endures. In *Andenken*, he does not speak of himself and the other poets as prophets, like Pindar, Horace or Ovid. Therefore, a *durat opus vatum* is not a statement equivalent to the final verse.[71] It is neither an *imitatio* nor an *aemulatio* of ancient or contemporary poetry.

Although *Andenken* contains traditional motifs and metrical patterns interwoven with its very essence, it is self-sufficient about antiquity and its time. *Andenken* can directly express what is human thanks to its simple way of speaking: absence of love, which appears as *Lieb'* when, despite all the courage and hope of the lovers, they lack caregivers, the wealth of experience gained by sea or land traced back to the source; uprootedness and loneliness. Active *Andenken* brings comfort. The external and internal coherence of the poem is strong, and individual verses and stanzas also display clear metrical and sensory links back to earlier lines in the poem. Counted as a Stromgedicht, *Andenken* is nevertheless unique, despite its essential affinity with the other Stromgedichte, because the localisation of the *Andenken* of Gontard on the distant river, qua *Gedächtniß* of the poet, creates a personal engagement.

---

70 A rare exception is M. Behre, *Hölderlins Stromdichtung. Zum Spannungsfeld von Naturwahrnehmung und Kunstauffassung*, in U. Beyer (ed. by): *Neue Wege zu Hölderlin*, Königshausen & Neumann, Würzburg 1994, pp. 17-40, p. 38s. Behre in addition to her review of "*Heidelberg*" and "*Der Ister*", briefly discusses "*Andenken*".

71 W. Killy, *Wandlungen des lyrischen Bildes*, Vandenhoeck & Ruprecht, Göttingen 1956.

Marcello Sessa

Vapors and Clouds
The 'Light' Morphological Paradigms of Eugenio d'Ors and Hubert Damisch

Und Greco wäre verloren,
wenn er nicht die Figurenbewegung
im eigentümlichen Zug der Wolken
am Himmel weiterleiten könnte[1].

Heinrich Wölfflin

E masimo le figure sono alte e in iscorcio ed ène altra cosa che a dipignere in tera[2].

Donato Bramante

I. *Reflections on Baroque between morphology and semiotics*

The intention of the present essay is to juxtapose the thought of two authors who are chronologically distant from each other, yet who touch at a specific point: the common attempt to reason in an oblique direction and in an eccentric sense about Baroque form; they are Eugenio d'Ors (1881-1954) and Hubert Damisch (1928-2017). Both of them elaborate, at different times and in different ways, what will be called here 'light morphological paradigms', that is, statutes of formal legality derived entirely from 'lightness' as a loss of weight and consistency. The particular character of this quality compels a reconnaissance of the 'dispute' around early and late Baroque that not only articulates itself on the bipolarity between 'light' and 'heavy' – between *levia*

1 H. Wölfflin, *Kunstgeschichtliche Grundbegriffe*, Bruckmann, Munich 1915, p. 64.

2 Quoted from a letter by Piero Roselli to Michelangelo Buonarroti, May 10, 1506: cf. *Il carteggio di Michelangelo*, ed. by G. Poggi, ed. by P. Barocchi, Ristori, Florence 1965, p. 16.

and *gravia* – but also renegotiates it *du côté aérien* to transcend its boundaries; indeed, d'Ors and Damisch's insistence on the marks of the intangibility of form is also justified in the name of overcoming disciplinary rigidities towards other, broad and all-encompassing fields of inquiry.

First, some brief questions of method. The Orsian approach to aesthetics is essentially of a phenomenological-morphological nature, and it is configured as a very personal declination of Johann Wolfgang Goethe's acquisitions – which are foundational of modern morphology[3] – on the trans-historical level of a "passage from General Philosophy to the Science of Culture"[4]. The Orsian project of a morphology of culture has developed to vanquish the barriers and partitions of historicism, and to realise it turns to form. A philosophy that "wants to be the philosophy of the whole, complete and true man"[5] analyses his cultural production as a whole, and thus finds the formal constants – invariant but subject to infinite variations – that recur in culture regardless of historical contingencies. To summarise: "d'Ors se interesó por la historia de la cultura, ya que consideraba la historia no solo como devenir, sino como serie de formas que se manifiestan ordenadas en el transcurso del tiempo en un repertorio de dominantes formales, con dos estilos generales y dominantes de la cultura: el clásico y el barroco"[6]. It is symptomatic – and of crucial importance to the subject of this study – that such a formulation refers back to the domain of style, and moreover to artistic bipartisanship[7];

3 On Johann Wolfgang Goethe's inaugural position on morphology, cf. P. Giacomoni, *Le forme e il vivente. Morfologia e filosofia della natura in J.W. Goethe*, Guida, Napoli 1993. On the overall relationships between morphology and philosophy, cf. *Morphology: Questions on Method and Language*, ed. by M. F. Molder, D. Soeiro, N. Fonseca, Lang, Bern 2013.

4 J.L.L. Aranguren, *La filosofia di Eugenio d'Ors*, transl. by L. Anceschi, Bompiani, Milan 1945, p. 126. [All translations, except where otherwise indicated, are mine. I chose to translate into English only the Italian texts; given the lack of official translations and considering the centrality of the author in this essay, I kept d'Ors prose in Spanish. The quotations in German are justified by the strong presence of schiolars of the specifical theoretical-artistic field, that of *Kunstwissenschaft.*]

5 Ivi, p. 115.

6 A.R. López, *La morfología de la cultura de Eugenio d'Ors: psicología histórica sensible*, in "El Alma Pùblica", (VII/ XIII) 2014, pp. 83-93, here p. 84.

7 "All of Orsian philosophy is penetrated by artistic meanings and, on the other hand, the same systematic criterion underlies the most important concrete applications of his thought: the basis of his aesthetics and his Ciencia de la Cultura, which corresponds to but does not coincide with the philosophy of history, lies in the search for a unity beyond plurality, for certain constants whose appearance only differs according to the circumstances of time, place, country, but whose substance is always identical", G. Zanoletti, *Estetica spagnola contemporanea*

d'Ors in fact reads every cultural phenomenon according to the Classical or Baroque hue that informs it[8].

Damisch – on the other hand, and after six decades since the beginning of the 20th century – addresses the artistic fact within the framework of semiotics, while problematising the tools of the discipline. He constantly questions the legitimacy of elaborating a "sémiologie de l'art"[9], and specifically of painting: he asks himself whether it is possible to "study painting as a *system of signs*"[10]. He wonders how the pictorial sign is organised in discourse, and what kind of reading the "system 'painting'"[11] lends itself to. He takes note of the iconic and artistic sign – which at the same time produces "a choice that one would like to be strictly sensitive, 'aesthetic'" and "a specific reading effect, or, to paraphrase Paul Klee, an initial 'acquiescence to the sign'"[12] – and of its irreducibility; in the pictorial sign *aísthēsis* and *logos* (perception and interpretation) are not mutually exclusive, but coexist and often overlap. In short, the semiotician

---

(Eugenio d'Ors – José Camón Aznar – José Ortega y Gasset). Volume primo, Lucarini, Rome 1978, pp. 59-60.

8 The invariant/variation dynamic allows d'Ors to interpret every type of phenomenon in a Classical/Baroque key; the spectrum ranges from the object (think for example of spectacles, liable to alter perception: "I hope I will not be accused of mania if I say that spectacles too, in their own way, a Baroque institution", E. d'Ors, *La vita di Goya*, transl. by E. De Zuani, in Id., *Epopea della Spagna*, Bompiani, Milan 1948, pp. 17-191, qui p. 139) to the behaviour (two-faced is that of Juan Donoso Cortés, Baroque from the rhetorical point of view and Classical from the political one: "Su arte, como retórico, es de un barroquismo formidable. Me recuerda en más de una ocasión el de la escultura policromada española. Cada página suya es un 'paso'; cada discurso, una procesión. Pero, como político, su manera de ver resulta admirablemente fría", Id., *Nuevo Glosario. Vol. I: 1920-1927*, Aguilar, Madrid 1947, p. 971); moving on to artistic manifestations proper, where the antithesis Classical/Baroque – to which we will return later – is embodied in the opposition between the painters Nicolas Poussin and El Greco (cf. ivi, pp. 372-373).

9 H. Damisch, *Théorie du nuage. Pour une histoire de la peinture*, Seuil, Paris 1972, p. 25. For a multi-voiced retrospective reconstruction of Damisch's heterogeneous interests, cf. G. Careri, G. Didi-Huberman (ed. by), *Hubert Damisch. L'art au travail*, Mimésis, Paris 2016.

10 H. Damisch, *Otto tesi pro (o contro?) una semiologia della pittura* (1974), transl. by I. Pezzini, in O. Calabrese (ed. by), *Semiotica della pittura*, Il Saggiatore, Milan 1980, pp. 123-139, here p. 124.

11 Ivi, p. 129. In the same place, he openly avoids reductionist perspectives: "The question of whether the system 'painting' can be reduced to units will therefore be answered negatively".

12 Ivi, p. 126.

needs "a different notion of sign from the strictly linguistic one"[13], which takes into account the fact that within it there is a "truth"[14] that is properly pictorial and, moreover, self-organised in a composition, in a "texture" in itself discursive "dans sa matérialité signifiante"[15]. Finally, the semiological discourse must start from the "constitutive gap [...] of pictorial textuality to the extent that it is interwoven with the visible and the legible", represented by the "iconic surplus value"[16] of the sign. Among the most liminal types of pictorial sign in this sense is "le /nuage/ – le graphe pictural dénoté *nuage*"[17]; it resorts in the Western figurative tradition in a disturbing way, and Damisch feels the need to dedicate a distinct study to it in order to verify its implications.

This is why we have chosen to call d'Ors and Damisch's theories on Baroque and proto-Baroque forms 'morphological paradigms': because both cannot be divorced from formal evidence. d'Ors is clearly a morphologist of appearances ("Toda obra importante [...] contiene una una especie de alusión implícita a algo que polariza los aspectos de su apariencia formal"[18]), while Damisch redeems formal materiality in interpretative discourse ("The question remains entirely one of how the form [...] will find a way to articulate itself on an economy"[19]). In mutually postulating "the possibility of an interpretative game, if not declarative, at least *monstrative*"[20], the two authors are close to Goethe's morphological warning that, when faced to forms, qualifies description – "the *darstellen* (displaying, describing, showing)" – and disqualifies explanation – "the *erklären* (explaining, i.e. tracing effects back to causes)"[21]. Moreover,

---

13 Ivi, p. 129.

14 Here Damisch refers to Paul Cézanne's formulation: "Je vous dois la vérité *en peinture* et je vous la *dirai*" , P. Cézanne to É. Bernard, October, 23, 1905, quoted in H. Damisch, *Otto tesi*, *op. cit.*, p. 123 [italics mine].

15 H. Damisch, *Théorie du nuage*, *op. cit.*, p. 27.

16 H. Damisch, *Otto tesi*, *op. cit.*, p. 127.

17 H. Damisch, *Théorie di nuage*, *op. cit.*, p. 27.

18 E. d'Ors, *Tres horas en el Museo del Prado* (1923), Tecnos, Madrid 2004, p. 296.

19 H. Damisch, *Otto tesi*, *op. cit.*, p. 133.

20 Ivi, p. 128.

21 A. Pinotti, *Memorie del neutro. Morfologia dell'immagine in Aby Warburg*, Mimesis, Milan-Udine 2003, p. 198; The lexicon is drawn from Goethe's *Maximen und Reflexionen* (1833). The volume offers an overview of philosophies and theories of art that descend from Goethe's morphology. Goethe himself summarised the essence of the latter as follows: "Ruht auf der Überzeugung daß alles was sei sich auch andeuten und zeigen müsse [...] Wir wenden uns gleich zu dem was Gestalt hat. [...] Die Gestalt ist ein bewegliches, ein vergehendes. Gestaltenlehre ist Verwandlungslehre", J.W. Goethe, *Morphologie* (1795-1798),

d'Ors and Damisch insist on Baroque forms precisely because of their 'monstrative' excess, which is likely to call into question the legality of the form itself, and they describe it by quite distinctive means.

II. *Two 'light' morphological paradigms*

d'Ors's aesthetic vision and morphological conception lay on a fundamental basic assumption; he believes that every form contains a "valor espacial" and a "valor expresivo", and that allows two distinct but polarised typological constants to be derived from each formal datum as complementary opposites. He thus connects 'spatial value' to the "dominio de la pura geometría" (concrete, effective, tangible) and 'expressive value' to "el campo de la pura significación"[22] (abstract, eidetic, conceptual). He hypothesises them as inherent to forms, but never balanced: one is always more accentuated than the other, depending on the degree to which it is developed. The oscillations between these poles determine a non-chronological unfolding of styles; thanks to their bipolar mechanism, they give themselves as ahistorical constants and categories of the spirit, liable to resurrect at any moment in time.

The author also declares his debt and the provenance of this approach from the distinction between "architectural value" and "functional value", made by Adolf von Hildebrand in *Das Problem der Form in der bildenden Kunst* (1893)[23], with which the domains of spatiality and expression are respectively associated. d'Ors's aesthetics is precisely influenced by the formalist art history and theory of mainly late 19th century German

in Id., *Goethe sämtliche Werke. Band 24. Naturkundliche Schriften II: Schriften zur Morphologie*, ed. by D. Kuhn, Deutscher Klassiker Verlag, Frankfurt a.M. 1987, p. 349.

22 E. d'Ors, *Tres horas en el Museo del Prado*, cit., p. 35.

23 Cf. *ibidem*: "Hildebrand afirmaba […] que esta […] forma encierra siempre dos 'valores': un *valor arquitectural* y un *valor funcional*. Por el primero, las obras se presentan en el espacio; por el segundo, encierran una expresión". For Hildebrand's essay, cf. A. von Hildebrand, *The Problem of Form in Painting and Sculpture* (1893), transl. by M. Meyer and R.M. Ogden, Stechert & Co., New York-London 1907. On the relationship between Orsian morphology and Hildebrandian theory we allow ourselves to refer to M. Sessa, *Camminare è descrivere. Il modello della* promenade *per l'ecfrasi filosofico-letteraria di Eugenio d'Ors*, in "Letteratura & Arte", 19 (2021), pp. 21-38, here pp. 26-28.

authors close to Hildebrand, such as Heinrich Wölfflin[24], Alois Riegl[25] and Wilhelm Worringer[26], and by a champion of early 20th century French formalism such as Henri Focillon[27]; he draws important concepts from all of them (mainly polarising oppositional pairs such as Hildebrand's), and spreads them throughout his writings in a constellative manner, in order to corroborate his theoretical edifice on the aesthetic side and to make up for its art-historical shortcomings, as did another morphologist perpetually torn between history and culture: Oswald Spengler[28].

---

24 The Wölfflian borrowings will be explained, here, when the Orsian interpretation of El Greco's work will be sketched out. Anyway, "la fecunda enseñanza de Wölfflin [on the Baroque], anuque no se llegase a fórmulas teóricas precisas, contribuyó mucho posteriormente a ampliar el cuadro donde había permanecido encerrada la misma", E. d'Ors, *Lo Barroco* (1935), Aguilar, Madrid 1964, p. 78.

25 Common to both d'Ors and Riegl is, for instance, dwelling on the organic and inorganic principles of forms. In ornamentation, for Riegl, the reproduction of organic motifs in all their momentary manifestations clashes with the use of crystalline motifs to fill a void, cf. A. Riegl, *Historische Grammatik der bildenden Künste* (1966), ed. by A. Pinotti, Mimesis Verlag, Milan-Udine 2017. d'Ors transposes the antithesis between the biological and the crystalline – as seen above – even to the political level: "Un buen revolucionario se embriagará siempre ante el espectáculo de la actividad de un organismo; pero un buen conservador puede que suspire a menudo por la perfección de los cristales", E. d'Ors, *Nuevo Glosario I*, cit., p. 37.

26 "Worringer descubre parentescos imprevistos entre dos manifestaciones históricas tenidas hasta entonces por inconciliables, entre el gótico y el Barroco", E. d'Ors, *Lo Barroco*, cit., p. 79. He obviously refers to W. Worringer, *Kritische Gedanken zur neuen Kunst* (1919), in Id., *Fragen und Gegenfragen. Schriften zum Kunstproblem*, Piper, Munich 1956, here pp. 86-105; but also to W. Worringer, *Form Problems of the Gothic* (1912), Stechert & Co., New York-London 1920.

27 Cf. M. Mazzocut-Mis, *Forma come destino. Henri Focillon e il pensiero morfologico nell'estetica francese della prima metà del Novecento*, Alinea, Florence 1998, p. 85: "Although it cannot be said that Focillon's *space as a limit* and *space as an environment* retrace the distinction between *spatial value* and *expressive value* of d'Ors [...] nevertheless some points for reflection can be drawn from it". The two concepts are equivalent, for the mature Focillon, to the two spatial configurations of form: "In the first case, space more or less weighs on form and rigorously confines its expansion. [...] In the second case, space yields freely to the expansion of volumes that it does not already contain: these move out into space and there spread forth even as do the forms of life", H. Focillon, *The Life of Forms in Art* (1934), transl. by J. Molino, Zone Books, New York 1992, p. 79. The same tones, low and high, that characterise heavy and light Orsian forms resonate here.

28 Also quoted by d'Ors: "La síntesis de Spengler descubre la inspiración barroca de ciertos fenómenos de historia de la cultura: la invención, por ejemplo, del paisaje y la del género pictórico conocido con el nombre de 'marina'", E. d'Ors,

For d'Ors, the two values of form – spatial and expressive – are, as we have said, constants, and "no aludimos a *leyes*, cuando hablamos de *constantes*, sino a *tipos*", i.e. to characteristics that recur throughout the history of culture by a "coeficiente de reapariciones"[29]. From the degree of Classical spatiality and Baroque expressiveness present in them, it is possible to interpret all phenomena in a dynamic sense, without inscribing them in categories but connecting them in "*sistemas*": in structures of thought that "juntan elementos distantes y disocian los elementos próximos o contiguos"[30]. Like the muscular, vascular, or nervous system, they regulate – with a metaphor that alludes to the birth of modern anatomy and its subduing of the partition into separate organs – the functioning of the entire phenomenal 'body'. Spatial classicism and expressive Baroque are thus also "sistemas sobratemporales"[31] that the philosopher calls, modelling himself on the Alexandrian tradition, "eónes"[32]: recursive and epiphanic cultural formations[33] justifying the "mutua oposición de los ideales"[34], by channelling them into a flexible synoptic-interpretive framework.

The dynamics of Classical and Baroque are assimilated by d'Ors – and this is the distinctive feature of his morphology – to gravitation: "Para entendernos más de pris, adelantemos que debe llamarse *Clasicismo* la tendencia a la supremacía de las formas que se apoyan, y *Barroquismo*,

---

Lo Barroco, op. cit., p. 79. Spengler's artistic appropriations (historical, critical, and theoretical) were already pointed out by L. Curtius, *Morphologie der antiken Kunst*, in "Logos" 9/2 (1920-1921), pp. 195-221. They are evident in the aesthetic section of *Der Untergang des Abendlandes*, for which cf. O. Spengler, *The Decline of the West. Form and Actuality* (1918, 1923), transl. by C.F. Atkinson, Knopf, New York 1945, pp. 217-296; their common matrix is Friedrich Nietzsche's Apollonian/Dionysian, as summarised by M. Guerri, *L'apollineo in Oswald Spengler*, in G. Marchianò (ed. by), *La pluralità estetica. Lasciti e irradiazioni oltre il Novecento*, Trauben, Turin 2001, pp. 161-173.

29 E. d'Ors, *Lo Barroco, op. cit.*, pp. 70, 71.

30 Ivi, p. 67.

31 Ivi, p. 68.

32 Ivi, p. 72-73: "Un *eón* para los alejandrinos significaba una categoría, que, a pesar de su carácter metafísico [...], tenía un desarrollo inscrito en el tiempo, tenía una manera de historia. [...] En el 'eón', lo permanente tiene una historia, la eternidad conoce vicisitudes".

33 Cf. J.L.L. Aranguren, *La filosofia di Eugenio d'Ors, op. cit.*, p. 64: "d'Ors replaces the old division of history into empirical chronological 'ages' with a vision that understands them as an alternation of 'epiphanies'. [...] Epiphany is the appearance in space and time, in history, of that which in itself is not spatial and temporal, but rather supra-historical, eternal".

34 E. d'Ors, *Tres horas en el Museo del Prado, op. cit.*, p. 33.

el de las formas que vuelan"[35]. They predominate one over the other according to the weight or lightness of the forms; not according to a rigorous alternation like Wölfflin's conceptual pairs[36] (from which the possible intermittence of the Classical and Baroque 'aeons' is undoubtedly derived), but with oscillations between gravitation and levitation that can affect both individual forms and their relationships. There is both a gravitation of forms (immanent to works of art) and a gravity of expressive forms (pertinent to the arts): "Cada época conoce a una [arte] a la cual tienden las demás, invadiendo fatalmente el campo de la inmediatamente vecina. Cambia la época, cambia el centro de atracción"[37]. Here are the attributes of each form's gravitational field:

> Ahora, si en toda forma, en cualquier obra, coexisten el elemento espacial o arquitectónico y el elemento expresivo o funcional – que podríamos llamar igualmente *musical* –, la respectiva proporción y dosis puede ser distinta, lo es naturalmente, en cada caso. En tales obras, en tales artistas, en tales países o épocas tenderá el arte a la gravidad arquitectónica ; en tales otras, se musicalizará. En éstas, se sentirá la emoción predilecta de vencer las fatalidades de la caída mediante el impulso que lleva a lo alto; en aquéllas, de vencerlas mediante el equilibrio. *Mundo de las formas que vuelan y mundo de las formas que se apoyan*, he llamado alguna vez a cada uno de ellos.[38]

Let us now emphasise the specificity of the Orsian Baroque. It is, in sum, a "culto de las formas que vuelan"[39], practiced on the double register just mentioned. In terms of individual forms, its characteristics do not deviate from those of Wölfflin's 'Grundbegriffe'; a move away from architectural and sculptural structural plasticity, a tension towards the 'painterly', the disempowerment of the circumscribing force of the line in favour of pure colour, dynamism, and movement of the masses:

35 Ivi, p. 36.

36 Which, as Arnold Hauser well points out, comes from Georg W.F. Hegel: "His formula reflects in essentials the self-movement of some higher super-individual principle, such as we find in Hegel's philosophy of history. The schematic sequence of styles repeats itself of necessity, and its periodic recurrence is a consequence of the inherent causation and the inner logic of the evolution. Wölfflin's well-known view of the parallelism by which 'Baroque styles' follow upon 'Classical styles' in a regular wave-like rhythm is the most striking instance of this theory", A. Hauser, *The Philosophy of Art History* (1958), Routledge, London 1959, p. 57.

37 E. d'Ors, *Nuevo Glosario I, op. cit.*, p. 381.

38 E. d'Ors, *Tres horas en el Museo del Prado, op. cit.*, pp. 35-36.

39 Ivi, p. 36.

> Cuando nos acercamos al límite opuesto [*scil.* to the opposite of Classical: to the expressive value], el dibujo es sacrificado al color; y, dentro del dibujo, el contorno es quien más padece; el intrés capital de la sensibilidad del artista dirígese al aire y a la luz; el ambiente desindividualiza, funde, hace vibrar los objectos.[40]

A decisive deviation: unlike Wölfflin, for whom it was only foreshadowed[41], d'Ors affirms the actual Baroque formal dissolution; if the form rises ever higher to the point of flying (if the expressiveness is exacerbated to the utmost), it reaches a "zona progresivamente romántica e inconcreta"[42]. The Baroque form is a "frontera"[43]: a threshold towards the intangible, paradoxically reached by the expressive *ductus* that eludes itself.

On the level of expressive forms, this translates into an ontological trespass of the plastic and figurative arts into music[44] and poetry, maybe[45], the 'abstract' arts par excellence: into "domains in which the expressive and

40 Ivi, p. 37.

41 Baroque pictorialism is for Wölfflin a declared display of appearances, which produces an autonomous formal domain. This enfranchisement whereby forms take their own independent direction envisages – if the divarication becomes more and more extensive – the possibility of the formless, because "in seiner letzten Konsequenz muss der malerische Stil die plastische Form ganz vernichten", H. Wölfflin, *Renaissance und Barock* (1888), Bruckmann, Munich 1908, p. 20. However, the complete dissolution is only overshadowed, keeping the concept of 'painterly' within an iconic, figurative, representative conception of the image.

42 E. d'Ors, *Tres horas en el Museo del Prado*, *op. cit.*, pp. 36-37. In many places in his production, d'Ors denotes Romanticism as hyperbole of the Baroque, further proving its trans-historicity. Cf. for example his writings dedicated to Goya: E. d'Ors, *La vita di Goya*, *op. cit.*; but also Id., *Tres horas en el Museo del Prado*, *op. cit.*, pp. 81-94.

43 Ivi, p. 71.

44 The juxtaposition of painting and music in the name of ideality and abstraction would later become a Romantic *topos*, cf. for example C.G. Carus, *Nine Letters on Landscape Painting* (1831), transl. by D. Britt, the Getty Research Institute, Los Angeles 2002; and post-Romantic, cf. for example W. Pater, *The School of Giorgione* (1877), in Id., *The Renaissance* (1888), University of California Press, Berkeley-Los Angeles 1980, pp. 102-122.

45 This passage clearly inverts the well-known and influential Gotthold. E. Lessing's dictate that separates "*painting or art of space*" that "*feigns* [...] *movement*" and "*poetry or art of time*" that instead "*lives movement*", as Anceschi points out: cf. L. Anceschi, *Rapporto sull'idea del Barocco*, (1945), in Id., *L'idea del Barocco. Studi su un problema estetico*, Nuova Alfa, Bologna 1984, pp. 7-30, here p. 15; and, more extensively in relation to the autonomy of the arts, Id., *Eugenio d'Ors e il nuovo classicismo europeo*, Rosa e Ballo, Milan 1945, pp. 63-75.

its function are preponderant"[46]; in a word, into *other* arts. The perennial flight of Baroque forms is always a flight upwards, towards heavens, and its points of arrival are the equivalent of the passages of state of water in physics: evaporation (from the liquid state of Classical art to the gaseous state of Baroque art), and even sublimation (if we consider the extremes mentioned above: from the solid state of Classical architecture and sculpture, to the gaseous state of Baroque music and poetry). With regard to Baroque painting, therefore, d'Ors elaborates a 'light' morphological paradigm on the pictorial sign as 'vapor'[47].

Damisch, as we have seen, thinks of the early Baroque 'cloud' sign as "un élément iconique"; although it acts "sur le double rigistre du signifié et du signifiant", it reveals at the same time a truth about images. It is the primary element for an investigation of the pictorial system in a semiological sense that is regulated, however, in a Wölfflinian way, by a logic intrinsic to iconicity: "l'étude de leurs principes formateurs et des traits constitutifs de l'apparence des choses tells que la peinture les donne à voir"[48]. The 'cloud' compensates the Cézannean 'truth in painting': it is a way of expressing it, and it does so precisely because "est connoté d'entrée du jeu comme élément hors la norme"[49]. Because of its working with pure sensation on the "*imagination matérielle*"[50], a certain type of depiction of clouds in relation to space – in the mid-16th century – breaks with the tradition of Classical style and Mannerism to inaugurate a divergent – in a word: Baroque[51] – path to representation. The 'cloud' is considered "as the key figurative object of 'another art', and more precisely as an object fundamental to a style of painting located at the opposite extreme

46 Ivi, p. 21.

47 On the "'corpulencias'" that "se evaporan" in El Greco's painting we will return later, but for now cf. E. d'Ors, *Tres horas en el Museo del Prado*, *op. cit.*, p. 77.

48 H. Damisch, *Théorie du nuage*, *op. cit.*, pp. 30, 21.

49 Ivi, pp. 55-56.

50 Ivi, p. 33.

51 Despite his open criticism of the limits of the concept of style ("La définition mal assure, l'extension très lâche assignée à la notion de *style* dans le champ de l'histoire de l'art font cette question, à la lettre, ni peut être *entendue*", ivi, p. 26), Damisch is unable to avoid confronting – and often even disengaging himself from – the theoretical achievements of late 19th century German formalism. In fact, he owes the assimilation of the 'cloud' to the Baroque and its anti-Classical connotation to a careful reading of Jacob Burckhardt, Wölfflin and Riegl: the same authors from whom d'Ors takes his cue. For Wölfflin's definition of the characteristics of the 'Classical style' and its exhaustion in the Mannerist 'thin crest', cf. H. Wölfflin, *Die Klassische Kunst*, Bruckmann, Munich 1899.

to that of perspective painting proposed by [Leon Battista] Alberti"[52]; it is a sign of an iconic paradigm other than perspective painting: "Le /nuage/, considéré en tant que graphe pictural, peut paraître contredire aux données et aux principes d'un art fondé sur la stricte délinéation des formes et de la perspective géométrique"[53].

To the perspective regime, Damisch contrasts the 'cloud' regime. The former is substantiated by a circumscribing pictorial graph derived from marquetry, from the "travail d'*intarsia*" of lines that set things in "dramatiques et scéniques"[54] relations of a theatrical matrix, such as those of linear perspective[55]; it is based on the contingent relations of figure/background and front/back. The second is materialised with the veiling/revealing pictorial graph mentioned above, which derives from attempts to render light with colour, and that "intervient dans le texte figurative là où est question non seulement des rapports entre la terre et le ciel, mais entre l'ici-bas et l'au-delà, entre un monde qui obéit à ses lois propres et l'espace divin dont nulle science ne saurait connaître"[56]. It is based on the transcendent correspondences of the depiction with the unrepresentable, modulated on low/high, and stands on the boundary of "the pictorial representation centred on the otherness of the visualization of the invisible"; speaking the lexicon of Victor I. Stoichita, it offers concrete means in "visualizing the Sacred"[57].

The new "art 'céleste'"[58], configured by the 'cloud' that obliterates geometric spatiality and illusion, is the first to reject the normativity of the Renaissance concept of perspective, and in this sense inaugurates artistic modernity. It surpasses Alberti's prescriptions – which are essentially selective: they subordinate colour to line and drawing, and exclude "l'élément aérien"[59] – because it makes representation arise from a field of forces susceptible to gravitational oscillations such as those described by d'Ors; it removes the aegis of the single, fixed point of view in favour of glimpses towards the infinite practised from within figurativeness: "Elle

52 V.I. Stoichita, *Visionary Experience in the Golden Age of Spanish Art*, transl. by A.-M. Glasheen, Reaktion Books, London 1995, p. 87.

53 H. Damisch, *Théorie du nuage*, *op. cit.*, p 29.

54 Ivi, pp. 164, 139.

55 Damisch has systematised his ideas on perspective in H. Damisch, *L'origine de la perspective* (1987), Flammarion, Paris 2017.

56 H. Damisch, *Théorie du nuage*, *op. cit.*, p. 147.

57 V.I. Stoichita, *Visionary Experience in the Golden Age of Spanish Art*, *op. cit.*, pp. 84, 86.

58 H. Damisch, *Théorie du nuage*, *op. cit.*, p. 29.

59 Ivi, p. 166.

entroduit dans le champ pictural une différenciation, quelque chose comme une faille, une rupture qui manifeste figurativement la précarité de l'ordre humain, constamment exposé à la déchirure du miracle"[60]. The form of the cloud breaks the illusion and recomposes the painting on an anti-anthropocentric – divine – scale; covering the pictorial space with painted clouds – making a sky out of them – is equivalent to the "moyen duquel les mesures humaines du drame sont localement suspendues"[61].

As in d'Ors, for Damisch, proto-Baroque and then Baroque forms escape; always mobile and impregnable they aim elsewhere, upwards. They do so by avoiding illusion and referentiality, by virtue of "une pratique dans laquelle les moyens d'expression sont mis en œuvre suivant des voies étrangères aux circuits ordinaires de la communication"; their graph is a type of form that "est à elle-même son propre contenu, d'une matière qui, d'entrée de jeu, fonctionne déjà comme forme, d'un signifié qui ne se laisse en aucun cas séparer du signifiant"[62]. In the context of a painting that is intended to be anti-Classical, the semiotician developed a 'light' morphological paradigm on the pictorial sign as a 'cloud'.

III. *Two reference artists*

It is worth emphasising a further parallelism between d'Ors and Damisch on the level of the relations that their respective artistic conceptions entertain with the figurative arts *stricto sensu*. The two authors do not limit themselves to selecting concrete examples endorsing their theories, but identify in two precise reference artists the exact homologues of their respective morphological paradigms: for d'Ors it is El Greco, for Damisch it is Correggio. Both, instead of relegating artistic facts to a secondary position as comments and corollaries of systems of thought, they use painting to make philosophy of art, therefore fully saving *aisthesis*. They appropriate El Greco and Correggio by making them their own, because the two artists perfectly embody the Baroque forms of 'vapor' and 'cloud', and dilute the categorical rigidity of philosophical dualism. Thus, d'Ors

60 Ivi, p. 148.

61 *Ibidem*.

62 Ivi, p. 46. Even Damisch refers to Focillon, by directly quoting from his *Vie des formes*, about the self-significant character of form: "A sign signifies an object, form signifies only itself. [...] Form has a meaning – but it is a meaning entirely its own, a personal and specific value that must not be confused with the attributes we impose on it", H. Focillon, *The Life of Forms*, *op. cit.*, pp. 34, 35.

and Damisch follow in the footsteps of many other thinkers who, since the beginning of the 20th century, have also turned to speculation from the iconic side by means of close comparisons with the work of painters; among them Georg Simmel with Rembrandt, Maurice Merleau-Ponty with Cézanne, Gilles Deleuze with Francis Bacon[63].

The reappropriation of El Greco by d'Ors is part of a relatively late modern process of rediscovery[64], crowned by a renewed popularity of the Cretan painter and culminating in a veritable 'Grecomania'. It took place between the 19th and 20th century and was characterised by a hermeneutic *querelle* around El Greco's 'blurred vision', which was antimimetic and therefore disturbing; it resulted in a "very strong polarisation of interpretations, which at the same time led to the extreme physiological approach" – El Greco's painting as "art of the (sick) body" – and "to his more spiritualistic readings related to the sphere of his alleged mysticism" – painting as "art of the (holy) spirit"[65]. d'Ors, as can be deduced, is assimilated to the

63 These are just a few of the philosophers who have been able to "recognise in the gesture of 'making visible' proper to painting a radical critique of our categorical habits, or – if you like – the need for their stupefying suspension", in favour of a surrender of the conceptual/linguistic to the iconic; cf. A. Pinotti, *Introduzione*, in Id. (ed. by), *Filosofia e pittura nel Novecento*, Guerini, Milan 1998, pp. 9-12, here p. 12. The volume is a good anthological compendium of the aforementioned aesthetological trend. As far as Simmel is concerned, it is appropriate to point out, in the economy of the present study, one of his particular declensions of gravitational polarity in an aesthetic key. In a very short essay significantly titled *Ästhetik der Schwere* (1901), he argues that "in our everyday surroundings, this typical fate of the soul continues. The movements of our limbs constantly show the struggle between physical gravity, dragging us downward, and psychic-physiological impulses, canceling out and deflecting a body's weight"; this antinomy has a counterpart in art: "the typical ways in which human beings present themselves and feature in diverse styles of art are decided by the particular manner in which these opposing forces encounter, divert, and thwart or sometimes foster or cede to one another and jointly create a unity of appearances in manifold combinations". Consistent with d'Ors and Damisch, when a style, for Simmel, "pushes psychic freedom and impulsivity to fuller expression by simple neglect of gravity", it tends towards the Baroque. Cf. G. Simmel, *Aesthetics of Gravity* (1901), transl. by A. Harrington, in Id., *Essays on Art and Aesthetics*, The University of Chicago Press, Chicago-London 2020, pp. 143-147, here pp. 143, 144, 145.

64 Well sythesized in E. Storm, *Julius Meier-Graefe, El Greco and the rise of modern art*, in "Mitteilungen der Carl Justi-Vereinigung", 20 (2008), pp. 113-133, now available at the following link: https://scholarlypublications.universiteitleiden.nl/access/item%3A3145764/view.

65 A. Pinotti, *El Greco at the Ophthalmologist's*, in "Predella", 35 (2014), pp. 3-23, here p. 4. The first tendency pertains to the 19th century, attempts to ascribe

spiritual side, as he frees El Greco from the encumbrances of classicism and naturalism, making him the painter of 'vapors' and 'flying forms'. He published his Grecian annotations from the beginning of the 1920s, but he was not alone; read for instance this page from the first part of Spengler's *Der Untergang des Abendlandes* (1918), which condenses the cogency of clouds and skies and El Greco's forerunner role for the Baroque transformation of Western art in a few lines:

> The same symbolic meaning attaches to clouds. Classical art concerns itself with them no more than with horizons, and the painter of the Renaissance treats them with a certain playful superficiality But very early the Gothic looked at its cloud-masses, and through them, with the long sight of mysticism and the Venetians (Giorgione and Paolo Veronese above all) discovered the full magic of the cloud-world, of the thousand-tinted Being that fills the heavens with its sheets and wisps and mountains. Grunewald and the Netherlanders heightened its significance to the level of tragedy. El Greco brought the grand art of cloud-symbolism to Spain.[66]

There is a difference, however, between them: for d'Ors El Greco is not just a symbol; he is the most vivid embodiment of Baroque aerial tension in formal bipolarity. His paintings are proof of how, with the lightening of forms, "va ascendiendo […] la escala de la expresividad"[67]. To the highest degree, up to the intangible; in front of the most audacious El Greco's experiments, one reaches "aquellas ardientes regiones en que la pintura, agitada por una ambición febril de expresión, está a punto de volatilizar su materia para convertirla en música o en poesía"[68]. d'Ors forcefully rejects the 'corporeal' interpretation and the hypothesis of astigmatism[69], siding

El Greco's expressionistic style to an alleged astigmatism of the artist, and is summarised and discussed in the early 20th century by D. Katz, *War Greco astigmatisch? Eine psychologische Studie zur Kunstwissenschaft*, Veit Verlag, Leipzig 1914. The second, on the contrary, justifies it in an anti-naturalistic key and is inaugurated in Spain by the so-called 'generation of intellectuals of 1898' (Miguel de Unamuno among the best known) and in France by Maurice Barrès (with his Greco ou le secret de Tolède, 1911). But – Storm points out – the revival of El Greco is fundamentally due to Julius Meier-Graefe, cf. E. Storm, *Julius Meier-Graefe, El Greco and the rise of modern art, op. cit.*

66 O. Spengler, *The Decline of the West, op. cit.*, pp. 239-240.

67 E. d'Ors, *Tres horas en el Museo del Prado, op. cit.*, p. 38.

68 Ivi, p. 71.

69 "Se ha dicho si era oftalmópata… No; lo que pasaba es que estaba bebido. Bebido de zumos de Dios y crepúsculo. En esta situación, las cosas pierden su peso; y al perder el peso de las cosas, llaman – han llamado – los poetas: espiritualizar", E. d'Ors, *Nuevo Glosario I, op. cit.*, p. 372.

with a mysticism of the painter, which is patently and perspicuously present in his painting. A painting that is by no means aberrated vision; it has dignity as a style with non-Classical principles, by "fatalidad"[70] ascetically deforming[71] and dynamic[72]. Since the Classical/Baroque antithesis mirrors the "fundamental reason-life antithesis"[73], El Greco's mystical style sits "en el centro del turbulento dominio en que la irracionalidad enciende sus temblorosas hogueras"[74], and whose vitalism at once religious and irrational legitimises every expressive license.

On a formal level it happens that "las cosas contempladas" – if baroquely transposed into an image – "pierden su peso", and that the figures go – as we have shown – out of state; the solidity of the referent becomes gaseous: "Se evaporan [...] las [...] 'corpulencias', para dar paso a todo lo que en arte es cohibido y subterráneo, a la loca sensualidad del color"[75]. Form as 'vapor' is that which, precisely via iconicity (and in the case of El Greco even through deformation), succeeds in tending upwards, in going lighter and thinner until it becomes anti-form, following a "progreso ascético"[76]. In his aesthetic itinerary through the Museo del Prado, d'Ors takes the detail of the upper register of *Pentecost* (1597-1600; fig. 1) as an extreme example, making an ecphrastic microscopy of it[77]: "Estas mismas lenguas de fuego che aparecen [in *Pentecost*] [...] que antes ya han sido prefiguradas en todos los cuerpos de los hombres, de las mujeres y de los ángeles [of his previous paintings]"[78] are the borderline case of the Baroque 'aeon'.

70 E. d'Ors, *Tres horas en el Museo del Prado*, *op. cit.*, p. 76.
71 Cf. ivi, p. 77.
72 Cf. E. d'Ors, *Nuevo Glosario I*, *op. cit.*, p. 372: "Aquí triunfan lo dinámico, lo embriagado y mistico, la supremacía de la pasión".
73 L. Anceschi, *Eugenio d'Ors e il nuovo classicismo europeo*, *op. cit.*, p. 55.
74 E. d'Ors, *Nuevo Glosario I*, *op. cit.*, p. 371.
75 E. d'Ors, *Tres horas en el Museo del Prado*, *op. cit.*, pp. 74, 77.
76 Ivi, p. 77.
77 On the logic of ecphrasis in d'Ors, we refer again to M. Sessa, *Camminare è descrivere. Il modello della* promenade *per l'ecfrasi filosofico-letteraria di Eugenio d'Ors*, *op. cit.*
78 E. d'Ors, *Tres horas en el Museo del Prado*, *op. cit.*, p. 78.

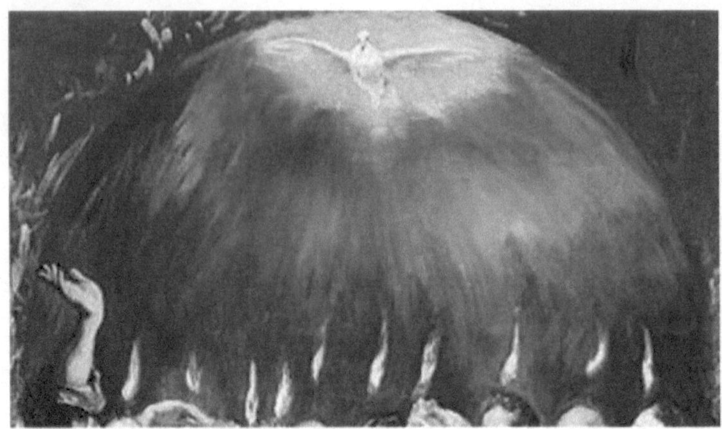

Fig. 1: El Greco, *Pentecost*, 1597-1600, oil con canvas, Museo Nacional del Prado, Madrid (detail).

In his evaluation of El Greco's form from a Baroque and 'aerial' perspective, d'Ors is close to two of the authors of his art-historical, critical and theoretical constellation: the aforementioned Wölfflin and Focillon. For Wölfflin, El Greco is the most peculiar "Vorläufer des Barock"[79] within the 16th century. He utterly contributes to that "Prozeß der Entwertung der Linie" that marks the transition from 'linear' to 'painterly'; he does not limit himself to destroy the "Flächenideal" as an instrument that adheres perfectly to a material referent: in El Greco "ist fast nichts mehr davon zu spüren"[80], because the contours of his figures dissolve into pure chromatism. With regard to the composition, Wölfflin has no doubts: in him, dynamism is clearly upwards oriented (and "*Hochdrangs*"[81] is a clear marker of the 'open form'): "Und Greco wäre verloren, wenn er nicht die Figurenbewegung im eigentümlichen Zug der Wolken am Himmel weiterleiten könnte"[82].

Focillon, in fact, includes him in the sphere of the so-called 'visionary' artists; those who "form an order apart" trans-historically, united by a shared anti-Classical and anti-naturalist figurative conception dictated by a perceptive exceptionality and an excess of vision. They "interpret rather

79 H. Wölfflin, *Kunstgeschichtliche Grundbegriffe*, *op. cit.*, p. 110.
80 *Ibidem*.
81 H. Wölfflin, *Renaissance und Barock*, *op. cit.*, p. 41.
82 H. Wölfflin, *Kunstgeschichtliche Grundbegriffe*, *op. cit.*, p. 64.

than imitate, and transfigure rather than interpret"[83]. In this group, El Greco stands out for his spatial approach to the painting, in which not surprisingly treats the human figure as "plastic matter" and "stretches [it] into death or dilates him through the sky, like the promise of the angel"[84]. The same characteristics of El Greco's form according to d'Ors reappear punctually: dynamism, mysticism, irrationality: "The dynamics and mysticism of space are of the same order as irrational perspectives"[85]. For Focillon, El Greco's forms are comparable to d'Ors's 'flying' ones.

From a broader perspective than that of pure form, the painting of the Cretan is one of the apexes of what Stoichita has called "'mystical style'"[86], i.e., of all the means employed in the Spanish *Siglo de Oro* to commence the challenge of representing the unrepresentable: the retentions of rapture and visionary experience – in short: the Sacred. This style is ontologically "nebulous": characterised by a "lack of clarity"[87]. Its figurative stratagems pertain to the depiction of clouds and skies and the rendering of light. El Greco, for instance, in the *Vision of St. Francis* (1600-1605; fig. 2, fig. 3), in the upper register of the painting "eliminated the figures" seen by the saint and replaces them with "a luminous tear in the dark heavens"[88]; in d'Ors's words: with a 'corpulencia evaporada' which tends to formless[89].

---

83 H. Focillon, *Estetica dei visionari* (1926), transl. by G. Guglielmi, Abscondita, Milan 2006, p. 13. Their "special optics" always reconfigure the real datum under the banner of "making visible" and renewing creation: "it alters [...] even the density of the sensible world", *ibidem*. Among them: Honoré Daumier, Rembrandt, Giovanni Battista Piranesi, William Turner, Tintoretto, and El Greco; all these artists "in general are more imaginative than sensitive", ivi, p. 15.

84 Ivi, p. 64.

85 *Ibidem*. In Focillonian morphology, the opposite pole – static, materialist, rational – is witnessed by Piero della Francesca. Speaking of his work, he expresses himself in terms once again similar to those of d'Ors: "The men and women [painted by Piero] weigh heavily on the earth, they rest heavily on the ground feet made for stable balance, for mountain stepping". Even when it must represent movement, Piero's painting remains heavy: "The movement of Piero's figures, instead of lightening the heaviness, completes and increases it". For Focillon, Piero della Francesca's forms are an analogue of d'Ors's 'heavy forms'. Cf. H. Focillon, *Piero della Francesca* (1934), transl. by F. Lanza Pietromarchi, Pratiche, Parma 1992, pp. 90, 91.

86 V.I. Stoichita, *Visionary Experience in the Golden Age of Spanish Art*, *op. cit.*, p. 80.

87 Ivi, p. 79.

88 Ivi, p. 82.

89 Cf. ivi, p. 83: "What can Francis see? Or, better still, can he see something, or is he only forcing himself to see? If he can see 'God' in one form or another, as

El Greco's works, to be 'flying forms' "en los misteriosos celajes"[90], redoubles and perpetuates asceticism; and it is precisely for this reason that it best embodies the Baroque morphological paradigm.

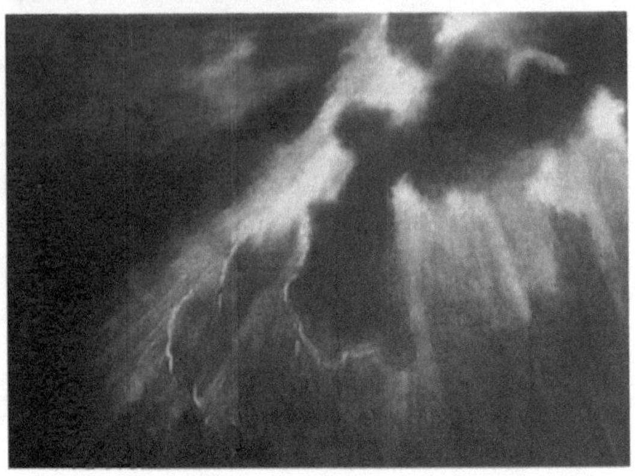

Fig. 2: El Greco, *Vision of Saint Francis*, 1600-1605, oil on canvas, Hospital de mujeres, Cadiz (detail).

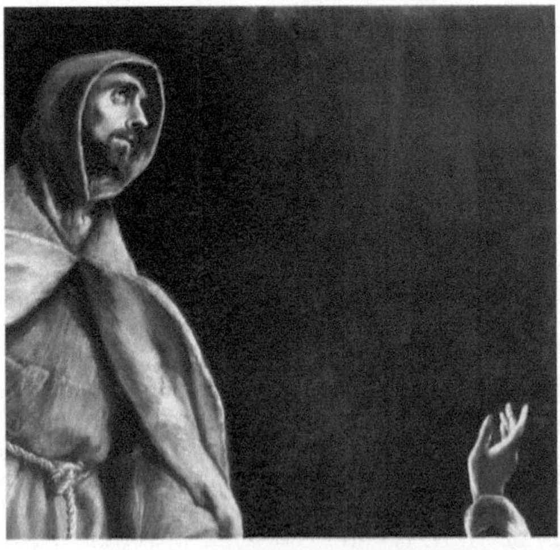

Fig. 3: El Greco, *Vision of Saint Francis*, 1600-1605, oil on canvas, Hospital de mujeres, Cadiz (detail).

his ecstatic manner might lead us to suppose, then he is seeing him more as an absence of form, without visible qualities, as a 'nothing'".

90 E. d'Ors, *Tres horas en el Museo del Prado*, *op. cit.*, p. 78.

Damisch, conversely, lingers on the figure of Correggio because of his exceptionality: his works, seen amid Western artistic production in general, have "une autre portée", to the point of "occuper une position décisive"[91]. This is due, as can be guessed, to the way the painter depicted clouds, especially in the famous two parmesan domes: that of the Church of San Giovanni Evangelista (1520-1524; fig. 4) and that of the Duomo (1526-1530; fig. 5). Such is the potential of Correggio's 'cloud' graph:

> Il permet en outre de soustraire les figures aux lois de la physique des corps et autorise nombre d'effets aériens, de transports, de ruptures et de juxtapositions paradoxales, ce n'est pas à dire que son occurrence, son maniement, son traitement même relèvent du seul caprice, de la 'manière' au sens péjoratif du mot. L''ivresse' à laquelle convie le Corrège est précisément calculée, et le *nuage* entre dans ce calcul à titre de vecteur libre qui prête ò des opérations dont Burckhardt a parfaitement reconnu la nature sémiotique, tout à la fois signalétique et syntaxique.[92]

Speaking then in Wölfflinian terms, Damisch counts Correggio's figurative machines among the first devices to reject Alberti's linear perspective and to propose, for them, a different conception of pictoriality:

> Au regard du concept d'un style 'baroque' ou encore 'pittoresque', 'pictural' (*malerisch*), et dont 'l'aversion pour toute délimitation précise est peut-être le trait le plus marquant', les coupoles du Corrège ne pouvaient manquer d'apparaître, historiquement parlant, comme une production inaugurale : l'une des premières manifestations, singulièrement précoce et décidée, d'un art où paraîtront se défaire les mesures du cube perspectif, de l'espace tectonique orthogonal et clos du Quattrocento.[93]

The 'cloud' is an essentially 'painterly' sign, in Wölfflin's sense, because it is capable of completely occluding – covering – the architectural space, and hence of entertaining with the support, with the specific medium of representation, a disturbing and perturbing relationship; it causes semiotic

---

91 H. Damisch, *Théorie du nuage*, *op. cit.*, p. 20.

92 Ivi, p. 29. Damisch quotes in full Burckhardt's description of the two domes of Parma of *Der Cicerone* (1855), ivi, pp. 12-14. The German historian already accords Correggio's clouds structural relevance: "La designation de l'espace, des supports e de l'assiette [*scil.* of Correggio's figuration], et de même les gradations, les nuances de la peinture, sont exprimées par des nuage, que Corrège traite comme des corps résistants", J. Burckhardt, *Der Cicerone* (1855), quoted ivi, p. 13.

93 Ivi, pp. 14-15. The intertextual quotation comes from Wölfflin's *Renaissance und Barock*.

short-circuits. Correggio's art "prend pour objet (pour référent) l'espace lui-même [...] la représentation des formes singulières telles qu'elles apparaissent et se découvrent dans une profondeur libre et indéfinie, considérée dans la substance lumineuse et aérienne"[94].

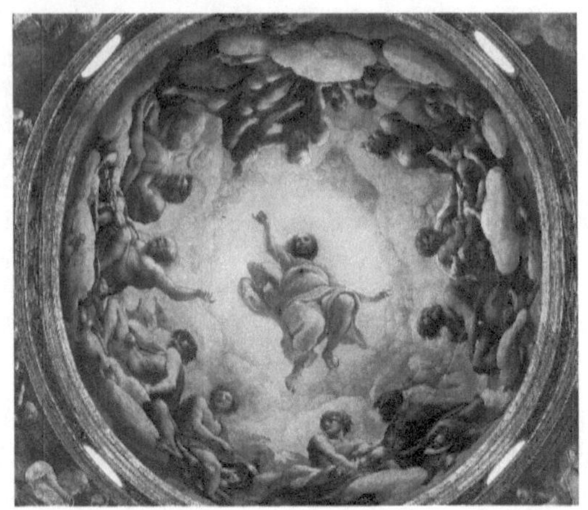

Fig. 4: Correggio, *The Ascension of Christ* or better *The Vision of Saint John in Patmos*, 1520-1524, fresco, Church of San Giovanni Evangelista, Parma.

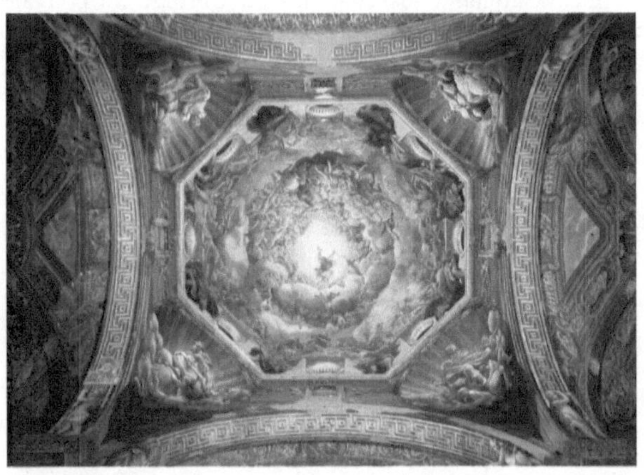

Fig. 5: Correggio, *The Assumption of The Virgin*, 1526-1530, fresco, Cathedral, Parma.

94 H. Damisch, *Théorie du nuage*, *op. cit.*, p. 22.

Correggio's 'cloud' is precisely the type of sign that allows for that effectively pictorial semiology Damisch promises himself; an interpretation of the iconic syntax founded on the immanence of the irreducible elements of painting; echoing Cézanne: a discourse that speaks the truth of painting. Therefore Correggio's 'cloud' is a 'light' morphological paradigm of the delegitimization of perspective; it shifts the attention on the frontline of the formless: "A vouloir saisir l'œuvre du Corrège dans son unité à la fois sensible et thématique sans doute prétend-on trop embrasser, au risque de n'étreindre que des formes, des structures inconsistantes"[95]. Correggio's 'cloud'. It is the ideal counterpart to the Grecian 'flying forms' for d'Ors, and it perfectly embodies the Baroque formal force, which is able to unmask the only presumed connaturality between representation and perspective illusiveness:

> Si le graphe pictural désigné comme *nuage* est souvent très éloigné de revêtir les dehors vaporeux et instables qui feraient cet élément connoter matériellement une effusion, et, dynamiquement, une ascension, force est alors d'admettre que le procès iconique ne se fonde pas nécessairement sur une analogie naturelle, une correspondance bi-univoque entre le signe et l'objet réel qu'il est censé représenter (dénoter).[96]

In assigning Correggio a decisive and anticipatory role in the transition from a Classical to a Baroque formal system, Damisch – just like d'Ors – genealogically relates to Wölfflin's dictate. For the latter, Correggio is the first in 16th-century Italy who "hat diese Schönheit zuerst geahnt": the beauty released by the "neuen Anschauung [way of seeing]"[97] of 'painterly' Baroque. As as written above about El Greco, the Italian painter also breaks through spatial depth by making it open, abandons line for chromatic masses, dissolves the pictorial surface in dynamism[98], and approaches the formless:

> Am weitesten von allen seinen Volksgenossen hat sich Correggio von der herrschenden Meinung freigemacht. Bei ihm merkt man deutlich, wie er die Linie als führendes Element zu überwinden versucht. Es sind zwar immer noch Linien, lange, durchlaufende Linien, mit denen er arbeitet, allein er kompliziert ihren Gang meist der Art, daß es dem Auge schwer wird, ihnen zu folgen, und in die Schatten und Lichter kommt jenes Lecken und Züngeln, als ob sie

95 Ivi, p. 40.

96 *Ibidem*.

97 H. Wölfflin, *Kunstgeschichtliche Grundbegriffe*, *op. cit.*, p. 128.

98 Cf. ivi, p. 110: in the same page, El Greco is linked to Tintoretto.

eigenmächtig einander entgegenstrebten und sich von der Form freimachen wollten.[99]

We recognise the opposition *gravia/levia* even in Wölfflin; the Baroque style becomes animated; it moves "zu der Massenhaftigkeit tritt Oberall eine ins Ungestüme und Gewaltsame gesteigerte Bewegung" that allows the forms to rise, unburdening themselves: in Correggio's paintings we find "ein Aufrauschen"[100]. Damisch, therefore, appropriates Correggio to make the 'cloud' the metonymy of a new figurative paradigm; but there is much more: the strategies that the painted clouds bring into play are "fonctions et relations dont la prise en consideration apparaît comme la démarche inaugurale d'une théorie de l'art"[101]. Just as in d'Ors El Greco and the 'flying forms' stand in the place of life (against reason), in Damisch Correggio and the 'cloud' stand in the place of art theory *tout court* (against a history of art that was born Classical and informed at its base by the 'perspectival reason').

The key role, in this passage, of both Correggio and the 'cloud', recalls the seminal studies of the English art historian John Shearman on the place and weight of clouds in early Renaissance and later Baroque figuration; a sketch of this analogy is therefore drawn. Shearman is convinced, like Damisch, that one can write a history of art modulated on clouds; they gave rise, from the 16th century onwards, to a "complex apparatus" of figurative choices that were then crystallised in the following century in Baroque form: "Who can imagine Baroque art without clouds?"[102]. 16th and Baroque clouds are an index of the mutations in the "relationship between observer and painted object"[103] that occurred in conjunction with the peak of the so-called *Maniera moderna*; they invite us to reflect on the interactions between function, abstraction, and illusion[104] and on how their

99 Ivi, p. 35.

100 H. Wölfflin, *Renaissance und Barock*, *op. cit.*, pp. 58, 59.

101 H. Damisch, *Théorie du nuage*, *op. cit.*, p. 40.

102 J. Shearman, *Raphael's Clouds, and Correggio's*, in M. Sambucco Hamoud, M.L. Strocchi (ed. by), *Studi su Raffaello. Atti del Congresso internazionale di studi (Urbino-Firenze 6-14 aprile 1984)*, QuattroVenti, Urbino 1987, pp. 657-668, here p. 657.

103 J. Shearman, *L'illusionismo del Correggio* (1980), in Id., *Funzione e illusione. Raffaello Pontormo Correggio*, trans. and ed. by A. Nova, Il Saggiatore, Milan 1983, pp. 171-184, 254-256, here p. 171.

104 Cf. *ibidem*: Illusionism is "one of the most ingenious, yet least studied inventions of Renaissance artists. If this subject has not been profoundly analysed, with the exception of the relationship with *linear* perspective, this is due, in my opinion, to

meaning is transformed in relation to the receptive side of the artistic fact, to fruition. Correggio must be interpreted, as "a great moment of synthesis of Italian art, akin, in this respect, to the work of Raphael"[105]; in the domes of Parma all the problems of illusiveness inherited from the Medieval tradition converge.

According to Shearman, when he comes to clouds, Correggio absorbed the lesson of Raphael's *Vision of Ezekiel* (1517-1518; fig. 6), who makes ingenious – and almost paradoxical – use of the naturalistic cloud to raise the form towards the unrepresentable: "In other words, it is the very naturalism of the cloud that most effectively signals the irrational magnitude of visionary Glory"[106]. The artist exploits this method and applies it in the particular context of dome decoration, that – Shearman stresses – brings the specifics of pictorial spatiality into play like few others.

By transposing this 'celestial' naturalism into the space of the dome, Correggio locates it in an equally evanescent vantage point; he satisfies what Shearman calls "the threshold instinct"[107]: he places the viewer in the most appropriate place to contemplate a painting that almost flies from how high up it is[108]. The main purpose of Correggio's decorative machines

---

the fact that contemporary art historians give more weight to abstractions than to representations of reality, and perhaps also to the fact that illusionism is regarded as a kind of miracle, better accepted as such and not susceptible to structural and historical analysis. On the contrary, I find both the mechanics and the psychology of illusionism interesting". It is necessary to note how for Shearman illusionism does not overlap with perspective representation, and that it is above all a mutable notion. On the complex topic of the meaning of illusion in relation to Renaissance perspective, one may refer, among many other contributions, to M. Kubovy, *The Psychology of Perspective and Renaissance Art*, Cambridge University Press, Cambridge 1988, in particular the chapters *The Arrow in the Eye* and *Illusion, Delusion, Collusion, & Paradox.*

105 J. Shearman, *L'illusionismo del Correggio, op. cit.*, p. 171.

106 Ivi, p. 662. For Shearman, Raphael "responds to the biblical text by describing the clouds as modern interpreters do, impressed by their naturalistic precision" to best render "the '*splendor quasi species electri*' revealed to Ezekiel in the clouds", ivi, pp. 662-663. Depicting Ezekiel's theophany, it is argued, engages the challenge of the "mystical style" – to make visible the unrepresentable – on which Stoichita dwelled, and which necessarily implies clouds: "Ezekiel's text is [...] central to the 'visualisation' of celestial Glory'", ivi, p. 661. The biblical lesson is contained in *Ez.*, III, 13.

107 J. Shearman, *Domes* (1988), in Id., *Only Connect... Art and Spectator in the Italian Renaissance*, Princeton University Press, Princeton 1992, pp. 149-191, here p. 166.

108 The "threshold instinct" "leads the artist to select the most natural viewpoint, which is at the first comfortable position from which the domed space becomes

is to make the celestial vision effective and actual for the spectator (by naturalistic means, it has been said): to make it, in practice, an experience. The relationship between the viewer and the painted subject has become "fully transitive": un "an empirically convincing continuum"[109], that encompasses both terms under the sign of pictorialism. Illusion, in Correggio, is not deception (what in English is called 'delusion'), but certainty; certainty, for those under the dome, that with the appropriate "elusive atmospheric transitions"[110] the painting can incarnate the Divine.

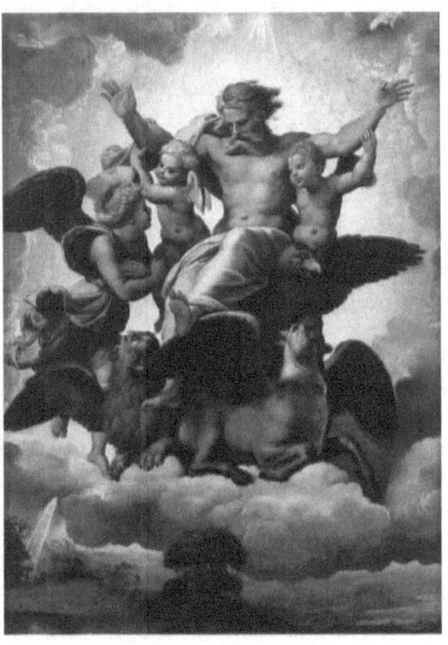

Fig. 6: Raphael, *Vision of Ezekiel*, 1517-1518, oil on board, Gallerie degli Uffizi, Florence.

It is recorded as crucial that, in order to achieve the result, the pictorial sign obliterates space and support in an anti-perspective manner: "Finally,

visible", *ibidem*. The enjoyment of domes – Shearman points out well – is painful: "It taxes the neck", ivi, p. 149. It entails a reversal of the phenomenological visual axis by forcing one to always look up, and it just distorts the gaze: "In a dome everything but this privileged area [*scil.* the decorated space] is necessarily, and in varying degrees, seen at an angle and distorted", *ibidem*.

109 Ivi, pp. 184, 186.

110 Ivi, p. 186.

it is remarkable how completely one loses all sense of the surface of the dome, a condition very important condition in the functioning of the illusion of transit"[111]. Even if Shearman focusses on the iconic device (dome/spectator), his Correggesque interpretation is not far from Damisch's, who insists on the system of signs (graph); the Shearmanian illusiveness "denoted as a bridge towards the sacred" collides with the Damischian 'cloud' connoted as "limite de la représentation, du *représentable*":

> Par-delà les nuées s'ouvre le règne de ce qui ne peut faire l'objet d'une representation parce qu'il ne peut recevoir de nom, l'espace infini, ou indéfini, dont le silence inquiétera les esprites classiques aussi longtemps qu'ils n'auront pas découvert un langage qui permît de l'interroger, de l'analyser, de le faire *parler.*[112]

Damisch's final characterisation of Correggio's 'cloud' as a liminal representation and diaphragm for the unrepresentable tinges his theory with a mystical afflatus, as it does for d'Ors and the Grecian 'flying forms'. The 'cloud' is also a 'mystical cloud'. Themes, problems, and methods are the same as those of d'Ors when he speaks of the spiritualisation of forms. And, later, of Stoichita, when he investigates a conceptual junction that has been a theme since the 'semiotics' of St. Thomas Aquinas, namely the pictorial (hence logically material) synthesis of the two aspects connatural in 'vision': "what the imagination or intellect perceives internally"[113] e "the visionary experience [which] is not necessarily an optical one, [and that even] though it remains the perception of an image, [...] can vary enormously"[114] (and which is therefore likely immaterial).

It is no coincidence that even Damisch, in a chapter of his book, invokes the "notional"[115] ecphrases of the apparitions of St. Teresa, 17th century Spanish painting, and even El Greco. The mystical 'cloud' is said to be an object that manifests the sacred, or that serves its manifestation, but "par

111 Ivi, p. 188.

112 H. Damisch, *Théorie du nuage*, *op. cit.*, p. 84.

113 Thomas Aquinas, *Summa Theologica*, I, q. LXVII, a, 1), quoted in V.I. Stoichita, *Visionary Experience in the Golden Age of Spanish Art, op. cit.*, p. 7.

114 *Ibidem.* Texts and painting that seek to describe or depict the mystical experience are "both problematic and paradoxical, since a priori, what they represent can neither be seen", *ibidem*.

115 Cf. J. Hollander, *The poetics of ekphrasis*, in "Word & Image: A Journal of Verbal/Visual Enquiry", 4:1 (1988), pp. 209-219, here p. 109. The account of the mystical phenomenon, by virtue of its intangible referent, can be ascribed to the domain of the 'notional'.

la grâce de l'image"[116]: through the intercession of the iconic that bears on its shoulders the weight of the divine to be made present. It also finds its place within the framework of the 'rhetoric of the unspeakable' that for Michel de Certeau is proper to the 'Fable mystique' (in the sense of discursive production, of storytelling) and that is classified in tropes: in true "phrases mystiques"[117]. Damisch even redefines the 17th century term "Iconomystica", or "science des images qui enseignent [...] les mystères de la foi", as "une iconographie toute ensemble mentale et figurative"[118]. The 'cloud' is a graph that finds a place in '*Iconomystica*' for 'gravitational' reasons similar to d'Ors's 'flying forms'. One need only sample the *Libro de su vida* (1565) of St. Teresa of Avila, and one will not struggle to find examples of clouds and skies as markers and vehicles of vision[119]. By the mystical subject, rapture in short, is always remembered as a lifting:

> Now let us return to raptures and speak of what is more common in them. I say that often, it seemed to me, the body was left so light that all its weight was gone, and sometimes this feeling reached such a point that I almost didn't know how to put my feet on the ground. Now when the body is in rapture it is as though dead, frequently being unable to do anything of itself.[120]

The enraptured body of the mystic rises from the ground, and his soul sees images such as the 'flying form' and the 'cloud'. Let us return for a moment to the pair of reference artists from which we started, as Damisch

---

116 H. Damisch, *Théorie du nuage*, cit., p. 65.

117 M. de Certeau, *La Fable mystique. XVIème-XVIIème siècle*, Gallimard, Paris 1892, p. 179. Modern mysticism itself, according to de Certeau, "prolifère autour d'une perte. [...] Elle rend lisible une absence qui multiplie les productions du désir", ivi, p. 25. Hence the need to "saisir aussi le cadre qu'il impose à la production mystique d'une lague nouvelle", ivi, p. 172. Cf. V.I. Stoichita, *Visionary Experience in the Golden Age of Spanish Art*, cit., p. 86, for the same reasoning applied to the strictly iconic side.

118 H. Damisch, *Théorie du nuage*, cit., pp. 72,73. The notion of '*Iconomystica*' was elaborated by the German Jesuit Jacob Masen in two books: *Ars nuova argutiarum* (1649), and *Speculum occultae, exhibens symbola, emblemata, hieroglyphica, oenigmata imaginum veritatis* (1650).

119 Cited among many occurrences are: the heavenly delights: "It seems to me the following comparison that now comes to mind is a good one, for these joys of prayer must be like those of heaven" and the understanding of heaven: "Returning then to the discussion of this kind of understanding, it seems to me that the Lord in every way wants this soul to have some knowledge of what goes on in heaven", Teresa of Avila, *The Book of Her Life* (1565), transl. by K. Kavanaugh and O. Rodriguez, Hackett, Indianapolis-Cambridge 2008, pp. 54, 180.

120 Ivi, p. 127.

understandably includes El Greco in his 'Iconomystica'. The artist paints "'corps sans surface'"[121]; his compositional formulas "ne laisse[nt] rien apercevoir du sol où sont établies les figures du régistre inférieur"; like those of the upper register, they ascend to the summit: "les figures se mêlent aux nuées"[122]. In every sense: they touch the sky, and are made of cloudy substance – in the same way as d'Ors's 'flying forms'. Damisch, however, enhances the oppositional aspect of El Greco's expression in relation to perspectivism and illusionism; although it refers to the supernatural, it is operative in iconicity as such: "S'il est une œuvre qui paraît satisfaire, dans son apparence même, à la définition d'un style fondé non plus sur la délinéation et le trompe-l'œil, [...] c'est bien celle du Greco"[123].

IV. *Conclusion*

A final trait unites the 'light' morphological paradigms just traced. It is only mentioned here, because it would require a separate space, but its importance demands, at least, a reflection; it is the intimate connection of the two morphologies, Orsian and Damischian, with the categories of modernity. For both authors, Baroque and proto-Baroque forms, as they describe them, not only trigger an aesthetic turning point: they are the premises of the modern painting and culture, and prefigurations of later artistic phenomena. According to them – but their voices are not isolated[124] –, Baroque, being anti-Classical, is intrinsically modern.

For d'Ors, this is primarily due to its trans-historical character, whereby the 'aeon' returns not only recursively but recurrently, regardless of the conditions of space and time; the morphological bipolarity guarantees the validity of its categories in eternity:

121 H. Damisch, *Théorie du nuage*, cit., p. 197. The expression is borrowed from a writing by Max Dvořák, another patron of the *Kunstwissenschaft*, cf. M. Dvořák, *Über Greco und den Manierismus*, in Id., *Kunstgeschichte als Geistesgeschichte: Studien zur abendländischen Kunstentwicklung*, Piper, Munich 1924, pp. 159-276.

122 H. Damisch, *Théorie du nuage*, cit., p. 198.

123 Ivi, p. 197.

124 One may think about the famous passage in which Walter Benjamin compares Baroque drama to Expressionism in the name of Riegl's *Kunstwollen*, cf. W. Benjamin, *The Origin of German Tragic Drama* (1928), transl. by J. Osborne, Verso, London 2003, pp. 54-55; or about Worringer analysing the psychologies of style of Gothic, Baroque, and Expressionism in texts assembled in W. Worringer, *Fragen und Gegenfragen*, cit.

> Y esta dualidad, esta multiplicidad de intenciones coexistentes, esta ruptura interior del espíritu, traducida por el antagonismo de las formas, ¿ no es la característica esencial de series muy diversas de obras de arte, obras humanas, a menudo muy separadas en el tiempo, pero unidas por una común aspiración?[125]

With its tendency to 'volatilise' the figurative work of art by poetising and musicalising it, the 'flying form' can lighten up in many ways. Baroque, therefore, are all the most daring artistic experiments, which, with a desire to lacerate the canons, intended to inaugurate new modernities. Baroque is thus Goya's painting – dangerously driven towards self-dissolution: "La pintura va a dejar de serlo"[126] –, but also, in part, that of Cézanne and Pablo Picasso: "Siempre, en todas estas investigaciones, la obra, en desacuerdo con el orden clásico, nos ha parecido en situación de interna ruptura, en tendencia hacia la multipolaridad"[127]. Marcel Proust's prose is even Baroque – we choose this entry from d'Ors's taxonomy because it is symptomatic –: "Así en la sintaxis de Proust, donde los incisos, lejos de subordinarse al discurso general, siguen un itinerario independiente, creando en su curso nuevos centros de atracción, ensanchándose en elipses, enroscándose en volutas"[128]. Forms can 'fly' and 'evaporate' incessantly and everywhere, since time immemorial.

Damisch's Baroque 'cloud' is modern because it first of all poses the conditions of possibility for dismantling a sign system such as that of perspective entirely based on referentiality; with its faculty of occlusion, it acts as a liberator that undermines the tyrant. And because, by contesting prospectivism at its roots and overthrowing it, it constitutes an order other than and entirely pertinent to iconicity; in this it puts the sensible, the perceived, "l'expérience préthéorique"[129] back into free play to the detriment of the rational, the constructed, the abstractness of science. Often silhouetted in painted skies over domes, the 'cloud' does not "ferme, clôture l'espace", but rather opens up a new "cosmique"[130] pictorial spatiality that is 'open', like the Wölffinian form, to future developments. It also poses some of the problems that will be of modern, if not modernist, painting. Such as John Ruskin's purported – and sometimes specious – obsession with clouds, his professing of "the service of clouds", and his claim that

125 E. d'Ors, *Lo Barroco*, cit., p. 109.
126 E. d'Ors, *Tres horas en el Museo del Prado*, cit., p. 81.
127 E. d'Ors, *Lo Barroco*, cit., p. 110.
128 *Ibidem*.
129 H. Damisch, *Théorie du nuage*, cit., p. 223.
130 Ivi, pp. 236-237.

the "cloudiness"[131] was typical of much up-to-date 19th-century landscape painting of a 'meteorological' stamp (fig. 7).

This is commendable as a

> étonnante formule, où s'affirme pour la première fois explicitement le préséance de l'ordre symbolique et le caractère non fonctionnel du signifiant, lequel se présente à vrai dire encore ici sous une masque emblématique : celui, précisément, du *nuage*, dont le peintre, après s'être si longtemps servi de lui, se veut désormais le serviteur.[132]

It is unfortunate because Ruskin, despite his *apologia* for nebulosity, does not disengage himself from the dictatorship of the contour, of the Wölfflinan 'linear', when he advises modern painters to make clouds "rapides at aussi précises que possible *dans le contour* (je souligne), au lieu de barbouiller (to daub down) ce qu'ils appellent des 'effets'", and not to be seduced by the "hasards heureux de l'invention, si brillante soit-elle"[133].

Fig. 6: John Constable, *Cloud Study*, 1821 circa, oil on paper, Yale Center for British Art, New Heaven.

131 A. J. Ruskin, *Modern Painters* (1856), quoted ivi, p. 257.
132 H. Damisch, *Théorie du nuage*, quoted p. 257.
133 J. Ruskin, *Modern Painters*, quoted ivi, p. 260

Many of the problems that Ruskin leaves open – subsumed in his question: "How is a cloud outlined?"[134] – would later be reactivated by 20th-century modernist painting; now when the 'cloud' informs styles and trends (with Tachisme and Informal art in the strict sense, for example), now when the autonomy of the sign is absolutely affirmed through abstraction: when "la reconnaissance de la peinture au titre de pratique signifiante spécifique"[135] takes place. Damisch warns us that if we look at the history of Oriental art – which never knew the primacy of perspective and *mimesis* like the West –, we realise that the 'cloud' has had a different trajectory; in Chinese painting, for example, that graph has always been used without reserve, because that other conception of figurativeness has never feared the "*inscription du vide*"[136] in pictorial space. In the arts, therefore, the 'cloud' expands according to the degree of freedom granted to it by each figurative reality. Finally, the metamorphic mobility of d'Ors's 'flying forms' and Damisch's 'cloud' can be ascribed to the 'lightness' that distinguishes these two morphological paradigms from every point of view: theoretical and historical. It can transcend space and time without losing its substance. The Baroque form thus conceived moves and transforms precisely for it perpetually seeks to shed its burdens, to lighten itself, and weigh as little as possible: to be as thin as air.

134 J Ruskin, *Modern Painters*, cit. ivi, p. 263.
135 H. Damisch, *Théorie du nuage*, cit., p. 310.
136 Ivi, p. 311.

MIMESIS GROUP
www.mimesis-group.com

MIMESIS INTERNATIONAL
www.mimesisinternational.com
info@mimesisinternational.com

MIMESIS EDIZIONI
www.mimesisedizioni.it
mimesis@mimesisedizioni.it

ÉDITIONS MIMÉSIS
www.editionsmimesis.fr
info@editionsmimesis.fr

MIMESIS COMMUNICATION
www.mim-c.net

MIMESIS EU
www.mim-eu.com

www.ingramcontent.com/pod-product-compliance
Lightning Source LLC
LaVergne TN
LVHW091125080826
845145LV00008B/2043

* 9 7 8 8 8 6 9 7 7 4 5 4 6 *